the
gap-year
guidebook
2010

Consultant Editor: Alison Withers
In-house Editor: Wendy Bosberry-Scott

John Catt Educational Ltd

JOHN
CATT
EDUCATIONAL
LIMITED

Published in 2009 by John Catt Educational Ltd,
12 Deben Mill Business Centre, Old Maltings Approach,
Melton, Woodbridge, Suffolk IP12 1BL

Tel: +44 (0) 1394 389850   Fax: +44 (0) 1394 386893
Email: info@gap-year.com   Website: www.gap-year.com

First published by Peridot Press in 1992; Eighteenth edition 2009
© 2009 John Catt Educational Ltd

British Library Cataloguing in Publication Data.

ISBN: 978 1 904724 704

Designed and typeset by John Catt Educational Limited, 12 Deben Mill Business Centre, Old Maltings Approach, Melton, Woodbridge, Suffolk IP12 1BL.

Printed and bound in Great Britain by Wyndham Grange, Butts Road, Southwick, West Sussex BN42 4EJ.

Contacts

Consultant Editor
Alison Withers

Executive Editor
Wendy Bosberry-Scott
Email: editor@gap-year.com

Production - Neil Rogers
Design - Scott James

Distribution/Booksales
Tel: +44 (0) 1394 389863
Email: booksales@johncatt.co.uk

Advertising
Tel: +44 (0) 1394 389853
Email: info@gap-year.com

visit: www.gap-year.com

contents

contents... continued

contents... continued

Your gap-year abroad

Your gap-year in the UK

contents... continued

Appendices

Preface

Any time you take time out from the normal pattern of your life to do something completely different –
that's a gap-

Preface

Research conducted by the Year Out Group, showed a 15% rise in the number of people who included a structured element in their **gap-**year programmes taken in 2008. While the majority of these people (75%) were aged between 18 and 24, there was a significant number (20%) aged between 25 and 40, many of whom were taking sabbaticals from work or seeking a change in career. Of the remaining 5%, many were in their late fifties, sixties or even seventies and were seeking to apply their skills and experience in a new, challenging environment. The research also revealed a further increase in interest in the **gap-**year concept across the globe, especially in the United States and western Europe, while numbers from Japan and China are small but rising.

In these difficult economic times, it is encouraging to see that people appreciate the benefits of including some structure in their **gap-**year programme. Those who have taken a structured **gap-**year arrive at university refreshed and focused, and they are more likely to complete their chosen course at university. They are more mature and globally aware, which enables them to take a broader perspective of their studies and make a greater contribution to their course. Some may take time to readjust to academic life but this is more than compensated by their social maturity.

Graduate employers actively seek to recruit former **gap-**year participants, who can demonstrate that they have developed key life skills such as teamwork, project management, negotiation skills, risk assessment, languages, cultural understanding and communication skills. Above all is the increased self-confidence that stems from a project that has been successfully conceived, planned and executed. Employers appreciate that those with a **gap-**year experience are more likely to adjust rapidly to the working environment and deliver.

A **gap-**year is an experience that is unique to the individual participant. A **gap-**year presents an opportunity for each participant to create a special programme of activities to meet their personal ambitions. The scope of activities on offer is

8

enormous and continues to expand. This has been made possible by the increase in comparatively cheap air travel and the opening of borders across all five continents. People have been inspired by media stories that highlight the scope for people to help those less fortunate than themselves, especially those in developing world. This is balanced by stories urging potential travellers to research and plan their **gap**-year programmes in as much detail as possible, and to be vigilant while they travel.

The broad spectrum of activities is open to everyone no matter what their age or circumstances. You can learn a skill or improve an existing one; you can be part of a cultural exchange or you can gain life skills and unique experiences by joining an expedition. Finally there are the opportunities for either paid or voluntary work, with numerous possibilities for community and conservation placements. In practice those with a full year or more at their disposal will have time for several activities, while others with less time will need to be more selective.

A **gap**-year is not for everyone. You cannot drift into a **gap**-year and expect it to be successful. A successful **gap**-year requires planning, commitment and an acceptance of responsibility: dropping out of a placement can be disruptive both for you and others. A **gap**-year should be a year out not a year off. If all you want to do is lounge around enjoying the sun, the beach and a few beers, best save your money for a holiday.

The key to a successful **gap**-year is detailed research and careful planning. There is a plethora of choice both in activities and destinations. A **gap**-year is a unique opportunity for each individual participant. Only through careful planning and preparation will you be able to make an informed decision and select a programme that best meets your individual needs. This is where the *gap-year guidebook* is so valuable. Use it as one of your research and planning tools. Use it as a checklist before you depart and take it with you as a reference book while you travel. The chances are that you will be rewarded with an exciting, challenging, valuable and enjoyable set of experiences that could, and probably will, change your life forever.

Richard Oliver
CEO Year Out Group
June 2009

the gap-year guidebook 2010

Jeremy,
Greenland ...
see page 331

Jeremy,
West coast of America ...
see page 331

Barry,
... Miami ...
see page 138

Rachael,
Mexico, South America ...
see page 263

Anna,
Travelling in South America ...
see page 354

Barry,
... Argentina ...
see page 138

Rachael,
China ...
see page 263

Barry,
... Asia ...
see page 138

David,
South Korea ...
see page 194

Claire,
A medical gap-
year in Uganda ...
see page 304

Katie,
A do-it-yourself
gap-year ...
see page 14

Katherine,
Took a career break
in Namibia ...
see page 68

Barry,
... Australia ...
see page 138

Many thanks to all those who have given their time, advice and expertise to help us keep this book as up-to-date as possible and to those who have shared their **gap-** adventures with us

They are:

Anna Would
Barry Sawyer
Claire Haddock
David Barratt
Jenny Vowles (UCAS)
Jude Hanan
Jeremy Hennell James
Karen Woodbridge (Hornet Solutions)
Katherine Parmley
Katie Norville
Linda Whittern (Careers Partnership UK)
Philip Taylor (Boxstore, Suffolk)
Rachael Gibson
Richard Oliver (Year Out Group)
Robert Ulph (Pennington Lettings, Ipswich)
Rona Cameron (Student Loans Co)

And ...for help in sourcing gapper case studies.... members of business networking groups Networking for Breakfast, Long Melford, Suffolk, and ABC Advantage Biz, Ipswich, Suffolk, and Emma Withers.

And a special mention to Rachael Gibson, one of our gappers, who has provided the photographs found on pages 8 and 256.

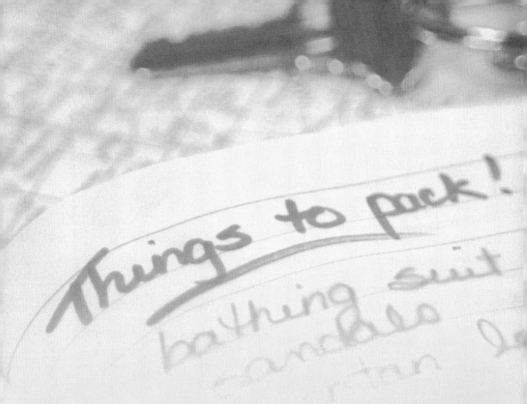

Chapter 1
Tips for travellers

A do-it-yourself gap-

Katie, 23, took a short, six week **gap-** after graduating with a degree in biology.

She visited three places in South Africa – Plettenburg Bay (the coast), Middelburg (in the Karoo) and Port Elizabeth.

She couldn't afford an organised volunteer placement and also had misgivings about whether she'd experience 'the truth' of the country that way, so bravely organised her own!

Here's what she had to say: "I used my own initiative to search (lots of Googling) for sanctuaries in Africa that weren't so 'commercial' and on a smaller, more local scale."

Luckily she made contact with an English woman who had set up a website about the two families she'd stayed with.

"These were two real South African families living very different lives that were asking a reasonable cost for your stay, literally to just cover your bed, board and provide a little towards the care of the animals.

"Both families shared an interest in primate conservation (Vervet monkeys and baboons which are horrendously and unfairly persecuted in this country).

"The BBC made a documentary on Karin Sachs' life with baboons (Baboon Woman - Channel 5) and it was lovely to see awareness being spread in this way."

She adds: "Myself and my friend stayed in Plettenburg Bay with Karin and John for a week…" and "…we experienced life 'back to basics'. There was no power and we lived very much in the Bush with Karin, John and their two Vervet monkey troops. We also did the 'tourist' things such as shopping at the traditional markets and volunteered for a day at Tenikwa, the cat (specifically cheetah) sanctuary.

"Life at Wilmar Animal Sanctuary with Willem and Margaret in Middelburg in the Karoo was a very different but also wonderful experience. We were living on the farm and walking the Karoo with the collies, helping with farm jobs and looking after all the animals: Wilmar took in orphaned, abandoned and abused Vervet monkeys and baboons. Cheaper living costs also meant we had more money to indulge on trips to the game reserves and other activities such as abseiling and shopping at the markets.

"I was lucky enough to have the amazing experience of surrogating a baby Chakma baboon whose mother had been shot. She came with me everywhere, slept with me at night and even had to come in the shower with me, as she would not leave me!

"Once the baby baboon selects you as mum and forms that bond with you they will not be parted from you.

"The family made us so wonderfully welcome. We … lived the African farm life as well as indulged in the 'tourist' trips too, such as visiting the game reserve Addo Elephant Park where we saw all the big five [animals]."

Katie describes her experience as: "The best experience of my life … I feel I experienced and lived the real South African experience, living in two very different places and living two very different lifestyles … I saw such beauty in the country as well as such poverty and cruelty and it was so enlightening"

Organising her own **gap-** turned out fine for Katie, as she and her friend were treated as part of the family.

Here's her advice for anyone wanting to try it: "Do your research and search around. There are so many **gap-**year programmes and companies [available for those not wishing to do it themselves] … I was in email contact regularly with the families for about eight months before I went out to Africa and you need to feel confident that you are going to stay with people you can trust and feel safe and secure with."

Readjusting on her return was difficult for a very special reason – being surrogate mum to a baby baboon named after her!

She said the most important thing she'd taken on her trip had been her camera.

She's now doing a PGCE, but plans to return as soon as she graduates, and hopefully visit the families once a year for as long as she can.

Tips for travellers

Beat the recession, take a gap-

The first signs of what was to turn out to be a severe global economic recession were just beginning when we were updating the 2009 edition of the **gap**-*year guidebook*.

A year on and we've had months of dire economic forecasts, rising unemployment and an ever-growing list of businesses going under. As even the emerging 'sunrise' economies (the BRIC - Brazil, Russia, India and China) have found their economies shrinking you might have expected a contraction also in the numbers of people taking a **gap-**.

However, that doesn't seem to have happened. Instead, there's been a slight shift in the kinds of people taking a **gap-**.

It seems that rather than plunge into a possibly fruitless and demoralising job search when there are few, if any, jobs to be had, people who have been asked by their companies to take a sabbatical or have been made redundant have been choosing to use their time to travel and get involved in structured projects abroad - perhaps in the hope that when they come back the signs might be more optimistic and in any case they will have something constructive and new to put on their CVs.

Richard Oliver, CEO of the voluntary **gap-** industry regulatory body Year Out Group, told us that VSO has reported that the average age of its volunteers has gone up over the past three years from 45 to 52.

According to Mr Oliver, YOG's 37 member organisations report an increase of some 15% in bookings for 2008-09 - a rise from around 46,700 to 53,000 people.

These figures obviously don't include those who went with non-YOG-affiliated **gap-** organisations, or those who organised their **gap-** independently, so the increase could have been even greater.

Gapadvice.org suggests the figure for UK citizens taking a **gap-** could add up to more than half a million people - 520,000.

It may be also that another worrying statistic has played a part - the prediction that the economic downturn could well plunge more than 53 million vulnerable people into poverty and malnutrition. So the need for volunteers has never been greater.

Let's start by defining a gap-

Although they're generally referred to as **gap**-years, it may be this is a habit, based on the history of travel throughout the centuries. Nowadays people travel to volunteer, work, study, see something new and it doesn't have to be for a year.

visit: www.gap-year.com

The one thing all such trips have in common is the fact that they're all about taking time out of the normal routine to do something different, challenging, fulfilling, memorable - so that is our definition of a **gap-**.

Who goes on a gap-?

Here are some more stats: Gapadvice.org estimates the figures as: young people 230,000, career breakers 90,000 and retired people 200,000.

We've known for several editions now that the biggest increases in numbers are among career breakers and mature travellers and, despite the last year having been so unsettled, this still seems to be the case.

So the answer is people of all ages, all walks of life, able bodied and disabled go on a **gap-**

Why take a gap-?

Time out before further study? A break from the daily work routine? A memorable experience? To give something back? To learn something new? Tick all that apply!

Whatever they've done, gappers all tell us it has been a life-changing experience.

Where to go and what to do?

To make the most of a **gap-**, whatever you want from it, you need to do something that you find exciting, fun and challenging.

It may be travelling, helping with conservation work nearer to home or learning a new skill you might not have had time for up till now. The point is to do what you think is right, something that gives you a sense of achievement.

Is a gap-year safe?

Accidents can happen anywhere and so can earthquakes, floods, cyclones and other random events.

But there are some risks you can avoid by being alert, informed and prepared. You should take personal safety seriously and not put yourself in danger by agreeing to anything, about which you have misgivings, just because you don't want to risk someone thinking that you're stupid or scared.

Tip: There's one rule: If in doubt - don't

The Foreign Office estimates that of the approximately 250,000 young people who take a **gap-** each year, around 75,000 are prone to a reckless spirit that it calls the 'Invincibles'.

This concern prompted the UK's first-ever Gap-Year Safety Conference in London in June 2009.

It brought together figures from the **gap-** industry, the FCO, British Standards and the British Safety Council to highlight the need for improved safety standards, including third party providers in Third World destinations.

Also at the conference was Ian French, father of Georgia, a young gapper who died in a bus crash in Peru in 2008. He has set up a not for profit website **www.gapaid.org** to highlight the issue.

Two useful initiatives offered by the UK's Foreign Office that have been running for some time are its Know Before You Go campaign, in which we at **www.gap-year.com** and *the gap-year guidebook* are partners, and Locate.

The FCO deals with an estimated 3.5 million enquiries, and supports around 85,000 Brits in difficulty each year. While support includes visiting those who have been admitted to hospital or arrested, to rescuing British citizens from forced marriages abroad, the FCO launched its service because it had found that the most common problems it was being called in on were the most preventable ones, such as inadequate or no insurance or lack of proper medical precautions.

Locate helps the FCO to track down Britons in the event of a crisis abroad. Again the need was revealed by a survey, which found that two thirds of us don't actually know where our travelling loved ones are and over half of us go abroad without leaving details of our trip with friends and family.

While the FCO deals with all travellers - not only those on a **gap-** - we agree with the message about being as prepared as possible before you go and that's what this guidebook is for.

We at **gap-year.com** also recommend that you consider taking a gappers' safety course before you go, to teach you how to recognise danger (from people as well as natural disasters), and how to look after yourself in a bad situation - it could be the thing that saves your life.

The point is that as long as you have done all you could to be well prepared with travelling essentials and knowledge, then you should go for it!

This first chapter is full of tips on planning your **gap-**, travel basics and will be useful whatever your age and for however long you are going.

There's lots of practical advice for those who haven't been on long trips abroad before, covering everything from taking care of essential documents and planning what to pack, to how to avoid offending local sensibilities.

For specific issues that concern people with more in the way of assets or responsibilities, take a look at Chapter 6 - Career Breaks and Mature Travellers.

Planning your gap- first steps

A good tip for the early stages of planning is to cut out and keep anything you find in magazines, brochures or newspapers that appeals to you - an article, a picture, an activity - and to make a note of anything you find interesting on the internet. These will help you build up a picture of where you want to go and what you might want to do.

It will help you clarify what you want from your **gap**-year and help you answer the following questions:

Time and Money

- Where do you want to go?
- What do you want to do?
- How long have you got?
- Are you a responsible/ethical traveller?
- How much do you want to spend?

Where do you want to go?

YOG's most recent research has found that the most popular countries for a structured **gap-** are:

South Africa (1st place), Canada (2nd) and Ecuador (3rd - up from 9th place in 2007), while Kenya and Ghana have dropped out of its top ten list altogether and New Zealand is a new entry (10th).

But if you want to visit several places you can let a cheap round-the-world ticket decide the framework for you. Otherwise you need to get your route clear in your mind.

Do you feel attracted to a particular area or to a particular climate? Unexplored territory or the popular backpacker places you've heard about?

If you're unsure, try connecting with people who've been, through the message board: **www.gap-year.com**

Heading for unknown territory off the backpacker routes in search of something more unusual will usually mean higher costs, perhaps a longer wait for visas and less efficient transport systems - therefore more preparation and travelling time. A bit of netsurfing, a check with any contacts who know a country and a chat with a travel agent will help you get a better idea of what this might mean.

Then there's the risk factor. Obviously family and friends will want you to avoid danger zones. The political situation in some places around the world is serious, unstable and can't be ignored.

You want your **gap-** travels to be stimulating, fun, to let you experience different cultures and meet new people, but do you really want to end up in the middle of a war zone with your life in danger? Foreign news correspondents and war reporters with large back-up organisations prepare properly, with proper insurance and safety and survival courses - and it makes sense for gappers too!

A good starting point is the Foreign Office website (**www.fco.gov.uk**) where you can find country profiles and assess the dangers and possible drawbacks to places you're thinking of. The FCO updates its danger list regularly as new areas of unrest emerge, but it's not, and never can be, a failsafe.

Rough Guide and *Lonely Planet* are probably the best-known guides and are excellent, as are the *Footprint* and Thomas Cook guides. Whatever your interests, these books will also give you relevant information about the places you want to go to - they too are all updated regularly but bear in mind the time it takes to gather, write and print the information.

What do you want to do?

- Work
- Volunteer
- Adventure
- Spiritual Retreats
- Study
- Free Spirit

This is a situation where knowing your own personality, your interests, your strengths and weaknesses will help you. Are you someone who likes to get stuck into something for a while or do you want to be on the move a lot?

If you're not confident about coping alone with unfamiliar situations you might want a more structured, group setting. On the other hand if you know you need time away from the crowds, you're bound to want to build in some independent travel.

YOG members report that the most popular choice for a **gap-** is volunteering and that since the onset of the recession teaching is the most popular volunteer option, placements having risen by 20%.

Or do you want to explore things you've always wanted to pursue but never had time? It could be anything from a spiritual retreat to meditation and yoga, art, photography, particular places and cultures.

Maybe you're particularly concerned about the state of the world and would like to do your bit environmentally or contribute to helping disadvantaged people?

The possibilities are endless and many gappers end up constructing a programme that combines several elements.

How long have you got?

Now you have at least a rough idea of where you want to go and what you want to do. The next step is to consider how long you might need to get it all in.

How much time you can spare depends on *when* you're taking your **gap-**. That's going to be dictated by when you have to be back for starting university or college or, for career breakers, how much time your employer's prepared to let you have, or even whether you're willing to risk quitting your job for more **gap-** time.

Some gappers just get a round-the-world ticket and take off for a year; others work for a while, go away on a placement, come back and earn some more then go again. Or you can work while you're away to finance the next stage of your trip. The essential point here is to be realistic about including time to raise the money as part of your **gap-** and, if minimising your carbon footprint is important to you, how much extra time you're going to allow for avoiding planes where you can so you can use more environmentally-friendly, and probably slower, local transport.

Maybe you'll have to refine or cut back the list, but remember, you don't have to spend a whole year on a **gap-**, it can be as short or as long as you want to make it.

How much do you want to spend?

Estimates vary widely, but the average cost for a full year's **gap-** is £3000-£4000 for young people, up to £7000 for career breakers and around £5000 for mature travellers.

Much depends on where you're going and what you plan to do, and these days, if you care about the planet, climate change and ethical travel, you need also to include the costs of carbon offsetting.

Some people work for a while to raise money for, say, a three-month activity, then come back to earn some more so they can go off again and do something different. The following are useful sources to at least start pinning down how much it's all going to cost.

21

For career breakers and mature travellers, who already have professional skills to offer, the United Nations Volunteer Programme is a good place to start looking at the options. UNV has links to local charities, NGOs (Non Governmental Organisations) and projects in countries all over the world. Some will be looking for people willing to work with them for living expenses; others will be looking for volunteers.

Travel guides are useful for copious information on towns, travel routes and budget hotels in the countries they cover. They'll help you work out some rough costs but remember some details will have changed when you get to where you are going.

You can also begin to contact **gap-** organisations specialising in volunteer projects, and/or work and study placements that interest you to find out more about their charges

Use our chapters on finance (see page 67) and our special chapter for career breakers and mature travellers (see page 151) to give you some ideas on how to raise the money for your **gap-**.

If you want to know more about all the implications of ethical travel, there's an excellent book called the *Ethical Travel Guide*, written by Polly Pattullo and Orely Minelli for Tourism Concern: ISBN: 9781844073214, published by Earthscan: **www.earthscan.co.uk**

Earthscan was founded in 1987 and is a leading publisher (in English) on climate change, sustainable development and environmental technology for academic and professional and for general readers.

Before you go...

... know where you're going

The more you know about your destination, the easier your trip will be: India, for example, is unbearably hot and humid in pre-monsoon April to June, Australia has seasons when bush fires are rampant and then there are the cyclone seasons in south Asia and rainy seasons in South America - and the consequent risk of flooding!!

It's also worth finding out when special events are on. It could be very inconvenient to arrive in India during Diwali - when everyone's on holiday and all the trains are full! Similarly Japan - gorgeous in cherry blossom season but avoid travelling in Golden Week.

Check out **www.whatsonwhen.com** - it's a great site, which lists all sorts of events around the world.

Before visiting any country that has recently been politically volatile or could turn into a war zone, check with the FCO for the current situation. Log onto **www.fco.gov.uk** for up-to-date information.

Note: If you're from a country that qualifies for a Visa Waiver for the USA (and that includes UK citizens) you must now register online your intent to visit the USA and you *must* receive travel authorisation. Authorisation still doesn't guarantee you'll be granted entry and you may still be asked to go to the US embassy for an interview, but you have to go through the process before you can do anything else. You'll find the details here:

www.usembassy.org.uk/dhs/ESTA_for_Visa_Waiver_Program_Travelers.pdf

If you're intending to visit for longer, or are planning to work, you will need the correct visa (see Chapter 7 - Working Abroad).

... sort the paperwork

If you need to get yourself a passport for the first time, application forms are available from Post Offices or you can apply online. But remember:

Passport interviews are a new part of the process and are required by all applicants, aged 16 or over, who are applying for a passport for the first time.

You can call 0300 222 1000 to make an appointment or for other enquiries about this, but remember also that first time applicants can't use the fast track service. There are 68 interview offices around the country and you have to go to the correct one for where you live - see the map on the IPS (Identity and Passport Office) website:

www.ips.gov.uk/passport/findinterviewoffices/

The standard adult ten-year passport currently costs £72 and you'll need your birth certificate and passport photos. It should take no more than a month from the time you apply to the time you receive your passport, but the queue lengthens coming up to peak summer holiday season.

You can use the Passport Office 'Check and Send' service at selected Post Offices throughout the UK or send it direct. The 'Check and Send' service gets your application checked for completeness (including documentation and fee) and is given priority by the IPS - they are usually able to process these applications in two weeks.

If your passport application is urgent and you're not applying for the first time, you can use the guaranteed same-day (Premium) service or the guaranteed one-week (Fast Track) service. Both services are only available by appointment at one of the seven IPS offices around the UK (phone the IPS Advice Line on 0300 222 0000), and both are expensive (£114 for Premium, £97 for Fast Track). The services are only available for renewals and amendments. And although you'll get a fixed appointment you'll almost certainly have to wait in a queue after this for your passport.

The IPS website is very helpful: **www.ips.gov.uk/passport/index.asp**

London Passport Office,
Globe House, 89 Eccleston Square,
London SW1V 1PN

What to take

Start thinking early about what to take with you and write a list - adding to it every time you think of something. Here's a general checklist to get you started:

- Passport and tickets
- Padlock and chain
- Belt bag
- Daypack (can be used for valuables in transit/hand luggage on plane)
- First aid kit: including any personal meds: split between day pack and rucksack/case
- Notebook and pen
- Camera
- Mobile phone and charger
- MP3 player - much less bulky than CDs
- Money: cards/travellers' cheques/cash
- Torch/candle
- Sheet sleeping bag
- Universal adapter
- Universal sink plug
- Spare specs/contact lenses
- Guidebook/phrasebooks - if doing several countries trade in/swap with other travellers en route
- Spare photos for ID cards *etc* if needed
- Photocopies of documents/emergency numbers/serial numbers of travellers' cheques
- Clothes and toiletries *etc*

Some of these checklist items will be more relevant to backpackers and people on treks, than to people on a work placement or staying in a family home. The list can be modified for your own particular plans.

Handy items

Every traveller has their own list of things they find particularly useful, and it varies from person to person, but these are things seasoned travellers say they've found really helpful:

- String that can double as a washing line and is handy for putting up mosquito nets.
- A universal sink plug.
- Universal adapter.

visit: www.gap-year.com

- A torch.
- A penknife with different functions (but don't carry it in hand luggage on planes, it will be confiscated).
- Duct tape/gaffer tape (handy for mending slashed rucksacks, sealing ant nests, fixing doors, sticking up mosquito nets).
- A padlock and chain to secure your rucksacks on long journeys and double lock hostel rooms.

There are mixed views about those security wire mesh covers you can buy for rucksacks. Some prefer a simple padlock and chain and say the security mesh covers are an open invitation to a thief armed with wire cutters, since they imply you're carrying something valuable. Others say the point is that they're slash proof, so useful as a short-term deterrent against thieves armed with a knife, when you're doing something where you might be distracted - like making a phone call.

One traveller we know has an ingenious solution - on the grounds that the mesh, padlock and chain methods advertise you as having something worth stealing he attaches a small bell to his backpack - he reckons it's a great deterrent since it makes the thief feel conspicuous and tells its owner someone's messing with his stuff!

We've come across a really useful, newly-launched, credit-card sized gadget called Traakit - a GPS-style tracker device which enables family to locate travelling loved ones via the internet, without making endless phone calls, when they're on a **gap-**.

David Clayton, whose Newmarket-based company, Radaw, developed the device (launched in May 2009), told us his nephew, Harry, is carrying one while **gap-** travelling in Australia. But perhaps even more useful, particularly for anyone travelling alone, is that Traakit can also be very easily set to secure belongings inside a 'virtual fence' so they can be left in a hotel or hostel room while you're off exploring wherever you are. If the secured items are moved outside the co-ordinates Traakit automatically sends a text to the owner's mobile phone, as well as an email alerting them and giving the items' new location. It costs £273.50 (including vat and delivery) to buy plus approximately £14 per month service charge, or it can be rented for around £50 per month. For more see: **www.traakit.co.uk**

- Water purifying tablets - useful but won't deal with all the possible waterborne parasites - sometimes boiling water and adding iodine are also necessary. It's best to stick to bottled mineral water if available - even for brushing your teeth - but always check that the seal is intact before you buy. That way you will be sure it's not a mineral water bottle refilled with the local dodgy supply. Lifesaver Systems (see directory page 58) produces a bottle that converts even the nastiest stuff into drinkable water without the use of chemicals. It's not cheap but being ill through drinking bad water while travelling can be expensive or even life threatening.

Remember it's easy to get dehydrated in hot countries so you should always carry a bottle of water with you and drink frequently - up to eight litres a day.

Less is best

As airlines struggle with rising fuel costs, and diminishing passenger numbers, they are becoming increasingly inventive in dreaming up extra charges. Excess and overweight check-in baggage is one particularly fruitful area - and it's confusing as the rules vary from airline to airline. This makes it even more crucial to think very carefully about what you need to take - and what you could do without.

Basically, some charge per piece and others by weight, but that's not all. Some carriers limit you to one check-in piece, others, like BA, allow two. It can also depend on your route and your destination. Weight limits vary from as little as 20kg per bag to 30 kg (Emirates to Asia). Charges can even be different on outward and return journeys, with some carriers charging as much as €30 per kilogram over the permitted weight, or £90 per extra bag. It won't take much to wipe out all the money you've saved by searching for the cheapest available flights!

Inevitably if you fly business or first class the allowances are more generous but the above assumes that most people on a **gap-** will be flying economy.

Packing tips

- Pack in reverse order - first in, last out
- Heavy items go at the bottom
- Pack in categories in plastic bags - easier to find stuff
- Use vacuum pack bags for bulky items
- Store toilet rolls and dirty undies in side pockets - easy for thieves to open and they won't want them!
- Take a small, separate backpack for day hikes *etc*. You can buy small, thin folding ones
- Keep spares (undies, toothbrush, important numbers and documents) in hand luggage
- Take a sleeping bag liner - useful in hostels
- Take a sarong (versatile: can be a bed sheet, towel, purse, bag...)
- Travel towels are lightweight and dry fast
- Remove packaging from everything but keep printed instructions for medications
- Shaving oil takes less space than cream
- Put liquids in squashy bottles (and don't carry liquids in hand luggage)
- Fill shoes, cups *etc* with socks and undies to save space
- Tie up loose backpack straps before it goes into transit

Now sit down and rationalise - cross off everything you don't really need. Pack enough clothes to see you through - about five changes of clothing should last you for months if you choose carefully. Don't take anything that doesn't go with everything else and stick to materials that are comfortable, hard-wearing, easy to wash and dry and don't crease too much. Make sure you have clothes that are suitable for the climates you are visiting and don't forget that the temperatures in some dry climates can drop considerably at night! You can find very lightweight waterproofs and thermals that can be rolled up easily.

Tip: Remember most places have cheap markets, not to mention interesting local clothes, so you can always top up or replace clothes while you are travelling.

Relax, you can't prepare for every eventuality if you're living out of a rucksack. The best way to know what you need is to ask someone who's already been on a **gap-** what they took, what were the most useful things, what they didn't need and what they wished they had taken.

Maps, directions and vital information

You won't need anything too elaborate: the maps in guidebooks are usually pretty good. A good pocket diary can be very useful - one that gives international dialling codes, time differences, local currency details, bank opening hours, public holidays and other information.

Take a list with you of essential information like directions to voluntary work postings, key addresses, medical information, credit card numbers (try to disguise these in case everything gets stolen), passport details (and a photocopy of the main and visa pages), emergency contact numbers in case of loss of travellers' cheques and insurance and flight details - and leave a copy with someone at home.

Another way of keeping safe copies of your vital documents (even if everything you have is lost or stolen) is to scan them before you leave and email them as attachments to your email address.

However, it is well known that you shouldn't send sensitive information via email and it's not clear whether that advice also applies to attachments, given that they're all stored on a remote server, so you might prefer one of the many online secure data storage options.

A quick internet search gave us these:

www.passportsupport.com/about/
www.omneport.com/

Or you could even put it all on a memory stick, which has the advantage of being small and easy to conceal and carry.

Those of you lucky enough to have one of those smart new phones or an MP3 player onto which you can download apps (you know which ones we're talking about...) will be able to input a mass of information and effectively 'carry' maps, timetables, hostel finders, information lists, and photographs of your valuable documents with you in one small, slim device.

The FCO's Locate service is free but only available to UK citizens. You fill in a simple registration form online giving your contact details and travel plans. You can also log in and update your details while you're travelling. The information's on a secure site, which is accessible only to embassy staff and the FCO's consular crisis group. If there's an unexpected crisis where you happen to be it means your friends and family can check whether you're okay and the nearest British Embassy can text you warnings and alerts.

Where to buy your kit

Some overseas voluntary organisations arrange for their students to have discounts at specific shops, like the YHA. The best advice on equipment usually comes from specialist shops, although they may not be the cheapest: these include YHA shops, Blacks, Millets and Camping and Outdoors Centres. Take a look in our directory on page 65 or at **www.gap-yearshop.com** for a specialist outlet selling over the internet.

Rucksacks

Prices for a well-stitched, 65-litre rucksack can vary greatly. Remember, the most expensive is not necessarily the best, get what is most suitable for your trip.

A side-opening backpack is easier than a top-opening one. You can get all sorts of attachments such as 'an integral pocket for your hydration bladder' but if you don't need it why pay for it? A good outdoor store should be able to advise you on exactly what you need for your particular trip. Most of these stores have websites with helpful hints and lists of 'essential' items.

You should be able to leave your rucksack in most hostels or guest houses, if you are staying for more than a day, or in a locker at the train station. *Always* take camera, passport, important papers and money with you everywhere, zipped up, preferably out of view.

Tip: If you're thinking of buying second-hand make sure you check that all fastenings work and that the frame is the right size for your height and weight.

Footwear

It's worth investing in something comfortable if you're heading off on a long trip. In hot countries, a good pair of sandals is the preferred footwear for many and it's worth paying for a decent pair, as they will last onger and be comfortable. If you're going somewhere cheap you could just pick up a pair out there but you're likely to be doing a lot more walking than usual, so comfort and durability are important.

Some people like chunky walking boots, others just their trainers, but it's best to get something that won't fall apart when you're halfway up a mountain. Take more than one pair of comfortable shoes in case they don't last, but don't take too many - they'll be an unnecessary burden and take up precious space in your rucksack.

Sleeping bags

Go to a specialist shop where you can get good advice. Prices vary widely and you can sometimes find a four-season bag cheaper than a one-season bag - it's mostly down to quality. You need to consider:

- Can you carry it comfortably and still have the energy to do all you want to do?
- Hot countries - do you need one? You may just want to take a sheet sleeping bag (basically just a sewn-up sheet).
- Colder countries: What will you be doing? Take into account weight and size and the conditions you'll be travelling in - you might want to go for one of those compression sacs that you can use to squash sleeping bags into.

For cold countries, you need heat-retaining materials. You can usually - but not always - rent down filled bags for treks in, say, Nepal.

the gap-year guidebook 2010

First aid kit

Useful basics:

- Re-hydration sachets (to use after diarrhoea)
- Waterproof plasters
- TCP/TeeTree oil
- Corn and blister plasters for sore feet
- Cotton buds
- A small pair of straight nail scissors (not to be carried in your hand luggage on the plane)
- Safety pins (not to be carried in your hand luggage on the plane)
- Insect repellent
- Antiseptic cream
- Anti-diarrhoea pills (only short-term; they stop the diarrhoea temporarily but don't cure you)
- Water sterilisation tablets
- Antihistamine cream
- Your own preferred form of painkiller

You can get a medical pack from most chemists, travel shops or online from MASTA (**www.masta.org**).

Homeway (see **www.gap-yearshop.com**) also specialises in medical kits for travellers: the contents vary from sting relief, tick removers, blister kits, sun block and re-hydration sachets to complete sterile medical packs with needles and syringe kits (in case you think the needle someone might have to inject you with may not be sterile).

You can also buy various types of mosquito net, water purification tablets and filters, money pouches, world receiver radios, travel irons and kettles. Not to mention a personal attack alarm.

Tip: If you take too much kit though, you'll need a removal van to take it with you!

Cameras

Picture quality on many mobile phones is now so good that you may not need to take a camera as well, especially if you're going to be uploading your pictures onto one of the many photo sharing websites now available.

If you do want the back-up of a camera check with your local photographic dealer about what will best suit your requirements. Make sure you get a camera case to protect from knocks, dust and moisture and don't buy the cheapest you can find. Cheap equipment can let you down and you need something that doesn't have software compatibility/connection problems. Here are a few other tips:

- Digital cameras use lots of power (especially if using flash). Take plenty of batteries with you or take rechargeable batteries and a charger (you'll save money in the long run but check they're usable in your particular camera).

- Don't risk losing all your photos! Back them up as you travel. Maybe visit an internet cafe occasionally and upload your best photos to a site such as Photobucket.com (which is free). Upload them onto your Facebook, myspace (or similar) site. Or even send them to your home email account.

- Don't walk around with your camera round your neck! Keep it out of sight whenever possible to reduce the risk of crime.

- Remember certain countries charge extra for using a camcorder at heritage sites, safari parks and monuments, but often they don't charge for stills cameras.

Leave someone in charge at home

Make sure you have someone reliable and trustworthy in charge of sorting things out for you - especially the official stuff that won't wait. Get someone you really trust to open your post and arrange to talk to them at regular intervals in case something turns up that you need to deal with.

However, there are some things you just have to do yourself, so make sure you've done everything important before you go. This particularly applies to any regular payments you make - check all your standing orders/direct debits and make sure to cancel any you don't need; and that there's money in your account for any you do need.

If you have a flat or house you're planning to sub-let, either use an accommodation agency or make sure someone you trust will keep an eye on things - it may be necessary to give them some written form of authority to deal with emergencies. There's more on all this in Chapter 6 - Career Breaks and Mature Travellers.

Looking after yourself...

Health

Note: Although we make every effort to be as up-to-date and accurate as possible, the following advice is intended to serve as a guideline only. It is designed to be helpful rather than definitive, and you should always check with your GP, preferably at least eight weeks before going away.

It's not only which countries you'll be going to, but for how long and what degree of roughing it: six months in a basic backpacker hostel puts people at higher risk than two weeks in a five-star hotel.

Before you go you should tell your doctor:

- your proposed travel route; and

- the type of activities you will be doing.

Ask for advice, not only about injections and pills needed, but symptoms to look out for and what to do if you suspect you've caught something.

Some immunisations are free under the NHS but you may have to pay for the more exotic/rare ones. Some, like the Hepatitis A vaccine, can be very expensive, but this is not an area to be mean with your money - it really is worth being cautious with your health.

Also, many people recommend that you know your blood type before you leave the country, to save time and ensure safety. Your GP might have it on record - if not, a small charge may be made for a blood test.

If you're going abroad to do voluntary work, don't assume the organization will give you medical advice first or even when you get there, though they often do. Find out for yourself, and check if there is a medically-qualified person in or near the institution you are going to be posted with. People who've been to the relevant country/area are a great source of information.

Some travellers prefer to go to a dedicated travel clinic to get pre-travel health advice. This may be especially worthwhile if your GP/practice nurse does not see many travellers.

Here are some options:

The Medical Advisory Services for Travellers Abroad (MASTA):
www.masta.org

For £3.99 you can register online, put in details of the countries you're visiting and get a health brief that contains recommended vaccinations for your journey, seasonal diseases, malaria advice, the latest travel health news and Foreign Office travel advice. The website also has a clickable map to find your nearest MASTA clinic.

The Liverpool School of Tropical Medicine:
www.liv.ac.uk/lstm/travel_health_services/travel_clinic/index.htm

Tel: 0151 708 9393 (for an appointment with its travel clinic)

Other useful websites include:

www.e-med.co.uk has a useful free travel service, which you can email for advice on immunisations, anti-malaria medication and what to watch out for.

www.fitfortravel.scot.nhs.uk

www.travelhealth.co.uk

Department of Health website
www.nhs.uk/LiveWell/TravelHealth/Pages/Travelhealthhome.aspx

For safety advice try the Foreign and Commonwealth Office:
www.fco.gov.uk/travel

Accidents/Injuries

Accidents and injuries are the greatest cause of death in young travellers abroad. Alcohol/drug use will increase the risk of these occurring. Travellers to areas with poor medical facilities should take a sterile medical equipment pack with them. As highlighted in Chapter 3, make sure that you have good travel insurance that will bring you home if necessary.

AIDS

The HIV virus that causes AIDS can be contracted from: injections with infected needles; transfusions of infected blood; sexual intercourse with an infected person; or possibly cuts (if you have a shave at the barbers, insist on a fresh blade, but it's probably best to avoid the experience altogether). It is *not* caught through everyday contact, insect bites, dirty food or crockery, kissing, coughing or sneezing. Protect yourself: always use condoms during sex, make sure needles are new and if you need a blood transfusion make sure blood has been screened, and don't get a tattoo or piercing until you're back home and can check out the tattoo shop properly.

Remember that AIDS is a fatal disease and though medical advances are being made there is no preventive vaccination and no cure.

Asthma and allergies

Whether you are an asthmatic or have an allergy to chemicals in the air, food, stings, or antibiotics, ask your GP for advice before you go. You will be able to take some treatments with you.

Allergy sufferers: if you suffer from severe shock reactions to insect bites/nuts or any other allergy, make sure you have enough of your anaphylactic shock packs with you - you may not be able to get them in some parts of the world.

Chronic conditions

Asthmatics, diabetics, epileptics or those with other conditions should always wear an obvious necklace or bracelet or carry an identity card stating the details of their condition. Tragedies do occur due to ignorance, and if you are found unconscious a label can be a lifesaver. See **www.medicalert.org.uk** for information on obtaining these items.

You should also keep with you a written record of your medical condition and the proper names (not just trade names) of any medication you are taking. If you are going on an organised trip or volunteering abroad, find out who the responsible person for medical matters is and make sure you fully brief them about your condition.

Contraceptives

If you are on the pill it is advisable to take as many with you as possible. Remember that contraceptives go against religious beliefs in some countries, so they may not be readily available. Antibiotics, vomiting and diarrhoea can inhibit the absorption of the pill, so use alternative means of contraception until seven days after the illness.

Condoms: unprotected sex can be fatal, so everyone should take them, even if they are not likely to be used (not everyone thinks about sex the whole time). Keep them away from sand, water and sun. If buying abroad, make sure they are a known brand and have not been kept in damp, hot or icy conditions.

Dentist

Pretty obvious but often forgotten: get anything you need done to your teeth before you go. Especially worth checking up on are wisdom teeth and fillings - you don't want to spend three months in Africa with toothache.

Diabetics

Wear an obvious medical alert necklace or bracelet, or carry an ID card stating your condition (preferably with a translation into the local language). Take enough insulin for your stay, although it is unlikely that a GP will give you the amount of medication needed for a full year of travelling - three to six months is usually their limit, in which case, be prepared to buy insulin abroad and at full price. Ring the BDA Careline to make sure the brand of insulin you use is available in the particular country you are planning to visit. Your medication must be kept in the passenger area of a plane, not the aircraft hold where it will freeze.

Diabetes UK,
10 Parkway,
London NW1 7AA

www.diabetes.org.uk

Careline: +44 (0) 845 120 2960, weekdays 9am-5pm.
Email: careline@diabetes.org.uk

Diabetes UK produces a general travel information booklet as well as specific travel packs for about 70 countries.

Diarrhoea

By far the most common health problem to affect travellers abroad is travellers' diarrhoea. This is difficult to avoid but it is sensible to do the best you can to prevent problems. High-risk food/drinks include untreated tap water, shellfish, un-pasteurised dairy products, salads, peeled/prepared uncooked fruit, raw/undercooked meat and fish. Take a kit to deal with the symptoms (your doctor or nurse should be able to advise on this). Remember to take plenty of 'safe' drinks if you are ill and re-hydration salts to replace lost vitamins and minerals.

If vomiting and/or diarrhoea continue for more than four to five days or you run a fever, have convulsions or breathing difficulties (or any unusual symptoms), get someone to call a doctor straight away. Seek advice on the best doctor to call; the British Embassy or a five-star hotel in the area may be able to offer some advice here.

Eyes

Contact lens wearers should stock up on cleaning fluid before going, especially if venturing off the beaten track; but if you're going away for a long period it might be worth switching to disposable types so there's less to carry - ask your optician for advice.

Dust and wind can be a real problem, so refreshing eye drops to soothe itchy eyes and wash out grit can be really useful. If you wear contact lenses, your optician should be able to offer you a range of comfort drops which will be compatible with your lenses.

Also most supermarket pharmacies, plus travel and camping shops, sell plastic bottles of mildly medicated hand cleanser that dries instantly. They're small and light to carry and you only use a small amount each time so it's worth packing a couple. They're really useful for cleaning hands before putting in contact lenses if the local water supply is suspect. It's also worth making sure you have glasses as a back-up, as it's not always possible to replace lost or torn contacts.

If you wear glasses consider taking a spare pair - they don't have to be expensive and you can choose frames that are flexible and durable. Keep them in a hard glasses case in a waterproof (and sand proof) pouch.

Malaria

This disease is caught from the bite of an anopheles mosquito and mosquitoes are vicious and vindictive. Highest risk areas are tropical regions like sub-Saharan Africa, the Solomon Islands and Vanuatu (Pacific), the Amazon basin in South America and parts of Asia. There's no jab, but your GP will give you a course of pills to take.

The most dangerous form of malaria is falciparum, which is particularly common in sub-Saharan Africa (places like Ghana, Gambia, DR Congo). It can cause liver, kidney, stomach and neurological problems and if left untreated, can be fatal.

One bite from a mosquito is enough. The parasite gets to your liver within 30 minutes and will reproduce there rapidly, infecting the blood stream. Once the parasites are in your blood stream you start to notice symptoms. Some versions can remain dormant in the liver, leading to repeat episodes of the illness.

The best protection is to try (as much as possible) to avoid being bitten.

Here are tips for how:

- Use insect repellent, preferably containing either at least 30% DEET (diethyltoluamide), or extract of lemon eucalyptus oil.

- Keep your arms and legs covered between dusk and dawn and use a 'knockdown' spray to kill any mosquitoes immediately.

- Mosquito nets are useful, but they can be hard to put up correctly. It is often worth carrying a little extra string and small bits of wire so that the net can be hung up in rooms that don't have hanging hooks. Ideally the net should be impregnated with an insecticide, you can buy nets that are already treated from specialist shops and travel clinics (see **www.gap-yearshop.com**).

- For some places, dual-voltage mosquito killer plugs are a good idea. Tests carried out for *Holiday Which?* by the London School of Hygiene and Tropical Medicine found four that gave 100% protection - Boots Repel, Jungle Formula, Lifesystems and Mosqui-Go Duo. They also tested hand-

held electric buzzers which claim to frighten off mosquitoes and found that they did not work on the anopheles mosquito.

- Another good idea is to spray clothes with permethrin - which usually lasts up to two weeks, although Healthguard has a product, called AM-1, which works for three months or 30 washes. Visit **www.healthguardtm.com** to find out more or call them on +44 (0)20 8343 9911.

The pills can be expensive, and some people, particularly on long trips, stop taking their pills, especially if they're not getting bitten much. Don't. Malaria can be fatal.

No one drug acts on all stages of the disease, and different species of parasites show different responses. Your GP, practice nurse or local travel clinic should know which one of the varied anti-malarials is best for you, depending on your medical history (*eg* for epileptics or asthmatics, for whom some types of anti-malarials cannot be prescribed) and the countries you are visiting. Visit your GP or travel clinic at least eight weeks before you go to discuss the options.

It's also worth doing a little research of your own before going to your GP or practice nurse. A very useful website is: **www.malariahotspots.co.uk/**

All the anti-malarial tablets have various pros and cons, and some of them have significant side effects. If you're going to an area where you have to use the weekly mefloquine tablets, MASTA recommends that you start taking the course two and a half to three weeks before departure. Most people, who experience unpleasant side effects with this drug, will notice them by the third dose. If you do have problems, this trial will allow you time to swap to an alternative regime before you go.

visit: www.gap-year.com

If you are in a malaria-risk area, or have recently been in one, and start suffering from 'flu-like' symptoms, eg fever, muscle pain, nausea, headache, fatigue, chills, and/or sweats, you should consider the diagnosis of malaria and seek medical attention immediately.

A traveller with these symptoms within several months after returning from an endemic area should also seek medical care and tell their doctor their travel history. The correct treatment involves the proper identification of the type of malaria parasite, where the traveller has been and their medical history.

Sunburn

Avoid over-exposure, especially on first arrival in a sunny country, and use sun creams and sun block frequently.

According to Cancer Research UK, malignant melanoma accounts for 3% of all newly-diagnosed cancer cases per year. In the UK each year, more than 8,900 people are diagnosed with melanoma. More women than men get melanoma in the UK. It is the seventh most common cancer overall; the sixth commonest cancer in women and the tenth most common in men. The number of people getting melanoma now is four times higher than in the 1970s.

Almost a third of all cases in the UK occur in people aged under 50 and, according to Professor Jillian Birch of Manchester University, an expert on teenage cancers, melanoma is increasing at the rate of 4% a year among people aged 20-29.

Don't think you're safe if you're spending three months as a skiing instructor either - snow can increase the amount of exposure to the sun's harmful rays significantly.

Tick borne encephalitis

Every year, as the summer travel season starts, we get a warning from the Tick Alert Campaign about the dangers of tick borne diseases in Europe. Ticks are second only to mosquitoes for carrying disease to humans. According to MASTA, changes in farming practices and global warming mean that there are more ticks in the countryside in many parts of the UK and Europe. This means that more UK travellers are at risk than ever when visiting Europe each summer. Leading scientists have confirmed that Tick Borne Encephalitis (TBE), which can lead to meningitis and, in serious cases, result in paralysis and death, is endemic in 27 countries across mainland Europe.

Ticks carrying the disease are found in many destinations now growing in popularity, such as Croatia, the Czech Republic and Slovenia and have also spread to parts of established holiday spots such as Italy, Greece and France.

Vaccinations

Ones to consider:

- Hepatitis (A&B)

- Japanese Encephalitis
- Meningitis
- Polio
- Rabies
- Tetanus
- Tuberculosis
- Typhoid
- Yellow Fever

Ask your GP for advice on vaccinations/precautions at least six to eight weeks before you go (some may be available on the NHS). Keep a record card on you of what you've had done. Certain countries won't admit you unless you have a valid yellow fever certificate.

Seeking medical advice abroad

You can expect to be a bit ill when you travel just due to the different food and unsettled lifestyle (painkillers and loo paper will probably be the best things you've packed).

While you're away:

- keep a record of any treatment, such as courses of antibiotics, that you have when overseas and tell your doctor when you get back;
- be wary of needles and insist on unused ones; it's best if you can see the packet opened in front of you, or you could take a 'sterile kit' (containing needles) with you; and
- if you don't speak the language, have the basic words for medical emergencies written down so you can explain what is wrong.

In-country advice...

Responsible travel, respect, behaviour and dress codes

Your first impression of some countries will be a swarm of people descending on you, pestering you to take a taxi or buy something - at night when you're tired from a long plane trip it can be quite scary. If you're not being met by anyone, check whether there's a pre-pay kiosk in the airport and pay for a ticket to your ultimate destination. That way the taxi driver can't take you on a detour since they won't get their money until you're safely delivered and your 'chit' has been signed.

Some people advise that, if you arrive alone in the middle of the night (which is often the case on long-haul budget flights), it might be safer to wait until daylight before heading onwards. That's not a pleasant prospect in most airports, but it may occasionally be the sensible option.

In many countries of the developing world, where there are no social security or welfare systems, life can be extremely tough and leave people close to despair. That's likely to be even more the case, in the face of growing food shortages and escalating fuel and food costs as a result of the ongoing global recession. What may seem like a cheap trinket to you may be enough to buy them a square meal for which they are desperate enough to steal from you violently, so it is sensible not to wear too much jewellery.

Equally, wandering around discarding uneaten food is a particularly tactless thing to do, when large numbers of people may not know where their next meal is coming from.

Bear in mind that, in most places, even the so-called First World, rural communities are usually far more traditional and straight-laced than city ones and casual western dress codes and habits can offend.

If you don't want to find yourself in real trouble, do some research. Each culture or religion has its own codes of behaviour and taboos and, while no one would expect you to live by all their rules, as an ethical and responsible traveller, showing respect for the basic principles is a must as a guest in their country, not to mention being a sensible precaution if you want to stay safe. Also remember that a country's native people are not just part of the landscape, they are individuals who deserve respect and courtesy, so if you want to take a photo of them - ask first, or at least be discreet!

These are the sorts of things you should bear in mind: in most Asian and African countries don't wear a bikini top and shorts in city streets if you don't want to attract the wrong kind of intrusive male attention. In any case an all-over light cotton covering will better protect you from sunburn and insect bites.

Men and women should dress modestly, particularly, but not only, in Muslim countries. Women especially should wear long sleeves and cover their legs. Uncovered flesh, especially female, is seen as a 'temptation' and you'll be more comfortable, not to mention finding people more friendly and welcoming if they can see you're sensitive to local customs.

You should also remember that, in Buddhist countries, the head is sacred and so it is unconventional to touch it.

Before entering temples and mosques throughout India and south Asia, you must remove your shoes. There are usually places at the entrances, where you can leave them with attendants to look after them. Women are also expected to cover their hair - and in Jain temples wearing or carrying anything made of leather is forbidden. Even in parts of Europe you'd be expected to cover your head and be dressed respectfully if you go into a church.

Open gestures of affection, kissing or even holding hands between married couples can be shocking to some cultures. This is particularly true of India, though it seems to be relaxing a little in the cities. However, you will often see men or boys strolling around hand in hand or with arms around each other's shoulders in India - don't misinterpret: they are friends, *not* gay couples! Remember also, that if you are speaking English with a local inhabitant, they may not understand or use a word with the same meaning as you do. Particularly in the area of emotional relationships and dating, remembering this and understanding the local religion, customs and morality can save a lot of misunderstanding, misery and heartache.

Sitting cross-legged, with the soles of your feet pointing towards your companions, is another example of a gesture regarded as bad manners or even insulting in some places and actually if you think about it, it's pretty logical if you're in a place where people walk around less than clean streets either barefoot or in sandals.

Since daily life and faiths are often closely interlinked, it helps to know a little about the major philosophies of life in the countries you visit so, to get you started, here's some very basic info about some of the main belief systems out of the many hundreds around the world. We use the term belief systems because, arguably, some of these are closer to being philosophies of life than to religions or faiths in the sense most people would understand them:

Bahá'i

God: a single God known through God's creation and prophets.

Foundation text: Bahá'is believe that all religions are different approaches to faith in a single God. So no core text, but Bahá'ís believe in unity, equality and human rights for all. The founder, Bahá'u'lláh, taught that world unity is the final stage in the evolution of humanity. There is no conversion and no requirement for followers to renounce their previous faith. Bahá'i originated in Iran, and is the world's youngest, and widely considered to be its fastest-growing, religion.

Place of worship: can be anywhere, but there is a stunning modern, pink marble building, the Lotus Temple, in Delhi.

Holy day: the main one is 29 May, which commemorates the founder's teachings and his death on that day in 1892.

Shinto

The official religion of Japan, it has no specific God, no founder and no specific core texts.

Beliefs: a three-level universe; the Plain of High Heaven; the Manifested World; and the Nether World, but with the invisible worlds seen as an extension to the visible world. Kami (gods and spirit beings which include the ocean, the mountains, storms and earthquakes) allow believers to regard the whole natural world as both sacred and material. Ethics start from the basic idea that human beings are good, and that the world is good. Evil enters the world from outside, brought by evil spirits. Shinto has no moral absolutes and assesses the good or bad of an action or thought in the context in which it occurs: circumstances, intention, purpose, time, location, are all relevant in determining whether an action is bad. Harmony depends on the group being more important than the individual.

Place of worship: shrines: an enclosed sacred area with a gate, an area for ablutions and a main sanctuary. There is an emphasis on ancestral spirits and on the importance of gratitude for the blessings of the kami.

There are many special prayers and rituals marking the various stages through life from birth to death.

Festivals: the main one is *Oshogatsu* (New Year) but there are festivals throughout the year marking spring and autumn as well as coming of age (*Seijin Shiki* or Adults' Day) and *Schichigosan* (when parents give thanks for their children's lives and pray for their future).

Taoism

God: *Tao* means 'the Way' and is a philosophy of living, but there is a concept of the Eight Immortal Beings (*Psa Hien*) who are the protectors of various aspects of life.

Core text: the *Tao Te Ching* (the *Book of the Way*, known in the West as the *I-Ching*) written by Lao Tzu.

Place of worship: everywhere - the Way is essentially a philosophy for living a life in balance.

Core beliefs: *Tao* is 'The Way' and the first cause of the universe, *Te* is the virtue of the person who lives in accordance with *Tao*. Taoists follow the art of *wu wei*, (*ie* to let nature take its course, but also to be kind to others because it will be returned) and the essential aim of Taoism is to achieve a world in equilibrium (a balance of Yin and Yang, the extremes of the universe such as the sun and moon, heaven and earth, chaos and order). There is no rigid division between body and spirit.

Mechanisms for achieving balance include meditation, breathing exercises, use of acupuncture, practising Tai Chi, and Feng Shui.

Confucianism

God: like Taoism, in China Confucianism is a philosophy for living life and therefore there is no concept of a God.

Place of worship: everywhere.

Core beliefs: based on the teachings of Confucius, who was a philosopher, moralist, statesman and educationist. The *Jen*, the essence of his teaching can be loosely translated as 'social virtue'. Like Taoism it strives for balance and harmony - by behaving towards others as one would want them to behave towards oneself. Confucius is believed to have met Lao Tzu and, by some accounts, to have been his disciple. His main concerns were with good order in human beings' principle relationships and with good government expressed in the values: *Li* (ritual, propriety, etiquette); *Hsiao* (love within the family, love of parents for their children and of children for their parents); *Yi* (righteousness); *Xin* (honesty and trustworthiness); *Jen* (benevolence, humaneness towards others); and the highest Confucian virtue, *Chung* (loyalty to the state *etc*).

Shamanism

In Latin America, particularly the area around the Peruvian Amazon basin, the traditional holistic belief system is called shamanism though the shamanistic tradition is not found only in Latin America.

Within the shamanist system, as in other traditional systems around the world, diet is important for both physical and spiritual wellbeing.

Shamans are found in many communities and act as a link to the spirit world, healing specific illnesses, both mental and physical, as well as officiating at important life moments, such as birth and death. Plants are the starting point for seekers of physical and spiritual health and the shaman will help select the one that is appropriate for an individual's needs.

Many shamans have expert knowledge of the plant life in their area, and a herbal regimen is often prescribed as part of the treatment. They often say they learn directly from each plant how to harness their effects and healing properties only after obtaining permission from its abiding or patron spirit. Each plant is believed to have a spirit and each is linked to treating a specific condition of the mind or body.

It's possible to join programmes in the Amazon basin but - a note of warning - there's a spiritual as well as dietary aspect to the treatment, sometimes using plants with hallucinogenic properties, which can be a test of mental strength and stability. Misuse and abuse of these powerful plant-based 'medicines' can have dangerous and even fatal consequences.

Humanism

Humanists are agnostic or atheist since they believe it is impossible to prove the existence of God and that it is possible to be good without the need for a God.

The essence of humanist practice is that it is about rational behaviour, rejecting both a supernatural being involved in human affairs and the idea of an afterlife.

Core texts: there are none, nor are there any declarations of faith.

Humanists regard themselves as independent thinkers who have arrived at a set of moral and ethical values and behaviours, which are shared.

They include accepting responsibility for one's actions and behaviour and that it is important to try to live a full and happy life and to help others do the same. They value human rights, freedom of communication, freedom from want and fear, education should be moral but free of bias from the influence of powerful religious or political organisations and that no doctrine, religious or political, economic or moral should be immune to critical scrutiny.

Zoroastrianism

God: Ahura Mazda.

Foundation text: the *Avesta*. There are few rules in Zoroastrianism, whose basic concepts are truth and purity and can be summed up as 'good thoughts, good words and good deeds'. Men and women are considered equal and with a responsibility for their own behaviour. The main thrust is to be the best one can be so there is a strong emphasis on education and on free will. Zoroastrianism is named after its founder the prophet Zarathustra and originated in Persia (now Iran). Many followers fled to India (where they are known as Parsis) following the Mongol invasion of Persia and its subsequent conversion to Islam.

Place of worship: Fire temple - the eternal flame is seen as a symbol of purity, but it is *not* worshipped. It is incorrect to call Zoroastrians fire worshippers.

Main festival: Noruz - New Year (around 21 March).

Prohibited food: none.

Islam

God: Allah.

Foundation text: the *Qur'an* transmitted by the Prophet Mohammed (the Messenger, Rasul, of God). It is customary when referring to the Prophet to add the words "peace be upon him".

Place of worship: Mosque. It is also a place of learning and teaching.

The five pillars of Islam: *Shahada* (declaration of faith); *Salat* (prayers five times a day); *Zakat* (charity tax for the poor); *Sawm* (fast during Ramadan); and *Haj* (pilgrimage to Mecca).

Holy day: Friday.

Main festival: Ramadan - a month when Muslims fast from dawn to dusk.

Greeting: *As Salaam aleikum* (Peace be upon you); reply *Wa aleikum salaam*.

Prohibited food and drink: pork, alcohol.

Jihad: literally means struggle - it does not mean holy war, though the term has been inaccurately used in that way by many people, Muslim and non-Muslim. The struggle is primarily a personal one against one's own faults and weaknesses.

Judaism

God: *Yhwh* (pronounced Yahweh).

Foundation texts: the Old Testament of *The Bible* and the *Torah*.

The Talmud: an explanation of the *Torah*, teachings and discussions of Jewish scholars.

Place of worship: the Synagogue, also used as a place of learning and teaching.

Holy day: Sabbath (sunset Friday to sunset Saturday).

Main festival: Yom Kippur - the day of atonement when Jews must seek forgiveness from those they have wronged.

Prohibited food: pork.

Zionism: an international political movement launched in 1897, by Austrian journalist Theodor Herzl, with the aim of establishing, in law, a Jewish homeland in Palestine. To be a Jew is not automatically to be a Zionist.

Hinduism

God: Brahman - represented by the 'Om' symbol, the creator and destroyer of life and the universe. The multiplicity of other 'gods' such as Brahma, Vishnu and Shiva, (the Trimurti) Parvati, Kali, Durga, Ganesha, to name but a few of the many Hindu deities, represent different paths to follow reflecting the variety of human life and the sense of personal responsibility for one's own actions.

Foundation literature: the *Vedas*, the core text representing an oral tradition coming direct from God.

Main festival: Diwali is the main one but there are many more.

Place of worship: temples to the many different deities are widespread and can be anything from tiny street shrines to huge, elaborately carved ancient monuments. People also have shrines in their homes. Many rivers, not only the Ganges, are also sacred.

Holy days: far too many to list. There is no specific day for prayer.

Prohibited food: beef (cows are sacred) but various peoples follow specific dietary requirements, from total vegetarianism through to eating of non-prohibited meats and fish, depending on the region they're from and their caste.

Essence of Hinduism: life is seen as an endlessly-repeating cycle of death and rebirth. Essentially the aim is to reach *moksha* and therefore release from the cycle of reincarnation. Karma is the accumulated result of a person's past action and determines the form in which they will be re-born. Dharma is the path of righteousness and duty, following which the individual can hope to improve their karma until they eventually reach *moksha*. This means that, as for other faiths, Hinduism is interwoven into the fabric of daily life and there is an emphasis on personal responsibility for one's behaviour, and therefore on modesty in dress and actions.

Buddhism

God: there is no name or central concept of a God. Buddhism is essentially a philosophy and a way of life leading to the goal of attaining nirvana - the release from the struggle to survive and from passion, aggression and ignorance.

Place of worship: although there are many shrines to the founder of Buddhism, Siddharta Gautama, he is not worshipped as a god nor is he

seen as one. The nature of Buddhism does not require a place of worship and the *stupas* (characteristic round towers) are sacred buildings housing relics or the remains of a saintly person. There is, however, a tradition of monastic communities, particularly found in the foothills of the Himalayas, in Thailand and in Tibet.

The essence of Buddhism: a philosophy for living summed up by the Four Noble Truths and the Noble Eightfold Path. The four truths were contained in the Buddha's first sermon and explain that suffering is part of life (the first truth) caused by the struggle to survive and by craving and aversion (second truth). That suffering can be overcome and we can become happy and free with more time to help others (third truth). The fourth truth is the way to achieve this - by following the Eightfold Path.

The Eightfold Path: Right View; Right Intention; Right Speech; Right Discipline; Right Livelihood; Right Effort; Right Mindedness; and Right Concentration.

Affirmation: Buddhists take five vows: to refrain from killing living beings; taking that which is not given; from sexual misconduct; from false speech; and from alcohol and drugs which confuse the mind.

Jainism

God: Jains believe in karma and there is no room in the belief system for a creator God. To follow the Jain faith is to follow a very rigorous and difficult way of life.

Place of worship: there are many ancient, beautiful and very ornate temples in India, particularly in Gujarat, but they are not quite places of worship in the sense generally understood.

45

The essence of Jainism: all beings, including inanimate objects, such as stones and earth, are alive and feeling. Consequently this is a strictly non-possessive and non-violent code of living.

Followers are divided into *sadhus* (monks), *sadhivas* (nuns), *shravak* (laymen) and *shravika* (lay women). The essence of Jainism is to strive for liberation of the self through right faith, right knowledge and right conduct (not unlike the Zoroastrian good thoughts, good words and good deeds).

The five great vows (*Maha-vratas*): right conduct includes not harming any living thing, not stealing, chastity, detachment from people, place and material things. Jains wear only white, usually with a mask over the nose and mouth to avoid inhaling insects. They also carry a soft brush to sweep any place they plan to sit to avoid harming any living thing.

Main festival: *Paryshana Parva* (August/September), which ends with people wishing each other *Michhami-Dudakam*, meaning: 'Forgive me if I have done anything wrong or hurt your feelings knowingly or unknowingly.'

Sikhism

God: Sikhism recognises one universal God of all nations, who has no name.

Place of worship: *Gurdwara* - this is both a temple and a community centre, a symbol of equality and fraternity. Many *Gurdwara* community kitchens, known as *Pangat*, or *Guru-Ka-Langar*, produce a daily meal to feed thousands of destitute people in their neighbourhoods. It's a religion firmly rooted in the world and so encourages work, enterprise and wealth.

Foundation text: the *Guru Granth Sahib*.

The essence of Sikkhism: the religion evolved in India at a time of considerable spiritual confusion, following the *Mughal* (Muslim) invasion into largely Hindu India. Sikkhism is open to anyone and is a faith rooted in optimism and in equal status, though with different roles, between men and women. Sikh unity and personality is based on the five Ks - *Kesha* (long and uncut hair); *Kangha* (a comb); *Kara* (a steel bracelet); *Kaccha* (special shorts worn as underwear) and *Kirpan* (the sword).

Prohibited: alcohol, tobacco, eating meat, and adultery.

Holy day: there is a daily service, called the *Granthi*, in the *Gurdwara* and Sikhs are expected to start their day with prayer, though they can visit the *Gurdwara* at any time of the day to pray. However what matters most is the way they live their daily lives.

Festivals: Vaisaki – harvest festival (around 13 April) and the celebration of the birth of the *Khalsa* (the brotherhood of those pure in word and deed).

For more information, or if you are interested in finding out about other religions, try: **www.bbc.co.uk/religion/religions**

Personal safety and security

Most of these are common sense, but are worth noting here. Our safety tips checklist is:

- At airports and terminals never leave luggage unattended or ask a stranger to 'keep an eye' on your belongings!
- Travel in pairs if you can. The more remote a place is, the more useful it is to have company.
- Never hitchhike or accept lifts from strangers.
- Be aware of your body language: walk confidently and purposefully, even if you're feeling nervous or unsure, inconspicuous clothing may help you blend into the crowd better.
- Avoid badly-lit streets after dark.
- Never discuss your own or your family's financial situation with strangers.
- Never try unknown substances.
- Never carry unopened parcels for people, especially when you fly.
- Always let people know where you are going and stay in touch with people back home regularly.
- Don't swim in strong currents, heavy waves or crocodile-infested waters.
- Check fire exit routes in hostels or other buildings where you plan to stay.
- Shake out clothes and shoes before you put them on: snakes, scorpions or allergy-causing plants may have got inside.
- If you don't like the look of some of the other people in a hostel, put your bed against the door at night.
- Keep windows open if you are in a room with a gas water heater, or other source of carbon monoxide, to let gases escape if the equipment is faulty.

Tip: It can help to arrive with some local currency in notes and coins. You can often change travellers' cheques in banks at airport arrivals halls.

Remember, anyone can get lost. When you are on the road don't panic. Always agree meeting places before you go somewhere and play safe by having a back-up plan. Then if you don't turn up reasonably on time someone will be alerted to raise the alarm.

Before you do anything or go anywhere think about the consequences - this isn't about not having a good time, or being boring - it's about getting through your **gap-** without taking foolish risks.

In many places, though, you'll find people are very hospitable and curious about you and you might find their unabashed and quite frank questions intrusive. While you have to be sensible about how much information you give, equally try not to be too suspicious about their motives. What feels like an invasion of your personal space, or probing questioning, doesn't automatically mean anything sinister - remember the British in particular can be quite reserved so you'll notice the contrast. It's all a question of balance and courtesy.

If you are offered strange drinks or drugs be sensible and think about your safety first. One of the biggest dangers in accepting a drink is that someone can slip in the so-called 'date rape' drug (Rohypnol). It doesn't taste of anything and you won't know you're taking it. Combined with alcohol, it can induce a blackout with memory loss and decrease your resistance, leaving you open to attack.

About ten minutes after ingesting the drug, you may feel dizzy and disoriented, simultaneously too hot and too cold, or nauseous. You might have difficulty speaking or moving and then pass out. Victims have no memory of what happened while under the drug's influence.

If you are tempted to try the local variety of cannabis in the belief that it is relatively harmless, remember that this isn't a view shared by everyone at home, never mind in other countries. Know what the local drug laws are and don't take risks. In many places in south Asia and south-east Asia, for example, it is illegal and possession carries stiff penalties in prisons where conditions are not remotely like they are in the UK. It's a shame to have to add this, but don't assume that a friendly Brit (who may or may not be a traveller) you might meet in a bar, on a beach, up a mountain *etc*, is any more trustworthy, genuine and agenda-free than a local. It's great to make conversation, break down barriers and feel 'at home' in a place - just exercise a degree of caution with any stranger!

If someone keeps pestering you with unwanted sexual advances after you have said no, get to somewhere where there are other people within earshot. Only use violence as a last resort - it's not worth fighting back against violent muggers. They're likely to be stronger than you and may be carrying a gun or a knife. Try to remain as calm and confident as possible - that way you'll be more likely to recall those useful tips you learnt on the training course you attended before you left.

Tip: Try to always carry a supply of small change and small notes in a pocket (trousers or jeans with deep pockets can be very useful) and not reveal that you are carrying larger notes.

Do not keep all your money in one place; distribute it between, say, a small daytime backpack, your rucksack or suitcase and a hidden belt bag so that if you are robbed, you still have some money in reserve.

If someone tries to snatch your bag throw it at them - it keeps as much space as possible between you and them and puts them off guard, giving you time to get away. Stick close to other people while you get back to base.

Money pouches worn around the waist under clothes are really good, though thieves have become much more expert at spotting them and removing them without you knowing, so it's a good idea to pass the straps through your belt loops.

Tip: One solution could be to buy some stick-on Velcro™ (or the stitch-on variety - more time-consuming but ultimately more secure) and attach a strip to the waistband inside all your trousers with the matching strip on the back of the belt bag.

If you have money, a camera or a passport stolen abroad (and the chances of this are high), report the theft immediately to the nearest police station and make sure you have some written record from them, giving the date that you did so, with all relevant details.

Police in popular budget destinations may have had to deal with hundreds of insurance scams in the past and may not be sympathetic. Dress smartly (and cover up; going in a bikini is not a good idea); stay polite and calm, but firm. It is very unlikely anyone will catch the thief or get your stuff back - all you need is a record of the police report for your insurance claim.

Ask someone back home to notify insurers and post or fax a copy of the police notification home. Many insurers will not pay up for loss or theft unless the police are notified (some policies won't pay out if you don't do this within 24 hours).

This also applies if you are involved in any accident likely to result in an insurance claim. Keep records of everything that might be important - better to throw it away later than not to have it when needed.

Keeping in touch

Spare a thought for those you're leaving behind - friends as well as family. Not only will they be worried about your safety, but they may actually be interested in your travels - most are probably jealous and wish they could go too.

It's not just about keeping them happy: make sure you tell them where you are and where you are going - that way if something does happen to you, at least they know where to start looking. Backpackers do go missing, climbers have accidents, trekkers get lost; at least if someone is concerned that you have not got in touch when expected, they can then alert the police. If you've promised to check in regularly with close family *make sure you do*, especially when you move on to another country. Of course, if you don't stick to what you agreed, don't be surprised if the international police come looking for you.

You can use a BT Chargecard to phone home from abroad from any phone - just call the operator and quote your pin number (having set it up before you left). The calls are charged to your BT phone account back home and are itemised on the bill; weekly limits can be set in advance. There are different types of Chargecard accounts you can set up, including limiting card use to one number or a set of numbers. For further details on BT Chargecards see: **www.payphones.bt.com/callingcards/prices/index.htm**

While you probably can't wait to get away, you may be surprised how homesickness can creep up on you when you're thousands of miles away. Getting letters or emails can be a great pick-me-up if you're feeling homesick, weary or lonely, so, in order to ensure a steady supply of mail, distribute your address(es) widely to friends and family before you go. If you're not able to leave behind an exact address then you can have letters sent to the local Poste Restante, often at a main post office, and collect them from there. Also, parcels do usually get through, but don't send anything valuable.

Keeping a diary/sketchbook to record places, projects, people, how you're feeling and the effect things are having on you, can help when you get an attack of the homesick blues or just feel a bit down.

49

Mobile phone basics

Make sure you've set up your account to allow you to make and receive calls and text messages in all the countries you'll be travelling to (and emails if you've got a WAP phone).

Try to limit use of your mobile to emergencies - they usually cost a fortune to run abroad as you pay for all the incoming calls at international rates too. (See Chapter 2 - Finance, for details on where to get an international sim card.)

It's worth insuring the handset, as mobile theft is common and if it's the latest model, try not to flash it around.

But don't rule out using your mobile phone as **gap-** kit; it might save your life if you break your leg halfway up a mountain and need to call for help (make sure you keep the battery charged).

If you are staying in one country for several weeks, consider getting either a cheap local mobile phone or a local SIM card for your UK mobile. Don't forget to alert friends back home to the new number! Local texts and calls tend to be very cheap and incoming calls from abroad are free, which avoids the massive charges when using your UK mobile.

Snail mail

Aerogrammes are a cheap way of writing from most countries. Registering letters usually costs only a few pence (or equivalent) from Third World countries, and is definitely worthwhile. Postcards are quick, cheap and easy - though not very private.

www.pc2paper.co.uk - This website allows you to send letters worldwide from the internet and store addresses in your account. You type your message and they then convert it into an actual letter and post it for you. The costs vary depending on weight and size.

Email

These days it's pretty unlikely you don't already have an email account from one of the free services, but here's a list of the more popular ones just in case:

www.googlemail.com

www.hotmail.com

www.uk.yahoo.com/

www.info.aol.co.uk/email

If you can get to a cybercafé or internet kiosk in an airport, hotel, university, office or home when you're abroad, you can simply log in to your mailbox (remember you'll need your User ID and password if these are part of the package). If you think getting to a cybercafé is going to be hard, there are always WAP phones (you need to register your email address before you leave).

Air Mail (**www.airmail.co.uk**) will forward emails to you as text messages sent to your mobile, and you can send emails by simply sending them a text message, which they will forward as an email. Check their website for their up-to-date tariff. In practice, however, if there are no internet facilities in the area then the chances are there won't be a mobile phone signal either, and you may have to resort to more traditional methods of communication.

Having said that, thousands of cybercafés now sprinkle the globe, and internet connections can be difficult in Delhi but perfectly okay in Bolivia, so you'll probably find somewhere that you can email home at some point.

Online journals

Another easy way to keep everyone up-to-date is to set up a travel blog - as many people now do. You can also sign up to Facebook or MySpace before you go (if you haven't done so already). On Facebook, your photos and comments will be available only to your 'friends' (unless you relax the privacy settings for a particular album) but there is the added advantage of being able to send messages and pictures to specific people without having to remember their email address, providing, of course, they too have a Facebook page.

Other sites you might like to check out are:

www.travelblog.org

www.yourtraveljournal.com

www.offexploring.com

www.fuzzytravel.com

www.twitter.com/

www.travoholic.com/articles/flashpacking.htm

If you're interested in cities have a look at the urban travel blogsite:

www.gridskipper.com/

And finally... back to earth after a gap-

We've talked to enough people, who've already taken a **gap-,** to know that a kind of reverse culture shock takes hold within a few days of your return home. Returning to ordinary life takes time. It doesn't matter when you took your **gap-,** you're likely to still go through the same sequence of feelings over the three months it generally takes to readjust.

How you respond, though, will depend on what you are returning to - if you went between school and university you might find yourself switching courses or storing up something else to explore later. Or you might be quite content to take up your course with renewed enthusiasm after a travelling break from study.

Coming back from a properly-structured **gap-** immediately after university is a great addition to a CV, but you already knew that when you used this guidebook to help you plan it, didn't you?

It's different again for people mid-career or over-50 mature travellers, but the pattern of adjustment is pretty much the same.

Prepare for crash-landing

The length of time you've been away makes no difference to the feelings you go through on your return and even after six months you may still need time to adjust.

We've talked to people who've taken a two week leave of absence from work through their company's charitable foundation and to people who've spent a year or more away. They all report coming back and finding themselves looking at everything through fresh eyes and questioning the importance of various aspects of homelife that they've previously taken for granted.

On average, it seems to take about three months on average between stepping off that last plane after a **gap-** and getting back into life's routines

To start with, a commonly-reported phenomenon is the odd sensation of the body decelerating while the brain's still on the move. So, after the first three weeks of initial euphoria and sharing, be prepared to come down to earth with a bump.

Here's one gapper's comment: "There is no feeling quite like it, I keep thinking about my next trip to keep me going!"

visit: www.gap-year.com

What do you do now?

This one depends on what you had planned before you left and whether the option's still there - and if you still want to do it - once you're back.

Some people advise that, if you can manage it, putting aside some money for about three months of living expenses for your return, as part of pre-**gap**-preparations, takes the pressure off if you're going to be job hunting. But if taking time out isn't an option, don't panic.

If you already have work to go back to you may have to combine the post trip elation with a fairly quick return to the 'rat race'. And you ll need to think about how you interact with your colleagues. How much do you say about your trip?

A spokeswoman for one major UK employer, which supports its staff in taking time out, and also has a foundation on whose projects they can do voluntary work, had this advice:

"When you are returning to work it is important to have a plan. Returning to work after 18 weeks or more can prove difficult on both a psychological and logistical level.

"Keep your line manager up-to-date with the timings of your return to work. This will ensure that they can factor you into their resource planning and also help you integrate back into the working environment.

"Do not rule out a degree of retraining when you return to work. Refreshing your skills will benefit most people in the work place, and, if you have been away from work for a long period of time, you should use the opportunity to familiarise yourself with new systems, procedures and practices.

"When you return to work take into consideration reverse culture shock. Whilst you might be keen to talk about your travels for many months to come, your colleagues may not be so keen to listen."

Karen Woodbridge, Director of Suffolk-based Hornet Solutions (an Independent HR/Employment Law Consultancy), also offers some important advice:

"Remember the old adage 'Out of sight, out of mind'. Your colleagues have been getting on with business whilst you've been away. There may even have been changes of personnel, for example your old team members or boss may have left the company. There certainly will be new alliances and different company politics. Don't expect people to remember that you were a 'star performer' before you left. That role may well be occupied by someone else now.

"So, in many ways it will help if you think about returning to your old position as if it were a brand new job, *ie* expect things to be new, to have changed and realise that it will be up to you, once again, to find out how everything works and prove yourself. Realising you may face these challenges and planning how to overcome them will help you to more successfully integrate and adapt to your return at work."

If you have to start earning as soon as you get back and your old job wasn't kept open for you, you can always consider temporary work. These positions are often available immediately and can be flexible enough to enable you to carry on with your permanent job search. And you never know, once working in a company, opportunities often come up that you'd never have expected.

However, when looking for that new permanent role, Karen Woodbridge says: "You need to carefully consider how to put together your CV. Unfortunately many people use the phrase 'travelling' to cover gaps; they may be using this term to hide an unsuccessful job which ended in their dismissal or possibly even time spent in prison! Consequently, recruiters can be cynical whenever they see 'travelling' on a CV, which may result in your CV, with its genuine period of travelling, being rejected before you are even given a chance to explain.

"The way to tackle this is to expand on your experience. Highlight all the positive things you did, discovered or learnt in your time away. Within the confines of the space (and CVs should usually be no more than two pages) make your experience seem very real and highlight how it has increased the contribution you can make to the role for which you are applying. I would also highlight the additional benefits your travelling experience will bring to your new employer on your covering letter. But remember, in a job search situation it's the benefits to the employer that will count, not how much fun you had."

How is it now? Deciding what next

While taking up the threads of life, you've no doubt been trying to process everything you've learned from your **gap-** experience.

How do you feel? What's changed? What's been confirmed? Where to now? Is there something new you want to do next as a result? How to go about it?

You'll almost certainly still be in touch with friends you made on your travels, maybe even had a couple of after **gap-** reminiscence meetings. Others may still be travelling and keeping you restless!

You may also still be in touch with the projects you worked on. It's a fairly common feeling to want to keep a link to something that's been a life changing, learning experience. Is this you?

The best piece of advice on dealing with the consequences of any life changing experience is to be patient and give it time. Nothing but time can make things settle into some kind of perspective and help you work out whether you are in the grip of a sudden enthusiasm or something deeper and more long-lasting.

The first reaction most people report is that it's whetted their appetites to hit the road again. But at the same time you need to be sure you're doing it for the right reasons. As one gapper told us: "There seemed to be a lot of lost souls who were running away from reality at home rather than going travelling for positive reasons. The problems will still be there when they get back home, and in many cases putting them off will only make things worse."

Change of direction?

In time you'll know whether your urge to travel has also become an urge to keep the links with the communities you visited now you're back.

What level of involvement do you want? Is it going to be something local like fundraising - doing local talks, letters to newspapers - or are you seriously looking to change career?

If you have come back with the germ of an idea for a career change as a result of a volunteer placement, for example, there's nothing to stop you slowly exploring the options and possibilities.

Have a look at your CV. Try to talk to people working in the field you're considering moving into. Armed with some basic information, you could also consider talking through issues such as what transferable skills you have to add to your volunteer experience, what training you might need and how affordable it is, with a careers counsellor or recruitment specialist - preferably with an organisation that specialises in aid/charity or NGO positions.

Try these links:

www.totaljobs.com/IndustrySearch/NotForProfitCharities.aspx

www.cafonline.org

www.charitypeople.co.uk/

www.peopleandplanet.org/ethicalcareers/

To keep you going you should also never underestimate the power of synchronicity. You may find unexpected connections and information come your way while you're getting on with other things. If it's meant to be, you'll find ways to make it happen.

For all the things you have in mind, and those you don't!

Exploring other cultures, meeting new people, extreme sports - we know there are plenty of things you want to cram into your travels. But with so much to see and do it can be easy to forget the practical things that need to be done BEFORE you leave - that is where GapAid can help.

Providing essential information for those considering a year out, from help with financial and insurance cover to what to pack and where to go - GapAid's website helps you prepare for an adventure of a lifetime.

READ, RESEARCH THEN TRAVEL

Being Safe

Adventure First Aid
15 Laskeys Heath, Liverton,
Newton Abbot, Devon TQ12 6PH

Travel first aid and crisis management courses over two days, delivered by experienced professional trainers.

Basis Training UK Ltd
18 Ael-y-Coed, Barry, Glamorganshire CF62 6LN

Company providing self defence training course which is tailored to the individual's requirements.

British Red Cross
44 Moorfields, Barbican, London EC2Y 9AL

The Red Cross (Charity No. 220949) offers first aid courses around the UK lasting from one to four days depending on your experience and the level you want to achieve.

Ecobrands
3 Adam & Eve Mews, South Kensington, London W8 6UG

Pharmaceuticals for the traveller available to buy online.

Gap Aid
PO Box 734,
Oxford OX1 9EY

Email: ally@gapaid.org
Tel: +44 (0)7903 285314
www.gapaid.org

Exploring other cultures, meeting new people, extreme sports- we know there are plenty of things you want to cram into your travels. But with so much to see and do it can be easy to forget the practical things that need to be done *before* you leave - that is where GapAid can help.

Providing essential information for those considering a year out, from help with financial planning and insurance cover, to what to pack and where to go - GapAid's website helps you prepare for an adventure of a lifetime.

Read, Research, then Travel.

InterHealth Worldwide
111 Westminster Bridge Road,
Lambeth, London SE1 7HR

InterHealth provide services such as travel health advice *eg* on immunisations, and support people worldwide.

57

Intrepid Expeditions
3 Chapel Court Cottages, Broadclyst,
Exeter, Devon EX5 3JT

Runs many different survival courses, including a first aid course, ranging from two to 14 days..

Lifesaver Systems
Old Bakery, 7 Tuddenham Avenue,
Ipswich, Suffolk IP4 2HE

All-in-one filtration system, in a bottle, which will turn the foulest water into safe drinking water without the use of chemicals.

Lifesavers (The Royal Life Saving Society)
River House, High Street, Broom
Alcester, Warwickshire B50 4HN

Contact them for information about qualifications in life saving, lifeguarding and lifesupport.

Mind The Gap Year
19-21 West House, West Street,
Haslemere, Surrey GU27 2AB

Email: info@mindthegapyear.com
Tel: +44 (0) 845 180 0060
www.mindthegapyear.com

We are a tailor-made combination of insurance and services for the gap-year traveller, promoting how to stay safe and prepare for your travels. Services include a free online planner, worldwide research tool, electronic document safe, discount off safety training and, most importantly, specialist backpacker insurance, plus much more.

Objective Travel Safety Ltd
Bragborough Lodge Farm, Braunston,
Daventry, Northamptonshire NN11 7HA UK

A fun one-day safety course for travellers, designed to teach them how to think safe and prepare for challenges they may face.

Remote Trauma Limited
2 Bridle Close, Surbiton Road,
Kingston Upon Thames, Surrey KT1 2JW

Specialist medical support and first aid training.

St John Ambulance
National Headquarters,
27 St John's Lane,
Clerkenwell, London EC1M 4BU

The St John Ambulance Association runs first aid courses throughout the year around the country. Courses last a day and are suitable for all levels of experience.

Suffolk Sailing
Unit 75, Claydon Business Park,
Gipping Road, Great Blakenham
Ipswich, Suffolk IP6 0NL

Although mainly suppliers of sailing safety equipment, Suffolk Sailing does offer a one-day RYA/DOT Basic Sea Survival Course for Small Craft.

The Instant Mosquito Net Company Ltd
25 Berkeley Close, Rochester, Kent ME1 2UA

Fully portable, self supporting mosquito net. Lightweight, easy to use and folds into its own carry bag.

The Year Out Group
Queensfield, 28 King's Road,
Easterton, Wiltshire SN10 4PX

Email: info@yearoutgroup.org
Tel: +44 (0) 1380 816696
www.yearoutgroup.org

See main entry under volunteering.

TravelPharm
Unit 10 D, Mill Park Industrial Estate,
White Cross Road, Woodbury Salterton, Devon EX5 1EL

Provides travellers with a range of medication and equipment at very competitive prices to make your journey both healthier and safer!

Ultimate Gap Year
5 Beaumont Crescent, Earl's Court, London W14 9LX

Personalised safety training suitable for anyone embarking on a gap-year. Training held at homes throughout south-east England.

YSP - Your Safe Planet Ltd
Bridgefield House, Spark Bridge,
Ulverston, Cumbria LA12 8DA

Website linking travellers to trusted local people worldwide, giving you access to local knowledge before you go.

Communication

0044 Ltd
2 Chapel Court, Holy Walk,
Leamington Spa, Warwickshire CV32 6EX

Their global SIM card could save you money on international calls.

aether mobile
8 Dianthus Place, Winkfield Row, Bracknell, Berkshire RG42 7PQ

Cheaper phone calls from abroad. Try their online Rate Checker to find out how much you could save.

CommsFactory
Oaklands, Shirlheath, Kingsland
Leominster, Herefordshire HR6 9RH

Produces foreign language and communications materials for emergency services and adventure travellers including the Lost For Words card.

iD-Everywhere Limited
65 Dundonald Drive,
Leigh on Sea, Essex SS9 1NA

Company offering a range of items, such as dog tags and ID cards, which enable you to access their secure website and store important information.

Internet Outpost
PO Box 4640,
Cairns, QLD 4870, Australia

Internet access and more available to travellers throughout Australia, New Zealand and Indonesia.

My Mate Back Home
PO Box 7143, Westbourne,
Bournemouth, Dorset BH4 0EA

A company that looks after your mail and makes sure that it gets to you, anywhere in the world.

PocketComms Ltd
The TechnoCentre,
Coventry University Technology Park, Puma Way
Coventry, Warwickshire CV1 2TT

A universal language system in pictorial form.

Sim4travel Ltd
SCN Ltd t/a SIM4travel, 4 Royal Mint Court,
London EC3N 4HJ

Stay in touch for less overseas. Use your own mobile and save up to 80% off standard call charges.

Planning The Route

Ants Media Group
Currumbin Sands Building,
71/955 Gold Coast Highway,
Palm Beach, QLD 4221, Australia

Australian TV company with a programme dedicated to backpackers.

60

British Educational Travel Association (BETA)
PO Box 182,
Carshalton, Surrey SM5 2XW

National body for youth, student and educational travel, representing over 120 members in various sectors.

Geography Outdoors
Royal Geographical Society (with IBG),
1 Kensington Gore,
South Kensington, London SW7 2AR

Provides information, training and advice to anyone involved in expeditions, field research or outdoor learning in the UK and overseas.

HnH Travellers Australia
18 Withington Street,
East Brisbane, QLD 4169, Australia

Information portal for all things Australian.

The Year Out Group
Queensfield, 28 King's Road,
Easterton, Wiltshire SN10 4PX

Email: info@yearoutgroup.org
Tel: +44 (0) 1380 816696
www.yearoutgroup.org

See main entry under volunteering.

Tourist Boards

This year we've included a selection of tourist boards for various countries. Although a **gap**-year is *not* a holiday, there may be things you want to do and see whilst in your chosen country, and these people should be able to help you.

Anguilla Tourist Board
c/o CSB Communications, 7a Crealock Street,
Southfields, London SW18 2BS

Email: anguilla@tiscali.co.uk
www.anguilla-vacation.com

China National Tourist Office
4 Glentworth Street,
Marylebone, London NW1 5PG

Email: london@cnta.gov.cn
www.cnto.org

Croatian National Tourist Board
Tourist Office, Lanchesters,
162-164 Fulham Palace Road,
Hammersmith, London W6 9ER

Email: info@croatia-london.co.uk
http://gb.croatia.hr

Cyprus Tourist Office
17 Hanover Street,
Mayfair, London W1S 1YP

Email: informationcto@btconnect.com
www.visitcyprus.com

Czech Republic Tourist Office
Czech Tourist Authority, 13 Harley Street,
Marylebone, London W1G 9QG

Email: info-uk@czechtourism.com
www.czechtourism.co.uk

Denmark Tourist Board
55 Sloane Street,
Belgravia, London SW1X 9SY

Email: london@visitdenmark.com
www.visitdenmark.com

Egyptian Tourist Bureau
170 Piccadilly,
St James's, London W1J 9EJ

Email: info.uk@egypt.travel

Embassy of Brazil in London
Tourist Office, 32 Green Street,
Mayfair, London W1K 7AT

Email: tourism@brazil.org.uk
www.brazil.org.uk/tourism/index.html

Estonian Embassy in London
16 Hyde Park Gate,
South Kensington, London SW7 5DG

Email: london@mfa.ee
www.estonia.gov.uk/tourism

Fiji Visitors Bureau United Kingdom
Lion House, 111 Hare Lane,
Claygate, Surrey KT10 0QY

www.bulafiji.com

German National Tourist Office
PO Box 2695,
Soho, London W1A 3TN

Email: gntolon@d-z-t.com
www.germany-tourism.co.uk

Government of India Tourist Office
7 Cork Street,
Mayfair, London W1S 3LH

Email: contactus@incredibleindia.org
www.incredibleindia.org

Greek National Tourism Organisation
4 Conduit Street,
Mayfair, London W1S 2DJ

Email: info@gnto.co.uk
www.gnto.co.uk

visit: www.gap-year.com

Hong Kong Tourist Office
6 Grafton Street,
Mayfair, London W1S 4EQ

Email: lonwwo@hktb.com
www.discoverhongkong.com/uk/

Iceland Tourist Information Bureau
Embassy of Iceland, 2a Hans Street,
Belgravia, London SW1X 0JE

Italian State Tourist Board
1 Princes Street,
Mayfair, London W1B 2AY

Email: italy@italiantouristboard.co.uk
www.italiantouristboard.co.uk

Japan National Tourism Organization
London Office 5th Floor, 12 Nicholas Lane,
London EC4N 7BN

www.seejapan.co.uk

Kenya Tourist Board
Colechurch House, 1 London Bridge Walk,
Southwark, London SEI 2SX

Email: kenya@hillsbalfoursynergy.com
www.magicalkenya.com

Latvian Tourism Bureau in London
72 Queensborough Terrace,
Bayswater, London W2 3SH

Email: london@latviatourism.lv
http://latviatourism.lv

Luxembourg Tourist Office
Sicilian House - Suite 4.1, Sicilian Avenue,
Holborn, London WC1A 2QR

www.luxembourg.co.uk

Norway Tourism Office
Charles House, 5 Lower Regent Street,
St James's, London SW1Y 4LR

www.visitnorway.com

Russian National Tourism Office
First Floor, 70 Piccadilly,
Mayfair, London W1J 8HP

Email: info@visitrussia.org.uk
www.visitrussia.org.uk

Singapore Tourism Board
Singapore Centre, Grand Buildings, 1-3 Strand
London WC2N 5HR

Email: stb_london@stb.gov.sg
www.visitsingapore.com

South African Tourism
PO Box 49110,
Wimbledon, London SW19 4XZ

Email: info.uk@southafrica.net
www.southafrica.net

Spain Tourist Board
PO Box 4009,
Soho, London W1A 6NB

www.spain.info

Sri Lanka Tourism Promotion Bureau
No 1, 3rd Floor, Devonshire Square
Broadgate, London EC2M 4WD

Email: infouk@srilanka.travel
www.srilanka.travel

Switzerland Tourism
30 Bedford Street,
Strand, London WC2E 9ED

Email: info.uk@myswitzerland.com
www.myswitzerland.com

The French Tourist Board
Lincoln House, 300 High Holborn,
Holborn, London WC1V 7JH

Email: info.uk@franceguide.com
http://uk.franceguide.com

Tourism Australia
Australia Centre, Australia House,
6th Floor, Melbourne Place, Strand
London WC2B 4LG

www.tourism.australia.com

Tourism Authority of Thailand
1st Floor, 17-19 Cockspur Street,
Trafalgar Square, St James's, London SW1Y 5BL

www.tourismthailand.co.uk

Tunisian National Tourist Office
77a Wigmore Street,
Marylebone, London W1U 1QF

Email: info@cometotunisia.co.uk
www.cometotunisia.co.uk

Turkey Tourism Office
29-30 St. James's Street,
St James's, London SW1A 1HB

Email: info@gototurkey.co.uk
www.gototurkey.co.uk

Visit Britain
Thames Tower, Black's Road, Hammersmith
London W6 9EL

www.visitbritain.co.uk

Visit Jamaica
1-2 Prince Consort Road,
South Kensington, London SW7 2BZ

Email: mail@visitjamaica.uk.com
www.visitjamaica.com

Visit Scotland
Level 3, Ocean Point 1, 94 Ocean Drive,
Edinburgh EH6 6JH

Email: info@visitscotland.com
www.visitscotland.com

What To Take

Adventure Centre
240 Manchester Road,
Warrington, Cheshire WA1 3BE

Top quality camping equipment available to buy at discount prices.

Attwoolls Camping & Leisure
Attwoolls, Bristol Road,
Whitminster, Gloucester GL2 7LX

A huge showroom south of Gloucester stocking tents, camping equipment, accessories and skiing equipment. You can also buy online.

Camping International
Clock Tower House, Watling Street (A2),
Gillingham, Kent ME5 7HF

Visit their branches, dedicated to outdoor equipment, in Gillingham and Horsham, or shop online.

Casey's Camping
Within Stephen Smiths Garden Centre,
Pool Road, Otley, Leeds, West Yorkshire LS21 1DY

Family camping specialists who sell a range of camping equipment and tents.

Coleman The Outdoor Company
Coleman (UK) Ltd, Kestrel Court Harbour Road,
Portishead Bristol BS20 7AN

Coleman offer outdoor products and camping accessories from tents and sleeping bags to kayaks and lanterns.

Cotswold Outdoor Ltd
Unit 11, Kemble Business Park, Crudwell
Malmesbury, Wiltshire SN16 9SH

Huge retail outlet for camping equipment, clothes, maps, climbing gear, footwear and more.

Craigdon Mountain Sports
Head Office, Unit 2, Burghmuir Circle, Blackhall Industrial Estate
Inverurie, Aberdeenshire AB51 4FS

Scotland's premier independent outdoor retailer, stocking a wide range of clothing and equipment.

Go Outdoors
Head Office, Hill Street, Bramall Lane
Sheffield S2 4SZ

Offer a wide choice of outdoor accessories and equipment, from tents, rucksacks, sleeping bags to clothing and brand labels.

Itchy Feet Ltd
4 Bartlett Street,
Bath BA1 2QZ

This company stocks a wide selection of equipment for all your travel needs. Also has a London branch.

Nikwax Ltd
Unit F, Durgates Industrial Estate,
Wadhurst, Sussex TN5 6DF UK

To clean and waterproof all your gear, extend its life and maintain high performance with low environmental impact - Nikwax it!

Nomad Travel & Outdoor
Unit 34, Redburn Industrial Estate, Woodall Road
Enfield, Middlesex EN3 4LE

As well as the usual stock of clothing, equipment, books and maps their stores also hold medical supplies and have in-store clinics.

Páramo Directional Clothing Systems
Unit F, Durgates Industrial Estate,
Wadhurst, Sussex TN5 6DF

Waterproof clothing, reversible shirts, windproofs, fleeces and other outdoor clothing.

Vango
2 Kelburn Business Park,
Port Glasgow PA14 6TD

Evergrowing range of tents, sleeping bags, rucsacks and outdoor accessories.

Yeomans Outdoors
Centenary House, 11 Midland Way, Barlborough Links,
Chesterfield, Derbyshire S43 4XA

Stocks a wide range of tents, camping equipment and outdoor clothing.

Chapter 2
Finance

A career break in Namibia

Kat, 32, took a career break for a few months mainly in Swakopmund, Namibia, but travelled around Africa when she could.

While there: "I helped out in a homework class every day after school.

"I also helped in the town's library getting lots of English books on the shelves, I also got some school kids to help me – we put a total of 592 books on the shelves, not bad considering each book took about two hours to process from start to finish!

"I worked with a group of ladies called the Busy Bees, putting on fundraising events where all the money went to local orphanages, charities or to buy wool so they could knit blankets for the orphanages."

She said it was: "Amazing. Humbling. Incredible. Brilliant… A real eye-opening experience that will stay with me for the rest of my life. I smile every time I think of my time there."

Her advice to gappers: "Make the most of every second – the time will pass really fast. Plan your trip well and above all research the culture and be safe."

And also: "I wish I had raised more money before I left so I could have stayed there longer. I also wish I had had the time to travel north to the Skeleton Coast, and visit more little towns."

Getting 'back to normal' was spurred on by the need to earn a living, she said, but in a way that actually helped: "I had to get a job after a few weeks of returning, and I was actually looking forward to it."

Would she do it again?

"I've been working since I got back, but do the lottery every week in the hopes that one day I will be able to do it again."

2 Finance

How much will you need?

It depends on what you're doing and for how long, but the average **gap**-year costs between £3000 and £6000.

What do you need to pay for?

A **gap-** needn't break the bank, but it helps if you start by making yourself a list of all the things you might need to pay for, and then research how much it all comes to. Then you can start looking at ways you can save some money by shopping around and keeping costs down. Here's a checklist to help you get started.

Before you go:

* Passport

* Visas and work permits (check the FCO website for the relevant embassy - **www.fco.gov.uk**)

* Insurance

* Flights

69

- Fees for placements/organised treks *etc*
- Special equipment if needed
- Vaccinations - they're not all free - and a travellers' medical pack

In country:

- Accommodation (if travelling independently)
- Transport (if travelling independently)
- Food
- Entertainment
- Shopping - gifts and souvenirs
- Emergency fund

Raising the money:

There's no doubt it's going to be harder to raise money for **gap-** travel during a recession, when the competition for even low-skilled or part-time work is likely to be intense, but here are some ideas to get you started:

- Part-time or full-time work (Supermarkets are always a favourite! But check out local job agencies for restaurant/factory/packing and casual work. If you can use a computer you could also pick up temp office work.)
- Babysitting (best to stick to friends and family for this.)
- Dog walking
- Car washing
- Ironing
- Office cleaning
- Ask for money or items you need as birthday/Christmas gifts
- Online auction sales (get rid of all that stuff you've stashed and never look at!)
- Car boot sales (ditto)
- Sponsorship (Try writing to your local paper to see if they'll do a story on your plans - better during the quiet news period in summer and also if you're planning to do something unusual for a worthwhile cause.)
- Sponsorship by local companies (Try approaching a few that operate in a field related to what you plan to do.)
- Sell the car (Drastic, but worth it if you're planning to be away for a year: think of the depreciation and the hassle of deciding what you're going to do with it if you don't.)

visit: www.gap-year.com

- Small change jar (Stick all your small coins in a big jar - you'd be surprised how quickly it adds up.)
- Can you do some seasonal work on your travels? (See Chapter 7 - Working Abroad.)

If you are planning to do a training course during your **gap-**year, you may be eligible for funding via a Career Development Loan. A CDL is a deferred repayment bank loan to help you pay for vocational learning or education. The Department for Children, Schools and Families pays the interest on your loan while you are learning and for up to one month afterwards. You can get more info from the National CDL enquiry line: 0800 585 505; or by visiting the government website:
www.direct.gov.uk/en/EducationAndLearning/AdultLearning/FinancialH elpForAdultLearners/CareerDevelopmentLoans/index.htm

Money savers

The International Student Identity Card (ISIC) gives you more than 40,000 travel, online and lifestyle discounts. It costs £9, is accepted in the UK and worldwide. There's also a 24/7 worldwide free call helpline for medical and legal assistance.

Many leading airlines also offer exclusive student/youth fares to ISIC (and IYTC) holders. Your travel agent can help you find the right one and advise if any age restrictions apply.

Your ISIC sees you right through the academic year: it's valid from each September, for up to 16 months, in other words until December the following year! You need to qualify for the year in which you'll hold the card:

- If you're a full-time student (15 hours weekly for 12+ weeks) at a secondary school, sixth form or further education college, language school, The Open University (60 points or more) or any UK university.
- If you've got a deferred/confirmed UCAS placement then you can grab an ISIC for your year away.

If you're neither of the above, but under 26, you can get an International Youth Travel Card (IYTC) with a similar range of benefits.

You can get the cards online at: **www.ISICcard.com** (mail order forms are also available from this site); or by phoning: 0871 230 8546.

As long as you live in the UK, you can also get these cards via STAtravel: **http://ibe.statravel.co.uk/AniteXmlGateway.aspx**

For budget flights and student discounts, you can check out the internet and we've included some hints in Chapter 4 – Travel.

If you're travelling independently, cut the cost of accommodation by: staying in the guest houses attached to temples and monasteries; camping or staying in a caravan park; as a guest in someone's home; sharing a room; or using budget hotels or hostels, but be careful to check for cleanliness and proper exits in case of emergency. (See Chapter 5 - Accommodation.)

the gap-year guidebook 2010

If you're a mature traveller, perhaps you could investigate a house swap for part of your time away, but see also Chapter 6 - Career Breaks and Mature Travellers for other ideas.

International sim card: if you have your mobile phone overseas enabled you'll pay for the roaming and on top of that all your calls are routed via your home country so you're paying two-way international rates (you pay for calls you receive as well as ones you make) and that's pretty hefty! It's cheaper to get an international sim card: here's a link to a site where you can buy one: **www.0044.co.uk**

This company also sells global phone cards, that can be used in 50 countries around the world, to make calls from 3p per minute from a landline.

However, at least one provider has recently abolished their roaming charges, making mobile calls from overseas no more expensive than UK based ones. Check with your service provider before you go.

Buy second-hand: rather than spend a fortune on a backpack, do you know someone who's just returned from a trip and might be willing to lend or sell you any equipment they no longer need? Check the classified ads in your local paper, buy on eBay (or similar) or try the **www.gap-year.com** message board. Make sure that whatever you buy is in clean, sound condition, that the zips work, there are fittings for padlocks, and it's right for your body weight and height. If it's sound but a bit travel-worn, so much the better - you'll look like a seasoned traveller rather than a novice!

Money security

Take a mix of:

- Cash
- Travellers' cheques
- Credit card
- Travel money cards

Cash: carry small change in pockets, *not* big notes. Distribute it between a belt bag, day pack and your travel bag so you have an emergency stash.

Travellers' cheques: record serial numbers and emergency phone number for the issuer in case of theft. You sign each one when you get them from the bank but then there's a space for a second signature. Don't sign this second box until you're cashing it - if you do and your cheques get stolen, they can be cashed and you invalidate the insurance cover. Only cash a couple of travellers' cheques at any one time - get a mix of larger and small change denominations - often street traders and snack stalls, or taxis and rickshaws, won't have change for a large note and it makes you vulnerable - you seem rich.

Hotel currency exchanges are more expensive, local banks can take a long time and require ID. If you can find a Thomas Cook centre they're the most efficient and speedy we've found. Street rates can be cheaper but be very careful. A lot of street money changers are trading illegally - don't hand over the cheque until you have your money and have counted it.

Credit card: essential back-up. The problem with a credit card is losing it or having it stolen - keep a note of the numbers, how to report the loss of the card and the number you have to ring to do so.

Both Visa and Mastercard are useful, in an emergency, for getting local currency cash advances from a cash dispenser at banks abroad. Remember, if you're using your credit card to get money over the counter then you're likely to need some form of ID (*eg* passport).

If you are paying for goods or restaurant meals by using your card, you should insist on signing bills/receipts in your presence and not allow the card to be taken out of your sight. This way you'll have no unpleasant surprises or mysterious purchases when you see your card statement.

Travel Money Cards: pre-pay travel cards are now a well-established alternative to travellers' cheques and can be used at an ATM using a pin number. The idea is that you load them with funds before you leave, but beware - like credit and debit cards, most charge for every reload and for cash withdrawals. To find out more check out the following:

www.iceplc.com/cashcard/

www.travelex.com/ae/personal/CP_default.asp?content=cp

www.postoffice.co.uk/portal/po/jump1?catId=19300207&mediaId=26800 661

Sticking to a budget

It sounds obvious but you can get a good idea of costs before you go from a gapper who's been there recently. Message boards like the one on **www.gap-year.com** are a good place to find such people. You can also get an idea of how far your money will go if you check an online currency converter like **www.xe.com**

As a general rule you'll find your money will stretch quite a long way in most of the less developed parts of the world, and once you're in-country you can find out fairly easily from other travellers/locals the average costs of buses, trains, meals and so on.

Having said that, the global recession and rises in oil and food prices have had an impact on most countries' economies. They've particularly hit costs in the less developed world and the signs are that it may take some time for things to settle down. As you're planning some months ahead of your trip it may be sensible to add a little extra for potential inflation when you're working out your minimum and maximum spend per day. The trick then is to stick to it.

Here are some tips:

Shopping: you're bound to find a zillion things that will make good souvenirs/gifts - best advice, though, is to wait. You'll see lots more wherever you are and the prices for the same goods in popular tourist and backpacker destinations will be much higher - and possibly of lower quality - than they will be in smaller towns and villages.

Do your buying just before you move on to the next destination, or return home, so you won't have spent too much money at the start of your trip, won't have to carry it all around with you and also by then you'll have an idea of what's worth buying and for how much. Another advantage of buying locally is that more of what you pay is likely to benefit the local community, and craftspeople, rather than the middle links in the chain.

If you buy souvenirs/gifts mid-trip, you could consider posting them home to save carrying them around with you but don't risk sending anything too valuable, and make sure you know what's permitted to send (and what's not) since you'll almost certainly have to fill in a customs declaration slip, which will be stuck to the outside of the parcel.

Bargaining: make sure it's the custom before you do, and try to find out roughly what it should cost before you start. Also try to look at yourself through local eyes - if you're wearing expensive jewellery and clothes and carrying a camera or the latest mobile phone you'll find it much harder to get a real bargain.

Whatever you do, smile and be courteous. The trader has to make a living, usually in pretty harsh economic conditions, and you're a guest in their country. Not only that, but if you're a responsible traveller then ethically you should be offering a fair price, not going all-out to grab a bargain you can boast about later.

Don't give the impression you really, really want whatever it is. Don't pick it up - leave that to the market trader, then let them try to sell it to you. They will tell how much they want and it's likely to be inflated, so you offer a price the equivalent amount below the figure it should be and that you're willing to pay.

visit: www.gap-year.com

If they start the process by asking you how much you're willing to offer then mention that you've asked around local people so you know roughly what it should cost, before you name a price a little below what you're prepared to pay.

From this point on it's a bit like a game of chess and it can be very entertaining - so don't be surprised if you collect an audience!

You might be told a heart-rending story about family circumstances or the trader's own costs, but you can counter that by saying that however much you like the article, you're sorry but it's outside your budget. Gradually you'll exchange figures until you reach an agreement.

One technique is to pretend you're not that bothered and start to walk away, but be prepared for the trader to take you at your word!

Not getting ripped off by cabbies: find out beforehand roughly what the local rate is for the distance you want to go. Then it's much the same principle as bargaining in a market. It's generally cheaper not to let hotels find you a cab - they often get a rake-off from the fare for allowing cabbies to park on their grounds so it will cost you more.

Agree a price before you get into the vehicle and if you're hiring a car and driver for a day (which can often work out cheaper especially if you're sharing with friends) usually you'll be expected to pay for a meal for the driver so make sure you agree that the price of a stop for food is included in the deal.

In India, there's a system of pre-pay kiosks, particularly at airport exits, where you can buy a chit - a paper that states a fair, and usually accurate, price for the journey. The driver can't cash it until you're safely at your destination, can't charge you more than is on the chit, and it has to be signed - usually by your hotel/accommodation before it can be cashed. So you can be sure you'll not be taking any long detours to bump up the cost. It's worth asking whether there are similar systems wherever you are.

Tipping: it's a bit of a minefield and you need to find out what the fair rate is. A tip should be a thank you for good service, so, for example, if you're in a restaurant and there's already a percentage on your bill for service you shouldn't pay more, unless of course you feel your waiter deserves it! Remember if you over-tip you raise expectations higher than other travellers - and locals - may be able or willing to pay.

Finding and affording a guide: find out if there's a local scheme for licensing/approving guides and what the 'official permit' looks like. Nearly always there will be any number of 'guides' at the entrances to any interesting place you might want to visit. Some will be official - others will be trying their luck. You'll usually find out when you pay the entrance fee.

Wiring money

If you find yourself stranded with no cash, travellers' cheques or credit cards, then having money wired to you could be the only option. Two major companies offer this service:

MoneyGram - **www.moneygram.com**

Western Union - **www.westernunion.com**

Both have vast numbers of branches worldwide - MoneyGram has 180,000 in 190 countries and territories and Western Union has 379,000 agent locations in 200 countries and territories.

The service allows a friend or relative to transfer money to you almost instantaneously. Once you have persuaded your guardian angel to send you the money, all they have to do is go to the nearest MoneyGram or Western Union office, fill in a form and hand over the money (in cash).

It is then transferred to the company's branch nearest to you, where you in turn fill in a form and pick it up. Both you and the person sending the money will need ID, and you may be asked security questions so you need to know what the person sending the money has given as the security question *and* its answer. Make sure they tell you the spelling they've used and that you use the same.

Older travellers with more assets will have specific financial concerns and perhaps more sources of funds than younger gappers, and we've included some detail in Chapter 6 - Career Breaks and Mature Travellers.

visit: www.gap-year.com

Finance

Exchange rates/conversion

There are many websites out there who offer this facility. Here are three that we have used ourselves.

www.xe.com/ucc

www.fairfx.com

www.oanda.com/convert/classic

www.x-rates.com/calculator.html

Career Development Loans:

UK government website providing information about career development loans and how you can apply for one.

www.direct.gov.uk/cdl

International Student Cards:

Website where you can apply for an international student identity card.

www.isiccard.com

Travel Money Cards:

Websites where you can apply for travel money cards.

www.iceplc.com/cashcard/

www.travelex.com/ae/personal/CP_default.asp?content=cp

www.postoffice.co.uk/portal/po/jump1?catId=19300207&mediaId=268 00661

Wiring money worldwide:

For when you need emergency cash transferred quickly overseas.

www.moneygram.com

www.westernunion.com

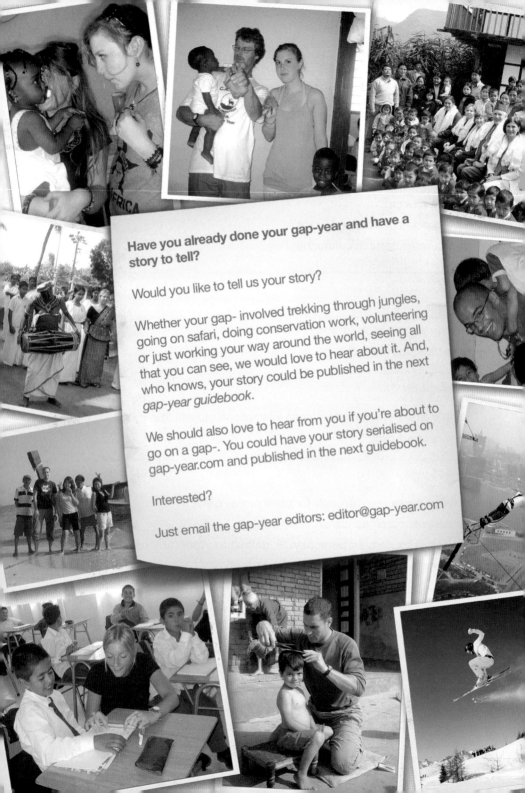

Have you already done your gap-year and have a story to tell?

Would you like to tell us your story?

Whether your gap- involved trekking through jungles, going on safari, doing conservation work, volunteering or just working your way around the world, seeing all that you can see, we would love to hear about it. And, who knows, your story could be published in the next *gap-year guidebook*.

We should also love to hear from you if you're about to go on a gap-. You could have your story serialised on gap-year.com and published in the next guidebook.

Interested?

Just email the gap-year editors: editor@gap-year.com

Chapter 3
Insurance

3 Insurance

Your insurance needs to be fixed before you go, but the range of policies is vast - and they all cover different things.

The basic things to check for are:

- Medical costs
- Legal
- Passport loss
- Ticket loss
- Cash loss
- Luggage
- Flight cancellation
- Missed flights
- Working abroad
- Hazardous sports
- Specific medical conditions

Other things you should ask:

- Is there a 24-hour helpline?
- Can you cover yourself for an unexpected return home so that you can continue your **gap-** later without losing your cover?
- Are there any special declarations you need to make on the health conditions of immediate family?
- Are there any conditions and requirements regarding pre-existing medical conditions?
- Are there any age restrictions or extra age-related costs on the policy? This is particularly important for mature travellers.

Some banks provide cover for holidays paid for using their credit cards, but their policies may not include all the essentials you'll need for a **gap-**year.

Banks also offer blanket travel insurance (medical, personal accident, third party liability, theft, loss, cancellation, delay and more). You may be able to get reductions if you have an account with the relevant bank or buy foreign currency through it.

Who to choose?

You don't have to buy a travel insurance policy as part of a travel package through a travel company and there is intense competition between insurance companies to attract your attention. It may be tedious but the best advice is shop around, check out the internet, talk to a broker and read the small print very carefully.

Medical insurance

If you're going to Europe you can get a European Health Insurance Card (EHIC), which allows for free or reduced cost medical treatment within Europe, should you need it. You can apply online: **www.ehic.org.uk**

Your card is valid for three to five years and should be delivered to you in seven days. Or you can telephone EHIC applications, Newcastle on Tyne, on 0845 606 2030. The EHIC card only covers treatment under the state scheme in all EU countries, plus Denmark, Iceland, Liechtenstein, Norway and Switzerland. You can also pick up application forms at your post office.

Countries with no health care agreements with the UK include Canada, the USA, India, most of the Far East, the whole of Africa and Latin America.

Wherever it happens, a serious illness, broken limb, or even an injury you might cause someone else, can be very expensive.

Medical insurance is usually part of an all-in travel policy. Costs vary widely by company, destination, activity and level of cover. Make sure you have generous cover for injury or disablement, know what you're covered for and

when you've got the policy read the small print carefully. For example, does it cover transport home if you need an emergency operation that cannot be carried out safely abroad?

Some policies won't cover high-risk activities like skiing, snowboarding, bungee jumping *etc* so you'll need to get extra, specific, cover and an insurance broker can help with this. Companies may also make a distinction between doing a hazardous sport once and spending your whole time doing them. Some insurance policies also have age limits.

If you have a medical condition that is likely to recur, you may have to declare this when you buy the insurance, otherwise the policy won't be valid. Also, check whether the policy covers you for the medical costs if the condition does recur, as some will not cover such pre-existing conditions.

Already covered?

If you're going abroad on a voluntary work assignment you may find that the organisation arranging it wants you to take a specified insurance policy as part of the total cost. You may also find you have a clash of policies before you even start looking for the right policy.

For example, if your family has already booked you a one-year multi-travel insurance policy to cover travel with the family at other times of the year, you

may find you are already covered for loss of life, limb, permanent disablement, some medical expenses, theft and so on. These multi-trip policies can be basic as well as quite cheap, but it's essential to check the small print of what the policy covers as it's possible that there may be a clause compelling the insured to return to the UK after a short period of time.

A lot of these policies only cover for trips of up to 60 days at a time, at which point travellers had to return to the UK. In other words, great for a holiday or two or for a business traveller but no use at all if you plan to be out of the country for the whole year.

In this case you can start by finding out (through the broker or agent who sold you the policy) if any additional cover can be tacked on to your existing policy, though this can be expensive and most off-the-shelf policies won't do it.

Try to find a policy that doesn't already duplicate what is covered by an existing policy (they don't pay out twice), but some duplication is unavoidable and it's obviously better to be covered twice than not at all.

Making a claim

Read through the small print carefully before you travel and make sure you understand exactly what to do if you need to make a claim - most policies will insist that you report a crime to the police where this is possible (often within a certain time period), and that you send in the police report with your insurance claim. What you don't want to happen is to have a claim dismissed because you don't have the right paperwork to back it up.

Insurers won't pay you money unless you have complied with all their rules and many travel policies impose conditions that are virtually impossible to meet.

For example, some policies demand that you report not only theft of items but also loss of items. Fine, but the police are likely to be pretty reluctant to write a crime report because you think you may have accidentally left your camera in the loo!

If you do have anything stolen and you have to get the local police to give you a report, it's a good idea to dress reasonably smartly when you visit them, be prepared to wait and try to be pleasant and polite no matter what!

The Foreign Office website (**www.fco.gov.uk/travel**) has a good page about insurance and is worth checking out for advice and links. In addition to a list of what your travel insurance should cover, which is similar to the one at the start of this chapter, it suggests the following extras, which are not always included:

- legal expenses cover - this can be useful as it will help you to pursue compensation or damages following personal injury while you're abroad - very important in countries without a legal aid system; and

- financial protection if your airline goes bankrupt before or during your trip - given the state of the airline industry this may be worth serious consideration for at least the next couple of years.

A spokesman for the Association of British Insurers told us: "The vast majority of travel insurance claims are settled quickly. However, the best way to avoid potential problems is to read the policy before you go, and ensure that you fully understand what you are covered for, and the terms and conditions. If anything is unclear, contact your insurer.

"Take a copy of the policy with you and make sure you know how to claim, especially any emergency contact numbers that you may need."

What to do if you get an emergency call to come home

We all hope there'll be no family crises while we're away on our **gap-** but it does occasionally happen that someone close is taken seriously ill, or even dies, and then all you can think about is getting home as quickly as possible. We've talked to a couple of insurers about this and they reinforce our advice to *always* read the policy carefully before you set off on your travels.

Generally speaking, your **gap-**year travel policy ceases once you return home, but some insurers offer extra cover for one extra trip home (or more, up to four, but the price rises with each one) without your policy lapsing. In a backpacker/adventure policy of three to 18 months, one home return is in the region of £5 and four would be around £24 extra on your policy.

Most insurers are used to dealing with sudden early returns and have a 24-hour emergency assistance company to help you through the whole process. You need to let them know anyway so you can set the ball rolling for claiming for the cost and they can deal with getting you from your **gap-** location to the airport, or, if you have one, you can use the help of your placement provider's in-country reps, or even a combination of the two, so *you* don't have to deal with transport hassles when all you can think about is getting home quickly.

However, there are often restrictions. First off, your family emergency has to affect an immediate relative - so husband, wife, mum, dad, grandparents, sisters and brothers, children, grandchildren - but *not* aunts, uncles and other extended family. It has to be serious injury, illness or death of a relative - family feuds and divorces do not count!

If you have home return extra on your policy you're covered for one extra flight home; you're *not* covered for an additional flight back to resume your **gap-**. But, if you have a return ticket, as most gappers do, the best way to go is to use your existing return, if the airline will reschedule, claim for it, then book another return flight. It's often cheaper to book a return flight than an extra one-way only.

If your ticket cannot be changed and you need to purchase a new ticket for your return journey, this can be arranged via a flight-ticketing agent or direct with the appropriate airline (subject to availability of flights and seats).

Websites such as Expedia and ebookers offer a wide selection of flights including single leg and one way tickets, which you can buy online and allocated e-tickets, or collect them from the airline sales desk at the airport.

During peak travel or holiday times you might find the quickest way to get home may be to go to the airport and wait to pick up a 'no show' seat on standby.

When submitting a claim for any additional travel costs incurred in getting back home, you could be asked to provide information relating to the medical history of the relative; all travel insurance policies contain health restrictions of some kind and you should check these when buying your policy.

As we have already said, some travel insurance policies contain a requirement to report pre-existing medical conditions. If the customer, any travelling companion, or a close relative has had a serious or chronic condition in the 12 months prior to buying the policy, or if they are waiting for, undergoing or recovering from, hospital, it should be mentioned in your application before you decide to buy. Insurers have screening services, who will advise whether the policy you're considering can be extended to cover these conditions.

There are now several insurers offering tailor-made insurance policies for **gap-**year travellers. You'll find them in the directory listings.

Insurance

ACE European Group Ltd
Customer Services, PO Box 1018,
Ashdown House, 125 High Street,
Crawley, West Sussex RH10 1DQ

Offers gap year/backpacker/student traveller insurance for ages 14 to 44 and traveller plus insurance for 45-55 years.

Blue Insurances Ltd
Suffolk House, Trade Street,
Cardiff CF10 5DT

E: info@multitrip.com
T: 0871 231 3222
www.multitrip.com/backpacker

Multitrip.com is a domain name of Blue Insurances, offering comprehensive backpacker/long stay cover at very competitive prices. Cover starts from as little as £23.99 which includes cancellation, medical, baggage, personal accident, personal liability, legal expenses, personal money, missed departure, catastrophe cover, holiday abandonment and hospital benefit. Blue Insurances has received numerous awards for Best Travel Insurance Product.

Boots UK Limited
1 Thane Road West, Beeston,
Nottingham NG90 1BS

Website has area dedicated to gap-year insurance and offers policies from three to 12 months.

BUPA Travel Services
Thames Side House, South Street,
Staines, Middlesex TW18 4TL

Offers Explorer to travellers taking a gap-year or career break, whether planning a three month jaunt or a trip around the world.

Club Direct Ltd.
Advertiser House, 18 Bartlett St,
Croydon, Surrey CR2 6TB

Affordable backpacker travel insurance for those who plan to travel abroad for an extended period.

Columbus Direct
Advertiser House, 19 Bartlett Street,
Croydon, Surrey CR2 6TB

Offers backpacker insurance for anywhere in the world from four weeks to a year. Also offers ski travel insurance and adventure travel insurance.

Dogtag Ltd
6 Magellan Terrace, Gatwick Road,
Crawley, Surrey RH10 9PJ

Insurance offered for 'action minded' travellers.

Downunder Worldwide Travel Insurance
Downunder Insurance Services Ltd,
PO Box 55605, Paddington
London W9 3UW

E: travel@duinsure.com
T: +44 (0) 800 393 908
www.duinsure.com

Gap-year/working holiday cover book online for a 10% discount.

Save up to 60% on High Street prices plus a further 10% discount if you book online. Comprehensive travel insurance for the adventurous traveller. Working holidays covered plus over 80 adventurous sports or activities. Medical emergency and money back guarantee. All their operators are seasoned travellers, so book with the experts on freephone 0800 393908 or check out their website.

They are a 'know before you go' preferred supplier to the backpacker market.

Endsleigh Insurance Services Ltd
Endsleigh Park, Shurdington Road,
Cheltenham Spa, Gloucestershire GL51 4UE

Endsleigh has tailored gap-year cover to suit you, with over 100 sports and activities covered as standard!

Essential Travel Ltd
Princess Caroline House, 1 High Street,
Southend on Sea, Essex SS1 1JE

Backpacker travel insurance policies for people aged under 45 available, and only for trips of up to 12 months.

Flexicover Direct
109 Elmers End Road,
Beckenham, Kent BR3 4SY

Gap-year travel insurance for those aged 18-45.

Globelink International Ltd.
84 Cannon Street, Little Downham,
Ely, Cambridgeshire CB6 2SS

They provide cover for backpacking and gap-years for up to 15 months in length, but extensions are available.

Go Travel Insurance
West Wing, Miles Gray Road,
Basildon, Essex SS14 3GD

Go Travel Insurance offers a flexible backpacker policy for ages 18 to 65.

Insure and Go
Maitland House, Warrior Square,
Southend on Sea, Essex SS1 2JY

Gap-year travel insurance for people aged under 36, also a policy for those over 36 and looking for longer trips.

JS Travel Insurance
Towerpoint, 44 North Road,
Brighton BN1 1YR

Provides comprehensive gap-year travel insurance.

Mind The Gap Year
19-21 West House, West Street,
Haslemere, Surrey GU27 2AB

E: info@mindthegapyear.com
T: +44 (0) 845 180 0060
www.mindthegapyear.com

We are a tailor-made combination of insurance and services for the gap-year traveller, promoting how to stay safe and prepare for your travels. Services include a free online planner, worldwide research tool, electronic document safe, discount off safety training and most importantly specialist backpacker insurance, plus much more.

MRL Insurance Direct
6 Magellan Terrace, Gatwick Road,
Crawley, West Sussex RH10 9PJ

Gap-year polices of between two and 12 months for under 45s. Over 60 activities including scuba diving and bungee.

Navigator Travel Insurance Services Ltd
19 Ralli Courts, West Riverside,
Manchester M3 5FT

Offers specialist policies for long-stay overseas trips, with an emphasis on covering adventure sports. These policies also cover casual working.

Right Cover Travel Insurance
2nd Floor, 31 Springfield Road,
Chelmsford, Essex CM2 6JE

Offers budget cover suitable for students or backpackers.

Round the World Insurance
Travel Nation Ltd, 8th Floor, Intergen House,
65-67 Western Road, Hove, Sussex BN3 2JQ

Specialist travel insurance designed for people on round-the-world or multi-stop trips.

Sainsbury's Travel Insurance
33 Holborn,
Holborn, London EC1N 2HT

They have a policy specifically for gappers.

Snowcard Insurance Services Limited
Lower Boddington,
Daventry, Northamptonshire NN11 6XZ

Travel and Activity insurance including long stays up to 18 months.

World Nomads Ltd
One Victoria Square,
Birmingham B1 1BD

Offers an insurance package specifically targeted at independent travellers.

Worldwide Travel Insurance Services Ltd
The Business Centre,
1-7 Commercial Road, Paddock Wood
Tonbridge, Kent TN12 6YT

This company offers travellers insurance from two to 18 months for long-haul travellers and backpackers, which also covers working overseas.

Chapter 4
Travel

Chapter sponsored by

Round-the-world trip

Sarah and Rob booked their eight month round-the-world trip with Travel Nation:

"When we first started planning our round-the-world trip we were somewhat daunted by the prospect. We had a good idea of where we wanted to go, but little or no understanding of how the tickets

worked, or even if what we wanted to do could be achieved on our limited budget. From the first moment we contacted Travel Nation they made the planning process simple. Our consultant had been to many of our destinations and quickly told us what was possible, and how much it would cost.

"On our must see list was the Trans-Siberian Railway, Angkor Wat in Cambodia, Kakadu National Park in the Northern Territory of Australia, Sydney, New Zealand, and The Inca Trail in Peru. After lots of phone calls and emails, our trip was planned to perfection – but it wasn't until we were away that we realized how important the advice we had received was. We were particularly grateful that we had booked so many things in advance as apart from making day-to-day budgeting simpler, this guaranteed that we did what we originally planned to do.

"We started in St Petersburg and joined the Trans-Siberian for our 18 day journey through Siberia, Mongolia and China. Our consultant had helped us sort all of our visas and made what is a complicated process very easy. The train itself was a real experience, but what made the trip were the

visit: www.travel-nation.co.uk

places where we got off the train for a few days. Seeing Lake Baikal (the world's largest fresh water lake) and staying in a Ger camp in the Mongolian Steppe were just two of the hilights.

"After seeing the incredible sights of Beijing we flew to Ho Chi Minh City where we joined an adventure tour through Vietnam, Cambodia and Thailand. Travelling through south-east Asia overland was a wonderful experience and visiting the temple complex at Angkor Watt fulfilled a lifelong dream. The expert guides really meant we got the most out of our time and didn't miss a thing.

"Then it was onwards to Australia and New Zealand. Here our consultant had recommended a mixture of flights and bus passes meaning we covered the massive distances in Australia with the minimum of cost and effort. The hop-on-hop-off bus pass meant we had prepaid our transport, but we could go at our own pace. This was particularly good advice in New Zealand as, in common with lots of other travellers we met in this beautiful country, we found we wanted more time here than we had allowed – which was no problem as we simply contacted Travel Nation and they changed the dates of our flights all via email.

"Our last destination was South America. By now we had confidence in our abilities as independent travellers so, other than the first few nights in Santiago and our five day Inca Trail trek, we booked our accommodation as we travelled. When we arrived in Cuzco we realized once again the quality of advice given by our consultant, as we met loads of people who had not been able to do the Inca Trail due to a lack of permits.

"Having the same person organise the trip from the very first phone call, all the way through to my hysterical queries in the middle of South America, took away so much of the stress of embarking on the journey.

"We have and will recommend Travel Nation to anyone we hear is travelling!"

Travel Nation
8th Floor, Intergen House,
65-67 Western Road, Hove,
East Sussex BN3 2JQ
Tel: 01273 320 580
Email: info@travelnation.co.uk

Round the World and Adventure Travel Experts

4 Travel

Global warming, climate change and the world's depleting energy resources continue to be a serious concern, regardless of the economic climate, and increasingly people want to know how to be environmentally friendly on their **gap-** travels. Nowhere is this likely to be more of an issue than in the types of transport you choose.

If you're hoping to travel to several destinations time is inevitably an issue, so it may not be practical to avoid air travel altogether, but there are ways you can minimise your carbon footprint.

If you're concerned about global warming, and want to do your bit, you can pay a small 'carbon offset' charge on your flight. If you want to know more try: **www.co2balance.uk.com/co2calculators/flight/**

The site has a calculator so you can work out how much to pay for journeys by car, train or air. It also has some simpler options - for example £50 will offset one long-haul one-way flight from London to Australia. Your money goes towards sustainable development projects around the world and there's a complete list of all current projects on the website: **www.co2balance.uk.com/carbon-offset-projects/projects-overview/**

They are all managed by co2balance, but are also all independently validated and verified by international standards organisations. Projects include providing energy efficient woodstoves in east Africa, wind power in India and renewable energy projects in China.

The UK's Green Traveller website includes a list of top ten fair trade holidays worldwide and lots more advice if you want your travel to be as environmentally friendly as possible: **www.greentraveller.co.uk/node/487**

To find out more about sustainable and responsible travel you could also look at the website of the International Ecotourism Society, which has a lot of tips for responsible travel both en route and in-country: **www.ecotourism.org**

Another option for responsible travellers is to make the journey part of your **gap-**, if you have time; for example, plan a rail route with stops along the way allowing you time to explore. There's more on this in the trains section below.

You may also be able to combine different forms of transport to get to your destination and while you're in-country. We've had a look at some other transport options and these can be found in the following pages.

Getting about

Planes

The internet is invaluable when searching for ticket information, timetables, prices and special offers, whether you're travelling by air, sea, train or bus.

Because the internet gives customers so much information to choose from, travel companies have to compete harder to win your booking. The internet shows you what flexibility is possible (a lot), so you could find your decision-making turned upside down.

When booking flights, have a look at special offers for round-the-world tickets first, find out how far in advance you can book, then plan your destinations to fit.

If one of your destinations has a fixed arrival and departure date - for example if you're signed up for a voluntary project - you could try asking for a route tailor-made for you using the prices you find on the web.

Make sure you check out the company making an offer on the web before you use internet booking procedures (does it have a verifiable address and phone number?). Remember, under EU law company's *must* publish a contact address on their website. So, unless the company in question is a household name, or you are able to locate a legitimate address via another source, think twice before handing over your hard earned cash.

It's important - as ever! - to read the Terms and Conditions to see what you're paying for and whether you can get your money back before you agree to buy - just as you would outside the virtual world.

What to watch out for

Once you've booked a flight online, especially if you do it through an agent such as **www.lastminute.com**, rather than direct with the airline, you may have to pay extra fees for rescheduling, not to mention date restrictions if you need to change the date. Unless you have a good, solid reason for cancelling - and most airlines define such reasons very narrowly - you also risk losing the money you've paid.

As we mention in Chapter 1, increasingly airlines are covering their additional fuel costs and taxes by adding charges for different services - like in-flight baggage storage, airport duty, seats next to each other (if you're not travelling alone) - you need to have your wits about you when you're going through the online booking forms as these extras can add a substantial amount to the final total, making that budget deal significantly more expensive than you originally thought (up to £100 at best and almost equalling the flight cost at worst).

Remember, the ads usually say 'flights from…£XXX' and *that's* your clue to watch out for extras.

Bargain flights: Scheduled airlines often offer discount fares for students under 26 so don't rule them out. Other cheap flights are advertised regularly in the newspapers and on the web. All sorts of travel agents can fix you up with multi-destination tickets, and student travel specialists often know where to find the best deals for **gap**-year students.

It's worth checking whether a particular flight is cheaper if you book direct with the airline - and if you are using a student travel card you may find that you have to do it this way to get the discount, rather than using one of the budget deal websites.

Above all, travel is an area where searching the internet for good deals should be top of your list - though it works best for single-destination trips rather than complex travel routes.

Trains

Travelling by train is one of the best ways to see a country - and if you travel on an overnight sleeper it can be as quick as a plane. India's train network is

visit: www.travel-nation.co.uk

simply world-famous and an absolute must experience! But don't think you can't use trains in other parts of the world. What follows is just a taster.

Inter-railing - Europe and a bit beyond

If you want to visit a lot of countries, one of the best ways to travel is by train on an InterRail ticket. With InterRail you have the freedom of the rail networks of Europe (and a bit beyond), allowing you to go as you please in 28 countries.

From the northern lights of Sweden to the kasbahs of Morocco, you can call at all the stops. InterRail takes you from city centre to city centre - avoiding airport hassles, ticket queues and traffic jams, and giving you more time to make the most of your visit. Passes are available for all ages, but you need to have lived in Europe for at least six months.

Overnight trains are available on most of the major routes, saving on accommodation costs, allowing you to go to sleep in one country and wake up in another!

Supplements apply so ask when you book. You will have to pay extra to travel on some express intercity trains or the Eurostar. Most major stations such as Paris, Brussels, Amsterdam and Rome have washing facilities and left luggage.

The InterRail One Country Pass can be used for the following countries:

Austria, Belgium, Bulgaria, Croatia, Czech Republic, Denmark, Finland, France, Germany, Great Britain, Greece, Hungary, Italy, Luxembourg, Macedonia (FYR), Netherlands, Norway, Poland, Portugal, Republic of Ireland, Romania, Russia, Serbia, Slovakia, Slovenia, Spain, Sweden, Switzerland and Turkey.

The alternative choice is the InterRail Global Pass, which is valid in all participating InterRail countries. Available for several lengths of travel it is ideal for gappers wanting to explore several, or even all, European countries in their year out.

One Country Pass Prices

Second class prices vary by the country and range from £29 (under 26)/£45 (over 26) for three days in one month, to £69/£109 for eight days in one month in Bulgaria, to £115/£175 in France.

Belgium, The Netherlands and Luxembourg are combined as the InterRail Benelux Pass. For Greece you have the option to order a Greece Plus Pass, which includes ferry crossings to and from Italy.

Global Pass

For second class travel, over 22 continuous days, prices range from £289 (under 26) to £435 (over 26) and are valid from five days to one month.

For further details on prices and how to buy an InterRail pass, visit their website: **www.interrailnet.com** and **www.raileurope.co.uk/inter-rail/**

Eurostar

The Eurostar train is a quick, easy and relatively cheap way to get to Europe. You can get from London to Calais from £59, and the trains are comfortable and run frequently. Tickets can be purchased online at **www.eurostar.com**, in an approved travel agency, or at any Eurostar train station.

Trans-Siberian Express

If you're looking for a train adventure - and you have a generous budget to play with - what about the Trans-Siberian Express? You could do a 14 day Moscow-Beijing trip. Do this as a 'full-on' or a 'no-frills' package:

Included in the trip:

Full on Trip

TRAIN: Second class, four berth, rail journey.

MOSCOW: Transfers on arrival and departure. Two nights stay in a three star hotel, breakfast included. Three hour personalised guided walking tour of the city.

COSTS: One person £1855; two people £1300 each; three to nine people £1235 per person.

No frills trip

TRAIN: Second class, four berth, rail journey.

MOSCOW: Transfer on arrival. Two nights stay in a one star hotel, breakfast not included.

COSTS: One person £1105; two people £950 per person; three to nine people £903 per person.

You can also choose from a range of other trips lasting from nine to 26 days.

On top of this you will need some money for food and drink, visas, airfare, *etc*. For China, Russia and Mongolia you'll need to have a visa for your passport to allow you into each country. Contact each relevant embassy to find out what type of visa you will need (*ie* visitors or transit). It's probably easiest to arrange for all your train tickets, visas and hotel accommodation through a specialist agency, about six months before you leave. Your journey will be a lot easier if you have all your paperwork in order before you leave - although it will cost you more to do it this way.

The trains can be pretty basic, varying according to which line you're travelling on and which country owns the train. On some trains you can opt to upgrade to first class. This should give you your own cabin with shower, wash basin and more comfort - however, although you'll be more comfortable, you may find it more interesting back in second class with all the other backpackers and traders.

If you're travelling in autumn or winter make sure you take warm clothes - the trains have rather unreliable heating. If you travel in late November/December you may freeze into a solid block of ice, but it will be snowing by then and the views will be spectacular. Travelling in September will be warmer and a bit cheaper.

If you want to read about it before you go, try the *Trans-Siberian Handbook* by Bryn Thomas. (You can buy it on Amazon.) It's updated frequently and it has details about the towns you'll be passing through, and includes the timetables.

There are several websites you can look up, but **www.trans-siberian.co.uk** is one of the best out there. For cheaper options you could also try Travel Nation, which has a useful page of FAQs on the Trans-Siberian Moscow to Beijing rail trip: **www.travel-nation.co.uk/trans-siberian-train/faqs.htm**

India and the rest of the world

Tell anyone you're going to India and you'll invariably be told you must try a train journey! Indian trains are the most amazing adventure - with all sorts of extras - like a meal included in the price on the Shatabdi Express intercity commuter trains, or the vendors who wander the length of the train with their buckets of snacks, tea or coffee, calling their wares "*chai, chai, chai*" as they go.

But Indian trains get booked up weeks or months in advance, especially if you're planning to travel during any major public festival like Diwali, which is a national holiday. You need a seat or berth reservation for any long-distance journey on an Indian train; you cannot simply turn up and hop on. Bookings now open 90 days in advance. Reservations are now completely computerised and a tourist quota gives foreigners and IndRail pass holders preferential treatment. Go to: **www.irctc.co.in/**

There's also a unique reservation system. After a train becomes fully booked, a set number of places in each class are sold as 'Reservation Against Cancellation' or 'RAC'. After all RAC places have been allocated, further prospective passengers are 'wait-listed'. When passengers cancel, people on the RAC list are promoted to places on the train and wait-listed passengers are promoted to RAC.

If you want to try your hand at organising your own train travel in India you can get a copy of the famous *Trains at a Glance* from any railway station in India for Rs 35 (50p) or you can download it as a PDF from: **www.seat61.com/India.htm**

But beware, it contains every train timetable (94 in all) for the sub-continent and it's very long!

The Man in Seat 61 is possibly the most incredibly comprehensive train and ship travel website ever. It literally covers the world from India to Latin America, Africa and south-east Asia. It's not only about times, costs and booking, it goes into some detail about the kinds of conditions you can expect.

It's written by Mark Smith, an ex-British Rail employee and former stationmaster at Charing Cross. He has travelled the world by train and ship and it's a personal site run as a hobby, so he pledges it will always remain freely available. It won the 'Best Personal Contribution' category in the First Choice Responsible Tourism Awards 2006. Readers of *Wanderlust* magazine also voted it Top Travel Website in 2007 and 2008 and gave it a bronze award in 2009, and it won the *Guardian* and *Observer* best travel website award in 2008. **www.seat61.com**

Buses/Coaches

Getting on a bus or coach in a foreign country, especially if you don't speak the language, can be a voyage of discovery in itself. UK bus timetables can be indecipherable, but try one in Patagonia!

Get help from a local you trust, hotel/hostel staff, or the local police station if all else fails. In developing countries, locals think nothing of transporting their livestock by public transport, so be prepared to sit next to a chicken! That said, some buses and coaches can be positively luxurious and they do tend to be cheaper than trains.

The 'Old Grey Dog'

Greyhound buses have air conditioning, tinted windows and a loo on board, as well as a strict no smoking policy. Greyhound offers Hostelling International members a discount on regular one-way and round-trip fares. They have a Discovery Pass, which allows seven, 15, 30 and 60 days unlimited travel. There's the usual 10% discount for ISIC and Euro 26 ID cardholders (go to **www.discoverypass.com**).

The bus company operates outside America too, with Greyhound Pioneer Australia (**www.greyhound.com.au**) and for South Africa there's Greyhound Coach Lines Africa (**www.greyhound.co.za**). Check out their websites or contact them for information about their various ticket options.

See also **www.yha.com.au** (Australia) and **www.norcalhostels.org** (USA).

Greyhound Lines, Inc
15110 North Dallas Parkway, Suite 600, Dallas, TX 75248, USA
Tel. 972-789-7000; Fax 972-387-1874
www.greyhound.com

And...

Here's a website we found that's worth a look if you're going to South Africa. Baz Bus is a hop-on, hop-off touring bus service between Cape Town and Port Elizabeth and is billed as a backpacker favourite. **www.bazbus.com** It was founded in 1995 by a former backpacker, Barry Zeidel and has a fleet of 19-seater buses with on-board TV and even has trailers able to carry surfboards and bicycles.

You can buy passes for travel in any direction you want, and as often as you like, within the time period. You get picked up and dropped off at the door of your backpacker hostel. The travel pass starts on the first day of your travel and is valid for seven or 14 or 21 consecutive days.

We have found similar services in Australia, New Zealand and France (see directory page 107) and are keeping our eyes out for more.

Student gappers could also check out **www.istc.org** (International Student Travel Confederation) for useful information and advice on special travel deals and discounts - planes, trains, coaches and ferries. Other useful sources of information are:

www.statravel.co.uk
www.studentflights.co.uk
www.thebigchoice.com/Travel/

Car

Another popular option is to travel by car, though it has to be said, mostly around Europe. It means you have somewhere to sleep if you get stuck for a bed for the night, you save money on train fares and you don't have to lug your rucksack into cafés.

If you are considering it, you need to know the motoring regulations of the countries you'll be visiting - they vary from country to country. Check that you are insured to drive abroad and that this is clearly shown on the documentation you carry with you.

The AA advises that you carry your vehicle insurance; vehicle registration documents and a current tax disc in the car and, of course, take your driving licence with you. If you still have an old paper licence you might want to consider

visit: www.travel-nation.co.uk

getting it updated to a photo licence before you go, but make sure you leave enough time for this - the DVLA isn't known for its speedy processing.

It is also advisable to take an International Driving Permit (IDP) as not all countries accept the British driving licence. In theory you don't need one in any of the EU member states, but the AA recommends having an IDP if you intend to drive in any country other than the UK. And, as it only costs £5.50, it's better than getting into trouble and being fined for driving without a valid licence.

An IDP is valid for 12 months and can be applied for up to three months in advance. The AA and RAC issue the permits - you must be over 18 and hold a current, full, UK driving licence that has been valid for two years. You'll need to fill in a form and provide your UK driving licence, passport and a recent passport-sized photo of yourself, which you can take to a participating Post Office. Be warned, you need to allow at least ten working days for processing, so don't try and do this at the last minute.

The AA website has loads of info about the permit, and driving abroad in general, and you can download the application form here: **www.theaa.com/getaway/idp/motidp002.html**

It's a good idea to put your car in for a service a couple of weeks before you leave and, unless you're a mechanic, it's also worth getting breakdown cover specifically for your trip abroad.

Any of the major recovery companies such as the AA, RAC or Green Flag offer this service. Remember, without cover, if you end up stuck on the side of the road it could be an expensive experience.

The RAC recommends taking a first aid kit, fire extinguisher, warning triangle, headlamp beam reflectors and spare lamp bulbs. These are all required by law in many countries and make sense anyway. for more information telephone: +44 (0)8705 722 722; or check out their website: **www.rac.co.uk**

Unless you're a very experienced driver, with some off-road experience, we wouldn't advise hiring a car and driving in many places in the developing world. South-east Asian, south Asian, south American and African roads are often little more than potholed tracks, and you really have to know what you're doing when faced with a pecking order decided purely by the size of your vehicle and the sound of your horn - not to mention negotiating wandering livestock, hand-pushed carts, overloaded local buses and trucks, and pedestrians with no road sense whatsoever.

In India, for example, this means road rules operate on a 'survival of the fittest' basis - big gets precedence and you better get out of the way if you're in something smaller. The only exception is cows, which are sacred, and if a cow decides to sit down in the middle of the road then everyone stops or goes around it. Heaven help you if you ever collide with one!

But often you'll find you can hire a car and a driver pretty cheaply for a day or two and then you'll be an ethical traveller contributing to the local economy. There's advice about how to negotiate in Chapter 2 – Finance.

Ships

If you want to get to the continent, taking a ferry across to France or Belgium can be cheap - but why not sail free as a working crewmember on ships? Before you leave the UK, contact the head offices of shipping companies to find out the procedures before you leave the UK and how to book a passage from a foreign port.

Or how about getting to grips with the rigging on a cruise yacht? There are numerous employers and private vessel owners out there on the ocean wave who take on amateur and novice crew. In this way you could gain valuable sailing experience and sea miles. You can also make some useful contacts on your way to becoming a professional crewmember. And have the time of your life.

A couple of useful sites where you can register, if you like this idea, are:

www.yachtcrew-cv.com/wordpress/?p=99 (it costs £10.95 to post your CV online but you do get a free downloadable copy of Jennifer Enrico's book, *Working on Yachts and Superyachts.*)

www.globalcrewnetwork.com (registration fee: £35 for six months and £45 for 12 months.)

Then there's the 'Classic Sailing' **gap**-year challenge. If you're over 18, in good health and have a sense of adventure, you could join other amateurs helping an expert crew to cross the ocean in a beautiful tall ship (be it a brigantine or a schooner): from the Azores to Bermuda to Charleston, South Carolina. Learn the ropes and find your sea legs! Find out more at:
www.classic-sailing.co.uk

visit: www.travel-nation.co.uk

Hitch hiking

Hitch hiking more or less died out after its heyday in the late 1960s and 1970s - partly out of safety concerns and partly as more and more young people became car owners. But with the onset of the recession it's become a regular feature of the travel pages in many national newspapers.

It costs nothing, except being a friendly and courteous passenger, and losing a bit of time waiting around for a ride, but you need to know what you're doing - and you need to know that in some countries it's illegal and that the usual sticking-your-thumb-out signal used in the UK is considered extremely rude in some countries.

There are no hard and fast rules about getting a lift, but above all you do need to think about your safety if you're going to try it - we wouldn't advise hitching alone for either men or women but on the other hand, if there are more than two of you, you might have trouble persuading a driver to stop.

If you are going to try it, make sure you know the basics. There are two useful websites:
www.hitchwiki.org/en/Main_Page
www.digihitch.com

Motorbike tours

If you're a keen biker and want to include your bike in **gap-** travel plans, there aren't many places you couldn't go. There's an excellent website by UK couple Kevin and Julia Saunders who are double *Guinness Book of Records* winners for their bike expeditions around the planet. The site offers plenty of advice as well as the opportunity to join expeditions with guides and team leaders: **www.globebusters.com**

Bicycles

If you're feeling hyper-energetic, you could use your pedal-pushing power to get you around town and country. This is really popular in north Europe, especially Holland, where the ground tends to be flatter. Most travel agents would be able to point you in the right direction, or you can just rely on hiring bikes while you are out there - make sure you understand the rules of the road.

With a globally growing 'green awareness', there's been a real surge in promoting cycling in the UK and abroad. Weather and terrain permitting it's a wonderful way of seeing a city, or touring a region, be it Portugal, Sweden, Provence, Tuscany…

But why confine it to Europe? There are many places where bicycles can be hired and it's a great way of getting around.

You can also participate in some amazing **gap**-year programmes, such as cycling to raise sponsorship for worthwhile charities and community projects worldwide. But charities aside, just get on your bike and enjoy a closer contact with nature and its vast range of spectacular scenery - getting ever fitter - for example, the USA's Pacific West Coast, Guatemala to Honduras, the Andes to the glaciers of Patagonia, Nairobi to Dar es Salaam, Chiang Mai to Bangkok, the South Island mountains of New Zealand…

Take a look at:

www.responsibletravel.com for cycling and mountain biking holidays;

also:

www.imba.com (the International Mountain Biking Association)

and:

www.cyclehire.co.nz/links.htm (independent cycle tours in New Zealand and worldwide links.)

visit: www.travel-nation.co.uk

Car Hire

Ezy Car Hire
PO Box 68199, Newton,
Auckland, New Zealand

Leading car rental company in New Zealand. Budget prices for cars from NZ$19. Campers suitable for two to six people available for hire from NZ$29.

Rent-a-Dent - Auckland Airport
PO Box 53-084,
Auckland Airport, New Zealand

One of many offices around New Zealand where you can hire budget vehicles including four wheel drive and mini buses.

Spaceships
31 Beach Rd,
Auckland 1010, New Zealand

Company offering campervan rentals in New Zealand and Australia.

Travellers Auto Barn
177 William Street, Kings Cross,
Sydney, NSW 2011, Australia

E: info@travellers-autobarn.com.au
T: +61 2 8323 1500 (outside of Australia)
T: 1800 674 374 (within Australia)
www.travellers-autobarn.com.au

Six branches in: Sydney, Brisbane, Cairns, Darwin, Perth and Melbourne.

There is no cheaper way to travel Australia than in one of our campervans, campers, wagons, stationwagons or cars. All of our campervans and wagons come with the ability to sleep in the vehicle... meaning big savings on your accommodation budget. We also offer a range of campervans and cars/stationwagons for sale with a guaranteed buyback.

Getting about

British Midland Airways Ltd
Donington Hall, Castle Donington,
Derbyshire DE74 2SB

Low cost flights to Europe and America.

Cheap Flights
49 Marylebone High Street,
Marylebone, London W1U 5HJ

This useful website does not sell tickets but can point you in the right direction to get the best deal.

the gap-year guidebook 2010

EasyJet Plc
Hangar 89, London Luton Airport,
Luton, Bedfordshire LU2 9PF

Offers cheap flights to European destinations with further reductions if you book over the internet.

Ebookers (Flightbookers Ltd)
5th Floor, 140 Aldersgate Street,
London, EC1A 4HY UK

Cheap flights can be booked through their website.

Florence by Bike
Via San Zanobi, 120 ,
Firenze, Tuscany 50129, Italy

Scooter, motorbike and bike rental company in Florence. Also sells clothing and accessories as well as bike parts.

International Rail
Chase House, Gilbert Street,
Ropley, Hampshire SO24 0BY

InterRail Pass provides unlimited travel on the sophisticated European Rail network. The pass is very flexible allowing you to choose either one country or all 30 countries.

See page 97 for more information.

Kiwi Experience
195 Parnell Road, Parnell ,
Auckland 1052, New Zealand

Extensive bus network covering the whole of New Zealand. Passes valid for 12 months.

Magic Travellers Network
120 Albert Street, PO Box 949,
Auckland, New Zealand

Flexible transport company for backpackers and independent travellers around New Zealand.

Oz-Bus
Unit 6A, Home Farm,
Diddington, St Neots
Cambridgeshire PE19 5XU

Oz-Bus operate the only regular hop on/hop off bus service between London and Sydney for all ages of Adventure Travellers.

Oz-Bus also offer The Hippie Trail, Oz-Bus Africa and Oz-Bus Down Under.

Rail Europe Ltd.
34 Tower View, Kings Hill,
West Malling, Kent ME19 4ED

Specializes in selling tickets and passes for travel throughout Europe by train. Available to buy online or via their call centre.

Ryanair
Satelite 3, London Stansted Airport,
Stansted, Essex CM24 1RW

Low cost airline to European destinations – many outward flights are actually free! – but make sure you check how much the return flight will be.

Stray Ltd
31 Beach Road,
Auckland Central, New Zealand

Stray is New Zealand's fastest growing backpacker bus network - designed for travellers who want to get off the beaten track

Thomas Cook
The Thomas Cook Business Park, Coningsby Road,
Peterborough, Northamptonshire PE3 8SB

General travel agent with high street branches offering flights and late deals.

Travellers Contact Point
7th Floor, Dymocks Building, 428 George Street
Sydney, NSW 2000, Australia

A specialist travel agency for independent and working holiday travellers. We have shops in Australia, New Zealand and the UK.

Ze-Bus
203 rue des artisans,
St Jean de Luz 64 500, France

Flexible transport enabling you to discover France. No fixed routes are involved as the passengers decide where to go, where to start and where to stop. Pass and tickets are valid for the entire season.

Tours

Acacia Adventure Holidays
LGF 23a Craven Terrace,
Lancaster Gate ,
Bayswater, London W2 3QH

Acacia offers exciting and affordable overland tours and small group safaris across Africa. Enjoy game viewing, desert adventures, beach breaks, dive courses or trekking!

visit: www.travel-nation.co.uk

Adrenaline Tours
Unit 412, MSK House, 13 Bultengracht Street
Cape Town 8000, South Africa

Based in Cape Town, and is your one stop shop for all your touring needs. Extreme activities, sporting events, football matches, music concerts, cultural tours and more...

Adventure Tours NZ
50 Fort Street,
Auckland 1010, New Zealand

Offers specialised small group nature-based tours for the active traveller on a budget. Go off the beaten track, see unique scenery and wildlife.

Adventure Travellers Club P Ltd
PO Box 12205, Nayabazaar,
Kathmandu, Nepal 12205

Offers trekking and adventure tours in Nepal, Tibet, Bhutan and Indian regions. Includes camping, peak climbing, jungle safaris, river rafting and much more.

Afreco Tours
2 Manor Mews, Shalstone Manor,
Main Street, Shalstone MK18 5LT

Afreco Tours specialises in African safari ranger training and wildlife adventures - from four days to one year.

Africa Travel Co
PO Box 50425,
Cape Town 8002, South Africa

Specialists in trips around Africa ranging from three to 56 days.

African Horizons
PO Box 61170, 216 Mosi O Tunya Road,
Livingstone, Zambia

E: horizons@zamnet.zm
T: +260 213 323 433
www.volunteerzambia.com

Volunteer Zambia staff have over ten years experience dealing with toursim/eco-tourism and volunteer support within Zambia.

Projects are available year round for our volunteers to work within schools, orphanages, sports education and wildlife education/research. Programmes from two weeks to three months in duration.

Alaska Heritage Tours
509 W 4th Avenue,
Anchorage, AK 99501, USA

At Alaska Heritage Tours we strive to give you the best of Alaska, the way you want it – with pre-packaged Alaska vacations and itineraries. Explore Alaska's top destinations.

Alpine Exploratory
9 Copperfield Street,
Wigan, Lancashire WN1 2DZ

Specializes in self-guided walking and trekking tours in Europe. Full programme of guided tours also offered, as well as bespoke holidays.

Andean Trails
The Clockhouse, Bonnington Mill Business Centre,
72 Newhaven Road
Edinburgh, Midlothian EH6 4JG

Owner run specialist adventure travel company organising small group tours to Peru, Bolivia, Ecuador, Cuba, Guyana and Patagonia.

Australia Travel Plan
7th Floor, Intergen House,
65-67 Western Road
Hove, East Sussex BN3 2JQ

T: +44 (0)1273 32 2055
www.australiatravelplan.co.uk

Create your own trip in Australia. For independent travellers who don't want to do a group tour.

Backpacker Travel Auctions
Safari Pete, PO Box 1465,
St Kilda South, VIC 3205, Australia

Safari Pete can offer you directions to the best deals on tours around Australia and New Zealand.

Bicycling Empowerment Network
PO Box 31561, Tokai,
Cape Town, Western Cape 7966, South Africa

BEN, a non-profit organisation, promotes the use and sale of refurbished bicycles. They conduct Bicycle Township Tours empowering local people and winning International Responsible Tourism Awards.

Black Feather - The Wilderness Adventure Company
250 McNaughts Road, RR#3,
Parry Sound ON, P2A 2W9, Canada

Company offering canoeing and kayaking trips and expeditions to remote artic locations. Offer women-only trips and will do a customized trip for groups of four or more.

Borneo Anchor Travel & Tours/Sabah Divers
G27, Ground Floor, Wisma Sabah,
Kota Kinabalu, Sabah 88000, Malaysia

They offer various wildlife, nature and adventure packages all over Sabah, Malaysian Borneo.

BridgeClimb Sydney

5 Cumberland Street, The Rocks,
Sydney, NSW 2000, Australia

BridgeClimb provides the ultimate experience of Sydney, with guided climbs to the top of the world famous Sydney Harbour Bridge. Climbers can choose between the Express Climb, The Bridge Climb or The Discovery Climb.

Cambodia Travel Plan

7th Floor, Intergen House,
65-67 Western Road,
Hove, East Sussex BN3 2JQ

T: +44 (0)1273 322 042
www.cambodiatravelplan.co.uk

Create your own trip in Cambodia. For independent travellers who don't want to do a group tour.

Cape York Motorcycle Adventures

PO Box 105,
Clifton Beach,
QLD 4879, Australia

Motorcycle tours from one to eight days duration. Private charter also available. They have their own motorbikes and a support vehicle that accompanies the longer excursions.

China Travel Plan

7th Floor, Intergen House,
65-67 Western Road
Hove, East Sussex BN3 2JQ

T: +44 (0)1273 322 048
www.chinatravelplan.co.uk

Create your own trip in China. For independent travellers who don't want to do a group tour.

Cordillera Blanca Trek

Av Interoceanica 198, Nueva Florida,
Huaraz, Ancahas, Peru

Offers treks to Machu Picchu, a volcanco tour and more.

Do Something Different

Third Floor, 16 Bromells Road,
Clapham, London SW4 0BG

Want to dog sled in the Rockies? Take a Hong Kong Island or helicopter Tour? Or climb Auckland Harbour Bridge?

Dolphin Encounter

96 Esplanade,
Kaikoura 7300, New Zealand

Swim or watch dolphins in Kaikoura. You do need to book in advance as there is a limit to how many swimmers are allowed per trip.

Dorset Expeditionary Society/Leading Edge Expeditions
Lupins Business Centre, 1-3 Greenhill,
Weymouth, Dorset DT4 7SP

Dorset Expeditionary Society promotes adventurous expeditions to remote parts of the world. Open to all. May qualify for two sections of the Duke of Edinburgh's Gold Award.

Dragoman
Camp Green,
Debenham, Suffolk IP14 6LA

Overlanding is stil the most authentic and accessible way of discovering new countries, their people and culture.

Join us in Africa, South America and Asia.

Eco Trails Kerala
Tharavadu Heritage Home, Kumarakom,
Kottayam, Kerala, Alleppey Kumarakom 686563, India

This tour company provides budget holiday tour packages in the Kumarakom and Alleppey Backwater areas.

Egypt Horse Tours
Giza, Cairo, Egypt

We offer Egyptian horse riding (desert and sightseeing tours). We have well kept horses to suit all abilities we welcome those who have experience with horses to work in our stables.

Equine Adventures
Long Barn South, Sutton Manor Farm,
Bishop's Sutton, Hampshire SO24 0AA

Horse riding tours available, in Australasia, Asia, Africa, Europe and the Americas.

Equitours - Worldwide Horseback Riding Adventures
PO Box 807, 10 Stalnaker Street,
Dubois, WY 82513, USA

With over 30 years experience, Equitours offer tested and tried horseback tours on six continents. Rides from three to eight days (or longer) for riders of all experience.

Explore Worldwide Ltd
Nelson House, 55 Victoria Road,
Farnborough, Hampshire GU14 7PA

Company organising special tours in small groups. Types of worldwide tours available are walking holidays, dog-sledding, wildlife and railway tours amongst others.

Fair Dinkum Bike Tours
PO Box 7442, Cairns, QLD 4870, Australia

Offer a range of tours using local guides to cater for all levels.

visit: www.travel-nation.co.uk

Flying Kiwi Wilderness Expeditions Ltd
48 Forests Road, Stoke, Nelson, PO Box 680, New Zealand

Bus tours around New Zealand offer a unique and fun experience. Camping or cabin options are available in exciting locations and usually meals are included.

Fräulein Marias Bicycle Tours
Dipl.Sptl.Rupert Riedl,
Meeting Point Mirabellgardens,
Salzburg, Austria

Maria's Bicycle tours take you to the main attractions from the film *The Sound Of Music*! The tour lasts three hours with stop points along the way and operates between May and September.

Go Differently Ltd
19 West Road,
Saffron Walden, Essex CB11 3DS

Company offering small-group, short-term volunteering and tailor-made holidays based on the appreciation and respect of the local environment and people.

Grayline Tours of Hong Kong
5/F, Cheong Hing Building,
72 Nathan Road,
Tsim Sha Tsui, Hong Kong, China

Special day tours around Hong Kong such as the Bun Festival and island hopping tour or a tour to Po Lin Monastary on Lantau Island.

Haka Tours
115 Hulverstone Drive, Avondale,
Christchurch 7, New Zealand

Haka Tours represents the ultimate in New Zealand adventure holidays, from small group adventures to New Zealand snow tours exploring the impressive Southern Alps and the active volcanoes of the North.

High & Wild
The Well House, Chydyok Road,
East Chaldon, Dorset DT2 8DN

High and Wild plan some of the most unusual and exciting adventures to destinations worldwide.

High Places Ltd
Globe Centre, Penistone Road,
Sheffield, West Yorkshire S6 3AE

Independent specialist trekking company organising tours to 22 countries.

Highland Experience Tours
Loch Ness Discovery Centre,
1 Parliament Square, High Street, Edinburgh,

Travel company offering one day and private tours around Scotland, such as a two day highland tour, a whisky tasting tour, or a tour of Scotland personalised to your own requirements.

In the Saddle Ltd
Reaside, Neen Savage,
Cleobury Mortimer,
Shropshire DY14 8ES

Specializes in horse riding holidays all over the world, catering for all levels of experience. From ranches in the Rocky Mountain states of Montana and Wyoming, to expeditions in remote and unexplored parts of the world.

India Travel Plan
7th Floor, Intergen House,
65-67 Western Road
Hove, East Sussex BN3 2JQ

T: +44 (0)1273 322 044
www.indiatravelplan.co.uk

Create your own trip in India. For independent travellers who don't want to do a group tour.

Indonesia Travel Plan
7th Floor, Intergen House,
65-67 Western Road
Hove, East Sussex BN3 2JQ

T: +44 (0)1273 322 052
www.indonesiatravelplan.co.uk

Create your own trip in Indonesia. For independent travellers who don't want to do a group tour.

Intrepid Travel
76 Upper Street,
Islington, London N1 0NU

Variety of worldwide tours on offer ranging from 'comfort' to 'intrepid'.

Joint Ventures
Joint Ventures, Gwexintaba, Lusikisiki
Port St John's 5120, South Africa

Their vision is: 'Bringing people together to experience the natural beauty of most extreme nature in untouched state, to enhance the outdoor activities and to empower and facilitate the lives of those living the ways of ancient civilization.'

Jungle Surfing Canopy Tours
Keydane Pty Ltd, 24 Camelot Close,
Cape Tribulation, QLD 4873, Australia

Night walks in a tropical rainforest or jungle surf through the Daintree Rainforest.

Kande Horse Trails
Box 22, The Stables,
Kande, Nkhata Bay District, Malawi

Experience the Malawi bush on horseback. All ages and riding abilities catered for.

Kenya Travel Plan
7th Floor, Intergen House, 65-67 Western Road
Hove, East Sussex BN3 2JQ

T: +44 (0)1273 322 053
www.kenyatravelplan.co.uk

Create your own trip in Kenya. For independent travellers who don't want to do a group tour.

KT Adventure
869-HongHa-HoanKiem,
Hanoi 84, Vietnam

KT Adventure, part of Vivu Travel, offer specialised tours in Vietnam, from adventure tours to motorbiking.

Kudu Expeditions Ltd
Unit 13, Court Farm Business Park,
Bishops Frome, Worcestershire WR6 5AY

Explore the world by motorcycle. Amazing trips, from two week multi-country tours to four month trans-continental expeditions, designed to challenge and inspire you.

Kuoni Challenge for Charity
Kuoni House, Deepdene Avenue,
Dorking, Surrey RH5 4AZ

Kuoni's challenge for charity webpage lists various opportunities for people to raise money for a charity of their choice in exotic destinations.

Laos Travel Plan
7th Floor, Intergen House, 65-67 Western Road
Hove, East Sussex BN3 2JQ -

T: +44 (0)1273 322 043
www.laostravelplan.co.uk

Create your own trip in Laos. For independent travellers who don't want to do a group tour.

Live Travel
154 Nelson Road, Twickenham, Middlesex TW2 7BU

Personalised travel plans offered as well as group tours.

Malaysia Travel Plan
7th Floor, Intergen House, 65-67 Western Road
Hove, East Sussex BN3 2JQ

T: +44 (0)1273 322 054
www.malaysiatravelplan.co.uk

Create your own trip in Malaysia. For independent travellers who don't want to do a group tour.

Melbourne Street Art Tour
110 Franklin Street,
Melbourne, VIC 3000, Australia

Melbourne Street Art Tours, led by one of Melbourne's elite street art stars, gives you an overview of the Melbourne underground street art scene.

Mexico Travel Plan
7th Floor, Intergen House, 65-67 Western Road
Hove, East Sussex BN3 2JQ -

T: +44 (0)1273 322 046
www.mexicotravelplan.co.uk

Create your own trip in Mexico. For independent travellers who don't want to do a group tour.

Morocco Travel Plan
7th Floor, Intergen House, 65-67 Western Road
Hove, East Sussex BN3 2JQ

T: +44 (0)1273 322 056
www.moroccotravelplan.co.uk

Follow the Berber Trail through Atlas Mountain villages, sleep in Sahara Desert tents and traditional *riads*, munch couscous in the souqs and take it easy on the beaches of Agadir. We'll help you build your own Morocco adventure.

Mountain Kingdoms Ltd
Old Crown House, 18 Market Street,
Wotton-under-Edge, Gloucestershire GL12 7AE

Himalayan Kingdoms is the UK's foremost quality trekking company, running treks and tours to the great mountain ranges of the world.

Nepal Travel Plan
7th Floor, Intergen House, 65-67 Western Road
Hove, East Sussex BN3 2JQ

T: +44 (0)1273 322 045
www.nepaltravelplan.co.uk

Create your own trip in Nepal. For independent travellers who don't want to do a group tour.

Olympic Bike Travel
Adelianos Kampos 32,
Rethymnon, Crete GR-74100, Greece

A variety of bike tours available for all ages. From a ride down the highest mountain in Greece, Psiloritis, to a bike and hiking tour to the Myli gorge.

On The Go Tours
68 North End Road,
West Kensington, London W14 9EP

Special tours such as solar eclipse tours and railways of the Raj can be arranged.

Outbike
The Adventure Collective, PO Box 848,
Unley BC, SA 5061, Australia

Bike ride across Australia. Definitely a once in a lifetime experience.

Overland Club
PO Box 755, 3a-5a Front Street,
Sedgefield, Cleveland TS21 3AT

Overland Club provide the ultimate in adventure style group tours and expeditions.

Palmar Voyages
Alemania N31-77, Avenue Mariana de Jesús,
Quito, Ecuador

Tailor-made programmes for tours in Ecuador, Peru, South America, the Andes and the Galapagos Islands.

Peregrine Adventures Ltd
First Floor, 8 Clerewater Place, Lower Way ,
Thatcham, Berkshire RG19 3RF

Peregrine offer a vast range of tours from polar expeditions to trekking the Himalayas.

Pura Aventura
18 Bond Street,
Brighton, Sussex BN1 1RD

Various beautiful tailor-made tours in exotic locations. Career break to fulfil a long held dream or a special diversion on your gap-year perhaps?

Rickshaw Travel
8th Floor, Intergen House,
65-67 Western Road,
Hove, Sussex BN3 2JQ

E: info@rickshawtravel.co.uk
T: +44 (0) 1273 320 580
www.rickshawtravel.co.uk

Rickshaw Travel is a UK based ABTA/ATOL bonded travel operator, that uses locally owned accommodation with an authentic feel that is a cut above the usual backpacker haunts. Customers can create their own trip by selecting from a range of bite-sized adventures, lasting between two and five days each.

Ideal for travellers who want see and do lots in a short time, but don't want to do a group tour.

Ride With Us
PO Box 936,
St Albans, Hertfordshire AL1 9GL

Organised motorcycle holidays around western and eastern Europe that offer something for everyone regardless of their touring experience.

Saddle Skedaddle
Ouseburn Building, East Quayside,
Newcastle upon Tyne,

Some say there is no better way to see a country, its culture, its wildlife and its people, than by bike! This company offers off-road, road or leisure cycling.

Safari Par Excellence
UK Head Office, Ermington Mill,
Ivybridge, Devon PL21 9NT

Safari company with a 'no fuss or frills' ethos. They cover Zimbabwe, Zambia, Botswana, Namibia and other countries in Africa.

Sahara Travel
Sahara House, Macetown, Tara, Republic of Ireland

Discover spectacular landscapes and mysterious cultures on a unique Desert Safari, Camel Trek or Short Break. Spend time with the Berbers, sleep under millions of stars and explore the culture and history of North Africa.

Scenic Air AG
PO Box 412, Interlaken, 3800, Switzerland

Thinking of spending time in Switzerland? Fancy scenic flights, glacier trekking, sky-diving or other adventurous activities?

Selective Asia
69 Grand Parade, Brighton, Sussex BN2 9TS

Offers a range of unique, privately guided tours and adventure holidays in Cambodia, Laos, Vietnam and Thailand.

South Africa Travel Plan
7th Floor, Intergen House,
65-67 Western Road
Hove, East Sussex BN3 2JQ

T: +44 (0)1273 322 047
www.southafricatravelplan.co.uk

Create your own trip in South Africa. For independent travellers who don't want to do a group tour.

Southern Cross Tours & Expeditions
MD Jones, 841-9100 Trelew,
Chubut, Argentina

Palaeontology tours in South America.

Specialtours Ltd.
Specialtours at The Ultimate Travel Company,
25-27 Vanston Place, West Brompton, London SW6 1AZ

International art and cultural tours. Access wonderful private houses, art collections and gardens. Most tours are accompanied by an expert lecturer. Why not try tours such as 'Sicily in the Spring' or 'Art & Architecture in New York'.

Suntrek
Sun Plaza, 77 West Third Street,
Santa Rosa, CA 95401, USA

Adventure tours arranged in the USA, Mexico, Alaska, Canada, Central and South America and Australia.

visit: www.travel-nation.co.uk

Sunvil

Sunvil House, Upper Square,
Old Isleworth, Middlesex TW7 7BJ

A range of active holidays/trips available including sailing holidays around the world
and sporting breaks worldwide.

Thailand Travel Plan

7th Floor, Intergen House,
65-67 Western Road
Hove, East Sussex BN3 2JQ

T: +44 (0)1273 322 040
www.thailandtravelplan.co.uk

Khao Yai jungle trails and island hopping to hidden paradise. Sleep in floating huts
along the River Kwai and try a real Thai homestay.

We'll help you build your very own Thailand adventure.

The Adventure Company

Cross & Pillory House, Cross & Pillory Lane,
Alton, Hampshire GU34 1HL

Offers inspirational holidays and trips worldwide that venture off the well trodden
tourist trails.

The Bundu Safari Company

c/o Intrepid Travel, 76 Upper Street,
Islington, London N1 0NU

The Bundu Safari Company has teamed up with Intrepid Travel to offer exciting safari
adventures.

The Imaginative Traveller

1 Betts Avenue, Martlesham Heath, Suffolk IP5 3RH

Individual, escape and volunteering tours available.

The Oriental Caravan

35 Vanburgh Court, Kennington, London SE11 4NS UK

The Oriental Caravan is a truly independent adventure tour operator specialising in
escorted small group travel in the Far East.

The Russia Experience

Research House, Fraser Road,
Perivale, Middlesex UB6 7AQ

The Trans-Siberian is a working train covering 9,000 km, ten time zones, 16 rivers and
some 80 towns and cities.

A once in a lifetime experience.

Timberline Adventures

7975 E Harvard, Suite #J, Denver, CO 80231, USA

Hiking and cycling tours in the USA.

the gap-year guidebook 2010

Travel Nation
8th Floor, Intergen House,
65-67 Western Road,
Hove, East Sussex BN3 2JQ

E: info@travelnation.co.uk
T: 01273 320580
www.travel-nation.co.uk

Independent specialist travel company providing expert advice and the best deals on round-the-world trips, multi-stop itineraries, overland/adventure tours and Trans-Siberian rail journeys.

Booking agent for all of the major overland and adventure tour operators; no booking fee and you can take advantage of independent and neutral advice.

Travellers Connected.com
Queensgate House, 48 Queen Street,
Exeter, Devon EX4 3SR

A totally free community site for gap-year travellers. Register and contact travellers around the world for to-the-minute advice on the best places to go and best things to do.

TrekAmerica
Grange Mills, Weir Road,
Balham, London SW12 0NE

Offering more than 60 itineraries from one to nine weeks in TrekAmerica's fun, free, and flexible small group adventure tours are the ideal way to explore North America.

Tribes Travel
12 The Business Centre,
Earl Soham, Woodbridge, Suffolk IP13 7SA

A Fair Trade Travel company with lots of exciting tours for you to choose from. Such as budget priced walking safaris to the more expensive once in a lifetime trips.

Tucan Travel
316 Uxbridge Road, Acton, London W3 9QP

Offer a wide range of tours at low prices.

Vietnam Travel Plan
7th Floor, Intergen House,
65-67 Western Road, Hove, East Sussex BN3 2JQ -

T: +44 (0)1273 322 041
www.vietnamtravelplan.co.uk

Meet the hilltribes of Sapa and drift along the Mekong to tropical Phu Quoi Island. Try Anchors Away in Halong Bay and learn to dive on tiny Palm Island.

We'll help you build your very own Vietnam adventure.

Vodkatrain
Unit 1 St George's Court, 131 Putney Bridge Road,
West Brompton, London SW15 2PA

Experience the Trans-Mongolian railway and the Silk Road, travelling with local people, sampling local food and travel at local prices.

Volcanoes Safaris
PO Box 16345,
Belgravia, London SW1X 0ZD

Eco-tourism is the key here. Their eco-lodges in Uganda offer comfortable accommodation without disturbing the surrounding environment. They also work closely with conservation organisations specifically those involved with Gorillas and Chimpanzees.

Walks Worldwide
12 The Square, Ingleton,
Carnforth, Yorkshire LA6 3EG UK

Offers different types of walking expeditions around the world, from walking across the Swedish coastal peninsulas to trekking to Everest base camp.

Wayward Bus Touring Company Pty Ltd
119 Waymouth Street,
Adelaide, SA 5000, Australia

Offers tours between Melbourne and Adelaide via the Great Ocean Road and Coorong. They also go to Kangaroo Island, Kakadu and a variety of other places.

Wild at Heart Youth Adventures
Kruger Office, Orpen Road,
Kruger Park Area, Limpopo province, South Africa

Wild at Heart Youth Safaris is a well-established South African based youth adventure company. From helping at a monkey sanctuary to working at a reptile farm there are many different opportunities available.

Wind, Sand & Stars
PO Box 4322,
Bath BA1 2BU

A specialist company that organises group journeys within the desert and mountain areas of Sinai, Egypt.

World Expeditions
81 Craven Gardens,
Wimbledon, London SW19 8LU

Adventure travel company offering ground breaking itineraries on every continent. They offer exciting all inclusive adventures and challenges worldwide.

Yomps
10 Woodland Way,
Brighton, Sussex BN1 8BA

Yomps offer adventure travel and interesting gap-year and career break experiences.

123

Travel Companies

Goa Way
111 Bell Street,
Marylebone, London NW1 6TL

Goa Way specialises in organising travel to Goa and Kerala. You can book flights, hostels or even package tours.

Greyhound Lines Inc
PO Box 660691, MS 470,
Dallas, TX 75266-0691, USA

The most famous and largest bus company in America. Book online and join the millions of others who travel across America on the 'old grey dog'.

See editorial on page 101.

Inside Japan Tours
Lewins House, Lewins Mead,
Bristol, Gloucestershire BS1 2NN

Specialist company offering tours of Japan, including small group tours and individual, self-guiding tours.

You can also book a Japan Rail Pass online here.

Journey Latin America
12-13 Heathfield Terrace,
Chiswick, London W4 4JE

JLA is the UK's major specialist in travel to Latin America. Its 'Open-Jaw' transatlantic tickets permit you to fly into one country and out of another.

Kumuka Worldwide
40 Earls Court Road,
Kensington, London W8 6EJ

Kumuka Worldwide is the leading specialist tour operator for activity holidays and adventure holidays in small group travel, around the world.

Mountain Beach Mountain Bike Holidays
13 Church Street,
Ruddington,
Nottinghamshire NG11 6HA

Find the mountain biking holiday of your dreams with Mountain Beach.

Neilson Active Holidays Ltd
Locksview, Brighton Marina,
Brighton, Sussex BN2 5HA

This company offers a selection of worldwide sporting holidays, all year round.

Oasis Overland

The Marsh,
Henstridge, Somerset BA8 0TF

E: info@oasisoverland.co.uk
T: +44 (0) 1963 363400
F: +44 (0) 1963 363200
www.oasisoverland.co.uk

Looking for an exciting and affordable adventure travel experience, where you'll work as part of a team with like-minded travellers as you explore different cultures and regions? Oasis Overland has the trip for you.

Overland trips range from two to 40 weeks in Africa, South America and the Middle East.

STA Travel

52 Grosvenor Gardens,
Victoria, London SW1W 0AG

This company has branches or agents worldwide and a Help Desk telephone service, which provides essential backup for travellers on the move.

Travel Nation

8th Floor, Intergen House, 65-67 Western Road,
Hove, East Sussex BN3 2JQ

E: info@travelnation.co.uk
T: 01273 320580
www.travel-nation.co.uk

Travel Nation provide expert advice and great deals on round-the-world flights and multi-stop tickets, adventure tours, accommodation, travel insurance and discounted long-haul flights.

Their staff are all well seasoned travellers who will be able to offer any destination advice needed. They have outstanding customer service levels and you'll deal with the same person for the life of your booking.

Travel Talk

Hudavendigar Cad, No 6 Kat 2 Sirkeci,
Istanbul, Turkey

Turkish travel agency specializing in the Mediterranean and fun, adventure tours.

Travelbag Ltd

373-375 The Strand, London WC2R 0JE

Book flights, hotel, holidays and even find insurance on their website.

USIT

19/21 Aston Quay,
Dublin, County Dublin 2, Republic of Ireland

Irish travel agents offering cheap flights from Dublin, Cork and Shannon specifically aimed at students.

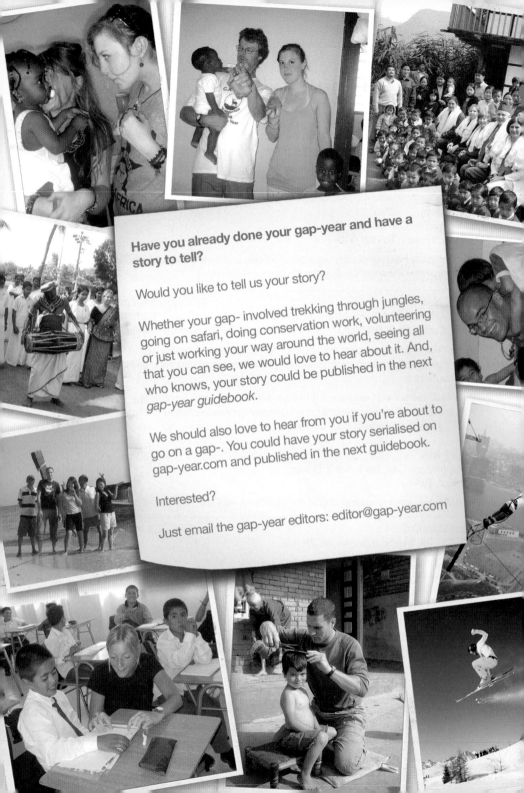

Have you already done your gap-year and have a story to tell?

Would you like to tell us your story?

Whether your gap- involved trekking through jungles, going on safari, doing conservation work, volunteering or just working your way around the world, seeing all that you can see, we would love to hear about it. And, who knows, your story could be published in the next *gap-year guidebook*.

We should also love to hear from you if you're about to go on a gap-. You could have your story serialised on gap-year.com and published in the next guidebook.

Interested?

Just email the gap-year editors: editor@gap-year.com

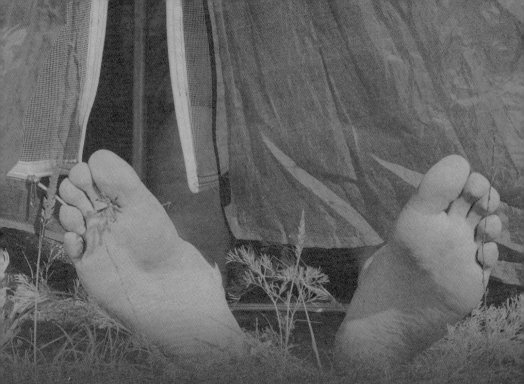

Chapter 5
Accommodation

Chapter sponsored by

Say HI to the world

Increasing numbers of people choose to take a **gap-** as a break from studying or an opportunity to fulfil an ambition. Travelling during your **gap-** can be one of the most rewarding and exciting adventures you'll ever experience - and staying safe is key to enjoying the ride.

Hostelling International has spent a century helping people of all ages discover this planet we call home. HI is the only global network of Youth Hostels - 4000 HI Hostels in 90 countries. HI Hostels adhere to our industry-leading Assured Standards, so you can be sure of a safe, clean, comfortable stay and a consistent level of services and facilities wherever you travel.

Many gappers travel alone - but you will never be lonely if you make HI part of your **gap-**! HI Hostels are open to all, enabling people of all nations, ages and cultures to share experiences and learn more about themselves, each other and their surroundings. Many HI hostels organise trips and activities - so you can see the sights and enjoy an adrenaline rush with new-found friends!

HI Hostels are a great way to cut accommodation costs without compromising on quality, comfort or our precious environment. All HI Hostels adhere to the HI Environmental Charter, taking great care to operate HI Hostels in ways sympathetic

to the environment - including solar power, water-saving devices, low-energy lighting and recycling.

Hostelling International is one of the world's biggest membership organisations for young people, and it offers a wealth of benefits. For starters, HI members save on overnight rates

visit: www.hihostels.com

in HI Hostels. And the savings continue throughout your **gap-** – with thousands of discounts worldwide on buses and trains, must-see sights and museums, tours and adventure activities, in shops, cafés and entertainment venues.

Wherever your **gap-** takes you, HI membership opens the door to amazing hostels in great places! No other hostel operator can match HI for sheer quality or variety of accommodation, combining local culture with international ambience. Here are a few ideas to whet your appetite:

- Traditional tatami rooms and food in Japan…
- A stunning modern hostel on an archaeological site in the heart of Sydney, Australia…
- Historic houses in China…
- A colonial building in the Bolivian Andes…
- A 15th century castle (with 21st century mod cons) in Ireland…
- A comfy cottage in Corbett National Park, India…
- An Afro-Victorian mansion in South Africa…
- A poolside retreat close to Brazil's spectacular Iguaçu Falls…
- Historic lodges in the heart of Canada's Rocky Mountains…
- Modern accommodation by the Red Sea, Israel…
- Ship hostels in Portugal, Sweden, Hungary…

For the full story, let us inspire you on **www.hihostels.com/gap**! You can also download free hostel guides and travel tools - like the handy HI Widget and friends @ hihostels Facebook application!

Hostelling International is a non-governmental, non-profit-making organisation recognised by UNESCO. Registered Charity no. 1117014.

5 Accommodation

Traditionally, hostels are the first option that springs to mind, whenever gappers or backpackers are looking for cheap accommodation.

Today there is a range of hostels available, which offer clean, safe and reasonably priced accommodation, some even have 'luxury' extras, such as internet connection, games rooms and laundry facilities.

However, safety can still vary widely and gappers often rely on *Rough Guide* or *Lonely Planet* guidebooks, or the word-of-mouth recommendations from other backpackers to find a suitable one.

Use your common sense and always check where the fire exits are when arriving at a hostel, because it's too late to look if there's already a fire and you're trying to get out of the building.

If you do find you're staying in a basic, no frills-style hostel, it's wise to make sure there's some ventilation when you have a bath or shower - faulty water heaters give off lethal and undetectable carbon monoxide fumes and will kill you without you realising it as you fall gently to sleep, never to wake up again.

Use your instincts - if you think the hostel's simply not up to scratch and too risky, go and find another one.

To book ahead try that well known favourite:

Hostelling International
2nd floor, Gate House, Fretherne Road
Welwyn Garden City, Hertfordshire AL8 6RD
Tel: +44 (0) 1707 324170
Fax: +44 (0) 1707 323980

Email: office@hihostels.com
www.hihostels.com

Hostelling International represents 4000 youth hostels, run by member associations in over 90 countries, and co-ordinates quality and the global booking system on: **www.hihostels.com**.

The basic YHA membership has been frozen at the same rate for the fourth consecutive year: for an individual it's £15.95, but there are several alternatives - from £9.95 for a year's membership (for under 26-year-olds) to £22.95 for a family membership. You can join online, by phone, or by post; membership applications are only accepted from an address within Europe. Non-EU residents can buy membership at a hostel in their home country or take out international membership on arrival at a hostel. Remember that a year's membership is valid for 12 months only from the date of issue and cannot be post-dated.
www.yha.org.uk/yha-membership/membership-types-and-prices/index.aspx

visit: www.hihostels.com

But there are other options from bed and breakfast to an Amazonian ecolodge, a monastery to a family-owned guesthouse.

For general information about interesting places to stay try:

www.gonomad.com/lodgings/lodgings.html

Camping

It's worth considering this option as it can cost as little as £6 per night. There are quite a few blogs where you can find out, from those that have tried it, what it's really like in the developed and developing world. Check out these websites:

www.campingo.com/campsite.html
www.internationalcampingclub.com/
www.eurocampings.co.uk/en/europe/
www.rentocamp.com/
www.trav.com/Campsites/Asia

Or how about camping Bedouin style in Jordan? There's a site about ten miles north of Petra: **www.bedouincamp.net/enter.html**

According to the website Associated Content, many campsites are replacing tents with huts; usually they're in places close to hiking areas. You'll get a bed in a hut, and use of other facilities, so you only need a sleeping bag - no need to carry a tent. There's more on:

www.associatedcontent.com/article/16737/hut_hiking_around_the_world.html

We've listed some campsites in the directory (page 142) and these are also included on **www.gap-year.com**, which is regularly updated. If we haven't yet

the gap-year guidebook 2010

covered a country you are interested in, check back or, better still, if *you* know of a good campsite let us know.

Caravan Parks

Renting a caravan is another possibility, but a quick web search suggests caravan parks are mostly to be found in the UK, Ireland, USA and in Australia. These websites are good places to start looking:

www.allstays.com/Campgrounds-Australia/
www.familyparks.com.au/
www.takeabreak.com.au/caravanparks.htm

Temple and monastery guesthouses

The main consideration for deciding to stay in a monastery or temple guesthouse, should not be your budget, though there's no denying that it's affordable for the budget traveller. It's also pointless to pretend that a male dominated culture doesn't exist in many parts of the world and guesthouses attached to temples and monasteries are therefore excellent places for women travelling alone to stay. Indeed for anyone wanting some place to be able to relax and not be constantly on guard, or if you're seeking a peaceful sanctuary and simplicity, religious guesthouses are ideal.

Some places prefer that you have *some* link with their faith, even if only through a historic extended-family link, but there is a strong tradition of offering refuge, safety and peace in any religious community that isn't a closed order.

Historically, the religious communities and monasteries of many faiths have provided hospice and hospital services to their surrounding communities. Much of our early medical knowledge developed from here too.

Changing economics have also meant their costs have risen and many temples and monasteries have had to be practical about raising income for their communities and for the upkeep of buildings, whose antiquity makes them costly to maintain. Most are therefore open to guests regardless of faith.

Having said that, if you are considering this option, be prepared for rooms and meals to be simple, facilities to be austere and for the community to be quiet at certain times of the day. There will be daily rituals to the life of the community and, like anywhere else, it's only polite to respect their customs. Obviously it's not an option that would suit some gappers.

But a chance to think, to recharge the spiritual batteries, to learn more about oneself or a particular faith, maybe to learn yoga or meditation, is what some gappers are looking for and it can be worth considering this option as part of a **gap-** programme.

Here are a couple of weblinks to give you a start:

www.gonomad.com/lodgings/0010/davis_monastery.html
www.salon.com/travel/advisor/1999/10/07/advisor/index.html

This link is to an article that will give you the basics on staying in religious guest houses and mentions several useful guidebooks, which list such lodgings, though these are mostly in Europe: **www.smartertravel.com/travel-advice/are-monasteries-and-convents-an-affordable-lodging-secret.html?id=2613061**

Hotels

If you've been on the move for several weeks and careful with the budget, you can find your spirits are flagging from coping with the often Spartan conditions in budget hotels, hostels and the like.

A couple of days of comfort in a good hotel can be a worthwhile investment as a tonic, to give you time out to sort your stuff, get some laundry done, have a decent shower and sleep in a clean, comfortable bed before you set off again.

Most hotels around the world use the familiar one to five star rating system, where five is luxury and one is likely to be a flea-pit! But the symbols used can be anything from stars, diamonds and crowns to keys, suns, dots, rosettes and letters.

visit: www.hihostels.com

As with most things in life you get what you pay for, but prices will vary wildly depending on whether you're in peak tourism season or off-peak, currency rates and the costs of living in the country you're visiting, so you may be pleasantly surprised by the rates in some of the better hotels and find you can stretch your budget without reaching breaking point.

But equally, hotel ratings are done by human beings, and they can vary wildly depending on who did them and which search engine you might have used, a point well made by:
www.independenttraveler.com/resources/article.cfm?AID=629&category=13

Their advice is to look for reviews or ratings from ordinary hotel guests who have actually stayed in the hotel - and slept in the beds!

There are several sources of independent information. Most of the travellers' guidebooks have lists of hotels within the different price ranges, but you have to bear in mind that, particularly in the tourism and hospitality industries, things can change between the time of printing and when you arrive.

If you want to check out a hotel while you're travelling, try this website: **www.tripadvisor.com**

What makes this site special is that it's all written by travellers from their own experiences and it pulls no punches. There are more than 15 million posts on just about every place or topic you can think of, covering destinations all over the world - including some that might surprise you, like the Middle East, (Saudi Arabia, Jordan, United Arab Emirates to name a few). You just click on a map to research the area of the world you're interested in.

It contains information on the best - and worst - of hotels, from top ranking to budget hotels as well as B & Bs, hostels and speciality accommodation. It has forums where you can ask a question and get advice on medical and safety issues, specific to the country or city you're interested in.

For example, did you know that you can quell the worst symptoms of traveller diarrhoea with neat lime juice? This was a tip we found posted by a traveller in a forum on Egypt:

"Squeeze a couple of limes and drink the juice concentrated, with no water, a few times a day. It will act as a disinfectant and also will decrease the diarrhoea …

"Lime juice is an excellent natural disinfectant. So it is a good idea to buy some limes (vegetable sellers or supermarket), wash them and have them with you. If in doubt of anything that you are going to be eating or drinking (including water or drinks with ice) cut the limes and squeeze one or two on what you are going to consume. Have [often] used this trick and it never failed."

Other websites you could try for travellers' reviews are:
www.travelpost.com/

visit: www.hihostels.com

www.cranley.com/about_cranley.htm - This site was founded by Mike Murray and Joaquim Rodrigues, two British Chartered Accountants, following extensive research on travel trends and consumer needs, as well as their own personal travel experiences across over 70 countries, which they found highlighted a need for more detailed and consistent independent on-line hotel information *and* globally consistent independent hotel ratings. They have devised their own 12-point rating system with this in mind.

Useful websites for last-minute and affordable accommodation are:

www.japaneseguesthouses.com - has over 600 *ryokans* (inns) all over Japan and an English language site where you can easily make a reservation.

'Bargain Rooms' – **www.roomauction.com** - you pay below the standard room rate by making the hotel a discreet offer, 'bidding' for the room.

www.laterooms.com - discount hotel rooms in UK and abroad; the low prices are genuine as they would rather see their rooms let out than not at all.

If you also have concerns about ethical tourism, whether it is the hotel's environmental impact or the conditions of its workers, the Ethical Consumer website has a report on these issues, which is downloadable as a PDF (cost £3) from:

www.ethicalconsumer.org/FreeBuyersGuides/traveltransport/hotels.aspx

www.realtravel.com - has info on hotels and advice blogs from travellers.

Couch Surfing

This is the ultimate in finding free accommodation and, although there were safety concerns when this service first started, it's noe had more than a million satisfied customers.

But this not-for-profit organisation has a philosophy that's about more than that - it's about creating friendships and networks across the world.

Here's what they say on the safety issue:

"CouchSurfing has implemented several precautionary measures for the benefit of its surfers, hosts, and community. Every user is linked to the other users he or she knows in the system, through a network of references and friend links. In addition to the solid network with friend link-strength indicators and testimonials, we have our vouching and verification systems."

There's a lot more information on their website that should answer all your questions: **www.couchsurfing.org/about.html**

the gap-year guidebook 2010

An independent career break

Barry, 41, took a nine-month career break to travel the world independently, visiting South Africa, Japan, Hong Kong, China, Vietnam, Laos, Cambodia, Thailand, Malaysia, Bali, Singapore, Australia, Argentina and Miami, using a round-the-world ticket.

He'd previously done a similar independent travel trip in Australia and New Zealand eight years before, but this **gap-** was more challenging: "I had a few reservations … and thought the places I was going to would be more difficult to get around. It had its moments but everywhere is so geared up for travellers it was fine."

There's a reason for Barry's reservations – what you can't see from his pictures is that he walks with the aid of crutches after suffering a childhood virus similar to polio.

So dealing with a backpack and the Great Wall of China was always likely to be something of a challenge!

visit: www.hihostels.com

But he found there were always willing hands if the going got tough: "I think my main concerns were the age thing (no worries, although the further south I went the younger fellow travellers were) and physically getting around, but none of my worries materialised.

"If anything Asia was easier to get around than Oz. I went through periods when I hardly had to even pick up my rucksack due to the obliging locals and their waiting tuktuks."

His advice to gappers: "Just do it. I had lots of 'should I/what if' moments before I went but it went without a hitch, apart from the ones that make it memorable.

"Don't over plan. I had a round-the-world ticket but apart from that my route was fairly open with vague timings. The best times were when I didn't have a point I had to make for on a certain date. So different to normal daily life!

"Make sure you have periods where you have a rest from sightseeing. Believe it or not you will get sick of it. ...and don't take any white clothes (like I did). You'll dump them in days."

If he did it again, he said that, apart from the white clothes, he might also have avoided some of the "more touristy" places, where he felt people had a "different mindset".

He'd been back at work for a month when we spoke to him, but his first thoughts were: "I am still getting back to normal. Although in some ways life is too normal. When I tell people where I went I feel like I'm making it up. After the initial euphoria of seeing people again and enjoying my flat it all seems a bit mundane."

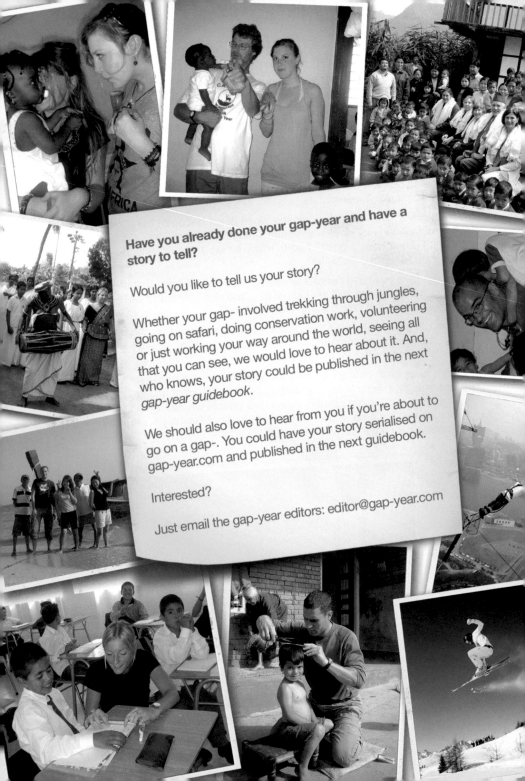

Have you already done your gap-year and have a story to tell?

Would you like to tell us your story?

Whether your gap- involved trekking through jungles, going on safari, doing conservation work, volunteering or just working your way around the world, seeing all that you can see, we would love to hear about it. And, who knows, your story could be published in the next *gap-year guidebook*.

We should also love to hear from you if you're about to go on a gap-. You could have your story serialised on gap-year.com and published in the next guidebook.

Interested?

Just email the gap-year editors: editor@gap-year.com

Accommodation

African Horizons
PO Box 61170, 216 Mosi O Tunya Road,
Livingstone, Zambia

E: horizons@zamnet.zm
T: +260 213 323 433
www.volunteerzambia.com

Fawlty Towers offers affordable accommodation options for all. Quiet, secure gardens, crystal clear swimming pool, excellent meals, wi-fi internet. On site is a dedicated activities and safaris booking office for assistance with tours and travel within Livingstone and throughout southern Africa. En suite rooms from US$25 to US$45 per night.

Billabong Resort
381 Beaufort Street,
Perth, WA 6003, Australia

A four star backpackers hostel in Perth. Beds from AU$22 per night. All rooms have en suite bathroom, linen, air conditioning, phone and balcony.

Cape Trib Beach House
MS 2041, Cape Tribulation, QLD 4873, Australia

Offers a huge range of accommodation styles to suit every budget from dormitory style to deluxe romantic beachfront cabins.

Cruize-Inn Beach House
122 Middleton Road,
Albany, WA 6330, Australia

Four bedroomed beach house with a fully equipped kitchen, dining area, laundry, living room with piano and open fire. TV, video, stereo and barbeque. Bike, board and fishing rod hire available.

North Borneo Cabin
1st & 2nd Floor, No 74 Jalan Gaya,
Kota Kinabalu, Sabah 88000, Malaysia

Accommodation with 24 hour reception service, a communal living area, internet access, cable TV, kitchen, luggage storage, laundry service, shower room and complimentary drinking water, coffee and tea.

Thai Cozy House
111/1-3 Tanee Road, Taladyod, Pranakorn
Bangkok, 10200, Thailand

Family run guesthouse. Rooms each have colour TV (including cable/satellite), air-conditioning, shower room and fridge.

They also offer a laundry service, wi-fi and their own restaurant.

The Furnished Property Group
Suite 111, The Manning Building, 451 Pitt Street,
Sydney, NSW 2000, Australia

Furnished housing perfect for the studying or working traveller with a minimum of one month's stay.

The Witch's Hat
148 Palmerston Street,
Perth, WA 6000, Australia

Four star backpacker hostel with double, twin and dorm rooms. Has a TV lounge and internet facilities, fully equipped laundry, movie nights, 24 hours check-in and a job/notice board which is regularly updated.

Campsites

Akaroa Holiday Park
96 Morgans Road, (Off old coach road), Akaroa 7542
Christchurch, New Zealand

Campsite on south island only 85k from Christchurch. Offers cabins as well with full facilities available for all, including laundry, wi-fi, BBQ, pool and TV.

Albany Happy Days Caravan Park
1584 Millbrook Road,
Albany, WA, Australia

Campsite places, backpacker caravans for two persons available, also chalets and excellent facilities.

Albany Holiday Park
550 Albany Highway,
Albany, WA, Australia

Campsite rates for two people per night from AU$28-AU$35, additional people at AU$8 per person per night. Campers' kitchen on site with gas cooker, microwave and fridge, also games room.

Blue Lake Holiday Park
723 Tarawera Road, Blue Lake,
Rotorua 3076, Central North Island, New Zealand

Holiday park located near Okareka, Tarawera and Blue lakes. Facilities include, spa, boat hire, wi-fi, laundry, bike hire and BBQ.

Bryher Campsite
Bryher,
Isles of Scilly TR23 0PR

Find a traditional camping experience on the isle of Bryher with basic facilities and isolated coves. Open April-December.

visit: www.hihostels.com

Cala Llevado Campsite
PO Box 34,
Tossa de Mar (Costa Brava),
Girona 17320, Spain

Campsite on the Spanish Costa Brava with sea views and great facilities including a swimming pool, restaurant and even washing machines.

Camping Antiparos
Camping Antiparos,
Antiparos, Cyclades, Greece

This family run campsite in Greece is low priced and offers washing facilities, a mini-market and a self-service restaurant.

Camping Glavotock
Camping Glavotock,
Glavotok 4, Malinska 51511, Croatia

This seasonal Croatian campite is open between February and July, and set in six acres of oakwood.

Camping Les Criques de Porteils
Camping Les Criques de Porteils,
Corniche de Collioure,
Argelès-sur-Mer 66700, France

A quiet camping and caravanning site by the sea, with mountain views. It has two heated swimming pools and electrical hook-up. Priced from €20 per day.

El-Bahira Camping
C.da Makari, Loc. Salinella,
San Vito Lo Capo,
Trapani (TP) 91010, Italy

Campsite with big pitches amongst olive trees. It has electrical hookup, a choice of food, laundry service, supermarket, swimming pools, sports and musical entertainment.

Enjoy-Lichnos Camping & Apartments
PO Box 50 P.C.,
Lichnos, Parga 48060, Greece

Campsite near Parga, western Greece, offers modern facilities, a beach bar, sports equipment and a restaurant serving traditional food.

Eurocamp
Hartford Manor, Greenbank Lane,
Northwich, Cheshire CW8 1HW

For those of you with your own tent, Eurocamp have a choice of over 150 campsites across Europe.

Lakeland Camping Barns
Lakeland Camping Barn Booking Office
c/o The Booking Portal, Horse & Groom Court,
Market Place, Egremont, Cumbria CA22 2AE

If you would rather a solid roof overhead, why not try a camping barn? Throughout Cumbria and the Lake District there are a variety of farm buildings.

Les Romarins Campsite
Les Romarins, Grande Corniche,
250 Av. Diables Bleus, Eze 6360, France

This campsite has modern facilities and is located on the Mediterranean coast between Nice and Monaco. Priced from €15 per night.

Mala Milna Auto Camp
Mala Milna Bay,
Mala Milna, Starigrad,
Island of Hvar, Croatia

This small family run Croatian campsite has an in-house restaurant offering organic food grown on site and fresh fish.

Morere Camping Ground
State Highway 2,
Morere, Northern Hawkes Bay,
New Zealand

Campsite alongside a stream in native bush area near Morere's Hot Springs. Room for 30 tents. Tea Rooms on site offering meals seven days a week.

Mountain Valley Adventure Lodge
McVicar Road, Te Pohue, RD2,
Napier, New Zealand

Camping site in Hawke's Bay, New Zealand. They cater for everyone, including backpackers.

Müllerwiese Camping & Caravan park
Familie Hans Erhard, Hirschtalstrasse 3,
Enzklösterle, D-75337, Germany

Situated within the Black Forest Nature Reserve this is a small but beautiful campsite with simple facilities, family-run, with around 75 pitches.

Pod Maslinom Camping
Božo & Mirko Dobroeviæ,
Na Komardi 23,
Orašac, 20234, Croatia

This low priced campsite is situtated in the Croatian village of Orašac and has 30-35 pitches.

ReserveAmerica
40 South Street,
Ballston Spa, NY 12020-9904, USA

Website where you can book a place in over 100,000 campsites throughout the United States.

Riva di Ugento - Camping Resort
73059 Ugento (Lecce),
Litoranea Gallipoli - S.M. di Leuca, Italy

This Italian campsite is located within a pinewood close to the beach. Facilities include a restaurant, supermarket, internet access and sports.

Stella Mare Camping Village
Camping Stella Mare ,
Loc. Lacona, Isola d'Elba, Italy

Camping Village on the island of Elba within the Tuscan Archipelago National Park. Equipped with all the comforts required for a relaxing stay.

Tartaruga Camping
Tartaruga Camping,
Lithakia, Zakynthos, Greece

Pitch a tent under shady olive trees at this quiet and relaxing Greek campsite near the beach. Enjoy Greek cuisine and hospitality in the tavern.

Te Anau Great Lakes Holiday Park
Corner Luxmore Drive and Milford Road, PO Box 205,
Te Anau, New Zealand

You can camp or take a bed in their backpackers dorm for about NZ$25 per night. Other, more luxurious, options also available.

Hostels

Agron Guest House
Agron 6,
Jerusalem 94265, Israel

The Agron Guest House lies in the centre of Jerusalem. It has 55 rooms all with air conditioning, shower/bath rooms, television and internet connection.

An Óige - Irish Youth Hostel Association
61 Mountjoy Street,
Dublin 7, Republic of Ireland

The Irish YHA consists of 26 hostels throughout Ireland. They have a range of hostels, from large city centre buildings to small hostels in rural settings.

Online booking available.

145

Annie's Place - Adelaide
239 Franklin Street,
Adelaide, SA, Australia

Character building with original polished floors and stained glass windows. Each room has air conditioning, TV and coded doors. Communal kitchen.

Annie's Place - Alice Springs
4 Traeger Avenue,
Alice Springs, Northern Territories, Australia

Hostel in centre of Alice Springs with 32 rooms sleeping up to 98 guests. Swimming pool on site, licensed bar, meals, laundry, communal kitchen, secure with no late night curfew.

Backpackers International Rarotonga
PO Box 878,
Rarotonga, Cook Islands 2220, New Zealand

As well as a complimentary airport pick-up service, this hostel offers a TV lounge, internet and moped hire. Bathrooms are shared and there is a large kitchen and dining area.

Barranco's Backpackers Inn
Mariscal Castilla 260, Barranco,
Lima, Peru

Ocean views, beach, in Bohemian neighbourhood. English and Spanish speaking staff. One minute walk to plaza for bars, live music, clubs and restaurants.

Base Backpackers
234 Sussex Street,
Sydney, NSW 2000, Australia

Base hostels are an exciting and fresh approach to budget accommodation. More than just a bed, Base has the best hostels in the best locations with the widest range of facilities under one roof.

Base Brisbane Central
308 Edward Street,
Brisbane, QLD 4000, Australia

Backpackers hostel with single, double, twin and dorm rooms. Shared bathroom facilities, laundry and self-catering kitchen. Cable TV and internet access.

Base Hot Rock Backpackers
1286 Arawa Street,
Rotorua, New Zealand

Overlooks the beautiful, historic Kuirau geothermal park. Many of the rooms have their own bathrooms, balconies and kitchens. Has internet access, a laundry and BBQ area.

Brodie's Hostels - Edinburgh
93 High Street, The Royal Mile,
Edinburgh, Midlothian EH1 1SG

Located in the heart of Edinburgh. Bed linen, hot showers, fully fitted kitchen and full laundry. Beds from only £10 per night.

Cossack Backpackers
Pearl Street,
Cossack, WA 6720, Australia

This independent hostel always gets rave reviews. Unfortunately, there's no website or email to be found so first point of call has to be the old fashioned way: by telephone or post.

Global Village Backpackers
460 King Street West,
Toronto ON, M5V 1L7, Canada

This hostel has nearly 200 beds, a 24-hour reception with swipe-card security, air-conditioning, kitchen, laundry, storage lockers, internet connection, breakfast included in the price and a bar on site.

Hostelbookers.com
52-54 High Holborn,
Holborn, London WC1B 6RL

Hostelbookers has a website giving access thousands of cheap hostels and budget properties worldwide catering for backpackers, students as well as the general budget traveller.

Hostelling International
2nd floor, Gate House, Fretherne Road
Welwyn Garden City, Hertfordshire AL8 6RD

E: office@hihostels.com
T: +44 (0) 1707 324170
F: +44 (0) 1707 323980
www.hihostels.com/gap

Hostelling International is the only global network of youth hostels. With 4000 safe, standards-assured HI Hostels in 90 countries, you will enjoy a world of adventure! There are HI Hostels in unusual buildings like castles, lighthouses, railway carriages and even on boats!

HI Hostels help stretch your budget further without compromising on quality, comfort or safety. HI Hostels are open to all, so you can meet people of all nations, ages and cultures, share experiences and friendship.

Book before you leave on www.hihostels.com and find out more about the countries you plan to visit. Registered charity No. 1117014.

Hostelling International - Canada
205 Catherine Street,
Ottawa ON, K2P 1C3, Canada

Contact details for the Canadian branch of this worldwide hostel service.

Hostelling International - Iceland
Sundlaugarvegur 34,
Reykjavik, 105, Iceland

Hostelling International Iceland has 25 hostels all around the country, offering comfortable, budget accommodation which is open to all ages.

Hostelling International - USA
National Administrative Office,
8401 Colesville Road, Suite 600
Silver Spring, MD 20910 USA

Hostelling International USA has a network of nearly 80 hostels throughout the United States that are inexpensive, safe and clean.

Jugendherberge Berlin - Am Wannsee
Bismarckstrasse 8,
32756 Detmold, Germany

Part of a large network of youth hostels in Germany any of which can be booked online before you go.

Mishkenot Ruth Daniel Guest House
Shderot Yerushalayim, corner of Ben Tzvi,
Jaffa, Israel

Has 66 high standard guest rooms all with air conditioning, shower/bathroom, TV, fridge and coffee making facilities.

Planet Inn Backpackers
496 Newcastle Street, Northbridge,
Perth, WA 6005, Australia

Party Hostel with rooms from AU$20 per night. Has laundry room, ceiling fans in all rooms and offers help in finding work.

Scottish Youth Hostel Association
7 Glebe Crescent,
Stirling, Stirlingshire FK8 2JA

There are over 70 SYHA hostels throughout Scotland. You can book online but you must be a member - you can join at the time of booking.

Registered Charity No. SC013138.

Swiss Youth Hostels
Schaffhauserstrasse 14,
8042 Zürich, Switzerland

They have 58 hostels which they divide into three categories: city, countryside and mountain. They range from traditional Swiss chalets, to modern buildings, large historic houses and even one or two castles.

149

Sydney Central YHA
11 Rawson Place,
Corner of Pitt Street and Rawson Place,
Sydney, NSW 2000, Australia

Easily accessible hostel opposite Central Station. Facilities include heated pool, sauna, kitchen, laundry, games room and more.

The Adventure Brew Hostel
Avenida Montes 533,
La Paz, Bolivia

Very popular hostel in La Paz, they urge you to book at least a day in advance. They have their own micro brewery on site!

Tokyo Yoyogi Hostel
c/o Olympic Centre, 3-1 Kamizono-cho,
Shibuya-ku
Tokyo, Japan

Part of Japan Youth Hostels Inc. All hostels can be booked online and range from traditional Japanese dwellings to larger more European style hostels. There are over 300 hostels all across Japan.

Youth Hostel Association New Zealand
National Office, Level 1,
166 Moorhouse Avenue,
PO Box 436
Christchurch, New Zealand

Budget accommodation in New Zealand. Hostels open to all ages. Book online before you go.

Youth Hostels Association of India
5 Nyaya Marg, Chanakyapuri,
New Delhi 110021, India

Youth Hostel Association in India. Over 200 hostels which can be booked online through their website.

Chapter 6
Career Breaks &
Mature Travellers

Chapter sponsored by

ProjectsAbroad

Time for a career break?

Career Breakers are joining Projects Abroad in increasing numbers. Some go away for as little as a couple of weeks whilst others will go away for three months or six months.

Ian Birbeck, Recruitment Director at Projects Abroad says: "In recent years we have seen a large increase in interest from mature travellers and career break volunteers. This is down to the wide variety of projects we offer and our flexible approach to volunteering."

The reasons for joining a project are different in almost every case. Some may have chosen to take time out voluntarily, or had to leave work for other reasons, such as redundancy, but the relative levels of skill and experience they bring with them means that career break volunteers are always greatly valued by the organisations we work with.

Pamela Jenner joined the care project in India:

"I decided to become a volunteer because I wanted a break from my job after 17 years. I wanted a challenge but I felt nervous about 'going it alone' and felt I needed the support of an organisation. My care project proved to be immensely varied and rewarding. I worked on a special complex in Tamil Nadu for children and young people with physical and learning disabilities. I took part in village outreach projects, held workshops with young women to help them build up self-esteem, and I taught English and learnt some physiotherapy techniques."

Lee Valentine decided to gain some experience teaching in South America:

"One of my most memorable experiences was genuine sadness shown by the students on my last day at the school. It showed to me how much help I had been to them and the shouts of "Please don't leave!" were touching. I wish I had done this years ago and would recommend others, regardless of age to give it a go!"

visit: www.projects-abroad.co.uk

Scott McQuarrie left his job working in a bank in Edinburgh to work on a sports project in Ghana:

"On leaving Accra someone asked me what my highlight had been – my reply, 'I'm not sure maybe the random acts of kindness from strangers, being amazed by how much women carry on their heads, rain that looks like a special effect from a movie, the colours, Ghana beating the Czechs in the World Cup, visiting the Liberian refugee camp, watching Cantonments under-12s win my first match ...' This isn't even scratching the surface; I would strongly recommend experiencing it for yourself! I had the best time of my life."

Projects Abroad can offer those wishing to take career breaks many opportunities. Whether you wish to change career or gain new skills in your chosen field there is an extensive range of medical, law and human rights, business and journalism placements on offer.

Skilled career break volunteers can really make a difference whether it is working on an IT project in Sri Lanka, a business project in Mongolia or working in a hospital in Mexico. Volunteering these days really isn't just for **gap**-year students.

Projects Abroad
Aldsworth Parade
Goring
Sussex BN12 4TX
Tel: +44 (0)1903 708300
www.projects-abroad.co.uk

the gap-year guidebook 2010

6 Career breaks and mature travellers

The benefits of being an older gapper:

- You're fit and healthy
- You have a lot of professional experience
- You have good people skills
- Taking a career break can add new skills to your CV
- You're retired but you have skills and wisdom to offer to people who may need them
- You can afford the time and cost
- You want to give something back
- You're never too old to learn something new

Are you an extravagapper? A flashpacker? These are just a couple of the latest terms to describe the more mature member of the **gap-** community!

Extravagappers are apparently newly-redundant city professionals with generous redundancy packages, who are taking the opportunity of a career break rather than plunge back into a possibly demoralising, recession-hit job market.

Wikipedia describes Flashpackers as: "...backpacking with flash, or style. ... travellers who adhere to a modest accommodation and meal budget, while spending freely, even excessively, for activities at their chosen destination..." But also: "...tech-savvy adventurers who often prefer to travel with a cell phone, digital camera, iPod and a laptop."

However, regardless of the definitions or their degree of affluence, older travellers generally have different considerations from younger ones when making their plans.

These include the effects of taking a **gap-** on careers, what to do about the house and mortgage, financial issues and whether or not to take the children, if this applies.

Taking a career break for three months to a year is the fastest-growing sector of **gap-**year activity and there's some anecdotal evidence that

visit: www.projects-abroad.co.uk

the global recession is increasing the numbers. So, if you're 50-plus it may be worthwhile considering something like this, if you've been made redundant or taken early retirement.

Several organisations that arrange places for people on overseas projects, have told us that more than half of their activity is now focused on helping place mature travellers and/or people who are taking a career break.

People are living longer and are also a lot healthier well into old age. Many, therefore, feel they want to continue to use their skills in places where they will do some good.

This, coupled with the issues of the retirement age being put back and worries about inadequate pension provision, has also prompted many older people to think about extending their working lives and perhaps also pursuing a different career altogether.

Taking a **gap-**, perhaps to volunteer in another country, is one good way of identifying skills, wisdom and knowledge gained over a working lifetime, that may be useful in another sector and this could lead to a new career.

It may be the perfect opportunity to do something you always wanted to do but couldn't while you were burdened with the responsibilities of family and mortgage.

Pre-travel prep checklist:

This list covers the extra responsibilities older people might have to consider. It only covers the basics of what you might have to organise - but we hope it will be a useful start for you to cherry-pick what's appropriate and no doubt add your own extras!

Work:

- Talk to your employer about sabbatical/career break options.

Career break:

- What do you want from it?
- What do you want to do?
- Where do you want to go?

Finance:

- Paying the bills.
- Mortgage.
- Financing and raising money for the trip.
- Insurance.
- Pensions and NI contributions.

The house: Are you going to let it? If yes, you need:

- To talk to an accommodation agency.
- Safety certificates.

- Insurance.
- To investigate tax exemption.

Storage of possessions:

- What do you want to store? And can it be stored at home?

Children:

- Talk to the school(s) about taking them.
- Find out about education possibilities where you're going.
- If they're coming, how long will the trip be?

Safety precautions:

- Wills and power of attorney.

Big decisions

So, how much risk are you taking if you decide to take a career break? Well, increasingly, employers recognise their value and some have well-organised schemes to allow their staff take a break.

Here's what some organisations told us:

"Once we had linear careers; now they move in zigzags. We're continually moving in and out of various forms of paid and unpaid employment. Offering career breaks is a critical attraction and retention tool in the highly competitive people market. It gives us a competitive edge over other companies and improves our employer brand."

visit: www.projects-abroad.co.uk

For the longer breaks, most companies told us that employees would have to resign but they would be encouraged to keep in touch and, if possible, efforts would be made to re-employ them once their break was over.

We've also heard that, during the current recession, some companies are offering time out to employees that they value, don't want to lose, but can't afford to have on the payroll for a while. In some cases, they were even offering a small financial sum to help people take a **gap-** and then come back in a year's time!

What if you can't arrange a sabbatical?

Karen Woodbridge, Director of Suffolk-based Hornet Solutions (an Independent HR/Employment Law Consultancy) says: "There is no obligation in law for companies to provide career breaks so you need to think about how your company and you would respond if your request is turned down. Would you resign? If not, and you decide instead to stay with your employer, how will they regard you? Will your rejected request affect your chances of further progress within the company? Might they consider that you lack long-term commitment to them?

"To help increase your chance of an employer agreeing to any **gap-** request, you should prepare and plan, in exactly the same way you would tackle any other work proposal. For example you must develop a really impressive answer to the question: 'How could this break increase the contribution I make to my employer?' Specifically address the issue of: 'What's in it for them?'"

One option you might consider if you can't arrange a sabbatical and are wary of just quitting is arranging a job swap with someone from another country in a similar industry. You need to consider:

• Where do you want to travel?

• Do you speak a second, third or fourth language?

• Will you need housing?

• Do you need to be paid while away?

• How long do you want to be away for?

This may be easier in an international company where there may even be opportunities to transfer to the overseas office. Many such companies offer formal secondment programmes so it's always worth exploring these first.

If the above options are not possible, and you are prepared to resign, you could investigate whether your company might agree to guarantee you a job on your return.

Reports we've seen of companies offering valued staff unpaid leave or sabbaticals, suggest that, even in the current climate, employers may be prepared to keep the door open. On returning to work after a career break, employees will be armed with new skills, a new perspective and also the experience and knowledge of the role that a new starter would not have.

However, Karen Woodbridge points out that, in this situation, you need to be aware that any resignation still breaks your continuity of service. "This

6

Career breaks and mature travellers | What if you can't arrange a sabbatical?

happened in the case of Curr vs Marks & Spencer Plc. Marks & Spencer agreed to guarantee Mrs Curr a job when she was ready to return after a career break and they duly honoured this agreement. Unfortunately two years later they made her redundant and she was then horrified to discover that her redundancy pay only reflected her last two years of service and not the 26 years she had accrued before she took her career break."

Even if they don't guarantee a position for you, have regular contact with the key decision makers whilst you are away by the occasional email *etc*. This will keep you in their minds and make it easier for you to approach them when you come back home, to see if they have any suitable job opportunities. Just remember, in job hunting, as in everything else, it's not *what* you know but *who*. So it's absolutely vital that you make the effort not to lose touch with your professional colleagues, networks and contacts whilst you are away. If you do, you'll regret it once you are back.

If you're not already signed up to LinkedIn, you might like to consider it. This website is the business world equivalent of Facebook. It's free to use and you can link to colleagues and business contacts and post recommendations about them and, importantly, get them to post recommendations about you. You can even upload your CV, and indicate that you are open to job opportunities. It could also be useful to add your list of contacts gained *whilst* you're on your career break, thus adding extra value to your LinkedIn profile.

If you're willing to quit and take your chances, what about finding work when the break's over?

Linda Whittern of Careers Partnership (UK) - a career counselling and job search support consultancy - advises using information on graduate employment trends and the small amount of research available on the value of a **gap-** to guide your decisions.

"When working lives last 30 years, and it's commonplace to change career at least three times, how can you decide whether a **gap-** this year would help or harm your career?"

Key information presented at a recent UVAC conference examining the government's high level skills strategy and in Dr A Jones' research (Review of Gap Year Provision) is as follows: 'The number of 18-year-olds in the population will fall by 16% in the period 2009-2020.'

Linda suggests this long-term reduction in the size of the available workforce will ease your re-entry into employment, regardless of the stage you've reached in your career and of employers' beliefs concerning the value of gaps.

"Eighteen million jobs will become vacant between 2004 and 2020 - half in the occupations most likely to employ graduates. In other words, there'll be plenty of good jobs to apply for, even at times when unemployment is high. In Careers Partnership (UK)'s experience, the employment prospects for many job hunters depend less on the state of the national economy than on the varying effectiveness of their job search.

"Forty percent of the adult working population will be qualified to graduate level by 2020. As a graduate, you are 5% more likely to get jobs and be in employment than your non-graduate peers. Research shows that taking a

visit: www.projects-abroad.co.uk

gap- further improves graduates' employability (though it doesn't boost the job prospects of non-graduates to the same extent).

"Employers share the general view that gaps enhance graduates' 'soft skills'; some blue chip employers actively encourage applications from 'gappers'. Employers' appreciation of the value of a **gap-** is often rather superficial and short-lived, however. Many employers have little understanding of the particular skill-sets recruits/employees have developed during their career breaks. They don't actively help staff transfer these skills to the workplace.

"Realising the full economic value of your **gap-** depends on choosing the break best aligned to your career plans and then properly marketing it to prospective and actual employers."

Linda advises: "The range of **gap-** activities on offer include teaching (circa 15%); conservation/environment (circa 15%); community (circa 37%); work experience (circa 11%); travel (circa 3%); leisure sports (circa 8%); and non-academic qualifications (circa 11%).

"When planning your **gap-**, work out precisely what the value of each proposed activity/experience will be to prospective employers. Decide what evidence will persuade employers that your **gap-** experience gives you 'added value' as a recruit. Highlight this evidence on your CV and during [your] interview. Once recruited, ensure your line manager and the training department know about the skill-sets you have built up during your **gap-** ... and put forward schemes for further developing these skills."

Finance

You've talked to your employer, perhaps also worked out what you hope to do - there are plenty of organisations to help you plan your chosen activities in the various sections in this book. The next crucial question is finance.

Obviously the amount of money you'll need depends on where you want to go, what you want to do, and how long you want to be away. At this point, drawing up a rough budget for how much it will cost would be a good idea. (See Chapter 2 - Finance, for a checklist.) Once you have this it's worth talking to your building society or bank to see whether they have any schemes that can meet your needs.

While banks often have student and graduate advisers who can advise on what to do about everything from travel insurance to suspending direct debits and deferring loan payment, they don't seem yet to have reached the stage of having advisers *specifically* for career breakers. They are, however, increasingly aware of the trend to take a career break and may well be able to use their experience of advising younger gappers to help you think the finances through.

A recent survey amongst older people in the UK revealed that a large majority are extremely pessimistic or fearful about the quality of their lives in old age. A significant number were taking the view that, if their old age was going to be so grim, why not have one last 'adventure'? Consequently, they were using annuities and equity release or lifetime mortgages to unlock money from their homes to boost their retirement income and pay for such adventures.

the gap-year guidebook 2010

This might seem like a good plan. However, there have also been many reports of schemes offering to buy people's homes and allowing them to rent them back for their lifetimes, only for them to be evicted after a few months or to find 'hidden charges' which meant they saw little money at the end of it. So beware! Read the small print *very* carefully.

Some companies offer lifetime mortgages, where you can release the value of your home and live in it without paying anything until you die, when the company will recover its money from the sale of the home.

Individual circumstances vary and if you feel you are 'asset rich but cash poor' it may be tempting to consider such options. You should only consider such a scheme with a reputable company and if the scheme includes protection against negative equity. We would strongly advise that if you are thinking of doing something like this you consult an independent financial adviser.

Maximise your funds: The chance for a good clear out

Is the garage crammed, are every drawer and cupboard stuffed? Is it all 'file and forget' or 'might come in handy' but never has? Admit it, you're one of those people who hasn't touched any of this stuff for years and you've kept saying you'd do a massive clear out. Aren't you?

But the more you add over the years, the more daunting it is and the easier it is to put off. We all do it. And how much houseroom do some of us give to all that stuff our children insist they have no space for but have sentimental attachments to?

Preparing for your year out is the perfect opportunity to de-clutter your life. Have a look at what you need to get rid of and turn into funding for your **gap-**. Consider raising some cash by selling items through online auction sites, such as eBay, holding a garage sale or a car boot sale.

You'll create space to store your precious items (the things you want to keep but not leave lying about), you'll add some cash to your travel fund, and you'll come back to a well organised home. Also, if you've decided to let your home empty (see below) you'll need less rented container space - and save yourself some money.

Consider selling the car

If you have a car it's likely to devalue in the year you are away, whether anyone is driving it or not, so you could sell it and put the money into your career-break fund. Leasing out your car is not an option - most insurers will not insure drivers of vehicles leased privately from their owners.

visit: www.projects-abroad.co.uk

Imaginative fundraising

If you've already settled on the kind of project you want to do and it involves raising a specific sum, as volunteer projects often do, you can hold fundraising events to help you raise the cash - the options are as limitless as your imagination!

You have an untapped resource where you work - you could try asking for a contribution from your employer. It's good PR to have a link with someone doing something for a worthy cause.

If your employer agrees, what about baking cakes to sell at coffee time or holding competitions (guess the weight/number of objects in a container) or even asking colleagues to sponsor you? Even simple things like putting all those irritating bits of small change that weigh down pockets, and cram purses, into a large pot or jar can mount up surprisingly quickly.

Pensions and National Insurance contributions

If you have an occupational pension and are taking a sabbatical you should check with your employer to see if they offer a pension 'holiday' and what that might mean to your eventual pension, but it might be possible to stop or reduce your payments while you are away. If you have been with the company less than two years, it might be possible to arrange a refund of pension contributions.

For the state pension you might want to look at two issues:

During the time you're away, you will be officially classified as living abroad and you won't be paying NI. However, you should check what that will do to your contributions' record and how it might affect your eventual state pension.

You can find out if there are gaps in your record by calling the HMRC (HM Revenue and Customs) helpline (0845 915 5996) and for more information. People living abroad should call: 0845 915 4811.

Once you have that information it's worth talking to the DWP (Department for Work and Pensions). They have a help and advice service (Tel: 0845 606 0265) and you can find out what you can expect by way of state pension. A DWP adviser told us that, from 2010, to get the maximum state pension both men and women will have to have paid NI for at least 30 years.

However, another useful fact, if you're likely to reach retirement age during your **gap-** and can afford it, is that there's an incentive for deferring your state pension. For every five weeks you agree to defer, you get 1% added to your eventual pension. After a year, you can either take that as a taxable lump sum or have it incorporated into your regular pension payments. You can defer for more than a year and continue to add this interest to your eventual state pension.

The Directgov website also has a useful page on pensions for people living abroad:
www.direct.gov.uk/en/BritonsLivingAbroad/Moneyabroad/DG_4000013

the gap-year guidebook 2010

Earning on your career break

It may even be possible to part-fund your career break by using your skills on volunteer and other projects.

United Nations Volunteers sometimes pay modest living or travel costs, for people with the skills they need for particular volunteer projects.

Have a look at their website: **www.unv.org/how-to-volunteer.html**

If you wanted a 'taster' before taking the big step of leaving the country, UNV also has a scheme for online volunteers, where you can become involved in worthwhile projects, using your computer in your spare time, at home: **www.onlinevolunteering.org/en/vol/index.html**

There are also organisations that can help with funding for specific projects: The Winston Churchill Memorial Trust is one of them.

It provides grants for people wanting to travel abroad and work on special projects that they cannot find funding for elsewhere and, crucially, then use the experience to benefit others in their home communities. Applicants must be British citizens, resident in the UK and must apply by October each year.

The Trust awards travelling fellowships to individuals of all ages wanting to pursue projects that are interesting and unusual. Categories cover a range of topics over a three-year cycle. Roughly 100 are awarded each year and they usually provide funds for four to eight weeks.

The Trust emphasises that fellowships are *not* granted to gappers looking to fund academic studies, attend courses or take part in volunteer placements arranged by other organisations.

The advice is to study the WCMT website for examples of projects that have been funded, as they are very wide-ranging and will help you come up with your own ideas.

To find out more you can contact the Trust at:

15 Queen's Gate Terrace, London SW7 5PR

Tel: +44(0) 207 584 9315
Fax: +44(0) 207 581 0410

Email: office@wcmt.org.uk
www.wcmt.org.uk

Tax issues

If you go to live or work abroad, and become non-resident in the UK, you might still have to pay UK tax - but *only* on your income earned in the UK (savings, dividends, rental income *etc*). If you do need to pay, you may need to complete a Self Assessment tax return.

This website explains the tax implications for all the circumstances in which you might be abroad, whether temporarily or permanently. It's particularly useful if you're thinking of renting out your home: **www.direct.gov.uk/en/BritonsLivingAbroad/Moneyabroad/index.htm**

visit: www.projects-abroad.co.uk

What about the house?

Some mortgage lenders may allow a payment holiday of up to six months without affecting your scheme.

Another option might be to rent out your house. You may need to check terms and conditions for subletting with your mortgage lender, but it can be a good way of covering the mortgage costs while you are away.

However, at the time of writing the government was planning a new registration scheme. If introduced, all private landlords would have to be licensed for a fee (estimated to be around £50), regardless of the reason for letting.

As it is your home and you need to be sure it will be looked after while you are away, the above reinforces our advice that, if you decide to rent, it's worth using an accommodation agent to take care of things and make sure you comply with all the regulations.

It would also be wise to check with the Inland Revenue to see whether you are eligible for a tax exemption certificate (on your rental income), which should be given to the accommodation agent.

Many letting agencies only operate in a local area and we asked Robert Ulph, Director of Pennington's, Ipswich, Suffolk, for some guidelines. He said an agent will generally take a six-week deposit from the tenant and will make sure the house is clean and the garden sorted out before you return:

"We come across this quite regularly. We see a lot of people thinking about letting their properties because they want to go off and do something different, especially people aged 50-plus. Actually it's very simple. I would say prepare in good time and, if you let to the right people who will take care of the property and pay the rent on time, you don't have any problem at all."

Firstly, he advised only using an agent who was a member of ARLA, the Association of Residential Letting Agents. They will usually charge 10-15% of the rental for their services, but they can guide you through the preparation as well as looking after things while you are away.

When letting a house there are some rules to abide by and some safety certificates you must have if you're going to take this route.

Mr Ulph said: "Generally people rent fully-furnished - otherwise think about the storage costs. But any furniture in the house which is made of foam, must comply with fire regulations. This also applies to anything, such as cushions, that you want to store. If they aren't made of fire retardant materials they cannot be stored in the house."

A second must-have is a current gas safety certificate for any appliances. You need one for the gas supply to the house, which costs around £80, and it is essential that you also have a certificate for each appliance in the house - roughly an extra £20 per appliance. A corgi-registered engineer must carry out the test and the certificate is valid for a year.

For electricity the regulations are different, and Mr Ulph said a certificate is not required *unless* you let to students or the property is a house in multiple occupancy (HMO). However, an electrician with a Part P qualification *must* carry out any new work and give you a certificate to prove that this has been done. Wiring has to be safe and if your wiring has been installed for 15-20 years it would make sense to have it checked.

A new regulation since our last edition is that landlords now have to get an Energy Performance Certificate (EPC). This new Act came into effect from the 1st October 2008 and requires all rental properties, with a new tenancy in England and Wales, to have an EPC, which can usually be organised by your lettings agent and looks similar to the energy labels found on domestic appliances such as fridges and washing machines; it will cost in the region of £95 and will last for ten years.

Another must is to tell your insurance company what you're planning. He said: "Some don't like it and you may have to take out specialised cover."

visit: www.projects-abroad.co.uk

Then there is the question of what to do with your personal property and who to let to. Thorough credit and reference checks are vital to get the right tenant.

Mr Ulph said: "It's important to get the right people and to be realistic. You are going to come back to some wear and tear. Don't expect the house to be exactly as you left it. Things do happen that are not the tenants' fault. But most people with proper references will take care of your property. It's a good idea to meet your tenants, then it becomes someone's home they're renting."

He said that leaving ornaments and pictures in place would also reinforce that message, but personal possessions and valuables should be packed away and stored - this can be the attic or basement (if you have one).

While this edition was being revised, an inquiry came in about insurers who specialise in cover for homes left empty. There are some but you should check them with the Association of British Insurers to make sure they're reputable. It's also possible to arrange with a lettings agency to do a once-a-week check on your property, if you do choose to leave your home empty, but we would advise you to consider this very carefully. It may not be an option if you're going to worry while you're away!

Another possibility is a house swap

Obviously you'd have to be careful in arranging this and in satisfying yourself that you're happy with the people you're planning to swap with, but we've found a number of agencies that can help you.

The following arrange holiday swaps in many countries around the world and have plenty of advice on how to go about it. You have to sign up as a member to access some information:

www.homelink.org - annual membership is £115. It has regional websites in 30 countries and has been operating for 50 years.

www.intervac.co.uk - annual membership is £49.99.

www.homebase-hols.com/ - annual membership is £29.

Household contents - storage

Two things to think about if you really want to clear your house before renting:

- Do you really want to add this to your list of 'things to do' before you go?
- Can you afford it?

We talked to an independent storage company with sites across the UK to get some idea of what's involved.

Sydney Hyams is managing director of Archival Record Management. His company rents ten, 20 and 40ft storage containers on managed sites - ie where there are security guards and your property is safeguarded from fire, flood and theft. He advises that you would need a 20ft container for the contents of an average house. The containers are 'self service' so you would have to pack, move and unpack yourself and therefore need to add the costs of van rental and transport to the container rental costs.

You would also have to arrange your own insurance, but, said Mr Hyams, normally you can extend your household contents insurance to cover property on secured sites.

It might be worth trying local independent storage companies in your area. Philip Taylor, of Boxstore, Rogers Farm, in Boxford, Suffolk, told us that renting out property when taking a **gap-** is proving more popular each year, and that when choosing where to store your possessions, it is worthwhile shopping around for the most competitive price.

He said: "Comparing like for like, smaller independent storage companies can be anything up to 50% cheaper than the larger ones. Once your belongings are in the van, travelling up to 50-100 miles is still an option to realise these savings, especially on the longer term."

National removals and storage companies, like Pickfords, also provide container storage on managed sites and can sell you the packing materials and boxes you might need as well. Prices vary according to the distance from the storage site, size of container and length of time and some self storage companies do not charge VAT on household storage, but others do. It is worth bearing in mind that storage alone for a year would come to over £1000.

But remember, on top of that you have to add the packing, loading, removal and unloading costs at each end of your career break. On average the process can cost £300-£400 more than an ordinary house move and prices vary depending on whether your dates fall into peak season for house removals - such as children's school holidays and the peak times of year for house sales.

There's more information here:
www.pickfords.co.uk/html/storage/removal-and-storage-company.htm

What about the kids?

There's some evidence that another growing trend is for families to take a **gap-** together, particularly while the children are young.

While it's virtually impossible to get reliable figures, there's a lot of anecdotal evidence from **gap-** providers.

Phil Murray, director of gapadvice.org, says: "gapadvice.org is asked from time to time for a view on whether or not such **gap-** years are advisable. The view is that as long as the children are safe, have access to medical facilities and their education development is not harmed, family **gap-**years can have very beneficial outcomes. Children are exposed to a variety of mind-broadening situations and their overall development can be very positive.

"Some **gap-**year companies might have a minimum age limit of eight years. It certainly is important to get the support of the school if children are being removed from mainstream education for a lengthy period."

Whether to take the children out of school is really up to you as parents. Much will depend on the length of time you plan to be away and the point your children are at in their education.

Essentially you need to balance the effects of taking a child out of school against the benefits of the 'education' they will get from seeing something of

the world. You also need to think through health and medical issues, but that may mean nothing more than carrying essential medical supplies with you, as all travellers are advised to do when travelling abroad.

It's also possible that you can get your child into a local school for some of the time they are away, or you can organise some basic study for them with the help of their school while you are travelling. The official view from the DCSF (Department for Children, Schools and Families) is that, ultimately, it is down to the parents, but that they should talk it through with their child's school or local education authority.

It is crucial that it's cleared with your child's school and Head teacher, who has to authorise it, if you don't want to face court action by the local authority and a possible hefty fine for taking a child out of school during term time

But parents who have done it, even with very small children, say that it has been a very worthwhile experience and brought them closer to their kids. A few **gap-** organisations are now providing family **gap-** volunteer placements.

It's worth remembering that most children are a lot more adaptable than parents think and really don't miss all the trappings of modern civilisation once they are in a new place. If you're thinking about it, there's some good advice for parents on: **www.netmums.com/h/n/HOLIDAYS/HOME/ALL/887/**

Safety precautions

You will find a great deal of advice on all aspects of planning your **gap-** in Chapter 1 - Tips for Travellers, as well as in-country advice and what to expect when you get back. Tips for Travellers is relevant to all travellers, whatever their age. We also cover the importance of getting the right kind of travel insurance and the questions you need answered in Chapter 3 - Insurance.

But there are some other issues that perhaps might be more important for older travellers to consider. You almost certainly have more in the way of assets than someone straight from school or university - things like a house, insurance and pension schemes; valuable personal property.

the gap-year guidebook 2010

In the unlikely event of something going wrong, it makes sense to ensure your affairs are in order and to have someone you trust authorised to take care of your affairs until you can do so for yourself. It will make things that much easier for those back home, who may be coping with the trauma of a loved one in hospital overseas, if they have some idea of how you want your affairs to be handled.

You should consider two things - making a will and possibly appointing someone with legal power of attorney.

Making a will

Points to remember when making a will:

- It doesn't have to be expensive.
- It can be amended later if your circumstances change.
- You can make it clear what you want to happen to your property.
- It prevents family squabbles.
- It allows you to choose executors you can trust.

You should:

- Give yourself time to think.
- Use a professional, preferably one experienced specifically with will preparation.
- Make sure you can update it without large additional charges.
- Make sure there's an opt out from executor or probate services if you don't need them - by the time the will is needed, which could be many years away, it may be that someone in the family, who was too young when you made it, who can deal with it.

visit: www.projects-abroad.co.uk

Power of attorney

Many people choose to make an informal arrangement with a family member to take care of things at home while they're travelling, but if you were to need someone authorised to pay bills at home or liaise with your travel insurance company, it might make sense to have a proper, formal arrangement in place before you go to give them the authority to act on your behalf.

You might be able to arrange with your bank to add them as a signatory to your account, in case it should be necessary, as long as you feel comfortable that the person you choose will make the right decisions about your money if you can't.

A more secure way is to appoint a power of attorney, but be warned it's a lengthy process, which can take up to five months to process. Until the documents are properly registered, whoever you appoint cannot act for you. There's no fast track procedure on compassionate grounds and the Public Guardians' Office website says: "Our target is to register and return 95% of valid applications to register an LPA within 11 weeks of receiving them, and improve this to 80% in eight weeks by March 2010.

"If there are no problems with the LPA or application, we are typically returning the registered LPA in around nine weeks from the date of receipt. If there are any problems with the LPA or application, we are currently informing the applicant within two weeks of receiving the application."

Getting it right when there are at least 30 pages of forms per person is no joke; and, if you're a couple, each one of you has to fill out a set. So to avoid delays and mistakes (with possible charging of repeat fees) it makes sense to get professional advice from a specialist.

The process is administered by the Public Guardians' Office, which charges a fee of £150. But compare that with having someone professional look after your property and personal welfare. It can cost as much as £1500 for a couple.

To find out more about the new legislation go to: **www.publicguardian.gov.uk**

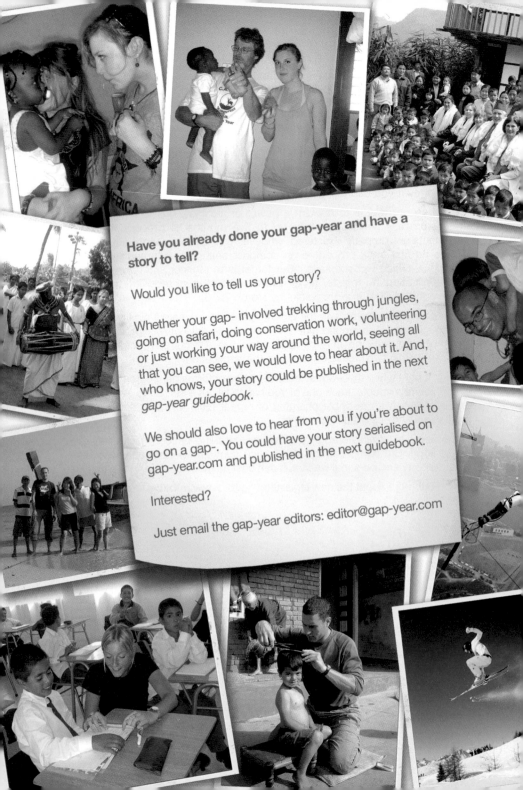

Have you already done your gap-year and have a story to tell?

Would you like to tell us your story?

Whether your gap- involved trekking through jungles, going on safari, doing conservation work, volunteering or just working your way around the world, seeing all that you can see, we would love to hear about it. And, who knows, your story could be published in the next *gap-year guidebook*.

We should also love to hear from you if you're about to go on a gap-. You could have your story serialised on gap-year.com and published in the next guidebook.

Interested?

Just email the gap-year editors: editor@gap-year.com

Career Breaks

Gap Year for Grown Ups
Zurich House,
1 Meadow Road,
Tunbridge Wells, Kent TN1 2YG

Company specialising in career breaks and volunteer work for the over 30s, hundreds of programmes in 30 countries from two weeks to 12 months.

JET - Japan Exchange and Teaching Programme UK
JET Desk,
c/o Embassy of Japan,
101-104 Piccadilly,
Mayfair, London W1J 7JT

The JET Programme, the official Japanese government scheme, sends UK graduates to promote international understanding and to improve foreign language teaching in schools for a minimum of 12 months.

NONSTOP Adventure Ltd
Unit 3B, The Plough Brewery,
516 Wandsworth Road,
Battersea, London SW8 3JX

Family owned company offering sailing, skiing and snowboarding training courses.

Projects Abroad
Aldsworth Parade,
Goring,
Sussex BN12 4TX

E: info@projects-abroad.co.uk
T: +44 (0) 1903 708300
F: +44 (0) 1903 501026
www.projects-abroad.co.uk

With Projects Abroad you can enjoy adventurous foreign travel with a chance to do a worthwhile job. Over 4000 places are available each year to teach conversational English (no TEFL required) or gain experience in medicine, conservation, journalism, business and many other professions.

Placements are available throughout the year and last from two weeks upwards. Volunteers receive substantial overseas support and are not isolated.

No teaching qualifications or local languages are needed. All degree disciplines welcomed.

Volunteers are needed in: Argentina, Bolivia, Brazil, Cambodia, China, Costa Rica, Ethiopia, Fiji, Ghana, India, Jamaica, Mexico, Moldova, Mongolia, Morocco, Nepal, Pakistan, Peru, Romania, Senegal, South Africa, Sri Lanka, Tanzania, Thailand and Togo.

Find out more at: www.projects-abroad.co.uk

171

Raleigh International

207 Waterloo Road,
Southwark, London SE1 8XD

E: info@raleigh.org.uk
T: +44 (0) 20 7183 1283
F: +44 (0) 20 7504 8094
www.raleighinternational.org

Since 1984 our youth and education charity has been helping people from all walks of life get out there and undertake challenging adventure expeditions. Volunteering on sustainable community and environmental projects you'll develop new skills, meet people from all backgrounds and make a real difference. You could be providing clean water for communities in Costa Rica, helping to conserve elephants with the WWF in India or protecting coral reefs in Borneo.

The Career Break Guru

Fairbank Studios, 65 Lots Road,
Chelsea, London SW10 ORN

The Career Break Guru was created to advise and guide grown-up gappers as they dream about, plan and create their ideal trip.

The Year Out Group

Queensfield, 28 King's Road,
Easterton, Wiltshire SN10 4PX

E: info@yearoutgroup.org
T: +44 (0) 1380 816696
www.yearoutgroup.org

See main entry under volunteering.

VentureCo Worldwide

The Ironyard, 64-66 The Market Place
Warwick, Warwickshire CV34 4SD

T: +44 (0) 1926 411122
F: +44 (0) 1926 411133
www.ventureco-worldwide.com

VentureCo provides the ideal combination for career break travellers who want to explore off the beaten track, learn about the host country and give something back to the communities they stay with. Ventures last between two and 15 weeks.

Spiritual Retreats

Beaver Lake Retreat

105 East Marble Street,
Marble, CO 81623, USA

Wilderness, well-stocked library, meeting rooms, peace, quiet and hot tub. Walks and more challenging activities are offered, but this is a definitely a retreat.

Dhanakosa

Buddhist Retreat Centre,
Balquhidder,
Lochearnhead FK19 8PQ

A registered Scottish charity, offering Buddhist meditation retreats, yoga, hillwalking and tai chi, (open to anyone).

173

Gaia House
Gaia House, West Ogwell,
Newton Abbot, Devon

Gaia House offers a sanctuary of contemplative calm and is open to all. Designed for both experienced meditators and beginners.

Heartspring
Hill House, Llansteffan, Carmarthen SA33 5JG UK

Welsh retreat offering rest, personal space and time to achieve clarity in your life.

Himalayan Healing Ltd.
Karen Williams, Suite 24, 151 High Street,
Southampton SO14 2BT

Learn Reiki in Nepal, gain a qualification and enjoy two weeks of healing and nurturing in the foothills of the Himalayas.

Hollyhock
PO Box 127, Manson's Landing,
Cortes Island BC, V0P 1K0, Canada

Buddhist teachings, massage, mediation and education.

Kagyu Samye Ling Monastery & Tibetan Centre
Eskdalemuir,
Langholm, Dumfriesshire DG13 0QL

Meditation, courses on Buddhism, yoga and tai chi. Kagyu Samye Ling was the first Tibetan Buddhist centre established in the west.

Mairela Retreat for Reiki Healing
Sara Gardner, Mairela Retreat, Puukkoistentie 485,
Kuhmoinen 17800, Finland

Stay in this retreat cottage in Finland and take a healing course in Reiki.

Purple Valley Yoga Retreat
142 Bairo Alto, Assagao, Bardez,
Goa, India

Purple Valley Yoga Retreat is the perfect place for a yoga holiday, offering accommodation, vegetarian meals, courses and relaxing treatments.

Rivendell Retreat Centre
c/o The Croydon Buddhist Centre,
96 The High Street,
Croydon, Surrey CRO 1ND

Retreat Centre housed in a former Victorian rectory offering yoga, meditation, vegetarian food and accommodation.

River Lodge Retreat
2111 Township Road 510, Rural Route 5,
Stony Plain AB, T7Z 1X5, Canada

Hidden away in the wilderness overlooking the north Saskatchewan river. There are places for meditation and trails for walking, saunas and massage.

Shambala Retreat Centre
Findhorn Bay,
Moray IV36 3YY

Retreat and centre for healing and developing universal compasssion.

Shiva Health
Shiva Rooms, 52a Old London Road,
Kingston-upon-Thames, KT2 6QF

Enjoy a relaxing yoga and meditation holiday on the island of Samos, Greece.

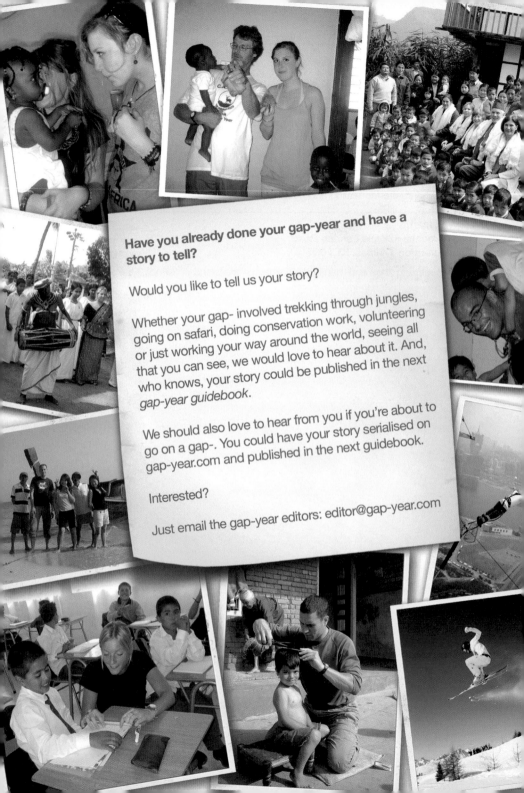

Have you already done your gap-year and have a story to tell?

Would you like to tell us your story?

Whether your gap- involved trekking through jungles, going on safari, doing conservation work, volunteering or just working your way around the world, seeing all that you can see, we would love to hear about it. And, who knows, your story could be published in the next *gap-year guidebook*.

We should also love to hear from you if you're about to go on a gap-. You could have your story serialised on gap-year.com and published in the next guidebook.

Interested?

Just email the gap-year editors: editor@gap-year.com

Chapter 7
Working abroad

Working abroad

Working abroad is a great option if you desperately want to go overseas, can't really afford it and the bit you have managed to save won't cover much more than air fare.

It's one of the best ways to experience a different culture; you'll be meeting locals and experiencing what the country is really like in a way that you can't do as a traveller passing through. Most jobs give you enough spare time, in the evenings and at weekends, to enjoy yourself and make friends.

You don't have to be tied to one place for your whole **gap**-year - you can work for a bit and save up for your travels. That way you can learn more about the place and get the inside information from the locals about the best places to see before you set off.

You cover at least some of your costs, and, depending on what you do, the work experience will look good on your CV - but even if you're only doing unskilled seasonal work, prospective employers will be reassured that you at least know *something* about the basics like punctuality, fitting into an organisation and managing your time.

An internship with pay is a good way to get work experience if you already have an idea about your eventual career and will help in those early stages of the catch-22 that affects many young people - when employers want experience but won't take you on so you can get it.

Older gappers, too, may find that, despite the current global economic problems, their skills and experience are in demand, particularly in developing countries.

Despite the economic downturn, at the time of writing, the construction industry is reporting a shortage of skilled workers. Australia also has a shortage of chefs and health care professionals. The Asia Pacific region (India, China, Malaysia, Australia and the Phillipines) has also identified skills gaps in IT, particularly in support, application development and system integration.

Another option is to look at working for one of the international organisations, such as the UN, IMF or British Council. There's a useful list of contacts for these, and similar organisations, here:
www.prospects.ac.uk/cms/ShowPage/Home_page/Working_abroad/info rmation_sources/p!eeXmbcL

Key questions to get started...

What kind of work do you want to do? There are some suggestions in this chapter but they're only a start.

* Is it to help pay your way on your **gap**-?

179

- Is it to get work experience/enhance your CV?
- Where do you want to work? (Don't forget to check **www.fco.gov.uk** for country info.)
- What skills and experience do you have?

It doesn't have to be work experience or education, don't forget hobbies and interests. If you can ride a horse, dance, draw, paint, or are good at a particular sport, you could use any of those skills as a basis for finding work.

Planning ahead

Choosing your destination

There are some jobs that always need to be done, whatever the state of the world, and if you're just looking at ways of funding your travel you could look for seasonal farm work.

In most cases, gappers intending to do seasonal work outside the EU need to have a job offer in order to get a visa. If you should find that, when you get there the job is no longer available, you can try elsewhere - but we would advise you to have a back-up plan before you set off on your travels (eg contacts, an emergency fund, names of companies that specialise in work overseas - see the list of websites below).

If you are a UK citizen, or hold an EU (European Union) passport, you can work in any other EU member country without a visa or work permit and there are countless jobs available to students who can speak the right languages. Not all European countries are EU members - go to the European Union website to check: **www.europa.eu/index_en.htm**

While even at the time of updating this guide there were beginning to be small signs that the global downturn was slowing, according to economic experts there is always a time lag between this and an upturn in job opportunities. However, some employers of seasonal workers specifically prefer backpackers, so there will still be jobs out there.

There have also been reports of hostility among local people to so-called 'immigrant labour'. If you find yourself facing this, try not to resent it - imagine how you'd feel if it was happening to you at home.

Speaking English is always an advantage for jobs in tourism at ski resorts, beach bars and hotel receptions and if you have a TEFL (Teaching English as a Foreign Language) certificate there's always the option of teaching.

You could try using the **gap-year.com** message board to find out what other gappers have done and what it was like.

If you want to be more adventurous and venture outside Europe, then check the Foreign Office website - **www.fco.gov.uk** - for the list of countries they consider are simply too dangerous to even go to.

visit: www.gap-year.com

Getting your paperwork sorted

Before you go, you should:

- Check whether you need to set up a job - you may need a confirmed work offer before you can get a work permit and visa - try **www.gap-year.com** for contact lists and more advice, or refer to the internship and graduate opportunities section in the directory of this guidebook (see page 198).

- Check on the work permit and visa regulations for the country you plan to work in and make sure you have the right paperwork before you leave. Remember, you don't need a work permit or visa if you're an EU citizen and planning to work in an EU country.

- Check if there's any special equipment or clothing you'll need to take, *eg* sturdy boots and trousers for manual jobs, reasonably smart clothes for office internships *etc*.

- When you're getting your insurance, remember to check that you'll be covered if you're planning on working. Working can invalidate a claim for loss or damage to your belongings on some travel policies. If in doubt, ask.

- Make sure you understand all the regulations and restrictions. You can get into serious trouble if you work without the necessary documents - you don't want to be deported during your **gap**-year! The best place to get information is the relevant embassy in London - there's a link on **www.gap-year.com** to the Foreign and Commonwealth Office website, where you will find links to all London based Embassies.

Finding a job

Finding a job may take time and effort. The more places you can send your CV to, the greater the chances of you getting a job. You can also register with international employment agencies but make sure you know what the agency fee will be if you get employment.

To find short-term jobs try:

www.transitionsabroad.com/listings/work/shortterm/index.shtml
www.pickingjobs.com/
www.seasonworkers.com/fe/
www.anyworkanywhere.com/
www.overseasjobcentre.co.uk/

If you use an agency, always insist on talking to someone who has used it before - that way you'll really find out what the deal is.

Do a search to see if there's a website for a particular area you want to go to and then send or email your CV, with a short covering note, to any interesting local companies. Don't expect to be flooded with replies. Some companies are simply too busy to respond to every enquiry, though it always helps to enclose a stamped addressed envelope. It's also true that you may get lucky and have exactly the skills or qualifications they're looking for. Some companies will also advertise vacant posts on specialist employment websites, which often have an international section. You can register with the sites too, usually for free.

Tell everyone you know, including relatives and your parents' friends that you are looking for a job abroad - someone may know someone who has a company abroad who can help you.

Check the local papers and shop window notices. Lots of jobs are advertised in the local papers, or by 'staff wanted' notices put up in windows. So if you get there, and hate the job you've got, don't put up with it, or come running home - see if you can find something better. It's always easier to find employment when you're living locally.

Over the next few pages we've listed ideas on types of employment, and any companies we know about, that offer graduate opportunities or work experience, can be found in the directory (page 198). Always ask an employment company to put you in contact with someone they have placed before - if they say no then don't use them: they may have something to hide.

Au pairing

Being an au pair is a good way to immerse yourself in a different culture, learn a new language and hopefully save some extra cash. You don't need any qualifications to be an au pair, although obviously some experience with children is a bonus. However, au pairing is a hard job and a big responsibility and you may well have to pass the equivalent of a Criminal Records Bureau (CRB) check.

In return for board, lodgings and pocket money, you'll be expected to look after the children and do light domestic chores like ironing, cooking, tidying

their bedrooms and doing their washing, for up to five hours a day (six hours in France or Germany), five days a week, as well as spending two or three evenings a week babysitting. If you are asked to work more than this then technically you are not doing the work of an au pair, but of a mother's help (which pays more). Remember that an au pair is classified as 'non experienced', and you should never be left in sole charge of a baby. If the family gives you more responsibility than you can handle say so. If they don't stop - quit.

Finding an au pair agency

It may be safest to look for a placement through a UK-based au pair agency. It's also better for the prospective family abroad, since they will be dealing with an agency (possibly working together with an agency in the family's own country) that has met you, interviewed you and taken up references; they will want reassurance before they trust you with their children.

What you should check:

- Does the agency you use have connections with another agency in the country where you'll be working?

- Can they give you a list of other local au pairs so you have support when you're out there?

- Take time finding a suitable family. The fewer children the better, and you should expect your own room.

- What is there to do in your free time? You don't want to spend every weekend in your bedroom because you're stuck in the middle of nowhere.

- Do you get written confirmation of the hours, duties and pay agreed?

- The number and address of the local British Consulate - just in case. (See Appendix 2.)

Check that the au pair agency is a member of either the Recruitment and Employment Confederation (which has a website listing all its members and covering au pair employment in many countries - **www.rec.uk.com/regions-sectors/sectors/childcare/faqs**), or of the International Au Pair Association (IAPA) which has a list of its registered agencies in 38 countries around the world:

International Au Pair Association
Bredgade 25H, 1260 Copenhagen K
Denmark

Tel: +45 3317 0066
Fax: +45 3393 9676
www.iapa.org

There are, of course, perfectly good agencies that do not belong to trade associations, either because they are too small to afford the membership fees, or because they are well-established and have a good independent reputation.

You can also find information on au pair work worldwide by using the internet. Registration is usually free and your details will be matched to the families

the gap-year guidebook 2010

around the world, that have registered on the site and that meet your specifications (but make sure you talk to both the agents, here and abroad, and the prospective family before you make your final decision).

However, if you are considering organising an au pair placement independently, you should be aware of the risks:

- High probability of unsuitable au pair or host family candidates.
- Absence of a written contract.
- Little or no experience in the au pair industry.
- Lack of professionalism or financial stability.
- Nonexistent standards or guidelines.
- Insufficient references and/or medical certification.
- Danger of document falsification.
- No rematch policy (secondary placement) if the initial placement is unsuccessful.
- No local support during the placement.
- Limited understanding of national au pair and visa regulations.

Remember also that au pair agencies operating in the UK and sending au pairs abroad cannot, except under specified circumstances, charge for finding you a placement.

If you have a complaint against a UK agency it's best to take it up with the Department for Business, Enterprise and Regulatory Reform's (BERR) Employment Agency Standards Helpline, Tel: +44 (0) 845 955 5105. It operates Monday-Friday 9.30 am to 4.30 pm.

You can find out more about your rights on: **www.berr.gov.uk/employment/employment-agencies/index.html**

Au pairing in Europe

There are EU laws governing the conditions in which au pairs can work:

- You must be 17 or over.
- You must provide a current medical certificate.
- You should have a written employment agreement signed by you and your host family; conditions of employment must be stated clearly.
- You should receive (tax exempt) pocket money.
- You should have enough free time to study.
- You should not be asked to work more than five hours a day.
- You must have one free day a week.

This is now the accepted definition for au pair jobs in the EU, but not necessarily in other countries. Some countries have different local rules.

Take a look at: **www.conventions.coe.int/treaty/en/Treaties/Html/068.htm**

visit: www.gap-year.com

for the details of the European Agreement and any local variations.

It's important to complete all the necessary paperwork for living and working in another country. Most agencies will organise this for you, and make sure the legal documents are in order before you leave. You should listen to any legal advice you are given by the agency you use. Many also now require written references, police checks and other proof of suitability - which is as much a protection for you as it is for the parents of the children you might look after.

Here's an example. Most French agencies require a set of passport photos, a photocopy of your passport, two references (preferably translated into French), and your most recent academic qualifications, as well as a handwritten letter in French to your prospective family, which tells them something about you, your reasons for becoming an au pair and any future aspirations.

The agency may also ask for a medical certificate (showing you are free of deadly contagious diseases, *etc*) dated less than three months before you leave, and translated into French. Au pairs also have to have a medical examination on arrival in France.

The French Consulate advises you to check that the family you stay with obtains a 'mother's help' work contract (*Accord de placement au pair d'un stagiaire aide-familiale*). If you are a non-EU citizen you are expected to do this before you leave for France, but British au pairs do not need to.

Au pairing in North America

All au pair programmes in America are legislated and regulated by US law, and all au pairs receive pocket money in return for a maximum of 45 hours work a week (no more than ten hours per day), regardless of the agency.

The pay is linked to the US national minimum wage, which from July 2009 is $7.25 per hour, so 45 hours per week would be $326.25 (£199.56 - exchange rate as at July 2009). This US Government website gives more details: **www.dol.gov/esa/whd/flsa/**

US Government regulations stipulate that au pairs must attend education courses (because au pair work is seen primarily as a cultural exchange) of at least six hours per week. This is financed by the host family up to a limit of US$500. Au pairs are not allowed to be placed with families who have a child aged under two years, unless they can prove they have at least 200 hours of documented childcare experience, or who have a child with special needs, unless the au pair has valid experience, training and/or skills in SEN and this has been confirmed by the host family.

You need to:

• Be between 18 and 26 years.

• Hold a valid driving licence.

• Speak English to a good standard.

• Have no criminal record.

• Commit to 12 months living with an American family.

• Have not previously been an au pair in America.

Please note: the US regulations on visas and work permits are very complicated. We strongly recommend you use the help of an au pair agency or consult the US Embassy: **www.usembassy.org.uk**

The US Department of State website has all the up-to-date legislation on au pairing in the US. See: **www.exchanges.state.gov/education/jexchanges/private/aupair.html**

Because of strict government regulations, most agencies that organise au pairs in the USA offer very similar services. However it's worth registering with a number of agencies, if only to have a range of 'perfect match' host families to choose from.

EduCare

If you want to combine au pairing with some study, EduCare places people with families who have school-aged children and who need childcare before and after school hours. Au pairs on the EduCare scheme work no more than 30 hours per week in return for roughly two thirds of the rates paid to au pairs. You must complete a minimum of 12 hours of academic credit or its equivalent during the programme year (financed by the host family for up to US$1000).

You can download a PDF about Educare here:
www.exchanges.state.gov/jexchanges/programs/aupair.html

Internships & paid work placements

- Are you at university?
- Are you a new graduate?
- Are you looking for work experience to land your dream job?
- Want to spend a year in another country?

Some careers, the media for example, are extremely tough to get into, so using your **gap**-year to get relevant work experience may be a good plan. You'll have the benefit of something to put on your CV and also get an idea of what the job is actually like. Internships are not usually open to people pre-university.

Many international companies offer internships but if you're thinking of the USA you should know:

1. Internships in the USA can be difficult to get without paying for the privilege, unless you have personal contacts within the organisation you hope to work for.

2. The USA has a strict job-related work permit system and won't hand out these permits for jobs that American nationals can do themselves.

3. The USA authorities also need to be convinced that the work experience offered provides an opportunity to the UK student that he or she cannot get back home.

If the companies listed in our directory can't help you try these websites:

www.cartercentre.org
www.summerjobs.com (enter internships in the search box)
www.internshipprograms.com
www.internabroad.com/search.cfm
www.soccerstreets.org/soccer_streets_internships.html
www.transitionsabroad.com/listings/work/internships/index.shtml

Before you sign up, make sure you're clear just what your placement will involve. An 'internship' should mean you are able to do interesting paid work related to your degree studies, current or future, for at least six months, but increasingly, even on some of the internship websites listed above, the distinction between a voluntary (unpaid) placement and an internship is becoming blurred so you may have to search for a while - or be creative and try a direct approach to companies in the fields that interest you.

Sport instructors

If you're already a qualified instructor in skiing, kayaking, diving, football, or any other sport for that matter, there are many places all around the world where you can use your skills.

Here are a few websites to get you started:

Skiing:

www.ifyouski.com/jobs/job/description/instructor/
www.jobmonkey.com/ski/html/instructors.html

Football:

www.deltapublications.co.uk/soccer.htm - soccer coaching in the USA

General Sports:

www.adventurejobs.co.uk
www.campjobs.com

Think further afield!

Skiing doesn't have to be in European resorts, don't forget there's the US and Canada, but there are also ski resorts in the foothills of the Himalayas!

For diving jobs you can go pretty well anywhere there's water and water sports!

Football's popular throughout Africa and Latin America, and there are now several football academies in India looking for help to spread the message of the 'beautiful game'.

But whichever sport is your passion, you can use it as part of your **gap**-year plan.

If you don't have an instructor's qualification you can still use your sporting skills as a volunteer, or take an instructor's course to qualify (see Chapter 9 – Learning Abroad). Many course organisers, particularly for ski instructors, will also help their graduates to find a job.

visit: www.gap-year.com

Teaching English as a Foreign Language (TEFL)

TEFL is one of the most popular ways of earning (and volunteering) when you travel, but you need to have a recognised qualification and it does help in getting a post abroad. It also has the advantage that, if you were thinking of teaching as a career, it's a good chance to find out if you like it before you begin your teacher training.

The two best-known British qualifications are:

• TESOL (a certificate from Trinity College, London)

• CELTA (Cambridge University certificate)

The USA has its own qualification and there are many private schools and colleges who offer their own certification. There are a great many colleges around the UK that offer TEFL courses but, ideally, you should check that the certificate you will be working for is one of these two.

It is worth doing your TEFL training within an accredited training centre, as most will help you find a placement once you qualify and face to face training can be more beneficial. One word of warning, if you were hoping to get a job with one of the many well known language schools around the world, some will insist that you undertake your TEFL training with them first. It's always worth checking this out, and deciding how you wish to use your training, before you sign up for a course.

How to find TEFL work

The availability of work for people who can teach English can vary, particularly outside the EU. In most countries it is possible to give private lessons. As stated before, if you wish to work for a language school or academy, find out what their requirements are before you begin your training. Most professional employers will expect you to have had some teaching practice before they will employ you. You should also find out more about the country you hope to find work in before you go. The contact details of the relevant embassies in the UK can be found on the FCO website - **www.fco.gov.uk** - and you should be able to obtain up-to-date details of visas, salaries, qualifications needed and a view about the availability of work in your chosen country. Rates of pay and conditions of employment will vary greatly from country to country and will most likely depend on your own education, training, experience and expertise.

In the UK, TEFL jobs are advertised in:

The Times Educational Supplement.

The Education Guardian.

In the education section of *The Independent.*

The *EL Gazette.*

www.eslbase.com/jobs/
www.cactustefl.com/
www.eteach.com/#International
www.english-international.com/
www.esljobfeed.com/

189

You could also check out the various 'blacklists' that have appeared on the internet in recent years. These list schools to avoid or watch out for. These are informal sites run by people with experience of TEFL teaching. They should be a good place to find out about language schools around the world and whether or not it's worth your time pursuing a vacancy there.

The most popular destinations for TEFL teachers are China, Hong Kong, Japan, Thailand and, of course, Europe. As the EU grows, so does the demand for English teachers, and the advantage of securing a job within the EU is that the UK is a member. This will give you some protection and should involve far less paperwork than if you applied to work further afield.

In China, you are more likely to find work in a private school, rather than the public schools system, as the latter is controlled by the Department of Education in Beijing.

Hong Kong is an obvious choice as it was once a British Colony and English is a second language for nearly everyone there. The added advantage for those with no Chinese language skills is that all the road signs, public transport and government information are in English as well as Chinese and most of the shops, agencies and essential services (such as police, doctors *etc*) employ English speakers.

There is also a daily English language newspaper, *The South China Morning Post* and it may well be worth checking their online jobs section for vacancies: **www.classifiedpost.com.hk/jshome_en.html**

If you want to take your skills and use them in Japan you should check out **www.jet-uk.org**. This is the Japanese Government's website for promoting their scheme to improve foreign language teaching in schools. You do have to have a Bachelor's degree to qualify though. The *Japan Times* (which is online) also lists job vacancies in English: **www.jobs.japantimes.jp/**

There is a great demand for English speakers in Thailand and so if you are taking your **gap-** in that country, and wish to earn money whilst there, TEFL could well be the answer, particularly as you will be unable to find work in a country where foreigners are forbidden from taking most unskilled occupations. The *Bangkok Post* lists job vacancies, including those for English teachers, in their online jobs section: **www.bangkokpost.net**

Teaching English in private lessons

If you decide to supplement your income in-country by giving private lessons, you can put notices in schools, colleges, newspapers and local shops but there are some basic safety precautions you should take:

1. Be careful how you word your ad - *eg* 'Young English girl offering English lessons' is likely to draw the wrong kind of attention.

2. If you arrange one-to-one tuition, don't go to your student's home until you've checked out how safe it would be.

3. Equally, if you're living alone, don't give classes at home until you've got to know your student.

190

4. Arrange classes in public, well-populated locations, which will also help as teaching aids (coffee bars, restaurants, shops, markets *etc*).

5. Make sure you're both clear about your fee (per hour) and when it should be paid (preferably these should both be put in writing).

Usually, you'll be inundated by friends of friends as word gets round there's an English person willing to give private lessons.

Seasonal work in Europe

Working in Europe offers endless possibilities - from fruit picking to hospitality and tourism, leading nature trips to teaching English (for more on this see our TEFL section above). Some non-EU members need work permits so you should check the regulations in the country you want to go to.

To find short-term jobs try:

www.transitionsabroad.com/
www.pickingjobs.com/
www.seasonworkers.com/fe/

Seasonal work in North America

Probably the most popular seasonal job for gappers in the US is working on a summer camp. The US has strict regulations on visas and work permits but summer camps are a well-established way of working for a short time.

US work regulations are very complicated, and specific, and this is one time where it would help to use a placement organisation to help you through the paperwork, but make sure you check out the small print about pay, accommodation and expenses.

If you don't fancy summer camp there are lots of other possibilities, from working on a ranch to cruise ship jobs. Have a look at:
www.jobmonkey.com/main/index.html

It covers all sorts of work from fishing jobs in Alaska, to working on a ranch, to casino and gaming clubs and cruise work. But check with the US Embassy to make sure you can get a visa or a work permit for the job you fancy. See:
www.usembassy.org.uk

Seasonal work in Australia and New Zealand

Periods of working and travelling in Australia and New Zealand are a very popular option and you can do everything from fruit picking to helping Amnesty International. However, you don't have to stick to the traditional backpacker temporary work - fruit picking, bar work or call centres. If you have a trade, IT skills or a nursing qualification they're also good for finding work.

Australia has a well worked-out system to allow you to work and travel. It's called the working holiday visa. From July 2008 the Australian Government changed the regulations so that you can qualify for any specified work and UK passport holders can apply online. Specified work is work, whether paid or

the gap-year guidebook 2010

unpaid, in certain specified industries or postcodes - for more details have a look at:

www.immi.gov.au/visitors/working-holiday/417/specified-work.htm

The main points are:

- You must be between 18 and 30.
  - It costs around £90 (AU$195). The charge is non-refundable.

You will also be required to have a health certificate before you apply for your visa.

What you can do:

- Enter Australia within 12 months of the visa being issued.
- Stay up to 12 months.
- Leave and re-enter Australia any number of times while the visa is valid.
- Work in Australia for up to six months with each employer.
- Study or train for up to four months.

To find out more go to:
www.immi.gov.au/visitors/working-holiday/417/eligibility-first.htm

Or call the High Commission in the UK:
Australian High Commission,
Australia House, Strand, London WC2B 4LA
Tel: 020 7379 4334
www.australia.org.uk

To find seasonal work try:
www.seasonalwork.com.au/index.bsp
www.workaboutaustralia.com.au/bwWebsite/default.asp

New Zealand has a similar scheme for either 12 or 23 months - and also a health certificate requirement. To qualify you must:

1. Usually be permanently living in the United Kingdom - this means you can be temporarily visiting another country when you lodge your application.

2. Have a British passport that's valid for at least three months after your planned departure from NZ.

3. Be at least 18 and not more than 30 years old.

4. Not bring children with you.

5. Hold a return ticket, or sufficient funds to purchase such a ticket.

6. Have a minimum of NZ$350 per month of stay in available funds (to meet your living costs while you're there).

7. Meet NZ's health and character requirements.

8. Satisfy the authorities your main reason for going to NZ is to holiday, not work.

9. Not have been approved a visa permit under a Working Holiday Scheme before.

The regulations for British Subjects are very clearly laid out on the NZ Government website:

www.immigration.govt.nz/migrant/stream/work/workingholiday/unitedkingdomworkingholidayscheme.htm

And here are a few websites to check for seasonal work in New Zealand:
www.picknz.co.nz/
www.seasonaljobs.co.nz/
www.backpackerboard.co.nz/work_jobs/seasonal_jobs_new_zealand.php

the gap-year guidebook 2010

A gap-year in South Korea

For the first time ever, we have the experiences of a gapper who spent a year in South Korea!

David, 24, took his **gap-** after graduating and doing a series of temp jobs to raise the money.

He spent most of it living in Incheon, South Korea, and he gave us his experiences while he was still on his **gap-** and as this book was being prepared. He'd also been to Hong Kong and was hoping to see one or two more countries his way home.

David was teaching English in a private English academy, or *Hagwon* (students aged from seven to 13).

Here's what he said: "All in all, it's been a thoroughly enjoyable and valuable experience. Staying in Korea for the whole of my **gap-**year has allowed me to learn a lot about the place and I feel quite settled here. I've had the opportunity to get used to Korean lifestyle, meet plenty of people and even pick up a little of the language.

"A year of teaching children has been tiring, but very rewarding, and in my opinion it's never a bad thing to have on your CV.

"Of course, another massive benefit of a working year out, is that it doesn't drain your funds in the way that other **gap-**years might. In fact,

I've been able to save a little money towards returning to university or travelling again when I finish here."

Although he was only part-way through his **gap-** when we spoke to him, he does have some advice for gappers: "I certainly think that research is the key. If you're planning your first extended stay out of the country, it's important that you choose the '**gap-**' that suits you in terms of duration and location.

"There's an abundance of information and offers available, so narrowing it down by choosing the type of **gap-** you want to take should help.

"Getting advice from others with experience is also a great way to get informed. I'd never even left Europe before coming here, so it was reassuring to speak to people who had done, or were doing, the very same thing.

"Internet forums are usually a good resource for this but beware of serial moaners who had one bad experience so want to put everyone else off!"

Anything he wished he'd taken with him? "Pictures of family and friends are one thing I regret not bringing with me, but my advice for anyone who chooses teaching in Korea, is to bring lots of deodorant. It's almost impossible to find and if you're lucky enough to come across some it will cost a relative fortune. Luckily, I was warned about this but, with three hot months remaining, I'm down to my last can so perhaps a few more were needed!"

Obviously he couldn't say how long it had taken to return to normal, but here are his thoughts: "I imagine that if 'back to normal' means my pre-**gap-** lifestyle then perhaps I'll never truly get back to normal. It sounds rather cliché but I'm sure my experience of living here, and being away from home for a long time, will shape decisions and plans I make in the future."

And actually, he is already considering whether to stay longer, as the school had offered to extend his contract, or whether to continue teaching English, but in another country!

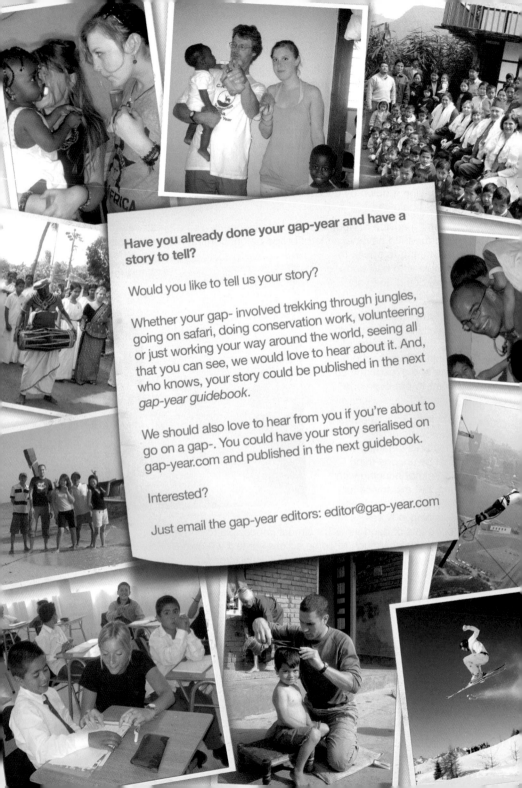

Have you already done your gap-year and have a story to tell?

Would you like to tell us your story?

Whether your gap- involved trekking through jungles, going on safari, doing conservation work, volunteering or just working your way around the world, seeing all that you can see, we would love to hear about it. And, who knows, your story could be published in the next *gap-year guidebook*.

We should also love to hear from you if you're about to go on a gap-. You could have your story serialised on gap-year.com and published in the next guidebook.

Interested?

Just email the gap-year editors: editor@gap-year.com

Au Pairing in Europe

Au Pair Ecosse
6 Park Place, King's Park,
Stirling FK7 9JR

Au Pair Ecosse places au pairs with families in Scotland and sends British au pairs to families in Europe and America using established, reputable agent partners.

Childcare International
Trafalgar House, Grenville Place,
Mill Hill, London NW7 3SA

Childcare International, together with their partner agencies abroad, arrange au pair placements in many EU countries including France, Germany, Holland, Italy and Spain.

Delaney International
Bramble Cottage, Thorncombe Street,
Bramley, Surrey GU5 0ND

Provides British au pair applicants with au pair positions in several EU countries including France, Germany, Italy and Spain.

Pebbles
35 rue pastorelli,
Nice 6000, France

Pebbles recruits au pairs through universities, schools, colleges and youth centres in England and France.

Planet Au Pair
Avenida Ausias March 32, Pta. 4,
Valencia 46006, Spain

Company placing au pairs throughout Europe and the USA.

Total Nannies
37 Leamington Avenue,
Morden, Surrey SM4 4DQ

This company places nannies and au pairs worldwide.

Au Pairing in North America

Au Pair in America (APIA)
37 Queen's Gate,
South Kensington, London SW7 5HR

Agency which specifically matches au pairs and nannies with families in America.

Internships & Paid Work Placements

AgriVenture
Speedwell Farm Bungalow, Nettle Bank,
Wisbech, Cambridgeshire PE14 0SA

E: uk@agriventure.com
T: +44 (0) 1945 450 999
www.agriventure.net

Spend your gap year getting fantastic work experience in South Pacific/North America/Japan/Europe. Work in agriculture or horticulture. Get paid for the work you do whilst living and working with one of our fully approved hosting enterprises. Great support and social network in your destination country plus we arrange it all for you.

Freephone for UK landlines: 0800 783 2186.

Gap Guru
Town Hall, Market Place,
Newbury, Berkshire RG14 5AA

Choose from a wide range of projects and select a programme duration from one month onwards - regular start dates every month for gap-year students or those on a career break to tailor-make their very own experience.

Global Choices
Barkat House, 116-118 Finchley Road,
Belsize Park, London NW3 5HT

Offers internships and working holidays in USA, Australia, Canada, UK, Ireland, Brazil, Argentina, Spain, Greece and Italy.

InterExchange
161 Sixth Avenue, New York, NY 10013, USA

InterExchange offers J-1 & H-2B visa programs throughout the US. Options include au pair, internship, seasonal work and travel and summer camp positions.

Invisible Children
1620 5th Ave, Suite 400,
San Diego, CA 92101, USA

Internships availabe in Uganda, specific to your abilities and strengths.

198

IST Plus
Rosedale House, Rosedale Road,
Richmond, Surrey TW9 2SZ

Internships in USA, Australia, New Zealand; Summer work in USA; Summer camp in USA; Gap-year work in Australia, New Zealand; Volunteer in Thailand; Teach in Thailand, China (for graduates).

Lucasfilm
One Letterman Drive, PO Box 29901,
San Francisco, CA 94129-0901, USA

As you can imagine, internships with Lucasfilm are few and far between. They are also quickly filled. See their website for further details.

Maasai International Challenge Africa
PO Box 14950,
Arusha, Tanzania 255

Offers low cost paid internships in Africa to students and graduates.

Mountbatten Institute
5th Floor, Michael House, 35-37 Chiswell Street
Clerkenwell, London EC1Y 4SE

Grab a whole year's worth of paid work experience through the Mountbatten Programme and enhance your CV.

Project O
PO Box 2082, Hillcrest,
Pinetown 3650, South Africa

A Christian organization who support AIDS orphans in Africa. They offer a three week internship programme.

The Foundation for Center for Research of Whales
1644 Plaza Way PMB 216,
Walla Walla, WA 99362, USA

Internships available in research and education.

The Institute for Public Policy Research (IPPR)
30-32 Southampton Street,
Covent Garden, London WC2E 7RA

The IPPR offers paid work placements throughout the year. See their website for more details.

Changing Worlds
Gap years

Hotels
Outdoor ed

www.changingworlds.co.uk
ask@changingworlds.co.uk
telephone: 01883 340960

The New England Wild Flower Society & Garden in the Woods
180 Hemenway Road,
Framingham, MA 01701, USA

The oldest plant conservation organization in the USA, and a leader in regional plant conservation programmes and native plant studies. They have volunteering and internship opportunities.

The Year Out Group
Queensfield, 28 King's Road,
Easterton, Wiltshire SN10 4PX

E: info@yearoutgroup.org
T: +44 (0) 1380 816696
www.yearoutgroup.org

See main entry under volunteering.

Twin Work & Volunteer
2nd Floor, 67-71 Lewisham High Street,
Lewisham, London SE13 5JX

Work and volunteer programmes listed.

Work the World Ltd
The Brighton Forum, 95 Ditchling Road,
Brighton, Sussex BN1 4ST

Organises healthcare and community development projects that provide maximum benefit to both the participants and the overseas communities they support.

Seasonal Work Down Under

Bellis Training Australia
Unit 7, 16-22 Miles Street,
Hawthorne, Brisbane QLD 4171, Australia

Offers paid work opportunities in Australia and training.

BUNAC (British Universities North America Club)
16 Bowling Green Lane,
Clerkenwell, London EC1R 0QH

Overseas work and travel programmes for people aged 18 and above. A BUNAC working holiday gives you the freedom and flexibility of spending an extended period of time living and working in another country.

Changing Worlds
11 Doctors Lane,
Chaldon, Surrey CR3 5AE

E: ask@changingworlds.co.uk
T: +44 (0) 1883 340 960
www.changingworlds.co.uk

Changing Worlds is a small, friendly organisation with charitable aims. We focus on providing a personal service – we know everyone on first name terms and handpick every group of applicants we send out. This ethos has successfully sent over 1200 people on once-in-a-lifetime trips, and we're proud to say that a quarter of our applicants come from recommendations.

We offer paid and voluntary placements: Argentina; Australia; China; Dubai; Ghana; Honduras; India; Kenya; Latvia; Madagascar; New Zealand; Romania; Serbia;South Africa; Thailand; Uganda;

So, if you like the idea of travel, meeting people and don't mind working hard then this is for you!

Go Workabout
PO Box 1865, Fremantle,
Perth, WA 6959, Australia

Arranges work in Australia for working holiday makers before they travel.

Immigration New Zealand
Mezzanine Floor, New Zealand House,
80 Haymarket
St James's, London SW1Y 4TE

New Zealand government website offering details on working holidays for visitors to the country.

Launchpad Australia
PO Box 2525,
Fitzroy, VIC 3065, Australia

Launchpad Australia provide working holiday, gap-year and career break adventures in Australia and abroad!

Oyster Worldwide Limited
Hodore Farm,
Hartfield, East Sussex TN7 4AR

E: emailus@oysterworldwide.com
T: +44 (0) 1892 770 771
www.oysterworldwide.com

Earn a wage and discover Australia with one of Oyster's two Aussie work programmes.

Those who love the outdoors, quadbikes, horses and a jackeroo lifestyle can apply for our Outback Programme. You'll work on farms and experience the big spaces and small communities of rural Australia.

Alternatively, those who love the buzz of the city can apply for our Sydney Programme. You'll work in catering, hospitality or office jobs in one of the best cities on earth.

In both cases you'll be looked after on arrival, undergo a training course, helped to find a job and have full support in the UK and in Australia.

The Year Out Group
Queensfield, 28 King's Road,
Easterton, Wiltshire SN10 4PX

E: info@yearoutgroup.org
T: +44 (0) 1380 816696
www.yearoutgroup.org

See main entry under volunteering.

Visas Australia Ltd
Lindum House,
44 Wellington Road,
Nantwich, Cheshire CW5 7BX

Specialises in processing and issuing all types of visas, particularly for gappers. Their service is approved by both the Australian Tourist Board and Australian High Commission.

Visitoz
Springbrook Farm,
8921 Burnett Highway,
Goomeri, QLD 4601,
Australia

E: info@visitoz.org
T: +61 (0) 741 686 185
F: +61 (0) 741 686 126
www.visitoz.org

Visitoz provides training and guarantees work for young people between the ages of 18 and 30 in agriculture, hospitality, child care and teaching all over Australia.

In 17 years no one has ever left without a job to go to after the training - there are 1800 employers all over Australia waiting for you!

Seasonal Work in Europe

Acorn Venture Ltd
Acorn House, Prospect Road,
Halesowen, West Midlands B62 8DU

Acorn Adventure runs adventure holiday camps from April until September based in eight centres in France, Italy, and the UK – their main customers are school/youth groups and families.

Beaumont Château Ltd (UK Office)
Weardale Business Centre, Martin Street, Stanhope
Bishop Auckland, County Durham DL13 2UY

Chateau Beaumont is a small friendly language and activity centre based in the Normandy region of France.

Canvas Holidays
East Port House, 12 East Port,
Dunfermline, Fife KY12 7JG

We have paid positions at over 100 campsites across Europe. We require a minimum of six weeks commitment between March and October.

Jobs In The Alps
3 Bracken Terrace,
Newquay, Cornwall TR7 2LS

Jobs in the Alps provide seasonal jobs in ski resorts for students who can speak French, German or Italian.

Mark Warner Ltd
20 Kensington Church Street,
Kensington, London W8 4EP

Leading independent tour operator with opportunities all year round in ski and beach resorts. Variety of hotel positions and fully inclusive benefits package on offer.

Natives.co.uk
263 Putney Bridge Road,
Putney, London SW15 2PU

Seasonal recruitment website for ski or summer resort jobs.

The Year Out Group
Queensfield, 28 King's Road,
Easterton, Wiltshire SN10 4PX

E: info@yearoutgroup.org
T: +44 (0) 1380 816696
www.yearoutgroup.org

See main entry under volunteering.

Seasonal work in North America

Camp America
37a Queen's Gate,
South Kensington,
London SW7 5HR

E: brochure@campamerica.co.uk
T: +44 (0) 20 7581 7333
F: +44 (0) 20 7581 7377
www.campamerica.co.uk

Be more than just another tourist this summer! Camp America has positions to suit anyone who wants to experience the fun and excitement of an American summer camp for nine weeks, as well as being able to explore the USA for up to ten weeks after camp! For more information see our website.

Camp Leaders In America
24-26 Mount Pleasant,
Liverpool L3 5RY

Activity leaders, camp counselors and support staff needed in their summer camps.

CCUSA
1st Floor North, Devon House,
171-177 Great Portland Street
Marylebone, London W1W 5PQ

Work in summer camps in beautiful locations in America. You don't need any experience or qualifications but you do need to be at least 18 years old. Also available, seasonal work down under and winter camps in Canada.

Oyster Worldwide Limited
Hodore Farm,
Hartfield, East Sussex TN7 4AR

E: emailus@oysterworldwide.com
T: +44 (0) 1892 770 771
www.oysterworldwide.com

Oyster offers challenging and rewarding paid work in Canada for the summer and winter seasons. You'll live and work in one of three world class resorts. Those with

the gap-year guidebook 2010

childcare experience can work for Whistler Kids and gain their Ski Instructors Level One Certificate.

Alternatively we'll find you work in one of Banff's hotels as a housekeeper. Opt for French speaking Tremblant in Quebec if you want to improve your French too. You're paid enough to live well and ski regularly.

Oyster offers a personal approach and organises your flights, work permit and provides full support throughout from their experienced destination managers and overseas representatives.

The Year Out Group
Queensfield, 28 King's Road,
Easterton, Wiltshire SN10 4PX
www.yearoutgroup.org

E: info@yearoutgroup.org
T: +44 (0) 1380 816696

See main entry under volunteering.

Sport Instructors

Britannia Sailing East Coast
Victory House, Shotley Marina,
Ipswich, Suffolk IP9 1QJ

Based at Shotley Marina near Ipswich, Britannia Sailing is a well-established company with first-class facilities offering all aspects of sailing instruction and yacht charter.

Crewseekers Limited
Hawthorn House, Hawthorn Lane,
Sarisbury Green
Southampton, Hampshire SO31 7BD

Work available as yachting crew cruising, racing, yacht delivering around the world. Beginners welcome.

Flying Fish
25 Union Road,
Cowes, Isle of Wight PO31 7TW

E: mail@flyingfishonline.com
T: +44 (0) 1983 280 641
www.flyingfishonline.com

Flying Fish trains and recruits over 1000 people each year to work as yacht skippers and as sailing, diving, surfing, windsurfing, ski and snowboard instructors. Combine professional training with international adventure and the chance to make money while having fun. Watersports courses are run in the UK, Greece and Australia while snow sports training takes place in Canada and France.

Goal-Line Soccer Clinics
PO Box 1642, Corvallis,
OR 97339, USA

Offers paid soccer coaching vacations for qualified applicants. Their programme operates in a number of communities in the Pacific Northwest of the USA.

International Academy
Sophia House, 28 Cathedral Road,
Cardiff, CF11 9LJ

E: info@international-academy.com
T: +44 (0) 29 2066 0200
www.international-academy.com

Become a ski or snowboard instructor on a five to 12 week gap year or career break course. Experience world class resorts and gain recognised CSIA, CASI, NZSIA or SBINZ instructor qualifications. Resorts include Banff/Lake Louise, Whistler Blackcomb, Sun Peaks resorts and Castle Mountain in Canada. Summer courses are also available at Mount Hood in the USA and Cardrona Alpine Resort in New Zealand.

PJ Scuba
Mermaids Dive Center S-2694,
PADI 5 Star Career Development Center,
Jomtien Beach Road, 75/124 Moo 12
Nongprue, Chonburi 20260,Thailand

Offers the chance to study scuba diving to instructor level (PADI) and then teach in Thailand, Vietnam or Cambodia.

Play Soccer
24 St Martins Drive, Unit 10,
Marlborough, MA 01752, USA

Play Soccer is New England's leader in soccer education, currently working with over 30,000 children each year.

Ski Academy Switzerland
6 Lane Side, Kirkburton,
Huddersfield, Yorkshire HD8 0TN

Provider of quality ski instructor programmes with work opportunities for gap-year students and for those on a career break or just fancy a challenge!

The Instructor Training Co
PO Box 791,
Queenstown, Otago 9348, New Zealand

The Instructor Training Co offers you the opportunity to train for your ski instructor qualification in New Zealand. Six, eight and eleven week courses available.

The Year Out Group
Queensfield, 28 King's Road,
Easterton, Wiltshire SN10 4PX

E: info@yearoutgroup.org
T: +44 (0) 1380 816696
www.yearoutgroup.org

See main entry under volunteering.

Ticket To Ride
263 Putney Bridge Road,
London SW15 2PU

A gap and career break company offering you the opportunity to experience great surfing.

Xtreme-gap.com
9 Victoria Terrace, Manchester M13 0HY

Gap company offering extreme sporting adventures.

TEFL

Adventure Alternative
PO Box 14,
Portstewart, County Antrim BT55 7WS

Teaching and volunteering in needy schools and orphanages in Kenya and in schools in Kathmandu (includes Himalayan trek).

CRCC Asia Ltd
106 Weston Street, Southwark,
London SE1 3QB

Organises paid internships and teaching placements in China and has both London and Beijing offices to ensure your programme goes smoothly.

Link Ethiopia
4 Orchard Mews, Islington, London N1 5BS

Experience Ethiopia and teach basic English to small groups on a very inexpensive three-month placement with us. Registered Charity No. 1112390.

Saxoncourt Training & Recruitment
59 South Molton Street,
Mayfair, London W1K 5SN

If you don't yet have your TEFL qualification, Saxoncourt runs full time four-week courses in London and Oxford, leading to either the Trinity TESOL diploma or the Cambridge CELTA qualification.

Syndicat Mixte Montaigu-Rocheservière
35 avenue Villebois Mareuil,
Montaigu, 85607 France

Receives local government funding to teach English in primary schools, offering four posts annually – and it also employs a fifth person to work as a language assistant in a local college and lycée.

Chapter 8
Volunteering
abroad

Chapter sponsored by

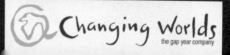

Volunteering placements in Kenya with Changing Worlds.

Nick Aspinal:

"Now I'm at home it has finally sunk in that I have left and may not see some of the friends or kids that I met again. It really was the best six months of my life and I have no regrets about any of it. The kids provide you with such entertainment and the representative and his family really are some of the nicest people I've ever met.

"My host family was incredibly welcoming and I have made really good friends there. They went out of their way to make us feel welcome and happy, very quickly it felt like home. I was lucky to experience the life of an African family and I will definitely keep in touch with them.

"The schools where I worked provided me with some of my best moments ever and saying goodbye to them was one of the worst.

"Without the support and planning of the staff in the UK this wouldn't have been possible. I can honestly say I don't think there is a better company than Changing Worlds!"

Becky Holden:

"Having to control and make yourself understood to large classes was sometimes challenging, but the school were so welcoming and easy to get along with that by having the motivation and enthusiasm to teach it was fairly easy to make the placement a success. Going with an open mind made it easy to adapt, and keeping busy kept us from feeling homesick. Plus, my host family were amazing!

"During the week I was at

visit: www.changingworlds.co.uk

school teaching, either until lunchtime or until the end of the school day. I went to St Stephen's Orphanage a few afternoons a week to play with the children once they had returned from school. At school I taught English, maths, PE and creative art. Lessons were 35 minutes long and I took four to six a day. In a typical English lesson I taught out of the textbook, with lots of children sharing each copy. We read from the book or completed an exercise before they wrote their answers. PE was less structured as all the children wanted to do was to play football! Average classes were 60/70 children.

"I stayed with three other volunteers to begin with. We had two bunk beds with mosquito nets, and a wardrobe with drawers that we shared. The room was fairly small for four of us so was usually quite a mess, but we all got on so well that we enjoyed sharing.

"About a month into our trip we went to the Masai Mara for a three day safari. Seeing the huge number of animals in their natural habitat was incredible. I especially loved seeing lions, cheetahs, elephants and giraffes. We stayed in little cabins. Later in our stay we chose to do another safari to Samburu where we camped in tents alongside the elephants!

"For me there was nothing which needed improving, although in Kenya don't expect things to run on time! I had the best six months of my life there and I will be recommending Changing Worlds and Kenya in particular to everyone I can."

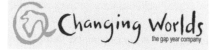

211

8 Volunteering abroad

Voluntary work abroad can be one of the most rewarding ways to spend all, or part, of your **gap**-year. You could find yourself working with people living in unbelievable poverty, disease or hunger. It can be a humbling and hugely enriching experience and it can make you question all the things you've taken for granted in your life. It's no exaggeration to say it can be life-changing.

Some people who have done it have ended up changing their planned course of study at university or even their whole career plan.

Year Out Group's members, who are all **gap-** providers, report that volunteering is the top **gap-** choice among all age groups and had risen by 20% in the last full year for which they carried out research.

Teaching and working with children are the most popular options, with requests for teaching placements going up by 10% since September 2008, according to statistics sourced from the Training & Development Agency in March 2009.

Interestingly, women gappers outnumber men, and women are also more likely to choose volunteering and expeditions rather than courses or cultural exchanges.

Here are a few comments from people who have done it:

"This year has given me the biggest confidence boost in so many different ways and I feel that I am now more focused and ready for whatever lies ahead at university."

"It was the most rewarding and fascinating trip of my life."

"I can honestly say that volunteering has changed my life. I feel a lot more grounded as a person. The simple things in life mean so much more."

Why volunteer?

There's no denying that the economic situation has also added to the need for volunteers, with organisations like the UN reporting that it has affected approximately 40% more of the world's most vulnerable people.

So volunteer help is likely to be even more needed and appreciated. Voluntary work abroad can also give you wonderful memories and a new perspective on the world.

On an organised voluntary project you often live amongst the local community and ten to get closer to daily life than you do as an independent traveller.

By taking part in an organised voluntary work project you can learn about a different culture, meet new people and learn to communicate with people who may not understand your way of life, let alone your language.

visit: www.changingworlds.co.uk

You will come away with an amazing sense of achievement and (hopefully) pride in what you have done.

Career breakers have also found that a volunteer **gap-** has not only been a satisfying experience but given them new ideas and attitudes too. A structured volunteer placement can also give a new dimension to the skills you can highlight on your CV.

Jude Hanan, 37, took a year's career break to volunteer on an AIDS project in Malawi. She said it was: "Tough... In fact, devastatingly heartbreaking. On some days, the perversity in attitudes to practising safe sex and those already with AIDS was just frightening.

"On other days, it was magic - there's something about Africa that calls to even the most cynical of souls. It's a cliché, but a child's smile when you've taken time to be with them is one of the most beautiful things I've ever seen."

And she certainly came back with a new perspective: "Things seemed so narrow, and after the excitement of being back wore off, life returned to how it was before I left.

"Sometimes, I felt like I was going backwards...

"Did it change me? Yes - I'd like to think that I'm more open now to what's going on in the world. At the same time, I don't know if I'd ever go back as it's often the mix of the people, the place and what you're doing at the time that makes a place. In saying that, one day I will."

Being realistic, voluntary work can be tough. You may be out in the middle of nowhere, with no western influence to be seen; food, language - the entire culture is likely to be totally different from what you're used to and there might not be many English speakers around: so you may have to cope with culture shock or feeling lonely, isolated and homesick at first, but if you stick with it you'll usually find those feelings will go as you get more involved in what you're doing.

the gap-year guidebook 2010

Are there ethical concerns?

The debate continues about the ethics of volunteering, and covers a variety of issues:

- Is it environmentally sustainable?
- Does it really benefit the people or is it creating a dependency culture?
- What's the 'benefit balance' between volunteer satisfaction and the community being helped?

The website **www.ethicalvolunteering.org/index.html** has some very sound advice on how to ensure you're an ethical volunteer. You can also download a PDF guide to ethical volunteering.

As a first step, they advise you to look at the ethics of the organisation you're thinking of going with. You can learn a lot from the tone of the words they use on their websites, not only about their own arrangements but the words they use to describe the host organisations they work with.

Be wary of promises to 'change the world' by going. You won't and these organisations wouldn't exist to send people out on volunteer placements if they didn't envisage doing it for some years.

Pictures, too, will tell you a lot, for example do they rely heavily on pictures of children to tug at your heartstrings or do they show pictures of volunteers working with children and the wider community? It's all about the balance.

You can also learn a lot from the way they prepare you for the trip and the kind of back-up they give you. Does it, for example, include some cultural acclimatisation to help you understand the situation of the people the project is designed to benefit?

Don't be afraid to ask questions - such as do they work with local organisations and do they actually make financial contributions to local volunteer programmes?

Equally ask yourself some questions - am I willing to do some research and learn all I can about the country and the conditions before I go? Am I willing to learn and be a good guest while I'm there? Am I willing to respect the local culture? Am I willing to be flexible and professional about what I'm doing?

What would you like to do?

Only you can decide what's most important to you, it depends on whether you're more into plants, animals and the environment, in which case you'd be happier on a conservation project. If you're a people person you might do something that helps disadvantaged people, whether they're children, adults, and disabled or able bodied.

Whichever you feel is right for you there's a huge range of companies and types of voluntary placements to choose from.

Even if you are straight from school or university and haven't yet had much experience of work-related skills you shouldn't underestimate the skills and qualities you may have, and take for granted, that can be far less accessible

visit: www.changingworlds.co.uk

to disadvantaged people in places where such things as access to education or to communications are not universally available.

How much time do you want to spend?

This is about how committed a volunteer you want to be. Would you feel more satisfied spending two weeks on a building project providing homes for people displaced by a natural disaster? Or are you the kind of person who wants to get stuck into a long-term project, where the results you see will be more gradual?

Because voluntary work is so popular with gappers, commercial companies offering volunteering packages exist alongside the more traditional not-for-profit organisations and the idealism associated with voluntary work, though still there, has come under some commercial pressure.

Some companies offer two- to four-week holidays combined with some voluntary work, but equally there are many organisations still committed to the idealism of volunteering, offering placements from a few months to up a year or more.

However, you may not want (or be able) to offer more than a few weeks or months of your time, so the combined holiday/short volunteering option might be for you. There's no point in committing yourself to a whole year only to find that, after a few weeks, you hate it and want to go home early. The two- to four-week option may also be a good 'taster' experience to help you decide whether to commit to something more long-term.

So, it's a good idea to be honest with yourself about what you want - there's nothing wrong with wanting to travel and have a good time. But, whatever you choose, make sure you are clear about what you will be doing *before* you sign up and part with your money.

When to start applying

Applications can close early, particularly for expeditions and conservation projects needing complex funding or for those tied in with international government programmes. If you'd like to go on one of these projects, planning should start about a year ahead, usually in the autumn term of the academic year.

Others can be taken up at very short notice. In fact, some organisations can take in applications during the August period (when you are getting A level results or going through clearing), and book you on a project that starts in September.

If you don't have much time before your **gap-** starts (maybe you didn't get the grades you expected, or you've made a last-minute decision to defer university for a year, or your company has offered you a sabbatical or made you redundant) it is always worth contacting a voluntary organisation about a project you're interested in. They may have had a last-minute cancellation.

Stiff competition

As more people are becoming motivated by the almost daily media reports on poverty in the developing world and on various global threats to the planet's climate, ecology and environment, to go out and do something, the

competition for places can be fierce. Companies can afford to be picky - you may find you have to prove to them that you should be selected to go before they will accept your money!

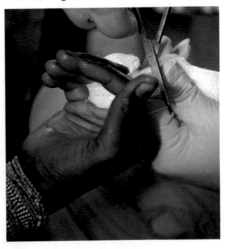

They have a point. Increasingly NGOs and volunteers are trying to make sure both sides benefit from the experience, so placement organisations put a lot of effort into checking and briefing as well as getting you out there and providing in-country support. If you can't stick it, everyone loses out - including the person who could have been chosen instead of you.

What's the cost?

It varies hugely - some companies just expect you to pay for the airfare - others expect you to raise thousands of pounds for funding. It can be hard to combine raising money with studying for A levels or with work, but there are a lot of ways to do it.

As usual, the earlier you start, the easier it will be. The organisation that you go with should be able to give advice, but options include organising sponsored events (abseiling down a tall building), writing to companies or trusts asking for sponsorship, car boot sales, or even just getting a job and saving what you can.

visit: www.changingworlds.co.uk

If approached, many local newspapers will do a short article about your plan if it's interesting enough - but it's better to ask them during the quieter news spells, like the summer holiday months, when they'll be more likely to welcome an additional story.

The last resort is to go cap-in-hand to your parents, either for a loan or a gift, but this can be unsatisfying and they may simply not be able to afford it. If your parents or relatives do want to help, you could ask for useful items for Christmas or birthday presents - like a rucksack.

Career breakers will have different considerations. There's more on this in Chapter 6 - Career Breakers and Mature Travellers, but if you work for a large organisation it's worth asking whether they have any links to projects, or run their own charitable foundation, which might offer placements to employees.

What to expect

Placements range from a couple of weeks to a whole academic year, but most provide only free accommodation and food - a very few provide pocket money.

You'll need to be resourceful, be able to teach, build, inspire confidence, communicate and share what you know. Physical and mental fitness, staying power and the ability to get on with people are essential.

This is what most placement organisers say: "We are looking for self-motivated and reliable positive thinkers. You need to be self-reliant and able to cope when you turn up at a Nepali school and find a basic room, no curtains and that the loo is a 'long-drop' down the garden."

Some other points worth emphasizing:

Big organisation or small specialist? You might feel safer going with a big voluntary organisation because they should be able to offer help in a nasty situation. Experience is certainly important where organisations are concerned. But often a small, specialist organisation is more knowledgeable about a country, a school or other destination.

Size and status have little bearing on competence. A charity can be more efficient than a commercial company. Conversely a commercial company can show more sensitivity than a charity.

There are few general rules - talk to someone who's been with the organisation you're interested in. Organisations vary as to how much back up they offer volunteers, from virtually holding your hand throughout your stay and even after you come back, to the 'sink or swim' method.

You need to know yourself if you're going to get the most out of your volunteering **gap-**. If you feel patronised at the slightest hint of advice then you might get annoyed with too much interference from the organisation. Though do bear in mind that they probably know more than you do about the placement, what sort of vaccinations you're going to need, what will be useful to take with you, and how to get the necessary visas and permits. Equally if you're shy or nervous it might be as well to go with an organisation that sends

the gap-year guidebook 2010

volunteers in pairs or groups. There's nothing wrong with either type of placement - it's about choosing what's right for you.

Talk to a few organisations before you decide which one to go with - and, probably even more useful, talk to some previous volunteers. They'll be able to tell you what it's really like; don't just ask them if they enjoyed it, get them to describe what they did, what they liked and why, what they didn't like and what they'd do differently.

Remember, wherever you're sent, you can't count on much. Regardless of the organisation, you will be going to poor countries where the infrastructure and support services can be minimal - otherwise why would they need volunteers?

Expect to be adaptable. Regardless of the reputation of the voluntary work organisation you choose, or the competence of voluntary work coordinators in a particular country, it's about your skills and human qualities and those of the people you'll be with so there's bound to be an element of chance as to whether the school you are put in, for example, really values you or whether you get on with the family you stay with. It's worth checking first what training is given and what support there is in-country, but be aware that you may not get what you expect - you need to be adaptable and make the most of whatever situation you find yourself in.

Safety first

If you're going with a good organisation they shouldn't send you anywhere too dangerous - but situations change quickly and it's always worth finding out for yourself about where you're going.

Check out the Foreign Office's travel advice pages on: **www.fco.gov.uk**

The Foreign Office site also has lots of advice on visas, insurance and other things that need to be sorted out before you go, and advice on what to do in an emergency abroad. There's much more on all this in Chapter 1 - Tips For Travellers.

Also, make sure you have proper insurance cover and that it is appropriate for where you're going, the length of time you'll be away and for any unexpected emergencies (see Chapter 3 - Insurance).

Conservation

African Conservation Experience
Unit 1 Manor Farm, Churchend Lane, Charfield
Wotton-Under-Edge, Gloucestershire GL12 8LJ

E: info@conservationafrica.net
T: 0870 241 5816
www.conservationafrica.net

Experience the wildlife of southern Africa up close and personal. Conservation projects range from studying elephants in Botswana to tracking cheetah in South Africa – and everything in between. A chance to work with and protect some of Africa's most vulnerable species and habitats. Placements suitable for all ages and levels of experience.

African Gap Year
PO Box 1312,
Cresta, Gauteng 2118, South Africa

Various opportunities to volunteer or work a gap-year in South Africa.

All Out Africa
PO Box 153,
Lobamba, H100, Swaziland

They run cutting edge wildlife conservation and social development projects in some of Africa's most amazing locations.

BSES Expeditions
at The Royal Geographical Society,
1 Kensington Gore,
South Kensington, London SW7 2AR

E: info@bses.org.uk
T: +44 (0) 20 7591 3141
www.bses.org.uk

BSES Expeditions organises challenging scientific expeditions to remote, wild environments. Study climate change whilst mountaineering or kayaking in the Arctic, measure biodiversity in the Amazon or investigate human interaction with the environment in the Himalayas. Achieve your DofE Gold Award Residential and Expedition sections. Open to all aged 16-23. Mentoring and fundraising support provided. Registered charity number 802196.

Coral Cay Conservation
Block 1, Elizabeth House, 39 York Road, Lambeth, London SE1 7NQ

Volunteer with award-winning specialists in coral reef and rainforest conservation expeditions. Scuba dive or trek in tropical climes and work with local communities to aid long-term conservation efforts.

CREES The Rainforest Education and Resource Centre
5-6 Kendrick Mews,
South Kensington, London SW7 3HG

Volunteering programme which combines conservation work with participation in local community projects.

Dyer Island Cruises
PO Box 78,
Gansbaai, 7720,
South Africa

Offer shark cage diving, boat based whale watching and also volunteer work.

Earthwise Valley
Earthwise Living Foundation,
PO Box 5,
Thames, 3540,
New Zealand

Join the Rainforest Sanctuary as a residential volunteer and experience New Zealand while making a real difference to our natural world.

Entabeni Nature Guide Training School
Entabeni Private Game Reserve,
Waterberg Escarpment,
South Africa

Situated on a private game reserve three hours drive from Johannesburg, Entabeni offer a series of programmes in nature guiding, weapons handling and other tailor-made courses.

Frontier
50-52 Rivington Street,
London EC2A 3QP

E: info@frontier.ac.uk
T: +44 (0) 20 7613 2422
F: +44 (0) 20 7613 2992
www.frontier.ac.uk

Frontier (The Society for Environmental Exploration), is an environmental NGO dedicated to conservation and development research. Their projects work towards safeguarding biodiversity and ecosystem integrity and building sustainable livelihoods for marginalised communities.

Since 1989 Frontier has, amongst other achievements, set up Tanzania's first multi-user marine park in partnership with the WWF, designed educational materials that were integrated into Vietnam's national curriculum, and produced over 300 technical papers and reports that have been published in major journals. Whilst having the opportunity of completing their dissertations and independent research credits, Frontier staff and volunteers carry out groundbreaking surveys in remote forest, savannah and marine environments.

221

Galapagos Conservation Trust
5 Derby Street,
Mayfair, London W1J 7AB

The Galapagos Conservation Trust has two aims: to raise funds to support the expanding conservation work and to raise awareness of the current issues the islands face.

Registered Charity No. 1043470.

Kwa Madwala Private Game Reserve
PO Box 192,
Hectorspruit, Mpumalanga 1330, South Africa

Kwa Madwala Private Game Reserve is located just south of Kruger National Park. They offer gap-year experiences for those interested in learning about African wildlife, conservation and eco-tourism.

ProWorld (Real Projects...Real Experience)
Globe II Business Centre, 128 Maltravers Road,
Sheffield, Yorkshire S2 5AZ

Projects offered: conservation, health care, education, human rights, journalism, and business. Programmes start every month of the year.

Rainforest Nature
Lima, Peru

Has conservation projects in countries such as Ecuador, Colombia, Chile, Brazil, Costa Rica, India, Panama, Peru and others.

ReefDoctor Org Ltd
14 Charlwood Terrace,
Putney, London SW15 1NZ

Become a volunteer ReefDoctor and contribute to marine research, education, conservation and sustainable community development alongside our team of local and international scientists.

Southern African Wildlife College
Private Bage X3015,
Hoedspruit,
Northern Province 1380, South Africa

Are you passionate about wildlife and wanting to learn more about conservation in Africa? This college is offering a unique opportunity to participate in a six month Game Ranger Course.

The Great Marine Project
Suite 6, 8 High Street,
Harpenden,
Hertfordshire AL5 2TB

Help save the turtles of the Perhentian Islands! Don't let the Green turtles follow the same fate as the Leatherbacks who are now extinct on the islands.

The Year Out Group
Queensfield, 28 King's Road,
Easterton, Wiltshire SN10 4PX

E: info@yearoutgroup.org
T: +44 (0) 1380 816696
www.yearoutgroup.org

See main entry under Volunteering.

Turtle Conservation Project
No 389 Godagama,
Kosgoda, Sri Lanka

Opportunities to measure turtles, undertake beach patrols and mapping, conduct education programmes, office administration, fundraising, and more.

Wilderness Awareness School
PO Box 5000, PMB 137,
Duvall, WA 98019, USA

The school offers courses for adults in tracking, wilderness survival skills and a stewardship programme. There are also monthly nature talks in Seattle, which are often free.

Volunteering Opportunities

2Way Development
2Way Space, 1-4 Pope Street,
Bermondsey, London SE1 3PR

2Way offer a support service to people looking for volunteering experiences worldwide.

A Broader View Volunteers Corp
1001 Dell Lane,
Wyncote, Montgomery, PA 19095, USA

Offer volunteering opportunites worldwide in a range of projects such as HIV/AIDS awareness, medical, education, conservation, community development and child care/orphanages.

Action Aid
Hamlyn House, Macdonald Road,
Upper Holloway, London N19 5PG

E: experiences@actionaid.org
T: +44 (0)20 7561 7571
www.actionaid.org.uk/experiences

Take part in ActionAid's First Hand Experience and change lives, including your own. ActionAid is offering volunteering opportunities in South Africa and Nepal, working alongside local people to build homes and centres to benefit whole communities for the better. No experience is necessary just enthusiasm, motivation and the desire to help make a difference. Charity number 274467.

Action Centres UK
King's Park Conference & Sports Centre,
King's Park Road, Northampton,
Northamptonshire NN3 6LL

Action Centres UK has been developing young people through gap-year and volunteer programmes since 1971 and still provides opportunities through its three UK based adventure and sports centres.

Africa & Asia Venture
10 Market Place,
Devizes,
Wiltshire SN10 1HT

Africa and Asia Venture enables motivated 18-24 year-olds to invest in their futures through three to five months of volunteering on teaching and sports coaching projects in Africa.

Environment and community projects also take place in Kenya.

African Conservation Experience

Unit 1 Manor Farm,
Churchend Lane, Charfield
Wotton-Under-Edge,
Gloucestershire GL12 8LJ

E: info@conservationafrica.net
T: 0870 241 5816
www.conservationafrica.net

Whether you want to get hands-on with hand rearing in a wildlife rehabilitation centre, use your DIY skills to help renovate an orphanage, experience life as a wildlife vet, or work on a research project to aid in the conservation of some of Africa's most iconic species – volunteering with African Conservation Experience allows you to make a real difference to wildlife and communities in South Africa. And in return for this invaluable contribution you will leave with memories and friendships that will last a lifetime.

Placements suitable for all ages and levels of experience.

African Conservation Trust

PO Box 310, Link Hills, Kwa Zulu-Natal 3652, South Africa

The mission of ACT is to provide a means for conservation projects to become self funding through active participation by the public.

African Impact

PO Box 1218,
Gweru, Zimbabwe

Various volunteering projects available in Zimbabwe, Kenya, Botswana, Mozambique and Zambia.

AIDE (The Association of International Development & Exchange)

1221 South Mopac Expressway, Suite 100,
Austin, TX 78746, USA

Alliance Abroad is a non-profit organisation that provides international teaching, work and volunteer placements. Our services include guaranteed placement and 24/7 personal assistance.

Amanzi Travel

4 College Road,
Westbury on Trym,
Gloucestershire BS9 3EJ

E: info@amanzitravel.co.uk
T: +44 (0) 117 904 1924
F: +44 (0) 117 959 4678
www.amanzitravel.co.uk

Leading Specialist in Volunteer Placements throughout Africa.

- Work with big cats at the Namibia Wildlife Sanctuary
- Look after AIDS orphans in Cape Town
- Teach disadvantaged children in schools in Tanzania
- Assist at the Zambia Medical Centre
- Help on the world's first Lion Breeding and Release Project

Amanzi Travel is passionate about the projects offered, ATOL licensed and offers a service that is second-to-none.

Asociacion Nuevos Horizontes
3a Calle, 6-51, Zona 2,
Quetzaltenango, Guatemala

Volunteers needed to help with the children in the shelter.

ATD Fourth World
48 Addington Square, Camberwell, London SE5 7LB

An international voluntary organisation working in partnership with people living in poverty worldwide.

Azafady
Studio 7, 1a Beethoven Street, West Kilburn, London W10 4LG

Pioneer Madagascar is a ten-week volunteer scheme that offers first-hand experience of frontline development and conservation work in beautiful and remote areas.

Be More - Volunteering in South Africa
Third Floor, 46 Berwick Street,
Soho, London W1F 8SG

A UK charity that supports grassroot development and HIV/AIDS relief organizations in Africa by providing funding and international volunteers. Registered Charity No. 1116179.

BERUDEP
PO Box 10, Belo,
Boyo Division, North West Province 237, Cameroon

BERUDEP's vision is 'to eradicate poverty and raise the living standards of the rural population of Cameroon's North West province'. They rely on volunteers to help them achieve this.

Blue Ventures
2D Aberdeen Studios, Aberdeen Centre,
22-24 Highbury Grove, Highbury, London N5 2EA

Blue Ventures runs award-winning marine research projects for conservation, education and sustainable development. Volunteers participate in diving and terrestrial activities in partnership with local communities.

BMS World Mission
PO Box 49, 129 Broadway,
Didcot, Oxfordshire OX14 8XA

BMS World Mission is a Christian organisation which sends out volunteers in teams and as individuals to over 40 countries worldwide.

Brathay Exploration Group
Brathay Hall,
Ambleside, Cumbria LA22 0HP

Brathay provides 'challenging experiences for young people' aged 15-25. It runs a range of expeditions from one to five weeks long which vary each year.

Cameroon Association for the Protection and Education of the Child (CAPEC)
BP 20646,
Yaounde, Cameroon

Volunteer to teach children in Cameroon. See website for vacancies and details of programmes available.

Camphill Community Ballybay
Robb Farm, Corraskea,
Ballybay, Monaghan, Republic of Ireland

Camphill Ballybay (registered charity CHY5861) is a caring community for adults with a variety of special needs.

Camphill Community Ballytobin
Callan, Kilkenny, Republic of Ireland

Camphill Communities work with people who are mentally handicapped. They are a registered charity (CHY 5861) who are always looking for volunteers in their communities.

Camphill Community Dingle
Beenbawn,
Dingle, Kerry, Republic of Ireland

Small rural life-sharing community with people with special needs, part of the Camphill Communities of Ireland (registered charity CHY5861).

Camphill Community Duffcarrig
Camphill Community Duffcarrig,
Gorey, Wexford, Republic of Ireland

Camphill Communities work with people who are mentally handicapped. They are a registered charity (CHY 5861) who are always looking for volunteers in their communities.

Camphill Community Dunshane
Brannockstown,
Near Naas, Kildare, Republic of Ireland

Training college, part of the Camphill Community (registered charity CHY5861), for young adults in need of special care.

Camphill Community Greenacres
1A Farmhill Park,
Goatstown, Dublin 14, Republic of Ireland

Camphill Community Greenacres is part of a unique, international, charity aiming to create a sustainable, inclusive and harmonious community. The community of about 20 people provides living and working opportunities with people with special needs.

Camphill Community Jerpoint
Thomastown, Kilkenny, Republic of Ireland

Jerpoint is part of the Camphill Communities (registered charity CHY5861). It is a small community where they live together with adults with disabilities. They have an organic garden, animals and are particularly caring towards the environment.

Camphill Community Kyle
Coolagh,
Callan, Kilkenny, Republic of Ireland

Kyle, part of the worldwide Camphill movement, is a life sharing community of 40 people, including 12 with learning disabilities. Everyone is supported through mutual relationships and contributes in shared work of various kinds. (Registered Charity CHY5861)

Camps International Limited
Unit 1 Kingfisher Park, Headlands Business Park, Salisbury Road
Ringwood, Hampshire BH24 3NX

Gap-year volunteer holidays available. Spend time in community and wildlife camps and still have the time and opportunity to trek mountains and dive in the ocean.

Carrick-on-Suir Camphill Community
Castle Street,
Carrick-on-Suir, Tipperary, Republic of Ireland

Small residential community in county Tipperary. Part of the Camphill Community (registered charity CHY5861) their emphasis is on living a caring and meaningful life.

Challenges Worldwide
54 Manor Place,
Edinburgh, Midlothian EH3 7EH

Volunteers with professional skills and experience needed to work on their many projects. Registered Charity SCO 28814.

Changing Worlds
11 Doctors Lane,
Chaldon, Surrey CR3 5AE

E: ask@changingworlds.co.uk
T: +44 (0) 1883 340 960
www.changingworlds.co.uk

Changing Worlds is a small, friendly organisation with charitable aims. We focus on providing a personal service – we know everyone on first name terms and handpick every group of applicants we send out. This ethos has successfully sent over 1200 people on once-in-a-lifetime trips, and we're proud to say that a quarter of our applicants come from recommendations.

We offer paid and voluntary placements in: Argentina; Australia; China; Dubai; Ghana; Honduras; India; Kenya; Latvia; Madagascar; New Zealand; Romania; Serbia;South Africa; Thailand; and Uganda;

So, if you like the idea of travel, meeting people and don't mind working hard then this is for you!

Cicerones de Buenos Aires Asociación Civil
J J Biedma 883,
Buenos Aires 1405, Argentina

Volunteering in Argentina: Cicerones in Buenos Aires works in a friendly atmosphere ensuring contact with local people, experiencing the city the way it should be!

City Year
Headquarters, 287 Columbus Avenue,
Boston, MA 02116, USA

City Year unites young people of all backgrounds for a demanding year of community service and leadership development throughout the US. This organisation recruits from US only.

CMS (Church Mission Society)
Watlington Road, Oxford, Oxfordshire OX4 6BZ

Offering more of a learning experience than a giving one, the CMS runs three- to four-week Encounter programmes in Africa, Asia, the Middle East and Eastern Europe for Christians aged 18-30.

Concordia International Volunteers
2nd Floor, 19 North Street, Portslade, Brighton, East Sussex BN41 1DH

Concordia offers the opportunity to join international teams of volunteers working on short-term projects in 60 countries in Europe, North America, Latin-America, Africa and Asia.

Conservation Volunteers Australia
PO Box 423, Ballarat, VIC 3353, Australia

Offers projects across Australia, including tree planting, wildlife surveys, track building, year-round. Contribution for meals, accommodation and travel applies.

Conservation Volunteers New Zealand
Conservation Volunteers Head Office, PO Box 423,
Ballarat, VIC 3353, Australia

Offers projects year-round, including habitat restoration, tree planting, track building. Contribution for meals, accommodation and travel applies.

Cosmic Volunteers

3502 Scott's Lane, Sherman Mills, Suite 3147,
Philadelphia, PA 19101, USA

American non-profit organisation offering volunteer and internship programmes in China, Ecuador, Ghana, Guatemala, India, Kenya, Nepal, Peru, the Philippines, and Vietnam.

Cross-Border Development

Level 20, AIA Tower, 251A-301 Av. Comercial De Macau,
Macau SAR, China

Offers volunteer and paid internship placements in Macau. A unique opportunity to gain work experience whilst travelling.

Cross-Cultural Solutions

Tower Point 44, North Road,
Brighton, Sussex BN1 1YR

E: infouk@crossculturalsolutions.org
T: +44 (0) 1273 666 392
F: +44 (0) 845 458 2783
www.crossculturalsolutions.org

Founded in 1995, Cross-Cultural Solutions now operates volunteer programmes in 12 countries in partnership with sustainable community initiatives. As a registered UK charity, CCS brings people together to work side-by-side with members of the local community while sharing perspectives and cultural understanding. Volunteer trips are available for 1-12 weeks year-round. Visit CCS online or call: 0845 458 2781 / 2782.

Cultural Canvas Thailand

1001 N. Barcelona Street, Pensacola, FL 32501, USA

Offers unique and meaningful volunteer experiences in Chiang Mai, Thailand. Placements are available in the following areas: hill tribe education, HIV/AIDS prevention, women's empowerment, and Burmese refugee education and assistance.

Discover Adventure Ltd.

Throope Down House, Blandford Road,
Coombe Bissett, Salisbury, SP5 4LN

Trips that are designed to be challenging, to push your limits. They are not holidays! They involve preparation in terms of fundraising and improving fitness. Discover Adventure challenges come in many varieties - trekking, cycling, horse-trekking, multi-activity, survival and sailing.

Discover Nepal

GPO Box: 20209, Kathmandu, Nepal

The aim of Discover Nepal is to provide opportunities for the involvement in the development process, and to practically contribute towards the socioeconomic development of the country.

Earthwatch Institute
256 Banbury Road,
Oxford OX2 7DE

E: info@earthwatch.org.uk
T: +44 (0) 1865 318 831
F: +44 (0) 1865 311 383
www.earthwatch.org.uk

Make a difference on your Gap Year! Work alongside leading scientists around the world and help solve pressing environmental problems. With hundreds of expeditions on over 50 research projects to choose from, conduct hands-on conservation research in stunning locations whilst having an experience of a lifetime. Find out more on our website.

Ecoteer
23 Bearsdown Close, Eggbuckland,
Plymouth, Devon PL6 5TX

Community-based placements in 40 plus countries and most are free! Volunteer with us and make everlasting friends across the whole world!

Ecuador Volunteer
Yánez Pinzón, N25-106 y Av. Colón, Quito, Ecuador

A non-profit organization that offers volunteer work opportunities in social, environment, educational and community areas around Ecuador.

EIL (Experiment for International Living)
287 Worcester Road,
Malvern, Worcestershire WR14 1AB

Worldwide volunteering. A typical programme lasts between two and three months. Host countries include Argentina, Brazil, India, Morocco, Nigeria and South Africa.

Essential Croatia
11, Plymouth Drive, Bramhall,
Stockport, Cheshire SK7 2JB

Griffon Vulture and nature protection programme. Volunteer opportunities available year round on the beautiful and upspoilt island of Cres-Croatia.

Fauna Forever Tambopata
TReeS-Peru, PO Box 28,
Puerto Maldonado, Madre de Dios, Peru

Volunteer researchers needed for wildlife project in the Peruvian Amazon. Fauna Forever Tambopata is a wildlife monitoring project based in the Amazon rainforest of Tambopata in south-eastern Peru.

Federation EIL International Office
70 Landmark Hill , Suite 204,
Brattleboro, Windham County VT 05301, USA

Volunteers required for their international partnership programme. They combine international community service projects with language training and homestay opportunities in 14 countries.

visit: www.changingworlds.co.uk

Friends of Conservation
Kensington Charity Centre, Charles House, 375 Kensington High Street
Kensington, London W14 8QH

There are some opportunities to volunteer on overseas projects such as the Namibian based Cheetah Conservation Fund. Volunteers are also needed in the UK and at their head office in London. Registered Charity No. 328176.

Gap Guru
Town Hall, Market Place,
Newbury, RG14 5AA

With a wide range of projects to choose from as a GapGuru volunteer, you could help provide street children education or track down a story for a local newspaper.

Gap Year South Africa
PO Box 592,
Cambridge CB1 0ES

Specialises in sports coaching, teaching, HIV/AIDS and health awareness, and environmental awareness projects in South Africa. Our project duration is between five weeks and three months.

Gapforce
530 Fulham Road,
Fulham, London SW6 5NR

Gapforce has established itself as a leading provider for enjoyable gap adventures worldwide including volunteering. It is the parent company of Trekforce and Greenforce.

Gapkenya.com
Old Farm House, Pen-y-Banc, Oakley Park
Llandinam, Powys SY17 5BE

Teaching, medical, community and sports projects from six weeks to three months, affordable, flexible placements with an experienced support team.

Glencree Centre for Peace and Reconciliation
Glencree, Enniskerry, County Wicklow, Republic of Ireland

Glencree welcomes international volunteers who provide practical help in exchange for a unique experience of working with those building peace in Ireland, Britain and beyond.

Global Action Nepal
Baldwins, Eastlands Lane,
Cowfold, West Sussex RH13 8AY

Projects are always closely in harness with grass roots level needs, focusing on community-led, participatory development. Registered Charity No. 1090773.

233

Global Vision International
3 High Street,
St Albans, Hertfordshire AL3 4ED

With unparalled in-country support, GVI volunteers benefit from exceptional training and a careers abroad job placement scheme.

Global Volunteer Network
PO Box 30-968,
Lower Hutt, 5040, New Zealand

Volunteer through the Global Volunteer Network to support communities in need around the world. Volunteer placements include schools, refugee camps, wildlife sanctuaries and nature reserves.

Global Volunteers
375 East Little Canada Road,
St. Paul, MN 55117-1628, USA

Have opportunities worldwide. The work is hard, rewarding and diverse, from repairing old school houses in Third World countries to social work within a Native American village.

Grangemockler Camphill Community
Temple Michael, Grangemockler,
Carrick-on-Suir,
Tipperary, Republic of Ireland

Part of the Camphill Community (registered charity CHY5861), situated in County Tipperary. A community for adults which places special emphasis on integration with the local community.

Greenforce
530 Fulham Road,
Fulham, London SW6 5NR

Greenforce is a not-for-profit organisation offering voluntary and paid work overseas. With ten years experience and a range of opportunities, Greenforce will have a programe to suit you.

Habitat for Humanity Great Britain
46 West Bar Street,
Banbury, Oxfordshire OX16 9RZ

Working in over 90 countries, Habitat for Humanity aims to eliminate poverty housing and homelessness. Volunteer teams travel to their chosen country to spend two weeks living and working alongside future homeowners and the local community. Charity Number 1043641.

Hope For The Nations Children's Charity
23 Caldervale, Orton Longueville,
Peterborough, Cambridgeshire PE2 7HX

Join our work with orphans and widows, feeding programmes and micro-enterprises in Sub-Sahara Africa.

i volunteer
D-134, 1st Floor, East of Kailash
New Delhi, 110065, India

Volunteering opportunites are shown on their website. You could end up working in an orphanage, on a helpline, on relief effort or in a school.

ICYE (Inter Cultural Youth Exchange) UK
Latin America House, Kingsgate Place,
London NW6 4TA

Sends people aged between 18 and 30 to work in voluntary projects overseas in including counselling centres, human rights NGOs, farms, orphanages and schools for the disabled. Registered Charity No. 1081907.

i-to-i
Woodside House, 261 Low Lane,
Leeds, Yorkshire LS18 5NY

At i-to-i, we work in partnership with locally run projects in over 30 countries offering you the chance to make a difference on your next trip in a safe, supported, and sustainable manner.

IVCS
12 Eastleigh Avenue, South Harrow, Middlesex HA2 0UF UK

IVCS is a small UK registered charity (No. 285872) supporting sustainable development projects in rural India, and offering opportunities to stay in one.

IVS (International Voluntary Service)
Thorn House, 5 Rose Street,
Edinburgh, Midlothian EH2 2PR

IVS exchanges volunteers with over 40 countries, mainly for international voluntary projects (living and working with a group on two to four week projects).

Josephite Community Aid
3 Nixon Avenue, Ashfield, NSW 2131, Australia

Australian organisation committed to helping poor and underprivileged with the aid of volunteers.

Karen Hilltribes Trust
Midgley House, Spring Lane, Heslington
York, North Yorkshire YO10 5DX

The Karen Hilltribes Trust (Registered Charity No. 1093548) sends volunteers to teach English in Thailand. You will live with a Karen Hilltribe family and your placement can be between six and ten months teaching five days a week.

Kings World Trust for Children
7 Deepdene, Haslemere, Surrey GU27 1RE

The Kings World Trust for Children is a UK-based charity (No. 1024872) which aims to provide a caring home, an education and skills training for orphaned and homeless children and young people in south India.

L'Arche
GY08, Freepost BD 3209,
Keighley, West Yorkshire BD20 9BR

E: info@larche.org.uk
T: +44 (0) 800 917 1337
F: +44 (0) 1535 656426
www.larche.org.uk

L'Arche is an international movement where people with and without learning difficulties share life together. There are communities in 34 countries. Volunteers are involved in all aspects of community life, are trained and supported, have free board and accommodation, a modest income and other benefits.

Latin Link Step Teams
Latin Partners, 87 London Street,
Reading, Berkshire RG1 4QA

Latin Link sends teams to work in mission with Latin American Christians every spring, from March to July, and summer for three to seven weeks. Registered Charity No. 1020826.

Lattitude Global Volunteering
44 Queen's Road,
Reading, Berkshire RG1 4BB

With 35 years of experience, Lattitude is a charity (No. 272761) which sends almost 2000 young people on overseas volunteering placements annually. Typical projects last four to nine months and are open to all young people aged 17-25.

Madventurer
Mad HQ, The Old Smithy,
Corbridge, Northumberland NE45 5QD

Offer group community projects in towns and villages in Ghana, Kenya, Uganda, Tanzania, South Africa, Fiji, Peru, Thailand, Vietnam and India.

Oasis UK
75 Westminster Bridge Road, Lambeth, London SE1 7HS

A Christian charity (No. 1026487) offering volunteering opportunities in the UK and worldwide, from two weeks to two years.

Orangutan Foundation
7 Kent Terrace, Regent's Park, London NW1 4RP

Participate in hands on conservation fieldwork that really makes a difference and see orangutans in their natural habitat.

Outreach International
Bartlett's Farm, Hayes Road,
Compton Dundon, Somerset TA11 6PF

Outreach International places committed volunteers in carefully selected projects on the Pacific coast of Mexico, Sri Lanka, Cambodia, Costa Rica, Ecuador and the Galapagos Islands.

Oyster Worldwide Limited
Hodore Farm,
Hartfield,
East Sussex TN7 4AR

E: emailus@oysterworldwide.com
T: +44 (0) 1892 770 771
www.oysterworldwide.com

Oyster is the specialist gap-year provider with links to over 40 volunteer projects. Oyster offers a distinctive personal approach from their experienced destination managers and overseas representatives who will offer support and guidance from application to completion of the placement.

Our unique voluntary placements range from working with bears in Europe to orphanage work in Africa. Placements with carefully selected groups of likeminded individuals ensure a fantastic experience with returned participant contact and advice.

Oyster's longer placements (three to six months) allow for immersion into a new culture.

Oyster include a one to one briefing, group pre-departure safety and skills course, return flights and language training where necessary.

Peace River Refuge & Ranch
PO Box 1127, 2545 Stoner Lane,
Zolfo Springs, FL 33890, USA

Peace River Refuge & Ranch is a non-profit-making exotic animal sanctuary located in Florida.

Its all-volunteer staff provides long-term care for confiscated, abused, neglected or unwanted exotic animals (from tigers to bats) to prevent them from being destroyed.

Pepper
Hazelpits Farm, Ulcombe Road,
Headcorn, Kent TN27 9LD

Pepper is a unique gap-year and adventure travel company offering tailor-made one to three month experiences, as well as custom trips, in South Africa.

Peru's Challenge
(Ultimate Tours),
Urb. Ingenieros D-2-12, Larapa,
San Jeronimo, Cuzco, Peru

Join a volunteer and travel programme and assist the work of charity organisation, Peru's Challenge, in rural communities in Peru.

Project Trust
The Hebridean Centre,
Isle of Coll, Argyll PA78 6TE

Project Trust (Charity No. SC025668) offers placements in over 20 countries departing in January, August or September.

Projects include teaching, social work, outdoor activities instruction, journalism, conservation and medical projects.

Projects Abroad
Aldsworth Parade,
Goring, Sussex BN12 4TX

E: info@projects-abroad.co.uk
T: +44 (0) 1903 708300
F: +44 (0) 1903 501026
www.projects-abroad.co.uk

With Projects Abroad you can enjoy adventurous foreign travel with a chance to do a worthwhile job. Over 4000 places are available each year to teach conversational English (no TEFL required) or gain experience in medicine, conservation, journalism, business and many other professions.

Placements are available throughout the year and last from two weeks upwards. Volunteers receive substantial overseas support and are not isolated.

No teaching qualifications or local languages are needed. All degree disciplines welcomed.

Volunteers are needed in Argentina, Bolivia, Brazil, Cambodia, China, Costa Rica, Ethiopia, Fiji, Ghana, India, Jamaica, Mexico, Moldova, Mongolia, Morocco, Nepal, Pakistan, Peru, Romania, Senegal, South Africa, Sri Lanka, Tanzania, Thailand and Togo.

Quest Overseas
15a Cambridge Grove,
Hove, East Sussex BN3 3ED

E: info@questoverseas.com
T: +44 (0) 1273 777 206
F: +44 (0) 1273 204 928
www.questoverseas.com

Quest Overseas specializes in gap-year adventures into the very heart and soul of South America and Africa. With over ten years of experience, we offer volunteers the chance to understand life far removed from home. Our team projects and expeditions (six weeks to three months) take you to parts seldom visited by others, and all make a positive impact on the communities we work with.

'a rollercoaster ride!' Tom Sale, Borneo

- Sustainable community and environmental projects combined with adventure
- Borneo, Costa Rica & Nicaragua and India
- 10, 7, 5 and 3 and a half week expeditions available

raleighinternational.org
info@raleigh.org.uk
020 7183 1270

YEAR OUT
GROUP

Raleigh International
207 Waterloo Road,
Southwark, London SE1 8XD

E: info@raleigh.org.uk
T: +44 (0) 20 7183 1283
F: +44 (0) 20 7504 8094
www.raleighinternational.org

Since 1984 our youth and education charity has been helping people from all walks of life get out there and undertake challenging adventure expeditions. Volunteering on sustainable community and environmental projects you'll develop new skills, meet people from all backgrounds and make a real difference. You could be providing clean water for communities in Costa Rica, helping to conserve elephants with the WWF in India or protecting coral reefs in Borneo.

Real Gap Experience
1 Meadow Road,
Tunbridge Wells, Kent TN1 2YG

Real Gap offers a wide and diverse range of programmes. These include: volunteering, conservation, adventure travel and expeditions, sports, teaching English, round the world, paid working holidays and learning.

Rempart
1 rue des Guillemites, Paris, 75004, France

Rempart, a union of conservation associations organises short voluntary work in France. The projects are all based around restoration and maintenance of historic sites and buildings.

Skillshare International UK
126 New Walk, Leicester LE1 7JA

Recruits professionals from different sectors to share their skills, experience and knowledge with local partner organisations in Africa and Asia as volunteers.

Smile Society
Udayrajpur, Madhyamgram, 9 no railgate
Kolkata, West Bengal 700129 India

SMILE Society invite international volunteers and students to join us in our welfare projects, international work camps, summer camps, internship programmes and volunteer projects in India.

Spirit of Adventure Trust
PO Box 2276, Auckland, New Zealand

Become part of the volunteer crew on one of the Trust's youth development voyages around New Zealand each year.

SPW (Students Partnership Worldwide)
7 Tufton Street,
Westminster, London SW1P 3QB

SPW run Health Education and Community Resource Programmes in South Asia and Africa. Volunteers are asked to fundraise a donation to the charity.

Starfish Ventures Ltd
PO Box 9061,
Epping, Essex CM16 7WU

Starfish has a volunteer placement for you, whatever your skills, they can be put to good use in our various projects in Thailand.

Sumatran Orangutan Society
The Old Music Hall, 106-108 Cowley Road,
Oxford OX4 1JE

SOS works with local communities living alongside orangutan habitats, helping them work towards a more sustainable future for their forests. Registered charity No. 1085600.

Sunrise International UK Ltd
71a Church Road,
Hove, Sussex BN3 2BB

Specialist for volunteer projects in China, offering volunteer opportunities of two weeks to one year in social, environment, education, medical, journalism and community areas around China.

Tanzed
80 Edleston Road, Crewe, Cheshire CW2 7HD

Working alongside Tanzanian nursery teachers as a classroom assistant you will be living in a rural village with plenty of opportunity to contribute to the community using your energy and enthusiasm. Registered Charity No. 1064659.

Task Brasil Trust
PO Box 4901, Rotherhithe, London SE16 3PP

Charity helping impoverished children in Brazil. Volunteers always needed. Registered Number 1030929.

The Book Bus Foundation
c/o VentureCo Worldwide,
The Ironyard, 64 -66 Market Place
Warwick CV34 4SD

E: volunteer@thebookbus.org
T: +44 (0) 1926 411 122
www.thebookbus.org

Book Bus volunteers use storytelling, artwork, puppet-making and a host of other media to bring to life the worlds within storybooks. The Book Bus provides a mobile service and actively promotes literacy to underpriviledged communities in Zambia and Ecuador. We can take a maximum of 12 volunteers plus our permanent staff at any time. See also VentureCo. Registered charity no. 1117359.

visit: www.changingworlds.co.uk

The Bridge Camphill Community
Main Street,
Kilcullen, Kildare, Republic of Ireland

Registered charity (CHY5861) in County Kildare working with adults after they leave the sister community of Camphill Dunshane.

The Ethical Project Company
Stowford Manor Farm, Wingfield,
Trowbridge, Wiltshire BA14 9LH

Join a team of people of various ages on a trip to Tanzania or India to do a mixture of volunteering in primary schools and fair trade travel.

The Gorilla Organisation
110 Gloucester Avenue,
Camden Town, London NW1 8HX

Formerly the Dian Fossey Gorilla Fund, the Gorilla Organisation (Registered Charity No. 1117131) list various events where you can raise money for the fund. Also lookibng for volunteers.

The Leap Overseas Ltd
121-122 High Street,
Marlborough, Wiltshire SN8 1LZ

E: info@theleap.co.uk
T: +44 (0) 1672 519922
F: +44 (0) 1672 519944
www.theleap.co.uk

Team or solo placements in Africa, Asia or South America. Volunteer to get stuck into our unique mix of eco-tourism, community and conservation projects. Connect with local people and enjoy the satisfaction that comes from making a real impact.

The Worldwrite Volunteer Centre
Millfields Lodge, 201 Millfields Road,
Lea Bridge, London E5 0AL

Join WORLDwrite's campaign for young volunteers who feel strongly about global inequality, want to make an impact and use film to do it. Registered charity No. 1060869.

The Year Out Group
Queensfield, 28 King's Road,
Easterton, Wiltshire SN10 4PX

E: info@yearoutgroup.org
T: +44 (0) 1380 816696
www.yearoutgroup.org

Year Out Group is an association of the UK's leading Year Out organisations that was launched in 2000 to promote the concepts and benefits of well-structured year out programmes, to promote models of good practice and to help young people and their advisers in selecting suitable and worthwhile projects.

The Group's member organisations provide a wide range of Year Out placements in the UK and overseas that cover courses and cultural exchanges, expeditions, volunteering and structured work placements. All members have agreed to adhere to the Group's Code of Practice and more detailed operational guidelines for each of the four sectors mentioned above. The Group's website also contains planning advice and guidelines for students and their advisers. These include questions that potential participants should ask providing organisations as they look for the programme that best suits their needs. Year Out Group monitors information published by its members for accuracy.

Year Out Group members are expected to put potential clients and their parents in contact with those that have recently returned, and consider it important that these references are taken up at least by telephone and, where possible, by meeting face-to-face. Group members include their complaints procedure in their contracts. Year Out Group can advise on making complaints but is not itself able to deal with them, though half the members are now participating in the Independent Dispute Settlement scheme arranged by the group. Nor is Year Out Group able to 'police' the 30,000 placements provided by its members but it can take action if any member is shown to be consistently negligent.

Since Year Out Group was formed its members have worked hard and continue to do so, to improve the service they offer their clients. However there will always be less-than-perfect organisations among members of a trade association and good associations that are not. There are some small specialist organisations with excellent reputations that cannot afford the membership fees. Whether or not an organisation is a member of Year Out Group, the questions in the student guidelines can be used to advantage.

Travellers Worldwide
7 Mulberry Close,
Ferring, West Sussex BN12 5HY

Various projects including tailor-made voluntary placements available. Qualifications aren't required and full induction and 24/7 support is offered in country.

Trekforce Worldwide
530 Fulham Road,
Fulham, London SW6 5NR

Trekforce offers expeditions in the jungle, mountains and desert, survival skills, teaching, trekking and conservation and community projects, new languages, work aboard programmes and expedition leadership training also available.

Tropical Adventures
Apartado 8-7800,
Paraiso, Cartago, Costa Rica

Provides volunteer tour packages for individuals, families and groups interested in exploring the culture, language and natural beauty of Costa Rica.

UNA Exchange
Temple of Peace, Cathays Park,
Cardiff, Glamorgan CF10 3AP

Arranges international volunteer projects worldwide: from Armenia to Zambia. The work is usually unskilled and you do not need qualifications or experience in most cases.

Utila Centre for Marine Ecology
Sherborne, Petworth Road,
Witley, Surrey GU8 5LP

Dive spectacular coral reefs, survey mega-fauna, investigate island ecology and contribute to applied conservation research.

VAP (Volunteer Action for Peace)
16 Overhill Road,
East Dulwich, London SE22 0PH

Organises international voluntary work projects in the UK each summer and recruits volunteers to take part in affordable placements abroad that range between two weeks and 12 months.

VentureCo Worldwide Ltd
The Ironyard, 64-66 The Market Place
Warwick CV34 4SD

T: +44 (0) 1926 411 122
www.ventureco-worldwide.com

Gap-year specialists in South America. Founded in 1999 with a wealth of experience, VentureCo organise combined volunteering and exploration placements throughout Central and South America.

VentureCo's small groups travel from the height of Machu Picchu to the Galapagos, Amazon jungle and Patagonia. Ventures include learning Spanish, volunteering on an aid project and joining an expedition.

All groups are accompanied by an experienced leader. Training starts in the UK (included in the price) before flying out to Latin America, and all our groups consist of people on their gap-year. Everyone who works in our friendly Warwick office is an experienced traveller keen to assist you and offer advice at any time.

See also our sister project - The Book Bus.

Village Education Project Kilimanjaro
Kilimanjaro Tanzania, Ms Katy Allen MBE, Mint Cottage, Prospect Road
Sevenoaks, Kent TN13 3UA

Live on Mount Kilimanjaro and teach English to village primary schoolchildren. Training is provided. Costs include airfare but exclude visa, spending money and insurance.

Vivisto Ltd
80 High Street, Winchester, Hampshire SO23 9AT

You can make a difference volunteering on our conservation and community programmes in South Africa.

Volunteer Latin America
London WC1N 3XX

Volunteer Latin America provides a comprehensive and affordable solution to finding volunteering opportunities and Spanish language schools in Central and South America.

Volunteers Making a Difference - vMaD
MaD for Good!, c/o Siem Reap Post Office,
Siem Reap, Siem Reap Province, Cambodia

This is a non profit organization offering international volunteer work opportunities abroad in Siem Reap, Cambodia. vMaD placements are all in rural areas, so you'll get to see the real Cambodia and experience the local culture.

Voluntours
6 Visser Street, Vorna Valley, Midrand,
Gauteng, 1685, South Africa

Volunteer in South Africa with a multiple award winning organisation in their community, wildlife and marine projects. A variety of short, medium and longer-term placements are available.

VSO (Voluntary Service Overseas)
317 Putney Bridge Road, Putney, London SW15 2PN

VSO has volunteering projects in the UK as well as overseas. Registered charity No. 313757.

WaterAid
2nd Floor, 47-49 Durham Street, Vauxhall, London SE11 5JD

WaterAid is an international charity enabling the world's poorest people access to safe water and sanitation. You can volunteer to help them in the UK.

Whipalong Volunteer Program
Plot 42, P O Box 63,
Kampersrus, Hoedspruit 1371, South Africa

Volunteer programmes in South Africa.

Willing Workers in South Africa (WWISA)
P O Box 2413, The Crags,
Plettenberg Bay, 6600, South Africa

WWISA are a volunteering organisation based in South Africa. Their core aim is to help bring desperately needed community development services to the poorly provisioned and frequently overlooked historically disadvantaged rural townships of the Bitou and Tsitsikamma regions.

Worldwide Experience
Ashley Adams Travel (UK) Ltd, Guardian House, Borough Road
Godalming, Surrey GU7 2AE

Worldwide Experience specialises in volunteer gap-year placements in conservation, marine and community projects throughout South Africa, Kenya, Malawi, Sri Lanka and India.

WorldWide Volunteering for Young People
7 North Street Workshops,
Stoke sub Hamdon, Somerset TA14 6QR

Registered charity (No. 1038253), set up to help people of all ages to find their ideal volunteering project either in the UK or in any country in the world.

WWOOF (World Wide Opportunities on Organic Farms)
PO Box 2154,
Winslow, Buckinghamshire MK18 3WS

Join WWOOF and participate in meaningful work that reconnects with nature, share the lives of people who have taken practical steps towards alternative, sustainable lifestyles.

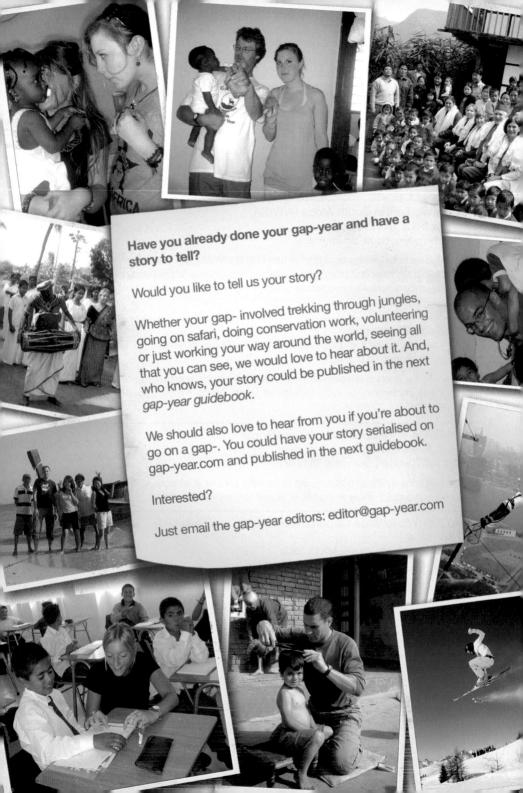

Have you already done your gap-year and have a story to tell?

Would you like to tell us your story?

Whether your gap- involved trekking through jungles, going on safari, doing conservation work, volunteering or just working your way around the world, seeing all that you can see, we would love to hear about it. And, who knows, your story could be published in the next *gap-year guidebook*.

We should also love to hear from you if you're about to go on a gap-. You could have your story serialised on gap-year.com and published in the next guidebook.

Interested?

Just email the gap-year editors: editor@gap-year.com

Chapter 9
Learning abroad

9   Learning abroad

While your **gap**-year will inevitably be about personal growth, because of all the new things you experience and see you, could build on this by using it as an opportunity to combine living and studying abroad.

This might not seem appealing if you've just 'escaped' from a period of intense study and exams, but consider this:

- The learning doesn't have to be goal oriented or laden with exam stress, you could learn a new skill and gain a qualification.
- You could pursue an interest, hobby or passion you haven't had time for before.
- You'll be able to explore and enrich your knowledge in your own way, rather than following a curriculum.
- You could also find you've added another dimension to your CV.
- You'll meet like-minded folk and have a lot of fun.

These are some of the things you could do:

Learn a language in-country, do a sports instructor course, music or drama summer schools, explore art, music, culture and learn about conservation. If you're not jaded with study or are at a time of life when a postgraduate qualification would be useful, and a career break possible, you could go for an academic year abroad. Another option for those of you who want to try to earn while you travel is to do a TEFL course.

Here's a good weblink for courses abroad: **www.studyabroaddirectory.com**

An academic year abroad

A good way of getting to know a place and its people in depth is to spend a whole academic year at a foreign school, either in Europe, the USA, or further afield. One possibility is an academic year before university:

- French Lycée.
- German Gymnasium.
- School in Spain.
- Spanish-speaking school in Argentina.

Which still leaves several months free for travel.

The most relevant EU education and training programmes are Comenius, ERASMUS, Lingua and Leonardo. For more information see:

Comenius: **www.britishcouncil.org/comenius.htm**

Erasmus: **www.britishcouncil.org/erasmus**

the gap-year guidebook 2010

Lingua:
www.ec.europa.eu/education/programmes/socrates/lingua/products_en.html

Leonardo:
www.ec.europa.eu/education/lifelong-learning-programme/doc82_en.htm

A scheme called Europass provides trainees in any EU country with a 'Europe-wide record of achievement for periods of training undertaken outside the home member state'. So ask the school: "Is this course recognised for a Europass?"

University exchange

If you want to spend up to a year abroad at a European university as part of the European Union's ERASMUS (EuRopean community Action Scheme for the Mobility of University Students) scheme, you'll need to have some working knowledge of the relevant language - so a **gap**-year could be the time to start, either studying overseas or in Britain. Information about Erasmus courses is usually given to students in their first year at university.

To apply for ERASMUS you must be an EU citizen. When you spend your time abroad, you continue to pay tuition fees or receive loans or grants as if you were at your university back home.

There's more information on: **www.britishcouncil.org/erasmus**

The scheme is also open to teaching and non-teaching staff at Higher Education and HE/FE institutions, as long as your home Higher Education Institution has a formal agreement with a partner in one of the eligible countries. It must also have an Erasmus University Charter awarded by the European Commission.

Postgraduate MA/visiting fellowship/exchange

Several universities in the UK have direct links to partnership programmes with others around the world, but if you want to widen your search, the Worldwide Universities Network (WUN) is a good place to start looking for exchange, overseas study and funding for research projects. It's a partnership of 16 research-led universities from Asia, Australasia, Europe and North America.

WUN's Research Mobility Programme funds a period of study overseas, for senior postgraduates and junior faculty, to establish and cultivate research links at an institutional and individual level between the partners in Europe, North America, south-east Asia and Australia. It is also

visit: www.gap-year.com

intended to encourage the personal and academic development of individuals early in their research careers.

Check out: **www.wun.ac.uk/aboutus.php**

Arts and culture

Art

If you want to go to art school, or have already been, no matter which art form interests you, travelling and soaking up the atmosphere is a good way to learn more and give you ideas for your own work. It's also a great opportunity to add to your portfolio.

You don't have to be an art student or graduate to enjoy the beauty of art and artefacts produced by different cultures. Most courses listed in this guidebook are open to anyone who wants to explore the arts in a bit more depth.

Culture

It's a cliché, but also true, that travel broadens the mind and you'll absorb much about the culture of the places you visit just by being there.

However, if you want to develop your understanding in more depth, maybe learn a bit of the language and discover some of your chosen country's history, then you could go for the cultural component of some of the language courses listed in the directory.

Design and fashion

Every year, when the new season's collections are shown on the world's fashion catwalks, it's clear that the designers have 'discovered' the fabrics, or decoration or style, of one region or another.

So for those with a passion for fashion a **gap**-year is a great opportunity to experience the originals for themselves. Wandering the streets in other countries, and seeing how other people put their 'look' together, can be an inspiration.

Then there's the opportunity to snap up, at bargain prices, all kinds of beautiful fabrics that would cost a fortune back home.

But if you wanted to use part of your **gap-** to find out more about fashion and design you could also join a fashion summer school in one of Europe's capitals, like the ones listed on this website:
www.learn4good.com/great_schools/fashion_design_career_courses.htm

Or why not India? The country's National Institute of Fashion Technology in Delhi runs summer schools for fashion stylists - here's the link: **www.nift.ac.in/**

Film, theatre and drama

If you're thinking of a short course in performing arts, the USA is one of the most obvious places to go - most famously the New York Film Academy, which has a very useful page for international students:
www.nyfa.com/film_school/student_information/international_student.php

The Academy runs summer schools in London, Paris, Florence, Colombia, China, Japan and South Korea

For a wider search try: **www.filmschools.com**

Or how about New Zealand? Try: **www.drama.org.nz**

If you want dance as well, the world's your oyster. You can learn salsa in Delhi (as well as in South America) and the traditional Indian Kathak dance in the USA. Here's a good place to start looking: **www.dir.yahoo.com/Arts/Performing_Arts/**

And then, of course, there's Bollywood. There are courses in film direction, cinematography, sound production and editing at the Film and Television Institutes of India, in Pune (south-west of Mumbai), which runs a number of courses for overseas students: **www.ftiindia.com**

Music

Whether you're into classical or pop, world music or traditional, there are vibrant music scenes all over the world.

From the studios that have sprung up in Dakar, the West African capital of Senegal, to the club scenes of Europe, to more formal schools, check out the opportunities to combine your interest with travel and maybe learn to play an instrument, if you don't already, or another one if you do.

We've checked online for short music courses, since the UNESCO site no

visit: www.gap-year.com

longer offers a directory, and although there are plenty out there, it's a case of searching by location.

Here's one for all UK summer schools, including music:
www.summer-schools.info/

Or how about helping out in a rock centre in Chennai, India?
www.unwindcenter.com

Media and journalism

Although the print media has been suffering from the global recession there are, of course, other options.

You may want to get into media/journalism but you're not the only one, so do thousands of others and the competition is intense. The skills you'll need could include media law, shorthand, knowledge of how local and national government works and, not least, the ability to construct an attention-grabbing story!

To get a job you may need to do more than gain a media studies degree or have on-the-job training in a newsroom.

It's, therefore, always a good idea to demonstrate your commitment and a **gap-** is a good time to do this. You can try contacting your local paper for a work experience placement, though don't expect to be paid!

Plus, if you search the internet there are plenty of internships in newsrooms - many of them in India, where there's still a lot of attachment to local and national newspapers.

We Googled 'journalism placements and internships' and found possibilities in Vietnam, Senegal, Hong Kong and California.

These websites may also be useful:
www.tigweb.org/resources/opps/
www.internews.org/default.shtm

Photography

Travelling offers you the chance to develop your skills as a photographer - after all almost everyone takes pictures to remember their travels.

But if you've always dreamed of turning professional, it's a chance to practice. You could be innovative by contacting a local newspaper or magazine and asking if they'll let you accompany one of their photographers on assignments. You won't be paid but you'll learn a lot and it might give you pictures to add to your portfolio.

For example, this year one of our gapper story contributors, Rachael, has provided some of the images to be found in this very guidebook. Can you tell which ones they are? Check out Rachael's story on page 263.

Languages

You learn a language much more easily and quickly if you're living in the country where it's spoken, but there's more than one reason to learn a new language. There's more to a language than just words: most language courses will include local culture, history, geography, religion, customs and current affairs - as well as food and drink. A language involves more than just translating your own thoughts into someone else's words. A new language brings a whole new way of thinking with it, and therefore a much deeper understanding of the people who shaped it and use it. For example, why do some languages have no future tense - is there a different way time is conceived?

Most people will know that the Icelanders have many different words for 'snow', but did you know that they have 85 words for 'storm'? You'll find plenty of local variations on that theme wherever you are.

Think laterally about where you want to study.

Spanish is spoken in many countries around the world, so you could opt for a Spanish course in South America, rather than Spain, and then go travelling around the country, or learn Portuguese in Brazil, where it's the main language, or perhaps French in Canada.

Be aware though that if you learn a language outside its original country you may learn a particular dialect that is only spoken in a specific region of the country as a whole. It may even be considered inferior by some people (or not understood) elsewhere in the country.

Finding the right place to learn

Universities often have international summer school centres or courses for foreign students, or there's the popular network of British Institutes abroad. And there are hundreds (probably thousands) of independent language colleges to choose from, either directly or through a language course organiser or agency in the UK.

The advantage in dealing with a UK-based organisation is that, if something goes wrong, it is easier to get it sorted out under UK law.

Using the internet

The following are some international language course websites that we have found from a basic internet search (but we've no idea how good they are - you need to check them out for yourselves):

www.languagecoursesabroad.co.uk
www.europa-pages.co.uk – for language courses in European countries.
www.ialc.org (International Association of Language Centres)
www.languagesabroad.co.uk
www.oise.com
www.cesalanguages.com

Living with a family

If enrolling on a language course sounds too much like school, another way of learning a language is staying with a family as an au pair or tutor (giving, say, English or music lessons to children) and going to part-time classes locally. See Chapter 7 - Working Abroad, for more details.

Language courses

Courses at language schools abroad can be divided into as many as ten different levels, ranging from tuition for the complete beginner to highly technical or specialised courses at postgraduate level. The usual classification of language classes, however, into 'beginner' or 'basic', 'intermediate' and 'advanced', works well. Within each of these levels there are usually subdivisions, especially in schools large enough to move students from one class to another with ease. When you first phone a school from abroad or send in an application form, you should indicate how good your knowledge of the language is.

You may be tested before being allocated your class, or you may be transferred from your original class to a lower or higher one, as soon as they find you are worse or better than expected.

Different schools will use different methods of teaching: if you know that you respond well to one style, check that is what your course offers. Foreign language lessons are often attended by a variety of nationalities, so they are almost always conducted in the language you are learning, forcing you to understand and respond without using English. In practice, however, most teachers can revert to English to explain a principle of grammar if a student is really stuck.

257

The smaller the class the better, though the quality of the teaching is most important - at more advanced levels, well-qualified graduate teachers should be available. Language schools and institutes show a mass of information, photographs and maps on their websites, so it's easy to find out if the school is near to places that interest you, whether it's in a city centre or near a coastal resort. The admissions staff should be happy to give you references from previous students.

Over the next few pages (and in the directory) we've listed some of the organisations offering language opportunities to gappers, from formal tuition to 'soaking it up' while you live with a family. We've split the organisations according to the languages they offer: Arabic, Chinese, French, German, Greek, Indonesian, Italian, Japanese, Portuguese, Russian and Spanish.

Arabic

Arabic is the language in which the *Qur'an* is written and, although there are translations into the local languages of Muslims around the world, there's also a lot of argument about the way they're translated. This has led to differences about what Islam means.

It's all a matter of interpretation of the roots of words and what's more there are two main versions of Arabic: Fousha - Modern Standard Arabic; and Aameya - Egyptian Colloquial Arabic. We've found one organisation that runs language courses in both: **www.languagesabroad.co.uk/egypt.html**

Chinese

As Chinese enterprises become global, the language is becoming a popular choice in UK schools, with as many as 400 state schools now offering lessons.

There are two main dialects: Cantonese: the language of most Chinese people living abroad, from Singapore to Europe and the USA. Cantonese is also spoken widely in the Guangdong and Guangxi provinces of mainland China and in Hong Kong and Macau.

Mandarin: is the official language of government, international relations and much education in China is undertaken in Mandarin. It is the more formal language and most students are advised to learn it.

Both languages are tonal (the same sound said in a different tone will change the meaning of a word) and therefore can be quite difficult for English-speakers to learn. The different tonal pronunciation, vowels and consonants effectively turn Mandarin and Cantonese into two different languages, although both use the same written characters. There are many, many other Chinese dialects, including Hokkien, Hakka, Wu and Hui.

You can find course information at:
www.mandarinhouse.cn/chinesecourses.htm

It has a choice of 12 different courses in Chinese, including one for expatriates, in Beijing or Shanghai.

visit: www.gap-year.com

French

Languages have changed over time as they have been introduced to other parts of the world from their home countries and then developed in their own directions. Then there are the local dialects. French covers French as it's spoken in France, but then there's also Swiss French, Belgian French and Canadian French.

There's a busy French community in the UK, a large French Lycée in London and more than one teaching institute run by French nationals, so there are plenty of opportunities to carry on developing your French language skills when you return to the UK.

German

German has many very strong dialects (particularly in Austria, Switzerland and much of south Germany), and it is important to bear this in mind if you want to study German academically, or use it for business, in which case you may need to be learning and practising *Hochdeutsch* (standard German).

Many universities in Germany, Austria and Switzerland run summer language schools for foreign students.

Contact:
German Embassy
23 Belgrave Square
Cultural Department
London SW1X 8PZ
Tel: +44 (0) 20 7824 1300.

Their website has a section on studying in Germany: **www.london.diplo.de**

There's also a lively German community in the UK and many courses run by the Goethe Institut (**www.goethe.de/ins/gb/lon/enindex.htm**). So, there are plenty of opportunities to carry on practising your German when you get back.

the gap-year guidebook 2010

Greek

The thoughts of the great philosophers such as Socrates and Aristotle, upon whose ideas the foundations of western values were built, were written in ancient Greek.

Democracy, aristocracy, philosophy, pedagogy and psychology are just some of the many Greek terms that are part of our culture and language. Modern Greek is spoken by ten million Greek citizens and by about seven million others spread around the world. The Centre for the Greek Language is a good starting point: **www.greeklanguagecentre.co.uk/**

Α Β Γ Δ Ε Ζ Η Θ
Ι Κ Λ Μ Ν Ξ Ο Π
Ρ Σ Τ Υ Φ Χ Ψ Ω

α β γ δ ε ζ η θ
ι κ λ μ ν ξ ο π ρ
ς σ τ υ φ χ ψ ω

Indonesian

Based on the Malay trade dialect, Bahasa Indonesia is the national language of the Republic of Indonesia. In a country of more than 230 million people, who speak over 580 different dialects, having a national language makes communication easier, in much the same way as Hindi does in India.

There's no general greeting in Indonesian; there are different words specific to the time of day. But it's said to be an easy language to learn and Indonesia is such a popular backpacker destination it's likely to be worth making the effort.

Here's a web link to get you started: **www.expat.or.id/info/bahasa.html**

Italian

Schools vary from the very large to very small, each with its own character and range of courses in Italian, Italian culture, history, art, cooking and other subjects. As in language schools across most of Europe, the language is often taught in the morning with extracurricular activities in the afternoon. If you want to do a course from March onwards it is advisable to get in touch with them at least two months in advance, as courses and accommodation get booked up early.

Most schools can fix you up with accommodation before your trip, either with a family, bed and breakfast, half-board, or even renting a studio or flat. If you're part of a small group, you might prefer to arrange accommodation yourself through a local property-letting agent, but this can be tricky unless you have someone on the spot to help.

Japanese

If you can get to the Japanese Embassy in London you can look up a comprehensive guide in its large library called *Japanese Language Institutes* [based in Japan]. The library also has material on learning Japanese and stocks Japanese newspapers including the English-language *Japan Times*, which runs information on jobs in Japan.

There's information about studying in Japan on the embassy website, with guidance on the type of visa you will need if you want to teach English as a foreign language or do other types of work there.

Japanese Embassy,101-104 Piccadilly, London W1J 7JT
Tel: +44 (0) 20 7465 6500
www.uk.emb-japan.go.jp/en/embassy

Portuguese

You don't have to go to Portugal to learn Portuguese - it's the main language of Brazil too, so if you're heading for Latin America on your **gap-** try:
www.linguaserviceworldwide.com/learnportuguesebrazil.htm
www.languageschoolsguide.com/Brazil.cfm

Russian

We suggest you check with the Foreign & Commonwealth Office before making any plans to travel to Russia to study.

That said, we found the following websites offering Russian language lessons in Russia:
www.abroadlanguages.com/learn/russia
www.eurolingua.com/learn_russian.htm
www.languagesabroad.com/countries/russia.html

Spanish

Spanish is the third most widespread language in the world after English and Mandarin Chinese. Over 400 million people in 23 countries are Spanish speakers - Mexico and all of Central and South America (except Brazil) designate Spanish as their official language.

Forms of Spanish can also be heard in Guinea, the Philippines and in Ceuta and Melilla in North Africa. But if you go to a language school inside or outside of Spain, you will probably be learning formal Castilian.

For information about universities and language courses, try:
Spanish Embassy, Education Department, 20 Peel Street, London W8 7PD
Tel: +44 (0) 20 7727 2462

If you want to learn it in Latin America try:
www.expanish.com
www.spanish-language.org/

Multi languages

There are companies offering courses in many different languages. When you're getting references, make sure they're not just for the company - but specifically for the country/course you're interested in.

the gap-year guidebook 2010

TEFL

Recent research has revealed that, within the next ten years roughly half the world will be using English, so there's never been a better time to do a TEFL course. Like having a sports instructors' certificate, a TEFL qualification is useful if you want to earn a little money for expenses on a **gap-** and it's a passport that will get you into many countries around the world and in close contact with the people. For more information on getting a TEFL qualification go to Chapter 7 - Working Abroad.

Sport

There are sports courses for all types at all levels, from scuba diving for beginners to advanced ski instructor qualification courses, in pretty much every country in the world. Of course, if you manage to get qualified as an instructor, you may be able to use it to get a job for the rest of your **gap-**year.

Make sure the course offers the qualifications that will be useful to you and check that the instructors are properly qualified. Most important is to make sure that you have the necessary insurance - take a look at any of the sport websites and you'll find out that accidents do happen (**www.bungeezone.com** - their disasters page is particularly scary) and if you slip whilst up a mountain, injuries tend to be a bit more serious - and expensive - than a sprained ankle.

That said, learning a sport abroad is a great way to meet new people, experience the local culture and have a really energetic, fun **gap-**year.

Around the world career break

Rachael, 28, took a career break to travel around the world, both independently and on some organised treks.

In her case, it was certainly a life-changing experience – she's now working in Australia!

Rachael visited Brazil, Argentina, Chile, Peru, Bolivia, Ecuador, Galapagos Islands, Peru, Panama, Costa Rica, Honduras, Nicaragua, Belize, Guatemala, Mexico, New Zealand, Australia and China.

She started her **gap-** with the Rio Carnival "quite a baptism of fire!" before joining an overland trip from Rio to Quito, then meeting up with her parents in the Galapagos Islands before doing an organised local transport tour from Panama City to Mexico City.

Rachael and a friend organised their own independent travel through New Zealand and Australia before going on an organised trip to China.

She said: "This was quite simply the best thing I have ever done in my life. I always said that I wanted to be able to travel and not worry about money, and be able to do whatever I wanted while I was away. I was lucky enough that this was the case. I got to meet people that are now some of my closest friends, and I got to see things that I had only ever dreamed of. I am still amazed at what I did, and saw and trying to digest it all- it doesn't seem real at times."

Her advice to gappers? "Make sure you plan well, especially budget wise! Pay for as much of it as possible before you leave, and make sure you have money for unforeseen circumstances such as ferries breaking down in the Caribbean and having to be airlifted off the island, not being able to get Russian visas and having to change your route home… Anything can happen!

"But most of all - do it. It is possibly the scariest thing I have done, and on my way to the airport I wondered what I was doing - leaving the security of everything behind, but it was the best experience of my life"

Anything she wished she'd done differently? "I wish I had packed less! I can't emphasise how heavy 20kg is when you have to carry it around with you everyday, and haul it onto the roof of chicken buses, or racks on Chinese sleeper trains."

As for returning to normal, well in Rachael's case – not really, not least because she's working in Australia: "I still consider myself to be on holiday, and try my best to make the most of being in a new city and country. Getting out at the weekends and being near new things to see and do makes it feel like the adventures are continuing."

And it's likely to stay that way: "I'm planning my next trip already! I was hoping that the travel bug would be out of my system after this trip, but it has just made me realise how big the world is and how many awesome things there are to see out there."

Rachael's dream is to become a travel photographer and we at **gap-**year think she's pretty good. She's contributed a couple of pictures, which appear in other places in this very book. Can you spot them? (Answer on page 12)

Academic Year Abroad

African Leadership Academy
PO Box 529,
Hurlingham, 2070, South Africa

Offers high school students worldwide the opportunity for an unparalleled African experience, by studying abroad or spending a gap-year with them.

Class Afloat
97 Kaulbach Street, PO Box 10,
Lunenburg NS, B0J 2C0, Canada

Sail on a tall ship to exotic ports around the world and earn university credits. Also offers Duke of Edinburgh's Award Scheme.

Council on International Educational Exchange (CIEE)
300 Fore Street,
Portland, ME 04101, USA

CIEE offer a wide range of international study programs such as study abroad programs for US students, gap-year abroad programs and seasonal work in the USA for international students.

Institute of International Education
1350 Edgmont Avenue, Suite 1100,
Chester, PA 19013, USA

Search for international education opportunities by country, language, subject and many other criteria.

Office of International Education, Iceland
Neshagi 16, 107 Reykjavík, Iceland

A service organisation for all higher education institutions in Iceland. From their website you can find information on all the higher education institutions in the country, as well as practical things to do before arriving, visas, admissions, residence permits, *etc.*

Queenstown Resort College
PO Box 1566, Queenstown 9348, New Zealand

Offers a diverse range of world class courses and programmes including diplomas, internships, a range of English language courses, leadership development programmes, and short courses for visitors.

265

Scuola Leonardo da Vinci
via Brunelleschi 4, Florence, 50123 Italy

One of Italy's largest provider of in-country Italian courses in Italy, for students who wish to experience living and studying in Italy.

The English-Speaking Union
Dartmouth House, 37 Charles Street,
Mayfair, London W1J 5ED

The English-Speaking Union organises educational exchanges in high schools (mostly boarding) in the US and Canada, awarding up to 30 scholarships a year to gap-year students.

The US-UK Fulbright Commission
Fulbright House, 62 Doughty Street,
Bloomsbury, London WC1N 2JZ

EAS is the UK's only official source of information on the US education system, providing objective advice through in-house advising and a variety of outreach events.

Where There Be Dragons
3200 Carbon Place, Suite #102,
Boulder, CO 80301, USA

Runs semester, gap-year and college-accredited programmes in the Andes, China, Himalayas and more.

Art

Aegean Center for the Fine Arts
Paros , Cyclades 84400 Greece

Offers small group and individualized study in the visual arts, creative writing and music. Facilities are located in two stunning locations: the Aegean islands of Greece and Italy's Tuscany.

Art History Abroad (AHA)
The Red House, 1 Lambsets Street,
Eye, Suffolk IP23 7AG

We specialise in taking students to the great centres of art in Italy. Our method of onsite study in groups no larger than nine is unique to AHA. Six week courses run throughout the year as well as shorter courses in the summer.

ARTIS - Art Research Tours
1709 Apache Drive,
Medford, OR 97501, USA

Provide high quality international art and cultural study abroad programmes at affordable prices, located in beautiful art capitals throughout the world.

Atelier Montmiral
Rue Gambetta, Castelnau de Montmiral,
81140, France

Atelier Montmiral offer painting and printmaking courses in south-west France. Courses offered are six or ten days in length and can accommodate all levels of ability.

Hellenic International Studies in the Arts (HISA)
Box 11, Paroikia, Paros, Cyclades, Greece

HISA endorses the gap-year concept and encourages students to immerse themselves in the culture, historical and classical landscape of Paros, Greece.

SACI Florence
Palazzo dei Cartelloni, Via Sant'Antonino, 11,
Firenze, 50123, Italy

A non-profit educational institution for students seeking fully accredited studio art, design, and liberal arts instruction.

SAI - Study Abroad Italy
7151 Wilton Avenue, Suite 202, Sebastopol, CA 95472, USA

In conjunction with Florence University SAI offer the chance for international students to live in the heart of this bustling Renaissance city while experiencing modern Florentine life.

Studio Escalier
Turner Towers - Suite 9H, 135 Eastern Parkway,
Brooklyn, NY 11238, USA

Admission to their three month intensive courses in painting and drawing is by advance application only. Anyone is welcome to apply who has a dedicated interest in working from the human figure.

SuperBon Painting Retreat
Atelier Snow and White, Le Château,
Saussignac, 24240, France

SuperBon painting retreat is located in south-west France and is a one-week hands-on learning experience designed to give the artist, more freedom of expression in their work.

The British Institute of Florence
Piazza Strozzi 2,
Florence, 50123, Italy

E: info@britishinstitute.it
T: +39 (0) 55 2677 8200
F: +39 (0) 55 2677 8222
www.britishinstitute.it

Located in the historic centre of Florence within minutes of the main galleries, museums and churches, the British Institute offers courses in history of art, Italian language and life drawing. Email and internet access, student support and accommodation service are available. Courses run throughout the year from one to 12 weeks.

The Marchutz School
The Institute for American Universities, 1830 Sherman Avenue,
Suite 402, Evanston, IL 60201, USA

Offers artists a unique opportunity to live, learn and grow in the incomparable Provencal setting of Aix-en-Provence, France.

The Year Out Group
Queensfield, 28 King's Road,
Easterton, Wiltshire SN10 4PX

E: info@yearoutgroup.org
T: +44 (0) 1380 816696
www.yearoutgroup.org

See main entry under volunteering.

Chinese

Hong Kong Institute of Languages
6/F Wellington Plaza, 56-58 Wellington Street,
Central, Hong Kong, China

Courses available in Mandarin and Cantonese. Good central location on Hong Kong Island.

Hong Kong Language Learning Centre
604, 6/F Emperor Group Centre, 288 Hennessy Road,
Wanchai, Hong Kong, China

Language school in Hong Kong which specialises in Cantonese and Mandarin conversation and Chinese reading and writing for expatriates, locals and overseas Chinese.

Talking Mandarin Language Centre
8/F, Full View Building, 140-142 Des Voeux Road,
Central, Hong Kong, China

Language school in Central, Hong Kong, that teaches both Cantonese and Mandarin.

WorldLink Education US Office
1904 3rd Avenue, Suite 633,
Seattle, WA 98101, USA

WorldLink Education's Chinese language programme immerses you in Mandarin Chinese through class instruction, after-class tutoring, language exchanges with native speakers and a range of optional extra activities.

Academic Programs International (API)
301 Camp Craft Road, Suite 100,
Austin, TX 78746, USA

An independent study abroad organization, offering living, travel, educational, and cultural opportunities for US students in Argentina, Costa Rica, England, France, Hungary, Ireland, Italy, Mexico, Poland and Spain.

Alderleaf Wilderness College
18715, 299th Avenue SE,
Monroe, Snohomish, WA 98272, USA

A centre for traditional ecological knowledge offering innovative wilderness survival, animal tracking and nature courses in the Pacific Northwest of the United States.

American Institute for Foreign Study (AIFS)
River Plaza, 9 West Broad Street,
Stamford, CT 06902, USA

One of the oldest, largest and most respected cultural exchange organizations in the world. Their programmes include college study abroad, au pair placement, camp counselors and staff.

Center for Purposeful Living
3983 HSA Circle,
Winston-Salem, Forsyth, NC 27101, USA

Provides full scholarships for a year-long service-learning experience that instils practical skills for a balanced and purposeful life.

Cultural Experiences Abroad (CEA)
2005 West 14th Street, Suite 113,
Tempe, AZ 85281-6977, USA

CEA sends thousands of students on study abroad programmes at multiple universities in 15 countries including Argentina, Australia, China, Costa Rica, Czech Republic, England, France, Germany, Ireland, Italy, Mexico, Poland, Russia, South Africa and Spain.

Eastern Institute of Technology
Private Bag 1201, Taradale,
Napier, Hawke's Bay, New Zealand

Te Manga Mâori - EIT in Hawke's Bay offers the opportunity to study the Maori language and culture from beginners through to advanced level.

9

Learning Abroad | Culture

El Casal
Balmes 163, 3/1,
Barcelona, 8008, Spain

Based in Barcelona, El Casal offers the chance to soak in Catalan culture through a programme specifically for gappers who want to learn Spanish.

Istituto di Lingua e Cultura Italiana Michelangelo
Via Ghibellina 88,
Florence, Tuscany 50122, Italy

The Michelangelo Institute offers cultural courses on art history, Italian language, literature, commerce and commercial correspondence, and *L'Italia oggi*.

Knowledge Exchange Institute (KEI)
63 Sickletown Road,,
West Nyack, NY 10994, USA

Study abroad and intern abroad programmes are designed to meet your academic, professional and personal interests.

Lexia Study Abroad
6 The Courtyard ,
Hanover, NH 03755, USA

Cultural study programmes that encourage students to connect with their community while pursuing academic research. Participate in the daily life and work of a community in countries worldwide.

Petersburg Studies
34 Wilkinson Street,
South Lambeth, London SW8 1DB

Offer a winter course designed to make St Petersburg accessible; its history, architecture, museums, music, literature and contemporary life are explored in the company of lecturers, guides and local contacts.

Road2Argentina
Anchorena 1676,
Capital Federal, Buenos Aires 1425, Argentina

Study abroad in Argentina and learn all about the country and its culture.

SIT Study Abroad
PO Box 676, 1 Kipling Road,
Brattleboro, VT 05302, USA

Offers undergraduate study abroad programmes in Africa, Asia and the Pacific, Europe, Latin America and the Caribbean, and the Middle East.

The John Hall Pre-University Course
9 Smeaton Road,
London SW18 5JJ

E: info@johnhallvenice.com
T: +44 (0) 20 8871 4747
www.johnhallvenice.com

John Hall Venice is an eight-week course held in London, Venice, Florence and Rome. The course includes lectures and visits by a team of world-class experts, covering painting, sculpture, architecture, music, world cinema, literature and global issues as well as practical classes in studio life drawing and portraiture, photography and Italian language.

Design & Fashion

Blanche Macdonald Centre
100-555 West 12th Avenue,
Vancouver BC, V5Z 3X7, Canada

Courses available in make up, nail techniques, spa therapy and fashion.

Domus Academy
Via Watt, 27,
Milan, 20143, Italy

Offers short courses with the University of the Arts - Central Saint Martin, but they also run a five day intensive course to Chicago for advanced students of fashion.

Florence Institute of Design International
Borgo Ognissanti 9,
Florence, 50123, Italy

New school of design in Florence.

Istituto di Moda Burgo
Piazza San Babila,
5-20122 Milano, Italy

A fashion design school in Milan offering summer courses for basic, advanced or professional level and private tuition in drawing techniques and pattern making.

Metallo Nobile
Via Toscanella 28/r,
Florence, Tuscany 50125, Italy

Summer course in jewellery design and creation, based in Florence.

NABA - Nuova Accademia de Belle Arti
Via C. Darwin 20,
Milano, 20143, Italy

NABA summer courses are divided into two levels: introduction and intermediate. They have courses in the design, fashion, graphic design and contemporary art.

271

Polimoda Institute of Fashion Design and Marketing
Polimoda via Pisana 77,
Firenze, I-50143, Italy

Based in Florence, Polimoda Fashion School offers a variety of summer courses for those interested in all aspects of fashion.

RMIT Training
PO Box 12058, A'Beckett Street,
Melbourne, VIC 8006, Australia

Has a Career Discovery Short Course in fashion. An intensive programme which includes lectures by experienced industry professionals alongside studio workshops.

Up To Date Fashion Academy
Corso Vittorio Emanuele II,
Milano, 15-20122, Italy

Learn about fashion in Milan! This academy has a variety of courses available.

Film, Theatre & Drama

Actors College of Theatre and Television
505 Pitt Street,
Sydney, NSW 2000, Australia

College specialising in acting, music theatre and technical production courses.

Ariège Arts
8 cours St Jacques ,
Léran, 9600, France

Ariège Arts offer the chance to make documentary films in the French Pyrenees. Students learn the techniques of narrative in film and experience tuition by broadcast professionals.

EICAR - The International Film School of Paris
The International Department, 50 avenue du Président Wilson,
Bât. 136 - BP 131, La Plaine Saint-Denis, 93214, France

Offers short summer workships taught in English during July and September in the following areas: filmmaking, script writing, editing, HD Video and sound.

Flashpoint Academy
28 North Clark Street, Chicago, IL 60602, USA

This is a two-year, direct-to-industry college focusing exclusively on the following disciplines: film/broadcast, recording arts, visual effects and animation and game development.

Full Sail University
3300 University Blvd., Winter Park,
FL 32792, USA

If you're after a career in music, film, video games, design, animation, entertainment business, or Internet marketing, Full Sail is the right place for you.

Hollywood Film & Acting Academy
1786 North Highland Avenue ,
Hollywood, CA 90028, USA

The traditional film school alternative, offering shorter more intense programme in feature films, movie making and acting.

NYFA (New York Film Academy)
100 East 17th Street, New York, NY 10003, USA

The New York Film Academy runs programmes all year round in New York City and at Universal Studios in Hollywood, as well as summer workshops worldwide.

PCFE Film School
Pstrossova 19, Prague 1, 110 00, Czech Republic

Offers workshops, semester and year programmes in filmmaking including directing, screenwriting, cinematography, editing and film history and theory.

The Acting Center
5514 Hollywood Blvd.,
Hollywood, CA 90028, USA

No audition is necessary but an interview is required. Classes are available in evenings during the week and on weekends.

The Los Angeles Film School
6363 Sunset Boulevard,
Hollywood, CA 90028, USA

Has degree programmes in filmmaking, game production and animation. International students must acquire a student visa before studying in the United States.

TVI Actors Studio - Los Angeles
14429 Ventura Boulevard, Suite 118,
Sherman Oaks, CA 91423, USA

Offers acting classes, workshops, and seminars for aspiring and professional actors.

Vancouver Film School
VFS Administration & Admissions Office, 198 West Hastings Street,
Vancouver BC, V6B 1H2, Canada

Centre for both training and higher learning in all areas related to media and entertainment production.

273

French

Accent Français
2 rue de Verdun, Montpellier, 34000, France

This school runs intensive French courses in Montpellier, particularly for non-French speakers, lasting between two weeks and three months.

Alliance Française de Londres
1 Dorset Square, Marylebone, London NW1 6PU

Alliance Française is a non-profit-making organisation whose goal is to teach French and bring cultures together (group classes and bespoke tuition available).

BLS French Courses
42 rue Lafaurie de Monbadon,
Bordeaux, 33000, France

Based in the heart of Bordeaux. You will be put up in a modest hotel or, more likely, with a host family, perhaps with another student.

CESA Languages Abroad
CESA House, Pennance Road,
Lanner, Cornwall TR16 5TQ

E: info@cesalanguages.com
T: +44 (0) 1209 211 800
F: +44 (0) 1209 211 830
www.cesalanguages.com

Check out CESA Languages for a fantastic gap-year in France See photo diaries from past gappers, read student reports, view all course options, start dates and prices on line. Quality French language tuition in fabulous locations throughout France (suitable for beginners/advanced abilities).

Perfect your French skills, experience the culture first-hand, get a French qualification (optional!) and have an amazing gap-year with CESA.

CMEF, Centre Méditerranéen d'Etudes Françaises
Centre Méditerranéen, Chemin des Oliviers,
BP 38 F - 06 320, Cap d'Ail, France

Located in the South of France between Nice and Monaco. An international language school with a long tradition on French language courses.

College Northside
CP 5158, 750 Chemin Pierre-Péladeau,
Sainte-Adèle PQ, J8B 1Z4, Canada

Northside offers an intensive French immersion camp through the summer geared towards the 16 to 18 age range. Located in the mountains in the French-speaking village of Sainte-Adèle.

En Famille Overseas
58 Abbey Close, Peacehaven, Sussex BN10 7SD

En Famille Overseas arranges for you to stay with a family in France as a paying guest for a week to a year, with the board and lodging costs negotiable if you stay more than a month.

Institut ELFCA
66 avenue de Toulon, Hyères, 83400, France

Located in Hyères on the Mediterranean coast. Tutition is in small groups. Students can take the Alliance Française exams or prepare for the DELF exams.

Institut Français
14 Cromwell Place, South Kensington, London SW7 2JR

The Institut Français is the official French Government centre of language and culture in London.

Institut Savoisien d'Etudes Françaises pour Etrangers
Domaine Universitaire de Jacob,
Chambery Cedex, 73011, France

An institute which specialises in teaching French as a foreign language to adults from non-Francophone countries.

Lyon Bleu International
54 Cours Lafayette, Lyon, 69003, France

Lyon Bleu International, in Lyon, is dedicated to teaching the French language and culture.

TASIS, The American School in Switzerland
6926 Montagnola, Switzerland

Each year, the TASIS schools and summer programmes attract over 2400 students representing more than 40 nationalities who share in a caring, family-style international community.

Vis-à-Vis
2-4 Stoneleigh Park Road,
Epsom, Surrey KT19 0QT

French courses offered in France. Various accommodation options are available, and there is the usual range of course length, level and intensity.

German

BWS Germanlingua
Hackenstr. 7, Eingang C, Munich, Bavaria 80331, Germany

BWS Germanlingua is based in Munich and Berlin; all staff are experienced teachers, and classes have a maximum of 12 students.

CESA Languages Abroad
CESA House, Pennance Road,
Lanner, Cornwall TR16 5TQ

E: info@cesalanguages.com
T: +44 (0) 1209 211 800
F: +44 (0) 1209 211 830
www.cesalanguages.com

Check out CESA Languages for a fantastic gap-year in Germany See photo diaries from past gappers, read student reports, view all course options, start dates and prices on line.

Quality German language tuition in fabulous locations throughout Germany and Austria (suitable for beginners/advanced abilities).

Perfect your German skills, experience the culture first-hand, get a German qualification (optional!) and have an amazing gap-year with CESA.

German Academic Exchange Service (DAAD)
34 Belgrave Square, Belgravia, London SW1X 8QB

The German Academic Exchange Service has an inforamtion portal for those interested in learning German in Germany.

Goethe Institut
50 Princes Gate, Exhibition Road, London SW7 2PH

The Goethe Institut is probably the best-known international German language school network

Greek

DIKEMES - International Center
for Hellenic and Mediterranean Studies
5 Plateia Stadiou,
Athens, GR - 116 35, Greece

E: programs@dikemes.edu.gr
T: +30 210 7560-749
F: +30 210 7561-497
www.cyathens.org

With a curriculum centred on three areas of study - ancient Greek studies, Byzantine and modern Greek studies, European and east Mediterranean studies - DIKEMES/College Year in Athens offers unparalleled learning opportunities for English-speaking students seeking a programme of study in Greece that encompasses an academic year, a semester, or a summer.

Greek Embassy Education Office
1a Holland Park,
Kensington, London W11 3TP

The Greek Embassy website has a link to the Greek Ministry of Education, where you can find a list of universities and schools in Athens, Thessalonika, Crete and the Greek islands among other places where modern Greek is taught.

Italian

Accademia del Giglio
Via Ghibellina 116,
Florence, Tuscany 50122, Italy

This quiet, small school takes about 30 students, taught in small classes. As well as Italian language courses, they offer classes in drawing and painting.

Accademia Italiana
Piazza Pitti 15,
Florence, 50125, Italy

An international design, art and language school, the Accademia Italiana puts on summer language courses as well as full-year and longer academic and Masters courses.

Centro Machiavelli
Piazza Santo Spirito 4,
Florence, 50125, Italy

Small language school in the Santo Spirito district of Florence. Set up to teach Italian to foreigners.

CESA Languages Abroad
CESA House, Pennance Road,
Lanner, Cornwall TR16 5TQ

E: info@cesalanguages.com
T: +44 (0) 1209 211 800
F: +44 (0) 1209 211 830
www.cesalanguages.com

Check out CESA Languages for a fantastic gap-year in Italy See photo diaries from past gappers, read student reports, view all course options, start dates and prices on line.

Quality Italian language tuition in fabulous locations throughout Italy (suitable for beginners/advanced abilities).

Perfect your Italian skills, experience the culture first-hand, get a Italian qualification (optional!) and have an amazing gap-year with CESA.

Europass
Istituto EUROPASS, Centro Studi Europeo, Via Sant'Egidio,
Florence 12 - 50122, Italy

Europass has offered individual and varied Italian language courses in the heart of Florence since 1992.

Il Sillabo
Via Alberti, 31,
San Giovanni Valdarno (AR), 52027, Italy

Il Sillabo, a small, family-run school, in San Giovanni Valdarno. Authorised by the Italian Ministry of Education.

Instituto Donatello
via Galliano 1, Florence, 50144, Italy

Italian language school in Florence.

Istituto Europeo
Piazza delle Pallottole n. 1 (Duomo),
Florence, 1-50122, Italy

Istituto Europeo has three language schools: two in Italy and one in Japan. As well as running courses on Italian wine and food, they have an art and music school.

Lorenzo de' Medici
Via Faenza 43,
Florence, 50123, Italy

The Lorenzo de' Medici's offers a combination of language and cultural courses and has a large library in the adjoining San Iacopo di Corbolini church.

Japanese

Kichijoji Language School
2-3-15-701, Kichijoji Minami-cho, Musashino-Shi
Tokyo, 180-0003, Japan

Language school in Tokyo which has been teaching non-native speakers the Japanese language and about Japanese culture since 1983.

The Yamasa Institute
1-2-1 Hanehigashimachi,
Okazaki-shi, Aichi-ken 444-0832, Japan

The Yamasa Institute is an independent teaching and research centre under the governance of the Hattori Foundation. It is APJLE accredited.

Just For Fun!

In this section we've listed fun things to do during your **gap**-year. Even if you don't actually want to learn anything in particular, something here might help you learn a little about yourself!

Adventure Bound
2392 H Road, Grand Junction, CO 81505, USA

Whitewater rafting in Colorado and Utah. Also kayaking on the Colorado and Green Rivers.

visit: www.gap-year.com

Alpin Raft
Hauptstrasse 7,
Interlaken, CH-3800, Switzerland

Located in Interlaken in the Swiss Alps, Alpin Raft offers fantastic fun and adventures - join us for some thrilling and scenic rafting, canyoning or bungy-jumping!

Appalachian Wildwaters
PO Box 100,
Rowlesburg, WV 26425, USA

White water rafting on the New River and Gauley River in West Virginia.

Cairns Dive Centre
121 Abbott Street,
Cairns, QLD 4870, Australia

CDC offers daily day or live aboard snorkel and dive trips to the Outer Great Barrier Reef.

Cape Trib Horse Rides
MS 2041, Cape Tribulation, QLD 4873, Australia

Experience where the rainforest meets the reef whilst on horseback! Ride through the rainforest and canter up the beach. We cater for beginners, intermediate and experienced rides.

Catalina Ocean Rafting
PO Box 2075,
Avalon, Los Angeles CA 90704-2075, USA

Half day and full day excursions around Catalina. Snorkelling trips also available.

Dart River Safaris
27 Shotover Street, PO Box 76,
Queenstown, New Zealand

Jet boat up the Dart River and kayak back or take the bus back. In between explore the ancient forest. The Dart River Valley featured in the Lord of the Rings films.

Dvorak Expeditions
17921 US Highway 285,
Nathrop, Chaffee, CO 81236, USA

White water rafting, kayaking and fly fishing trips offered in Colorado, Utah, New Mexico, Idaho and Texas.

Gravity Assisted Mountain Biking
Av 16 de Julio #1490, Edificio Avenida,
Planta Baja, Oficina #10
La Paz, Bolivia

Downhill mountain biking in Bolivia, also cross-country.

Harris Mountains Heli-Ski
The Station, Cnr Shotover and Camp Sts, PO Box 634
Queenstown, 9348, New Zealand

If you are a strong intermediate skier or ski-boarder, then try this for that extra thrill!

Hawaii Ocean Rafting
PO Box 381, Lahaina,
Maui, HI 96767, USA

Whale watching, rafting, sailing and speed boating all off the coast of Hawaii. Small groups only.

Kiwi River Safaris
PO Box 434,
Taupo, New Zealand

White water rafting, scenic rafting and kayaking trips in Taupo.

Mokai Gravity Canyon
PO Box 84,
Taihape, New Zealand

Mokai Gravity Canyon boasts three world-class adventure activities: our extreme flying fox, our mighty 80-metre bungy or feel the thrill of a 50-metre freefall on our bridge swing.

Ocean Rafting
PO Box 106, Canonvale, QLD 4802, Australia

Ocean rafting around the coast of Queensland and the Whitsunday Islands, which includes exploring Whitehaven Beach. They also offer snorkelling trips along pristine reefs and tropical island guided walks.

Pocono Whitewater Rafting
1519 State Route 903,
Jim Thorpe, PA 18229, USA

Trail biking, paintball skirmish, kayaking and whitewater rafting available in the LeHigh River Gorge.

River Expeditions
900 Broadway Avenue,
Oak Hill, WV 25901, USA

Rafting in West Virginia on the New and Gauley Rivers.

Taupo Bungy
PO Box 919, Taupo, New Zealand

Located in the Waikato River Valley, Taupo Bungy is considered one of the world's most spectacular bungy sites. Featuring the world's first cantilever platform and New Zealand's first 'splash cam'.

visit: www.gap-year.com

Whistler Summer Snowboard Camps
106-4368 Main Street, Suite 981,
Whistler BC, V0N 1B4, Canada

Summer camp for snowboarders who want to improve their skills.

Multi-languages

Caledonia Languages Abroad
The Clockhouse, Bonnington Mill, 72 Newhaven Road
Edinburgh, Midlothian EH6 5QG

Short courses in French, Italian, German, Russian, Spanish and Portuguese in Europe and Latin America, for all levels, start all year round, most for a minimum of two weeks.

CERAN Lingua International
Avenue des Petits Sapins ,
Spa, 27 4900, Belgium

CERAN runs weekly intensive residential language programmes in Dutch, French, German and Spanish.

EF International Language Schools
17 Havelock Road,
Hastings, Sussex TN34 1BP

On an EF International Language Schools programme you will immerse yourself in the language and culture of some of the world's most exciting cities.

Eurolanguages
Ido Language Travel Services Limited, The Enterprise Centre,George's Place,
Dun Laoghaire, County Dublin, Ireland

Have a website that helps you choose a language school and book a place on a language course. Read the reviews of fellow students.

Eurolingua Institute
Eurolingua House, 61 Bollin Drive,
Altrincham, Cheshire WA14 5QW

Eurolingua is a network of 70 institutes teaching nine languages in 35 countries. 'group programmes' give 15 hours of tuition a week according to your level.

Inlingua International
Belpstrasse 11, Bern, 3007, Switzerland

Inlingua International runs language colleges throughout Europe.

Language Courses Abroad
67 Ashby Road, Loughborough, Leicestershire LE11 3AA

Languages courses available in French, German, Greek, Italian, Portuguese, Russian, Spanish and others.

281

Learn Languages Abroad
'Sceilig', Ballymorefinn, Glenasmole
Dublin, 24 County Dublin, Republic of Ireland

Learn Languages Abroad will help you find the course best suited to your needs. Courses available range from two weeks to a full academic year.

Modern Language Studies Abroad (MLSA)
PO Box 548,
Frankfort, IL 60423, USA

Offers language study abroad programmes in: Spain, Italy and Costa Rica.

OISE Oxford
13-15 High Street,
Oxford OX1 4EA

Have their own unique teaching philosophy which leads students to gain confidence, fluency and accuracy when speaking another language taught by a native-speaker.

The Year Out Group
Queensfield, 28 King's Road,
Easterton, Wiltshire SN10 4PX

E: info@yearoutgroup.org
T: +44 (0) 1380 816696
www.yearoutgroup.org

See main entry under volunteering.

Music

Backbeat Tours
140 Beale Street,
Memphis, TN 38103, USA

Offer 'rockin' rides' through Memphis music history on a vintage 1950s bus. The three hour Hound Dog Tour follows in the footsteps of the King of Rock 'n' Roll, Elvis.

Country Music Travel
PO Box 10171, McLean, VA 22102, USA

Country music-themed vacations and escorted tours, from trips to Dollywood entertainment park, to music cities tours in Nashville, Memphis and Tennessee.

Jazz Summer School
41a High Street, Wanstead, London E11 2AA

Jazz Summer School offering places at the French jazz summer school in the South of France or The Cuban music school in Havana.

NashCamp
PO Box 210396,
Nashville, TN 37221, USA

Programmes offered in acoustic music and songwriting, inlcuding bluegrass and banjo playing.

Red Cedar Songwriter Camp
PO Box 135 , Pender Island BC, V0N 2M0, Canada

Learn the craft of songwriting, hone your guitar skills, hike and meet new friends.

Scoil Acla - Irish Music Summer School
Achill Island, County Mayo, Republic of Ireland

Summer school established to teach Irish Piping (Irish War Pipes), tin whistle, accordian, banjo, flute and harp.

Songwriter Girl Camps
PO Box 167, Old Hickory, TN 37138, USA

They offer weekend songwriting camps for girls and women of all ages and ability!

SummerKeys
c/o Bruce Potterton, 32 North Main Street,
Boonton, NJ 07005, USA

Music vacations for adults in Lubec, Maine. Open to all 'musical people' regardless of ability with workshops and private tuition in a variety of instruments.

SummerSongs Inc.
PO Box 803, Saugerties, NY 12477, USA

A not-for-profit corporation dedicated to the art and craft of songwriting.

Taller Flamenco
C/ Peral, 49, Seville, E-41002, Spain

Courses include flamenco dance, flamenco guitar, singing and percussion.

United DJ Mixing School
Level 10, 92-94 Elizabeth Street,
Melbourne, Australia

Offer an introductory course over two weekends, which gives the basics of DJ-ing and a longer comprehensive course that runs over twelve weeks.

Welsh Jazz Society
26, The Balcony, Castle Arcade, Cardiff CF10 1BY

Based in Cardiff the society promotes live jazz music of all styles and can keep you informed of gigs and jazz events going on in Wales.

World Rhythms Arts Program (WRAP)
Kalani Music, 11862 Balboa Blvd. Suite 159,
Granada Hills, CA 91344, USA

Classes develop your working knowledge of instruments, rhythms, dances, songs, styles, methods and applications.

283

Andalucian Photography Workshops
Calle Agua 12, Alhama de Granada,
Andalucia, 18120, Spain

Workshops are suitable for all abilities. The school is set in the stunning surroundings of Andalucia in southern Spain, which provide marvelous photographic opportunities.

Brooks Institute
27 East Cota Street ,
Santa Barbara, CA 93101, USA

This school offers training in filmmaking, graphic design and photojournalism. The courses are designed for anyone who aspires to a career in photography, filmmaking, visual journalism, or graphic design.

c4 Images & Safaris
Knoll Hill Cottage, Knoll Lane,
Corfe Mullen, Dorset BH21 3RF

Offers short photography workshops and wildlife safaris in South Africa with emphasis on helping you to improve your photography skills.

Europa Photogenica
3920 West 231st Place,
Torrance, CA 90505, USA

This company provides carefully planned, high quality, small group photo tours, designed for photographers of all levels who wish to improve their photographic skills using Europe as their classroom.

Joseph Van Os Photo Safaris
PO Box 655, Vashon Island,
WA 98070, USA

Joseph Van Os Photo Safaris guide you to some of the world's finest wild and scenic locations with the main purpose of making great photographs.

London Photo Tours & Workshops
APT Studios, 6 Creekside, Deptford,
London SE8 4SA

Offers short courses and photography workshops. Also specialise in small group photo travel with no more than eight photo travellers in their seven-day photo holidays.

Nigel Turner Photographic Workshop
3055 Evening Wind,
Henderson, NV 89122, USA

One- and two-week workshops on photographic technique based in Las Vegas. Your chance to capture some of the most breathtaking scenery the US has to offer, from Death Valley to Yosemite National.

Photo Holidays France
12 Middleton Grove,
Holloway, London N7 9LS

A private photography school in the south of France offering one to one photography tuition specialising in landscape and portrait photography.

Photographers on Safari
West End Studios, 55 Stapleford Road, Whissendine
Oakham, Rutland LE15 7HF

Offers a variety of exciting workshops in the UK and photography Safaris overseas, ideal for the wildlife lover.

Steve Outram Crete Photo Tours & Workshops
D.Katsifarakis Street, Galatas,
Chania, Crete 73100, Greece

Professional photographer Steve Outram uses his local knowledge of Zanzibar, Lesvos and western Crete to show you how to make the most of photographic opportunities and develop your skill as a photographer.

Venice School of Photography Workshops Ltd
26 York Street,
Marylebone, London W1U 6PZ

Photography workshops run throughout the year in Venice, London, Sicily, Namibia, Tuscany, Provence, New York and elsewhere.

Portuguese

CIAL Centro de Linguas
Av da Republica, 41 - 8° Esq.,
Lisbon, 1050-187, Portugal

With schools in Lisbon and Faro, CIAL organises courses in Portuguese for foreigners. Accommodation is in private homes at an extra weekly cost, which includes breakfast.

Russian

Obninsk Humanities Centre
Dubravushka, 249020 Kaluga Oblast,
Obninsk, Pionersky Proezd 29, Russia

An independent boarding school two hours from Moscow offering intensive and reasonably priced Russian courses.

The Russian Language Centre
5a Bloomsbury Square, Bloomsbury, London WC1A 2TA

Offers a range of courses for groups and individuals: intensive, accelerated and private.

Spanish

Academia Hispánica Córdoba
C/Rodríguez Sánchez, 15, Córdoba, 14003, Spain

Small-group language tuition to suit all levels.

AIL Madrid Spanish Language School
C/Doctor Esquerdo 33, 1a2, Madrid, 28028, Spain

They offer flexible gap-year programmes tailored to your needs.

Amigos Spanish School
Zaguan de Cielo B-23, Cusco, Peru

Non-profit Spanish school. With every hour of your Spanish classes, you pay for the basic care of a group of underprivileged children at their foundation.

Bridge Year, Spanish Programs
Roman Diaz 297, Providencia, Santiago, Chile

Study Spanish in Chile and Argentina! There are plenty of activities and excursions plus the homestay could be the most rewarding part of the experience.

CESA Languages Abroad
CESA House, Pennance Road,
Lanner, Cornwall TR16 5TQ

E: info@cesalanguages.com
T: +44 (0) 1209 211 800
F: +44 (0) 1209 211 830
www.cesalanguages.com

Check out CESA Languages for a fantastic gap-year in Spain. See photo diaries from past gappers, read student reports, view all course options, start dates and prices on line.

Quality Spanish language tuition in fabulous locations throughout Spain and Latin America (suitable for beginners/advanced abilities).

Perfect your Spanish skills, experience the culture first-hand, get a Spanish DELE qualification (optional!) and have an amazing gap-year with CESA.

Comunicacion Language School
Avda Las Marinas, 110, Roquetas de Mar, Almeria, 4740, Spain

Come and enjoy professional Spanish classes, a great beach and lots of outdoor and cultural activities in Almería province, Spain. Stay in an apartment, a hostel or with a Spanish host family.

Don Quijote
2/4 Stoneleigh Park Road,
Epsom, Surrey KT19 OQT

E: uk@donquijote.org
T: +44 (0) 20 8786 8081
F: +44 (0) 20 8786 8086
www.donquijote.org

Don Quijote is a leading network of schools teaching Spanish in Spain and Latin America. Quality Spanish courses from one to 48 weeks are available year-round for all levels. Programmes also include volunteer projects in Latin America and study-work opportunities in Spain. Accommodation available on all courses.

Enforex
C/Alberto Aguilera 26,
Madrid, 28015, Spain

Learn to speak Spanish in Spain or Latin America. Over 28 centres all in Spanish speaking countries. Summer camps also available.

Escuela Internacional
Central Office, Calle Talamanca 10,
28807 Alcala de Henares, Madrid, Spain

Learn Spanish in Spain or Latin America. Also offers Spanish cultural and literature courses.

Expanish
Viamonte 927, 1A ,
Buenos Aries, Argentina

Learn Spanish in Buenos Aires located in the city centre, home to some of the oldest historical sites in the city.

IndaPidal
C/ Granada 9, 1º Oficina 2,
Almería, 4003, Spain

Offer Spanish language courses in Almería, Spain.

International House Madrid
C/Zurbano, 8,
Madrid, 28010, Spain

Learn Spanish in Madrid.

287

Mente Argentina
Juncal 3184 piso 7,
Buenos Aires, C1425, Argentina

Visit Argentina and learn Spanish in 'a unique and different way'.

Pichilemu Institute of Language Studies
138 Agustin Ross,
Pichilemu, Chile

Offers group, private, and certified courses. Students can surf and experience rural Chile.

Simón Bolivar Spanish School
Mariscal Foch E9-20 y Av. 6 de Diciembre,
Quito, Ecuador

One of the biggest Spanish schools in Ecuador. Spanish lessons are offered at the main building in Quito, the Pacific coast and the Amazon jungle.

Spanish Study Holidays
67 Ashby Road,
Loughborough, Leicestershire LE11 3AA

Offers Spanish courses throughout Spain and central and south America lasting from a week to nine months.

Universidad de Navarra - ILCE
Institute of Spanish Language and Culture, Campus Universitario,
Edificio Central, Pamplona, Navarra 31080 Spain

A wide range of programmes are offered for people who wish to travel to Spain to learn about the culture and the language.

Sport - Air

Sports such as paragliding, skydiving *etc*

Fly Gap
Chalet Anguillita , Chemin de la Côte,
Le Chable, 1934, Switzerland

Paragliding school whose flying courses are specifically designed for British gap-year students.

Great Lake Skydive Centre
Taupo Airport,
Taupo, New Zealand

Freefall skydiving over Lake Taupo.

New Zealand Skydiving School
PO Box 21, Methven, Canterbury 7345, New Zealand

Jump start your career with a diploma in commercial skydiving. This comprehensive course includes 200 skydives. Graduates have proven to be highly employable in skydiving with employment rates exceeding 95%.

Nimbus Paragliding
25b Lower Sumnervale Drive, PO Box 17712,
Sumner, Christchurch, New Zealand

Paragliding courses, tandem paragliding flights and paragliding equipment sales in Christchurch, New Zealand. For those of you who wish to jump, no training is necessary and there are almost no age or size limits for tandem paragliding.

Nzone
PO Box 554, 35 Shotover Street,
Queenstown, New Zealand

Experience the ultimate adrenaline rush of tandem parachuting while on vacation in New Zealand. Or train to be a Sport Skydiver yourself with an Accelerated Freefall Course, no prior training needed.

Paul's Xtreme Skydiving
51 Sheridan Street, Cairns, Queensland, Australia

Challenge yourself to the thrill of a lifetime with an Xtreme Skydive with Paul's, the original North Queensland crew.

Skydive Arizona
4900 North Taylor Road, Eloy, AZ 85231, USA

Located halfway between Phoenix and Tucson is the largest skydiving resort in the world. The clear desert weather allows over 340 flying days a year.

Skydive Cairns
82 Grafton Street, Cairns, QLD 4870, Australia

Based in Cairns, North Queensland, this company specializes in tandem skydiving for both the novice and the professional skydiver.

Skydive Las Vegas
1401 Airport Road, Boulder City, NV 89005, USA

Skydive over the quiet and peaceful views of Hoover Dam, Lake Mead, the Colorado River, the Las Vegas Strip and the entire Las Vegas Valley. Tandem skydiving is the easiest, fastest, cheapest and safest way to make your first skydive.

Skydive Switzerland GmbH
PO Box 412, Interlaken, 3800, Switzerland

Learn how to skydive in Switzerland. Tandem jumps, fun and glacier jumps also available.

Skydive Taupo
Lot 26, Anzac Memorial Drive, PO Box 1525,
Taupo, New Zealand

Skydiving over the central plateau of New Zealand and Lake Taupo could be one of the most breathtaking experiences you'll ever have!

Wallaby Ranch
1805 Deen Still Road, Davenport, FL 33897, USA

Year-round tandem hang gliding flights and hang gliding instruction in central Florida.

Sport - Earth
Sports such as fitness training, polo, climbing *etc*

Action Professionals Ltd
9 Edwy Parade, Kingsholm, Gloucester, GL1 2QH

Get an internationally recognised qualification in Argentina or South Africa. The 12-week course in personal fitness training will give you the opportunity to enjoy a fully-inclusive gap-year experience.

Awol Adventures
PO Box 56207, Dominion Rd,
Auckland, New Zealand

Join us in the Waitakere Rainforest for an amazing Auckland Adventure in the rainforest and beach adventure zone of Piha. We offer canyoning and abseiling experiences, as well as boogie boarding and cater for any level of ability.

Bucks and Spurs
HC 71 Box 163, Ava, Missouri, USA

Horseback riding vacations in Missouri. Round up cattle, see a horse whisperer use his natural horsemanship, and enjoy the ride at this Missouri Dude ranch.

Hike Japan
89 Fleet Street, London EC4Y 1DH

This company offers guided walking holidays and tailor-made tours for individuals and small groups, from the island of Yakushima south of Kyushu, to the Kii and Hida mountain ranges in Central Japan, and the island of Hokkaido.

Jagged Globe
The Foundry Studios, 45 Mowbray Street, Sheffield, Yorkshire S3 8EN

Provides mountaineering expeditions and treks. They also offer courses which are based in Wales, Scotland and the Alps for both the beginner and those wishing to improve their skills.

Megalong Australian Heritage Centre
Megalong Road, Megalong Valley, Blue Mountains, NSW 2785, Australia

Horse riding in the blue mountains of New South Wales. Jackaroo and Jillaroo courses available. Also courses in how to work with horses.

Mountaineering Council of Ireland
Sport HQ, 13 Joyce Way, Park West Business Park
Dublin, County Dublin 12, Republic of Ireland

They have lists of mountaineering clubs in Ireland, useful information and can give advice on insurance.

PoloSkool Ltd
Sportskool, 37-39 Southgate Street, Winchester, Hampshire SO23 9EH

PoloSkool offers intensive polo tuition programmes in Argentina. Fully residential courses of two, four and ten weeks are available for players of all abilities.

Qufu Shaolin Kung Fu School China
Jubao Shanzhuang, Bei Wai Huan Rd,
Qufu, Shandong Province 273100, China

Shaolin Temple in Shandong, China, where you can learn Kung Fu and Mandarin Chinese.

Rock'n Ropes
Karetoto Road,
Wairakei, Taupo 3330, New Zealand

A Rock'n Ropes course is 'as exciting as skydiving or bungee jumping'.

Rua Reidh Lighthouse
Melvaig,
Gairloch, Ross-shire IV21 2EA

Courses in basic rock climbing available - one or two days also one to one teaching. Their one day course has a class limit of four people.

Shoestring Polo Ltd
2 Street Cottages, Wheatsheaf Lane, Oaksey
Malmesbury, Wiltshire SN16 9SZ

Playing polo in Argentina, the home of polo, is a fantastic opportunity for individuals regardless of previous experience.

White Peak Expeditions
Agents for Atlantic & Pacific Travel, 49 Conduit Street, Mayfair, London W1B

Specialists in trekking and climbing for small groups in Nepal, Tibet, Kazakhstan/Kyrgyzstan, Ecuador and Peru, climbs are suitable for the less experienced climber and are generally combined with trekking expeditions.

291

Sport - Snow

Sports such as skiing, snowboarding *etc*

Alltracks Limited
The Lawns, Longstock Road,
Goodworth Clatford, Hampshire SP11 7RE

This company runs high performance ski and snowboard instructor courses at Whistler, Revelstoke and Banff in Canada. Ideal for a constructive and fun gap-year.

Altitude Futures - Gap Course Verbier
Case Postale 55,
Verbier, 1936, Switzerland

E: info@altitude-futures.com
T: +41 (0) 2777 16006
F: +41 (0) 2777 16111
www.altitude-futures.com

Verbier's only officially recognized Snowsports School running 'in house' gap courses.

- Highest pass rates
- Work opportunities
- 210 on snow coaching hours
- Up to 40% discount on equipment
- 'Pub Mont Fort' discount card

Courses start on 29th November 2009, 3rd January 2010 and 8th February 2010.

BASI (British Association of Snowsport Instructors)
British Association Of Snowsports Instructors, Morlich House,
17 The Square, Grantown-on-Spey PH26 3HG

The UK authority for training, examining and grading snowsport instructors and its qualifications are recognised worldwide.

Cardrona Alpine Resort
PO Box 117, 18 Dunmore Street,
Wanaka, Central Otago 9343, New Zealand

Ski resort in New Zealand with ski school attached.

Deutsch-Institut Tirol
A-6370 Kitzbühel,
Am Sandhügel 2, Austria

E: office@deutschinstitut.com
T: +43 53 56 71274
F: +43 53 56 72363
www.deutschinstitut.com

Our gap-year course, set in the famous Austrian ski resort of Kitzbuehel, provides intensive German lessons followed by skiing or snowboarding tuition, sufficient to enable you to take the Austrian ski or snowboard instructors' exam, leaving you free to work as a ski/snowboard instructor for the whole winter season.

ICE Snowsports Ltd
3-4 Bath Place, Aberdovey, Gwynedd LL35 0LN

Ski instructor courses from eight to ten weeks in Argentina or Val d'Isere.

OnTheMountain Pro Snowsports Instructor Training in Switzerland
Neige Aventure Ski & Snowboard School,
CH-1997 Haute-Nendaz, Switzerland

Provides exceptional training and loads of fun, after training stay and enjoy the slopes until the end of the season at no extra cost.

Outdoor Interlaken AG
Haupstrasse 15, PO Box 451,
Interlaken-Matten, CH 3800, Switzerland

Ski/Snowboard school for complete beginners and for those who wish to brush up their skills. Have local guides who know the best trails, snow and shortest lift lines.

Ski le Gap
220 Chemin Wheeler, Mont-Tremblant PQ, J8E 1V3, Canada

Offers ski and snowboard instructor training courses based in popular Canadian resort of Tremblant.

Ski-Exp-Air
913 rue Senneterre, Québec PQ, G1X 3Y2, Canada

Ski-exp-air is a Canadian ski and snowboard school offering quality, professional instruction in a fun atmosphere.

SnowSkool
SportSkool, 37-39 Southgate Street,
Winchester, Hampshire SO23 9EH

Ski and Snowboard instructor courses in Canada and New Zealand. SnowSkool offers four, five, nine and eleven week programmes earning internationally recognised qualifications.

Snowsport Consultancy
Aandammergouw 13,
1153 PA Zuiderwoude, The Netherlands

Skiing lessons leading to ski instructor exams. Lessons are taught in German and so you will need a good working knowledge of the language.

The International Academy
Sophia House, 28 Cathedral Road,
CArdiff CF11 9LJ

E: info@international-academy.com
T: +44 (0) 29 2066 0200
www.altitude-futures.com

Become a ski or snowboard instructor on a five to 12 week gap-year or career break course. Experience world class resorts and gain recognised CSIA, CASI, NZSIA or SBINZ instructor qualifications. Resorts include Banff/Lake Louise, Whistler Blackcomb, Sun Peaks Resort and Castle Mountain in Canada. Summer courses are also available at Mount Hood in the USA and Cardrona Alpine Resort in New Zealand.

Sport - Various

Companies offering a range of sports

Adventure Ireland
Donegal Adventure Centre & Sports Training College, Bayview Avenue, Bundoran, County Donegal, Republic of Ireland

Live and work in Ireland. Learn to surf, climb, kayak. Classes on Irish culture, history, language and literature.

Avon Ski & Action Centre
Lyncombe Drive,
Churchill, Somerset BS25 5PQ

Centre is on the edge of the Mendip hills, where you can ski, snowboard, mountain board, as well as pursue archery, rifle shooting, power kiting, 4x4 driving, quad biking, rock climbing, abseiling and many more exciting outdoor pursuits.

Base Camp Group
Unit 30, Baseline Business Studios,
Whitchurch Road
Notting Hill, London W11 4AT

Instructor courses and performance camps in scubadiving, kitesurfing, surfing, windsurfing and waterskiing.

Bear Creek Outdoor Centre
45 Barnet Boulevard,
Renfrew ON, K7V 2M5, Canada

Offers courses in canoeing skills also swiftwater and rescue courses and wilderness first aid.

Camp Challenge Pte Ltd
1 Gunner Lane, Sentosa,
Singapore 99562

Organisation teaching young adults how to be good global citizens.

Canyon Voyages Adventure Co
211 North Main,
Moab, UT 84532, USA

River rafting, kayaking, canoeing, hiking, horseback, mountain bike and 4x4 trips available in the canyons of Utah.

Class VI River Runners
PO Box 88,
Lansing, WV 25854, USA

Organised sporting trips for students and also family and corporate groups.

Flying Fish
25 Union Road,
Cowes, Isle of Wight PO31 7TW

E: mail@flyingfishonline.com
T: +44 (0) 1983 280 641
www.flyingfishonline.com

Flying Fish trains and recruits over 1000 people each year to work as yacht skippers and as sailing, diving, surfing, windsurfing, ski and snowboard instructors. Combine professional training with international adventure and the chance to make money while having fun. Watersports courses are run in the UK, Greece and Australia while snow sports training takes place in Canada and France.

Peak Leaders
Mansfield,
Strathmiglo,
Fife-shire KY14 7QE

E: info@peakleaders.com
T: +44 (0) 1337 860 079
F: +44 (0) 1338 868 176
www.peakleaders.com

How about a day's heli skiing in New Zealand? Or riding in Whistler's famous Bike Park? All part of your experience on our ski, snowboard and mountain bike instructor programs.

Make the most of your once in a lifetime experience in some of the world's leading resorts whilst gaining internationally recognised instructor qualifications, plus plenty of CV enhancing extras.

Plas Menai
The National Watersports Centre,
Caernarfon, Gwynedd LL55 1UE

Offers a range of courses training people to work as watersports, yachting and adventure instructors abroad and in the UK.

Raging Thunder
PO Box 1109,
Cairns, QLD 4870, Australia

Selection of day tours, once in a lifetime experiences, available, such as Great Barrier Reef excursions, sea kayaking, ballooning and white water rafting.

Rapid Sensations Rafting
PO Box 1725,
Taupo, New Zealand

White water rafting, kayaking and mountain biking on offer. They also have a kayaking school.

River Deep Mountain High
Clocktower Buildings, Low Wood,,
Haverthwaite, Cumbria LA12 8LY

Outdoor activities and activity holidays in the Lake District. Where you can try canoeing, kayaking, gorge walks, abseiling, climbing, sailing, walking, trail-cycling or mountain biking

River Rats Rafting
PO Box 7208, Te Ngae,
Rotorua, Bay of Plenty 3402, New Zealand

River Rats are located in Rototua, New Zealand, and are specialists in rafting. They also offer a gondola ride up Mount Ngongotaha and Formula 1500 Sprint Car racing.

Rogue Wilderness Adventures
PO Box 1110, 325 Galice Road,
Merlin, OR 97532, USA

Hiking, fishing and rafting trips are designed to give you a thrilling, relaxing and fun experience. Based in Rogue River canyon.

Sport Lived Ltd
40 Broadgate , Beeston,
Nottingham NG9 2FW

Sporting gap-year company which arranges for young people to play sport overseas.

Surfaris
353 Loftus Road,
Crescent Head, NSW 2440, Australia

Company offering camping in remote areas and surfing off Byron Bay in New South Wales.

The Year Out Group
Queensfield, 28 King's Road,
Easterton, Wiltshire SN10 4PX

E: info@yearoutgroup.org
T: +44 (0) 1380 816696
www.yearoutgroup.org

See main entry under volunteering.

Torquay Wind & Surf Centre
Shop and Booking Office, 55 Victoria Rd, Ellacombe, Torquay,

Courses available in kitesurfing, kitebuggying, powerkiting and stand up paddle surfing.

Wilderness Aware Rafting
PO Box 1550 WS, Buena Vista, CO 81211, USA

Extreme tours, also downhill mountain biking, horseback riding, 4X4 tours and lost mine tours in Arkansas and Colorado.

Wilderness Escapes
PO Box 271, Taupo 2730, New Zealand

Kayaking, guided walks, abseiling, rock climbing and caving in Taupo.

Sport - Water

Sports such as sailing, rafting, kayaking *etc*

All Outdoors California Whitewater Rafting
1250 Pine Street, Suite 103,
Walnut Creek, CA 94596, USA

California River Rafting trips for the beginner, intermediate and experienced rafter.

Allaboard Sailing Academy
7 The Square, Marina Bay, Gibraltar

Tailor-made sailing courses available in Gibraltar.

AO Nang Divers
208/2-3 Moo 2, Ao Nang, Krabi 81000, Thailand

Learning to dive in Thailand at the Ao Nang diving school.

Aquatic Explorers
40 The Kingsway, Cronulla Beach 2230,
Sydney, NSW, Australia

Aquatic Explorers is an SSI (Scuba Schools International) Platinum Facility offering new divers, as well as local and international scuba divers, the best scuba diving training in Australia.

Barque Picton Castle
PO Box 1076, 132 Montague Street,
Lunenburg NS, B0J 2C0, Canada

Explore Europe, Africa and the Caribbean as crew on a square rigger. No experience needed. Join Barque Picton Castle. Come aboard, come alive!

Bermuda Sub Aqua Club
PO Box HM 3155,
Hamilton, HM NX, Bermuda

A branch of the British Sub Aqua Club and offers members a varied programme of club-organised dives; a safe, structured, proven training programme.

Cave Diving Florida
PO Box 519,
High Springs, FL 32655, USA

Full training offered in diving including cave diving. Guided dives available, for those who are already cavern or cave certified. Website also offers details of several other Florida caves.

Challenge Rafting

Queenstown Information Centre,
PO Box 634,
Queenstown, New Zealand

Challenge Rafting offers exciting half-day whitewater rafting trips on the Shotover and Kawarau Rivers.

Deep Sea Divers Den

319 Draper Street, Cairns, QLD 4870, Australia

Your guide to the finest Great Barrier Reef scuba diving and snorkelling off Cairns Tropical Queensland, Australia.

Dive Kaikoura

Yarmouth Street, Kaikoura, 7300, New Zealand

Professional instructors and small groups make Dive Kaikoura the ideal place to start your diving journey or advance your diving qualification.

Diversity

Local 125, Centro Comercial Puerto Colon,
Playa de las Americas
Tenerife, Canary Islands, Spain

A Gold Palm 5 Star resort based in Tenerife who offer the full range of PADI courses, including the PADI Open Water and PADI Dive Master.

Elite Sailing

Chatham Maritime Marina,
Leviathan Way,
Chatham, Kent ME4 4LP

Sailing school and RYA Training Centre based at Chatham, Kent. Suitable for absolute beginner to professional skippers and crew.

Gap Year Diver Ltd

Tyte Court, Farbury End,
Great Rollright, Oxfordshire OX7 5RS

Diver training and a wide range of activities and excursions included which make the entire experience more exciting and enjoyable.

Island Divers

Chao Koh Service Ltd Part,
157 Moo 7 T. Aonang, Muang,
Phi Phi, Krabi 81000, Thailand

E: info@islanddiverspp.com
T: +66 (0)898732205
F: +66 (0)75601082
www.islanddiverspp.com

Looking for a new adventure? Then join our friendly and highly qualified staff for dive courses and dive trips for all levels, from beginner to professional.

Divemaster internships are also available. In just two months Island Divers can take you from a novice diver to a dive professional with an international qualification.

Marine Divers (British Sub-Aqua Club School 388) Hong Kong
c/o United Services Recreation Club, Kings Park,
Kowloon, Hong Kong, PR China

Training and fun in Hong Kong, with optional five-day trip to the Philippines. Various packages.

Neptune's Dive College
PADI 5 Star Instructor Developement Center,
59 Calle Las Palmas,
Manzanillo, Colima Mexico 28860

Neptune's Dive College offers college or university credit eligible scuba instructor training and internships.

OzSail
PO Box 582, Airlie Beach,
QLD4802, Australia

OzSail presents an extensive range of sailing and diving holidays from which to choose.

Penrith Whitewater Stadium
PO Box 1120, Penrith Post Business Centre,
Penrith, NSW 2751, Australia

Introduction packages and courses in whitewater rafting and in whitewater kayaking offered.

Sabah Divers
G27 Wisma Sabah, Jln Haji Saman,
Kota Kinab Alu, Sabah 88000, Malaysia

Sabah Divers offer both PADI and SSI scuba diving courses in Sabah, Malaysian Bourneo.

Saracen Sailing Mallorca
Apartado 162,
Pollensa, Majorca E-07460, Spain

A RYA approved sea school whioh offers a broad range of practical tidal sailing courses aboard their yachts based in North East Mallorca all year round.

Scuba Junkie
PO Box 458, Block B Lot 36,
Semporna,
Semporna Seafront
Sabah, 91308, Malaysia

Scuba Junkie is a fully licensed and insured PADI operation offering courses for beginners to advanced in the Celebes Sea.

Straits Sailing
10 The Square,
Marina Bay, Gibraltar

Expert tuition with the full range of RYA courses.

Sunsail
The Port House, Port Solent,
Portsmouth, Hampshire PO6 4TH

Sunsail offers the full range of RYA yacht courses as well as their own teaching programmes. Their instructors are RYA qualified.

Surfing Queensland
PO Box 233,
Burleigh Heads,
QLD 4220, Australia

Surfing Queensland has a surf school system with 16 licensed surf schools operating on beaches from Coolangatta to Yeppoon.

Wavehunters UK
Animal Surf Academy,
6 Fore Street, Port Isaac,
Cornwall PL29 3RB

Wavehunters UK offer a complete package with selected lodges and surf academies.

TEFL

Academy of Prague Schools
Evropska 35, Praha 6, 160 00, Czech Republic

Dynamic private language school based in Prague 6, specializing in the Trinity Certificate in TESOL.

Cactus TEFL
Clarence House,
30-31 North Street,
Brighton BN1 1EB

Cactus TEFL is an independent advice and admissions service working with over 120 TEFL course providers in 34 different countries.

OxfordTEFL
6-7 Southampton Place,
Bloomsbury,
London WC1A 2DB

OxfordTEFL offer a four week training course, accredited by Trinity College London, at the end of which you should get a Certificate in TEFL.

The Language House
1 Bis, Rue de Verdun,
Montpellier, L'Herault 34000, France

TEFL/TESOL programme available. Also courses in French, Arabic, Spanish or Italian. Small classes.

The Year Out Group
Queensfield, 28 King's Road,
Easterton, Wiltshire SN10 4PX

E: info@yearoutgroup.org
T: +44 (0) 1380 816696
www.yearoutgroup.org

See main entry under volunteering.

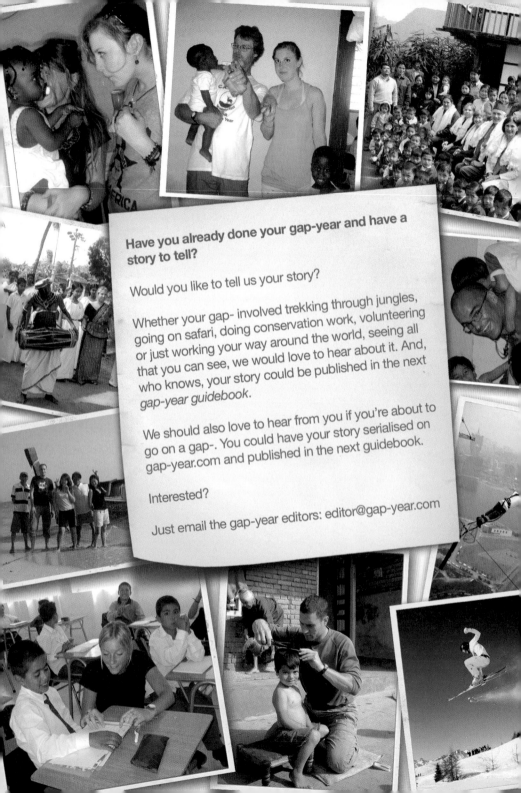

Have you already done your gap-year and have a story to tell?

Would you like to tell us your story?

Whether your gap- involved trekking through jungles, going on safari, doing conservation work, volunteering or just working your way around the world, seeing all that you can see, we would love to hear about it. And, who knows, your story could be published in the next gap-year guidebook.

We should also love to hear from you if you're about to go on a gap-. You could have your story serialised on gap-year.com and published in the next guidebook.

Interested?

Just email the gap-year editors: editor@gap-year.com

Chapter 10

Working in the UK

A medical gap- in Uganda

Claire, 22, took a **gap-** between her third and fourth years of a medical degree to spend six weeks in a remote hospital in rural Uganda for her medical elective.

She also took the opportunity to spend three weeks travelling on safari in Kenya/Tanzania and to visit a beach in Zanzibar. She said it took her about a week to get back to normal on her return.

Claire said: "Working in the hospital was incredibly scary and difficult, with a huge amount of responsibility, but it was the most rewarding thing I have ever done and I gained so much confidence.

"Travelling afterwards was a fantastic experience, and we saw some amazing sights."

Her advice to gappers: "Get a local SIM card for your phone, and search the internet before you leave, for independent telecom companies who offer very cheap international calls from the UK; really good for being able to keep in touch with people at home."

Anything she wished she'd taken?

"Some more treats/food from home – what little we had was very strictly rationed!"

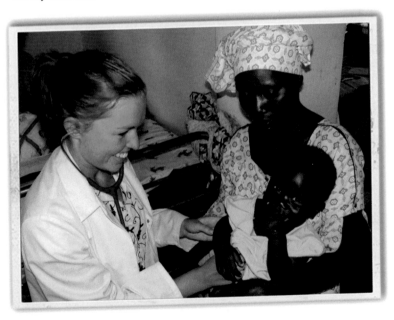

Working in the UK

Why work on a year out?

If you're not working to raise money for **gap-** travel and you've just finished school or university, you might want a break from study and take a deep breath or two for a while. But even though work doesn't seem too appealing, just try going through the complex claiming procedure for jobseekers' allowance and then living on it for a few weeks, and you'll soon see that work has its advantages,

To see what we mean look at: **www.jobcentreplus.gov.uk/JCP/index.html**

You now have to make your claim by telephone or online - and according to the advice on this website the phone call will take 40 minutes!

But there are plenty of much better reasons to use a **gap-** for work:

• Saving money for university

Going to university is an expensive thing to do. Today, the vast majority of graduates are heavily in debt and this burden will be with them for many years to come.

This extract is from an article in the online version of the *Birmingham Post* and illustrates the point: 'In 2004 the average graduate came out of university £12,000 worth in debt. The predicted amount of debt for a graduate leaving in 2009 is between £30,000-£40,000. It's an astonishing amount of money to pay back.'

So earning just a little bit now could really help your bank balance in the future.

• Showing commitment

If you're attracted to a career in popular professions like media, medicine and law, which are incredibly competitive and hard to get into, it could well prove necessary to grab any experience you can; paid or unpaid. It might make all the difference down the line when you have to prove to a potential employer that you really are committed.

• Work experience

Another consideration is the frequency with which people applying for jobs report being rejected at interview "because of a lack of work experience". A **gap-** is a great time to build up an initial experience of work culture as well as getting a foot in the door and getting recognised; in fact many students go back to the same firms after graduation.

• Not sure what you want to do?

If your degree left you with several possible options and you couldn't face the university final year/graduate 'milk round' or you're undecided what career direction you want to head in, then a **gap-** could be a great time to try out different jobs and to get a feel for what you might want to do in the future.

the gap-year guidebook 2010

Whatever your reasons for working during a **gap-** you should start looking early to avoid disappointment.

Writing a CV

Fashions change in laying out a CV and in what order you arrange the various sections.

The advice is that a CV should be no more than two A4 pages and also that it should be tailored to the sector you're applying for.

The thing to remember is that employers are busy people, so they won't have time to read many pages, especially if they're trying to create a shortlist of maybe six interviewees from more than 100 applications for just one job.

If you're at the start of your working life, there's a limit to how much tailoring you can do.

A good tip is to put a short summary of your skills, and experience to date, at the top so the recruiter knows what you can do. It can either be a bullet point list or a short paragraph, but remember that it's essentially your sales pitch explaining *why* you're useful to the company. It should only be a short summary of what's contained in the sections that follow.

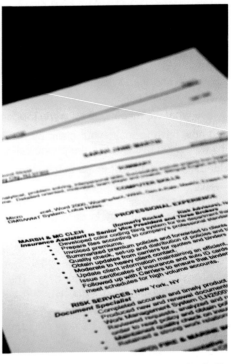

There are a number of online CV-writing advice sites and templates that can help you, but do check for any fees before you start.

Here's a selection:
www.careersadvice.direct.gov.uk/helpwithyourcareer/writecv/
www.cv-service.org/
www.alec.co.uk/cvtips/
www.soon.org.uk/cvpage.htm

Here's a list of headings for the details your CV should include:

• Personal details: name, address, phone and email. You do not have to include gender, age, date of birth, marital details or nationality nor send a photograph, in fact some employers actively discourage photos for fear of being accused of bias in selecting people for interview.

• Short skills paragraph or key skills bullet points (see above).

visit: www.gap-year.com

- Work experience and skills: in order with most recent first. You can include part time working that you've combined with education, as well as any voluntary work you've done, but if neither is directly within the job sector you're applying for, you need to focus on the transferable skills you got from it *eg*: familiarity with office routines, record keeping, filing, if you've been in an office, or people skills if you worked in a shop.

- Achievements: have you been on any committees? (student council?), organised any events or fundraisers? Again, concentrate on what you learned from it, such as organisational skills, persuading companies to donate prizes for a raffle, planning catering and refreshments.

- Other skills: such as the Duke of Edinburgh's Award Scheme, workshops you've attended, hobbies *etc*.

- Education: again most recent first, with subjects studied and grades.

- References: you usually need two, one of them a recent employer, the other from school or university, though on a CV you only need to say 'references can be supplied'.

Getting the job

How do you get that first job with no prior experience? What can you possibly offer?

The key is creativity. Show the company you're applying to that you can offer them something that nobody else can and do this by giving them an example.

Be creative: If you're applying to an advertising firm, for instance, then mock up some adverts to show them.

Want to go into journalism? Write some specimen articles and send them to local newspapers. Write to the editor and ask whether you could volunteer to help out in the newsroom to get a feel for the environment and the skills you'll need - a kind of extended work experience to add to what you should have had via school.

You could try this with companies in other fields you're interested in. Be proactive and persevering. It will show you have initiative and commitment and whatever your eventual career it will also help you to learn the basics of acting professionally in a professional environment.

Do the research: Whatever your chosen field, find out about the company and show your knowledge about the industry.

If you are going for an industry, such as medicine or law, then showing that you are more than competent and willing is all that you can really do. Saying this, you have to make sure that you stick out from other applicants.

Contacts

In the directory of this guidebook we list some companies that specifically employ **gap**-year students or offer graduate opportunities. But take this as a starting point - the tip of the iceberg - there are hundreds of other companies out there waiting to be impressed by you.

Research is crucial. Tailor your approach towards that specific company and never just expect to get a job; you have to work at it. The general rule is that nobody will call you back - be the one who gets in contact with them.

Job surfing

Most major job agencies, and many smaller ones, now have websites. You don't get the personal touch from a website that you do by going into a local branch and getting advice, or registering face-to-face, but recruitment websites are really useful if you know what you want to do and you have a 'skills profile' that one of their customers is looking for. Some of them are aimed at graduates and students, others at a general audience, others at specific areas of work (IT, for example).

Here are a few to start with:

Student summer jobs:

www.activate.co.uk
(This one contains **gap-**jobs, summer jobs, internships and jobs for new graduates.)

Graduate careers:

www.milkround.com
www.jobs.guardian.co.uk

General vacancies:

www.reed.co.uk
www.search.co.uk/jobs/
www.monster.com
(Good for jobs in UK, but also Europe and across the world.)
www.fish4jobs.co.uk
www.gumtree.com

Technology specialists:

www.agencycentral.co.uk/jobsites/IT.htm
(This site has a list of IT specialist recruiters.)

Finance - FT jobs site:

www.ft.com/jobsclassified

On spec

If you can't find what you're looking for by using contacts, advertisements, agencies or the internet there is always DIY job hunting. You can walk into shops and restaurants to ask about casual work or use a phone directory (*eg Yellow Pages*) to phone businesses (art galleries, department stores, zoos...) and ask what is available.

Ring up, ask to speak to the personnel or HR manager and ask if and when they might have jobs available and how you should apply. If they ask you to write in, you can do so after the call. If you go in, make sure you look smart.

visit: www.gap-year.com

Remember, opportunities in the big professional firms are not always well publicised.

Temporary jobs (except agency-filled ones) are often filled by personal contact. If you have a burning desire to work for an architects' or lawyers' firm, for example, and you find nothing advertised, you could try making a list and phoning to ask if work is available.

Think about people you might already know in different work environments and ask around for what's available.

Banking: approach your local branches for work experience. You can also try: **www.hays.com/banking/**

Education: most educational work experience is tied in with travelling abroad, to places like Africa or Asia, mostly to teach English. However, there are ways of gaining experience back home in England.

A very popular way is to see if the school that you have just left would like classroom helpers, or perhaps they need help in teaching a younger sports team. The key to this is to ask around and see what might be available.

But remember, for any work with children you will have to have a CRB (Criminal Records Bureau) check.

For more information, see: **www.crb.gov.uk**

As well as straight teaching, any experience with children can be very useful, so try looking at camps and sports teams that may need help - there are a few contacts for camps within the Seasonal Work section.

For jobs in education try: **www.tes.co.uk**

the gap-year guidebook 2010

Legal and medical: it's well known that studying for these two professions is lengthy and rigorous, so any amount of work experience could prove very useful. There's plenty available, but lots of competition for the places so you need to start looking early.

Nearly all NHS hospitals look for volunteer staff. So, if you can't find a worthwhile paid job, just contact the HR Manager at your local hospital.

Try also:

www.jobs.nhs.uk/
(for all NHS jobs)
www.lawgazettejobs.co.uk/content_static/home.asp
(for law jobs, including trainee positions)

Media, publishing and advertising: working on television or the radio is a favourite and it is no surprise that, because of this, the media is one of the hardest industries to break into.

Work experience is highly recommended. Many companies are very willing to try out **gap**-year students as trainees, as raw talent is such a limited commodity they want to nurture it as much as possible - plus it's cheap.

There are many websites dedicated to media jobs, but a good place to look for publishing vacancies is: **www.thebookseller.com**

Theatre: many theatres provide work experience for **gap**-year students, so it's definitely worthwhile contacting your nearby production company.

This industry recognises creativity and application probably more than any other, so starting out early and fiercely is the only way to do it.

Try also: **www.thestage.co.uk/recruitment/**

Interviews

Once your persistence has got you an interview, you need to impress your potential employers.

Attitude - confidence and knowledge are probably top of the list for employers, so that is what you must portray, even if you're a bag of nerves and haven't got a clue. They want to know you're committed.

Dress - make sure you are dressed appropriately (cover tattoos, remove nose piercings *etc*, don't show too much flesh, have clean and brushed hair - all the stuff that your teachers/parents tell you and really annoys you). If you're going for a creative job (advertising, art, *etc*) then you can probably be a little more casual - when you phone the secretary to confirm your interview time and venue, you can ask whether you'll be expected to dress formally. Alternatively, you could go to the company's offices around lunchtime (usually 1pm) and have a look at how people coming out are dressed.

Manner - stand straight; keep eye contact with the interviewer and smile.

Be positive about yourself - don't lie, but focus on your good points rather than your bad ones.

Be well prepared to answer the question: "So, why do you want this job?" -

remember they'll want to know you're keen, interested in what they do and what benefit you think you can bring to their company.

Gap-year specialists

If you would like to get a work placement from a **gap**-year specialist, the contacts listed in the directory sections in this guidebook are a good starting point for organisations to approach.

Another option is The Year Out Group, the voluntary association of **gap**-specialists formed to promote the concept and benefits of well-structured year out programmes and to help people select suitable and worthwhile projects. The group's member organisations are listed on their website and provide a wide range of year out placements in the UK and overseas, including structured work placements.

Year Out Group members are expected to put potential clients and their parents in contact with those who have recently returned. They consider it important that these references are taken up at least by telephone and, where possible, by meeting face-to-face.

The Year Out Group
Queensfield
28 Kings Road
Easterton
Wiltshire SN10 4PX

Tel: +44 (0) 1380 816696
www.yearoutgroup.org

Gap-year employers

In the directory we've listed companies that either have specific **gap**-year employment policies or ones that we think are worth contacting. We've split them into three groups: festivals, seasonal work and graduate opportunities and work experience.

This isn't a comprehensive list, so it's still worth checking the internet and your local companies (in the *Yellow Pages*, for example).

Festivals

Whether musical, literary or dramatic, there are all kinds of festivals taking place up and down the country every year. You need to apply as early as possible, as there aren't that many placements. Satellite organisations spring up around core festivals; so if you are unsuccessful at first, try to be transferred to another department. The work can be paid or on a voluntary basis. Short-term work, including catering and stewarding, is available mainly during the summer. Recruitment often starts on a local level, so check the local papers and recruitment agencies.

Seasonal and temporary work

A great way to make some quick cash, either to save up for travelling or to spend at home, is seasonal work. There are always extra short-term jobs going at Christmas: in the Post Office sorting office or in local shops.

In the summer there's fruit or vegetable picking for example. There's a website which links farms in the UK and worldwide with students looking for holiday work: **www.pickingjobs.com**

Another option, if you have reasonable IT skills, is to temp in an office. July and August are good months for this too, when permanent staff are on holiday. You can register with local job agencies, which will almost certainly want to do a simple test of your skills. Temping is also a great idea if you're not at all sure what sector you want to work in - it's a good chance to find out about different types of work.

Pay, tax and National Insurance

You can expect to be paid in cash for casual labour, by cheque (weekly or monthly) in a small company and by bank transfer in a large one. Always keep the payslip that goes with your pay, along with your own records of what you earn (including payments for casual labour) during the tax year: from 6 April one year to 5 April the next. You need to ask your employer for a P46 form when you start your first job and a P45 form when you leave (which you take to your next employer). If you are out of education for a year you are not treated as a normal taxpayer.

Personal allowances - that is the amount you can earn before paying tax - are reviewed in the budget each year in April. To find out the current tax-free personal allowance rate call the Inland Revenue helpline or go to: **www.hmrc.gov.uk/nic/**

Minimum wages, maximum hours

Since we published our last edition the Government has reviewed the minimum wage rate again from 1 October 2008, workers aged 16 and 17 should get a 'development rate' of £3.57 an hour; 18- to 21-year-old workers should receive £4.83 an hour; and workers aged 22 and over should get £5.80 per hour.

To check on how the National Minimum Wage applies to you, go to the Department for Business, Enterprise and Regulatory Reform (formerly called the DTI) website:

www.berr.gov.uk/employment/pay/national-minimum-wage/index.html

or phone the National Minimum Wage Helpline on 0845 6000 678.

If you think you are not being paid the national minimum wage you can call this helpline number: 0800 917 2368

All complaints about underpayment of the National Minimum Wage are treated in the strictest confidence.

The UK also has a law on working hours to comply with European Union legislation. This says that (with some exemptions for specific professions) no employee should be expected to work more than 48 hours a week. Good employers do give you time off in lieu if you occasionally have to work more than this. Others take no notice, piling a 60-hour-a-week workload on you. This is against the law and, unless you like working a 12-hour day, they must stop.

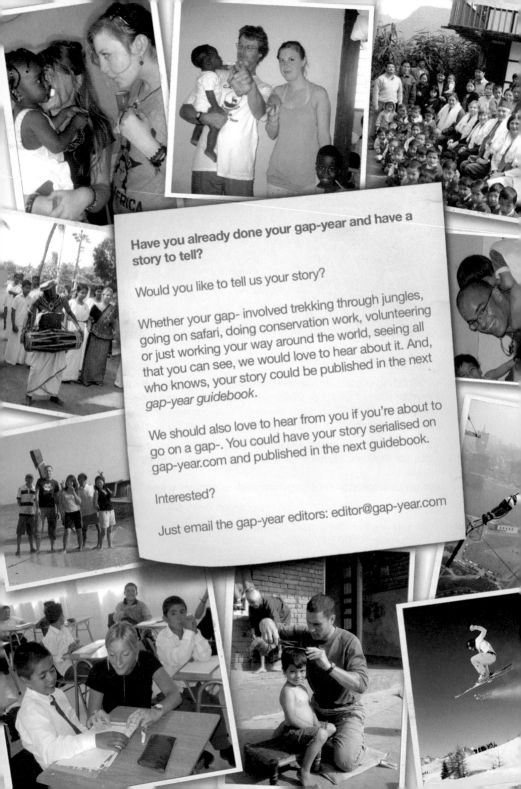

Have you already done your gap-year and have a story to tell?

Would you like to tell us your story?

Whether your gap- involved trekking through jungles, going on safari, doing conservation work, volunteering or just working your way around the world, seeing all that you can see, we would love to hear about it. And, who knows, your story could be published in the next *gap-year guidebook*.

We should also love to hear from you if you're about to go on a gap-. You could have your story serialised on gap-year.com and published in the next guidebook.

Interested?

Just email the gap-year editors: editor@gap-year.com

Festivals

Aldeburgh Music
Snape Maltings Concert Hall,
Snape, Suffolk IP17 1SP

Internships and work experience available in arts administration. Registered charity No. 261383.

Brighton Festival
12a Pavillion Buildings, Castle Square,
Brighton, East Sussex BN1 1EE

A handful of volunteer posts are open during the festival in May, working in the education and press office departments.

Cheltenham Festivals
Town Hall, Imperial Square,
Cheltenham, Gloucestershire GL50 1QA

This company runs festivals throughout the year, including jazz, science, music, folk, fringe and literary events. There are usually a number of placements available, although they tend to be unpaid.

Edinburgh Festival Fringe
180 High Street, Edinburgh, Midlothian EH1 1QS

Big and long-established late summer festival that has managed to stay cutting-edge.

Harrogate International Festival
Raglan House, Raglan Street,
Harrogate, Yorkshire HG1 1LE

Harrogate International Festival hosts a number of arts festivals, and offers six month internships and short-term work experience placements for three to four weeks during festivals.

Hay Festival
The Drill Hall, 25 Lion Street,
Hay-on-Wye, Herefordshire HR3 5AD

One of the most famous literary festivals in the UK. Most departments take on extra workers for festival fortnight, including stewards, extra staff for the box-office and the bookshop and three interns.

Holloway Arts Festival
c/o The Rowan Arts Project, 83 Sussex Way,
Holloway, London N7 6RU

Volunteering opportunities include being a steward for a day.

Ilkley Literature Festival
Manor House, 2 Castle Hill,
Ilkley, Yorkshire LS29 9DT

If you want to become a volunteer at the Ilkley Literature Festival fill in their online form. Jobs include stewarding and helping with mailouts.

Lichfield Festival
Festival Office, 7 The Close,
Lichfield, Staffordshire WS13 7LD

Volunteers required backstage, to assist with stage management and to help with the education programmes. Contact Richard Bateman, volunteer coordinator, for more details.

Mananan International Festival of Music and the Arts
The Erin Arts Centre,
Victoria Square, Port Erin,
Isle of Man IM9 6LD

Volunteers needed for stewarding duties, programme selling, transportation of artists, administration, catering, bar duties, technical support and manning galleries and shops.

Manchester International Festival
Festival Office, 3rd Floor, 81 King Street
Manchester, Lancashire M2 4AH

Your chance to volunteer to be a part of the world's first international festival of original, new work. Particularly good for those people interested in the arts or the cultural sector.

Norfolk and Norwich Festival Ltd
Festival Office, First Floor,
Augustine Steward House, 14 Tombland
Norwich NR3 1HF

Volunteers needed from January to May to help out with administration, marketing and even event production.

Portsmouth Festivities
Pippa Cleary, Administrator, 10 High Street,
Portsmouth, Hampshire PO1 2LN

Volunteers required to help out with the many varied festivities in Portsmouth.

Salisbury International Arts Festival
87 Crane Street,
Salisbury, Wiltshire SP1 2PU

Volunteering opportunities include stage manager, helping out with crowd management and leaflet distribution. Registered charity No. 276940.

Winchester Hat Fair
5a Jewry Street,
Winchester, Hampshire SO23 8RZ

This vibrant and entertaining festival takes over the centre of Winchester each year during the first weekend in July. Volunteers are needed to help out before and during the festival.

Youth Music Theatre
40 Parkgate Road,
Battersea, London SW11 4JH

Internships are available in their London office for recent arts graduates or for professionals looking to change career direction. Also need UK-wide volunteers for one to two days per week.

Graduate Opportunities & Work Experience

3M United Kingdom Plc
3M Centre, Cain Road,
Bracknell, Berkshire RG12 8HT

Industrial placement opportunities available, also graduate opportunities.

Accenture
60 Queen Victoria Street,
London EC4N 4TW

Apply for graduate placements with Accenture, a global management consulting, technology services and outsourcing company.

Alliance & Leicester plc
Carlton Park,
Narborough, Leicestershire LE19 0AL

They can't guarantee work but it will keep your CV on file in case a project comes up that needs extra staff, usually at the Narborough customer services centre.

Arcadia Group plc
Colegrave House, 70 Berners Street,
Soho, London W1T 3NL

They have placement postions in their finance and HR departments, suitable for those undertaking a year's placement as part of their degree.

BBC Recruitment
PO Box 48305,
Shepherd's Bush, London W12 6YE

Work experience placements available across the UK in all areas. These are unpaid placements that can last up to four weeks.

Competition is fierce so you need to apply at least a year in advance.

Cadbury Schweppes plc
Head Office, Cadbury House, Uxbridge Business Park,
Uxbridge, Middlesex UB8 1DH

Cadbury Schweppes places people on work experience in response to specific business needs. Contact the business units direct.

Cancer Research UK
PO Box 123, Lincoln's Inn Fields, London WC2A 3PX

Internships of 12 week duration for people who wish to gain valuable work experience in fundraising, as well as marketing, campaigning and communications. Registered Charity No. 1089464.

Civil Service Recruitment
HMGCC, Hanslope Park, Hanslope
Milton Keynes, Buckinghamshire MK19 7BH

The Civil Service website has no central contact office for recruitment. This address is for just one of the many different departments with vacancies for undergraduates and graduates. Check each department for details.

Colgate-Palmolive (UK) Ltd
Human Resources, Guildford Business Park,
Middleton Road, Guildford, Surrey GU2 8JZ

Twelve month placements offered to exceptional students wishing to acquire work experience. Send in your CV to Human Resources for consideration.

Deloitte
Stonecutter Court, 1 Stonecutter Street, London EC4A 4TR

This company runs a 'Scholars Scheme' which provides successful candidates the opportunity to combine travel during a gap-year with paid business experience.

Demos
Third Floor, Magdalen House, 136 Tooley Street
Southwark, London SE1 2TU

Independent social policy think tank and charity (Reg. No. 1042046) examining societal change and exploring public policy solutions. Internships available. Send CV and letter.

EMI Group plc
27 Wrights Lane, South Kensington, London W8 5SW

See website for details about a career or work experience with one of the largest record companies in the world.

Foreign & Commonwealth Office
King Charles Street, St James's, London SW1A 2AH

Careers and opportunities in the Diplomatic Service.

Future Publishing Plc
Beauford Court, 30 Monmouth Street,
Bath BA1 2BW

Work experience placements offered in their Bath and London offices. One week duration in all areas of publishing.

GlaxoSmithKline
GSK House, 980 Great West Road,
Brentford, Middlesex TW8 9GS

Industrial placements placement available.

HSBC Holdings plc
8 Canada Square, Canary Wharf, London E14 5HQ

HSBC has a worldwide graduate and internship programme.

IBM
UK Head Office, North Harbour, Cosham
Portsmouth, Hampshire PO6 3XJ

IBM run a number of Student Schemes for 'very talented individuals' in all aspects of their business.

IMI plc
Lakeside, Solihull Parkway, Birmingham Business Park
Birmingham, Warwickshire B37 7XZ

IMI operates a global graduate development programme and offers vacation work from June to September to penultimate year engineering (mechanical, electrical or manufacturing) students leading to possible sponsorship through the final year at university.

L'Oréal (UK) Ltd
255 Hammersmith Road, Hammersmith, London W6 8AZ

L'Oréal have over 2000 internships worldwide. Apply online.

Majestic Wine Warehouse
Majestic House, Otterspool Way,
Watford, Hertfordshire WD25 8WW

Majestic have a graduate recruitment programme and placement schemes for students needing work experience.

Marks & Spencer Plc
PO Box 288,
Warrington, Cheshire WA5 7WZ

They have a Student Support Scheme where they will give you a yearly grant providing you commit to 200 hours paid work in store and your parents have not gone to university. Places are limited. Gain valuable work experience with no obligation to join M&S when you graduate.

Penguin Group UK
80 Strand, London, WC2R 0RL

Has a variety of areas where you could gain valuable work experience. Placements are of two week durations and take place throughout the year. You must be 18.

PricewaterhouseCoopers
Southwark Towers, 32 London Bridge Street,
Southwark, London SE1 9SY

Worldwide company which was recently voted the number one graduate employer in the UK.

RAF
Walters Ash,
High Wycombe, Buckinghamshire HP14 4UE

Work experience places are available in RAF bases all over the UK. As each base runs its own work experience programme you need to check the RAF website to find one near you.

S & N Genealogy
West Wing, Manor Farm, Chilmark
Salisbury, Wiltshire SP3 5AF

Gap-year students required to do office work such as document scanning.

The National Magazine Company Ltd
National Magazine House, 72 Broadwick Street,
Soho, London W1F 9EP

Publishers of many of the UK's leading magazines, including *Esquire*, *Cosmo* and *Good Housekeeping*. To apply for work experience positions you need to email the editor of the magazine you are interested in.

The Random House Group Ltd
20 Vauxhall Bridge Road,
Westminster, London SW1V 2SA

Work experience opportunities are available in editorial, publicity and marketing. Complete their online form to apply.

UNHCR
Strand Bridge House, 138-142 Strand, London WC2R 1HH

The UNHCR have six month internships which give the participant the opportunity to gain valuable experience working with refugees.

Virgin Radio
Gareth & Hannah, Work Experience,
1 Golden Square, Soho, London W1F 9DJ

They have work experience places for over 18-year-olds currently studying media related courses. Send CV and covering letter.

Seasonal

Brightsparks Recruitment
Parsons Green House , 27 Parsons Green Lane,
Parsons Green, London SW6 4HH

Immediate vacancies in bar, waiting and hospitality work in the UK.

Facilities Management Catering
Church Road, Wimbledon, London SW19 5AE

If you would like to work at the most prestigious sporting event of the year then log onto our website now and click on the work opportunities page to apply online.

Hot Recruit
Beaumont House, Kensington Village,
Avonmore Road, Earl's Court, London W14 8TS

Search for temporary work, paid or unpaid, charity and fundraising jobs and seasonal holiday jobs abroad.

Kingswood Learning & Leisure Group
Kingswood House, Alkmaar Way, Norwich, Norfolk NR6 6BF

Kingswood offer an 'earn while you learn' development programme.

PGL Recruitment Team
PGL Travel Ltd, Alton Court, Penyard Lane
Ross-on-Wye, Herefordshire HR9 5GL

PGL runs activity holidays and courses for children. Each year the company employs over 2000 young people to work as instructors, group leader, catering and support staff at its centre in the UK, France and Spain.

Have you already done your gap-year and have a story to tell?

Would you like to tell us your story?

Whether your gap- involved trekking through jungles, going on safari, doing conservation work, volunteering or just working your way around the world, seeing all that you can see, we would love to hear about it. And, who knows, your story could be published in the next gap-year guidebook.

We should also love to hear from you if you're about to go on a gap-. You could have your story serialised on gap-year.com and published in the next guidebook.

Interested?

Just email the gap-year editors: editor@gap-year.com

Chapter 11

Volunteering in the UK

Volunteering in the UK

Volunteering doesn't have to be done in a developing country, amongst the poorest on the planet, to bring a sense of satisfaction. There are many deserving cases right on your doorstep. You might also find that, if you do voluntary work close to home, it will make you more involved in your own community.

What's more, the global recession that began towards the end of 2008 has prompted a greater need for volunteers, as charities have had to cut back on paid staff in the wake of reduced donations.

Equally some, like the British Red Cross, have also reported a huge increase in the numbers of potential volunteers - in some cases up to four times as many per month as they'd normally expect. Arguably this reflects the numbers of graduates coming out of university unable to find work as well as high numbers of reported redundancies.

A Red Cross spokeswoman said: "In response to the huge increase in applications from volunteers during 2009, we have increased the number of internships we offer, and have widened our volunteering roles to use the skills that people are offering us. We're seeing people coming from all sorts of occupations - banking, marketing, estate agents. These people have valuable skills to offer.

"Volunteer roles with the British Red Cross include first aiders, supporting emergency services, drivers, sales assistants, school and youth workers, refugee support, helpers for people recently discharged from hospital, fundraisers and office staff."

The charity offers training for qualifications and says volunteering could help people get back into work.

Some companies have also offered staff long holidays or sabbaticals in order to cut back on their salary bills during the downturn, in the hope of being able to take them back once the worst is over.

Benefits of UK volunteering

You can:

- Do some things you couldn't do abroad. Good examples are counselling, befriending and fundraising, all of which need at least some local knowledge.
- Have more flexibility: you can do a variety of things rather than opting for one programme or project.
- Combine volunteering with a study course or part time job.

325

- Get to know more about your own community.
- Get experience before committing to a project abroad.
- Develop career options - a now well-accepted route into radio for example is to do a volunteer stint on hospital radio.

It is sometimes argued that it's a little presumptuous to go off somewhere exotic, and help sort out the problems of the local disadvantaged people when things are plainly not all well in one's own backyard. While there may occasionally be some truth in this charge of 'cultural imperialism', it depends on what particular problems we're talking about and on the attitudes and knowledge of those seeking to help tackle them.

Equally there's no denying there are environmental issues, endangered species and disadvantaged people all over the world, and the skills of people willing to volunteer are desperately needed. So one element of deciding where to volunteer is likely to depend on your interests and skills.

If you choose to spend at least some of your **gap-** doing something for the benefit of others here in the UK, you'll get the same satisfying sense of achievement as volunteers who have been on programmes elsewhere. Wherever you are, volunteering is an opportunity to learn about other people and about yourself.

If you're just starting out on a career path and are unsure what you want to do, volunteering can be an opportunity to gain relevant work experience. If you know, for example, that you want a career in retail, a stint with Oxfam will teach you a surprising amount. Many charity shops recognise this and offer training. Careers in the charity sector are also extremely popular and can be quite hard to get into, so a period of voluntary work will demonstrate your commitment and willingness to learn.

Volunteering for a while can also be useful for those who are maybe thinking of a career change or development. For example you could use your skills to develop a charity's website, or perhaps you have experience of marketing or campaigning.

While you're volunteering your services you can also use the time to find out more about the organisation's work, whom to talk to about training or qualifications and about work opportunities within the organisation.

What can you do?

Before contacting organisations it is a good idea to think about what you would like to do in terms of the activity and type of organisation you would like to work for. There's good advice on this at:
www.volunteering.org.uk/IWantToVolunteer

visit: www.gap-year.com

The UK has its share of threatened environments and species, homeless people and the economically disadvantaged, and those with physical disabilities or mental health problems. In some ways, therefore, the choices for projects to join are no different in the UK from the ones you'd be making if you were planning to join a project abroad.

Cash strapped hospitals are always in need of volunteers - Great Ormond Street Children's Hospital in London is a good example. They look after seriously ill children and need volunteers to play with the children and make their stay less frightening. It also runs a hospital radio station - Radio Lollipop - in the evenings and on Sundays, for which it needs volunteers.

Or you could help with a youth sports team, get involved in a street art project, or with a holiday camp for deprived inner city youngsters - there are many options and there are any number of inner-city organisations working to improve relations between, and provide/identify opportunities for, people from different ethnic groups, faiths and cultures.

Remember, though, that any volunteer work you do that puts you directly in contact with young people and other vulnerable groups, such as people with mental health problems, or care of the elderly, is likely to mean you'll need a CRB (Criminal Records Bureau) check for both their protection and yours. In some cases, you'll have to pay for this yourself.

It costs £31 for a standard check and £36 for an enhanced check and you can find out more here:

www.crb.gov.uk/using_the_website/general_information.aspx

Where to start?

Your own hometown will have its share of charity shops on the high street, and they're always in need of volunteers. But you could also try local churches or sports groups. Check your local paper for stories on campaigns, special conservation days and other stories about good causes close to home that you might be able to support.

CSV - Community Service Volunteers - has a useful page on finding out more about types of volunteering that might interest you. It covers mentoring and befriending, environment, health and social care, media, schools and education: **www.csv.org.uk/Volunteer/Whats+Your+Interest/**

CSV also offers a variety of volunteer schemes appropriate to different lifestyles and age groups as well as training schemes to help you make the best of your skills.

What qualities does a good volunteer need?

The Samaritans is one organisation that's reported an upsurge in calls to its confidential helpline as a result of the recession - and if you've been in the position of losing your job, and are maybe thinking of volunteering to help others, it would be a good idea to think hard about whether you're able to offer what's needed.

Here's what the Samaritans have to say:

"Samaritans volunteers need to be able to listen. They are not professional counsellors. They can also:

- question gently, tactfully - without intruding;
- encourage people to tell their own story in their own time and space;
- refrain from offering advice and instead offer confidential emotional support; and
- always try to see the other point of view, regardless of their own religious or political beliefs."

From the Samaritans website:
www.samaritans.org/support_samaritans/volunteer.aspx

You can find out more here on the training and support you will be given before you are taken on.

ChildLine too has good advice for volunteers on its website and sees them as the essential basis of ChildLine's service. They need volunteers to speak to children and young people on their helpline, to work with them in schools, and to support fundraising, administration and management.

The charity provides full training and support, and has centres in London, Nottingham, Glasgow, Aberdeen, Manchester, Swansea, Rhyl, Leeds, Belfast, Exeter and Birmingham.

www.nspcc.org.uk/getinvolved/volunteer/childline/childlinevolunteering_wda56391.html

There's a need for volunteers to help with disadvantaged people of all ages and if you're older, and considering volunteering, your work skills could come in handy. Many charities may need professional advice from time to time. If you have expertise in accountancy, administration, construction and maintenance, the law, psychiatry or treasury you might be able to help.

Helping refugees

The International Red Cross has a long history of helping traumatised and displaced people around the world, from being the first port of call in an emergency to monitoring the treatment of political prisoners, it is often trusted as the only impartial authority allowed access to detainees.

The British Red Cross has a specific scheme dedicated to helping refugees adjust to life in the UK. Trained volunteers provide much needed support to thousands of people every year, helping them to access local services and adjust to life in a new country. The Red Cross' services provide practical/emotional help to vulnerable asylum seekers and refugees. This includes offering orientation services to help refugees adapt to life in the UK, providing emergency support for large-scale arrivals, providing emergency provisions for those in crisis and offering peer-befriending support to young refugees.

You can volunteer to help out in charity shops or with fundraising. There are also internships but the Red Cross doesn't send its volunteers overseas.

Here's what they say:

"The Red Cross Movement is made up of 179 National Societies, the British Red Cross being one of these. As each National Society has the capacity to draw upon its own body of volunteers, we don't send volunteers overseas. Not only does the Movement save time and money, but local volunteers have the advantage of speaking the language, knowing the region, and understanding the culture."

To find out more about volunteering with the Red Cross go to: **www.redcross.org.uk/TLC.asp?id=75777**

Conservation

Perhaps you're more interested in conservation work. The British Trust for Conservation Volunteers is a good place to start. It offers short (and longer) training courses which are informal and designed to be fun - including practical skills such as building a dry stone wall, creating a pond or a wildlife garden. It also has a number of options for volunteer schemes you can join: **www2.btcv.org.uk/display/volunteer**

Animals

Volunteer jobs with animal welfare organisations can vary from helping with kennel duties, assisting with fundraising events, carrying out wildlife surveys, to working on specific projects.

Animal Jobs Direct has information on paid work with animals but it also has a section for volunteers.

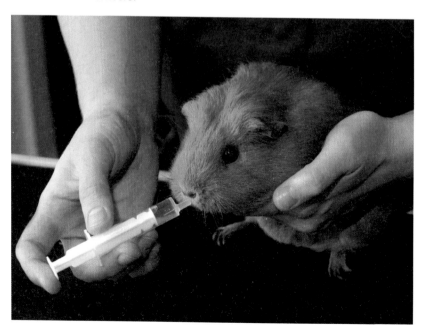

The web address below gives direct links to animal welfare and rescue charities that offer a variety of different and interesting volunteering opportunities - there are an amazing range of voluntary jobs available.

Remember, many animal charities exist on limited funds and therefore voluntary workers are much needed and appreciated.

To find out more, visit:
www.animal-job.co.uk/animal-volunteer-work-uk.html

Volunteering - with pay?

Although the definition for voluntary work is, strictly-speaking, work that you're not paid for, voluntary schemes (especially the government-inspired ones) will often pay you some pocket money and may also give you free meals and accommodation.

Each scheme varies in what it provides - there are no rules. The point is that these are not 'jobs'; what you will be doing is altruistic: helping someone or a specific cause, usually a charity, whether you're working on a nature reserve or doing the office filing.

For example, Shelter, the charity for the homeless, details the expenses it pays to its volunteers on its website:

www.england.shelter.org.uk/what_you_can_do/volunteer/expenses_for_ our_volunteers

In the directory we list the contact details of a number of charities and organisations that are grateful for volunteers. If you can't find anything that interests you there, then there are a number of organisations that place people with other charities or thta have a wide national network of their own - an internet search should give you a good list.

The following websites provide useful links and information about volunteering:
www.do-it.org.uk
www.ncvo-vol.org.uk
www.timebank.org.uk
www.vois.org.uk (specifically working with young people)
You have nothing to lose and so much to gain!

A three-part gap-

Jeremy was 43 when he decided he needed time out. He said: "[After] 20 years at the coal face - it was time for a break to recharge the batteries and to see what I wanted to do for the rest of my working life."

It was to be literally a life-changing experience. He'd negotiated a sabbatical with his then employer: "The deal I struck with my (now ex) employer was a guaranteed job after the year – though not the job I left."

But when he returned, he said: "In the end I was made redundant after two months searching within the business for a new role. I have now started my own photography business working for myself!"

Jeremy split his **gap**-year into three, one part of it to include his family. Here's what he did:

Part one: "Greenland via Reykjavik, Iceland (two weeks). I flew into a small hamlet (population 300) called Kulusuk on the east coast of Greenland, which is just south of the arctic circle, joining a photographic tour and travelled by small fishing boat into the fjords.

"[There were] two locations – one in an area of tundra and one at the foot of a glacier, where there was no vegetation as the rock had been exposed only in the last year. We camped at both and spent the days and nights (only about 1½ hrs) eating, sleeping and taking pictures. Came back with approx 3000 photos!"

Part two: "The alps in France to follow Le Tour – followed three stages of this legendary bike race in the mountains."

Part three: "Family Tour on the west coast of the US (one month) – landed in Las Vegas and went to Grand Canyon, Antelope Canyon, Yosemite, Lake Tahoe, Sonoma, San Francisco, Big Sur and flew out of Los Angeles – came back with approx 3000 photos!"

In between he spent his time planning the next stage, riding his bike and doing photography courses.

the gap-year guidebook 2010

His advice to gappers is to go for it: "If there is a way that you can afford it or circumstance conspires to make you take the chance. It will change you and the chance may never come again. There were a lot of jealous people when I left the office for the last time!

"A year flies by (even though it seems slow to start) so make sure you know what you want to get from it. This may change as the year goes on so be flexible enough to accommodate this."

Now he says it's: "One of the best things I ever did! Chance to unwind – I deliberately took no decisions for the first month. May seem a waste but this enabled me to truly unwind from the stresses of the job I had left. I have become a much more pleasant person – my view and those of friends!"

And as for getting back to normal: "I'll never go back to what I was doing so it will be a new normal."

Volunteering in the UK

Fundraising

Marie Curie Cancer Care (Head Office)
89 Albert Embankment,
Vauxhall, London SE1 7TP

Volunteer. Help in their shops, hospices and/or offices, or get involved in fundraising for Marie Curie (Registered Charity No. 207994).

Scope
6 Market Road,
Holloway, London N7 9PW

Cerebral palsy charity (No. 208231) which needs your help in raising funds.

SOS Rhino
Lot 15, Block B, 2nd Floor, Visa Light Industrial Centre,
Mile 5-1/2 Tuaran Road, Sabah 88856 Inanam, Malaysia

SOS Rhino needs donations to help them in their work to save the Sumatran rhinoceros. Why not choose them as your charity fundraising beneficiary?

War on Want
FAO David Rudkin, Development House,
56-64 Leonard Street, St Luke's, London EC2A 4LT

Fundraise for War on Want. Registered Charity No. 208724.

Wesser and Partner
St John Ambulance County HQ,
The White House, Argyle Way
Stevenage, Hertfordshire SG1 2AD

Wesser offers you the chance to fundraise for St John Ambulance, work outside, socializing and living with like-minded individuals and earning an uncapped sum of money. Be part of something worthwhile ...

Volunteering Opportunities

Amnesty International
The Human Rights Action Centre,
17-25 New Inn Yard, Shoreditch, London EC2A 3EA

Amnesty International (registered charity No: 1051681) have a selection of volunteering vacancies throughout their UK offices. Volunteer roles are advertised on their website. Speculative applications are not accepted.

Ashbourne Arts Ltd
St John's Community Hall, King Street,
Ashbourne, Derbyshire DE6 1EA

Ashbourne Arts is a not-for-profit company who rely entirely on volunteers.

Barnabas Adventure Centres
Carroty Wood, Higham Lane,
Tonbridge, Kent TN11 9QX

Opportunities are available to assist in the practical running of the Barnabas Trust centres. (Registered Charity No. 1107724)

Beamish, The North of England Open Air Museum
The Friends' Office, Beamish,
County Durham DH9 0RG

Beamish Museum is a unique place. A registered charity (No. 517147) they rely on volunteers to help them in their work: from taking visitor surveys to working on their many restoration projects.

Born Free Foundation
3 Grove House, Foundry Lane,
Horsham, West Sussex RH13 5PL

The Born Free Foundation has grown into a global force for wildlife. Volunteer with their major international projects devoted to animal welfare, conservation and education. They also list other possible overseas volunteering vacancies.

British Red Cross
44 Moorfields, Barbican, London EC2Y 9AL

'Volunteers are the lifeblood of the British Red Cross.' As well as volunteering, the British Red Cross (Charity No. 220949) offered internships and work experience opportunities for those still at school.

BTCV
Sedum House, Mallard Way, Potteric Carr
Doncaster, Yorkshire DN4 8DB

BTCV runs working conservation holidays in the UK and in more than 25 countries abroad working in partnership with other organisations.

Camphill Communities in the UK
Co-worker Development Office,
55 Cainscross Road,
Stroud, Gloucestershire GL5 4EX

Camphill is a worldwide network of communities dedicated to work and life with children, adolescents or adults with developmental and other disabilities.

Careforce
35 Elm Road, New Malden,
Surrey KT3 3HB

Each year Careforce recruits Christians aged 17 to 30 and places them at churches and community projects across the UK.

Cats Protection League
National Cat Centre, Chelwood Gate,
Haywards Heath, Sussex RH17 7TT

Volunteering opportunities available in a wide variety of roles, see their website for more details. Registered charity No. 203644.

Central Scotland Forest Trust
Hillhouseridge, Shottskirk Road, Shotts, Lanarkshire ML7 4JS

CSCT organises volunteers to help with ecological improvements in Central Scotland. Work includes fence repairing and path building. Reg Charity SC015341.

Centre for Alternative Technology
Llwyngwern Quarry, Pantperthog,
Machynlleth, Powys SY20 9AZ

CAT has volunteer placements from one week to six months in length. Registered Charity 265239

Children with Leukaemia
51 Great Ormond Street, Bloomsbury, London WC1N 3JQ

Britain's leading charity (Registered No. 298405) dedicated to the conquest of childhood leukaemia through pioneering research, new treatment and support of leukaemic children and their families.

Children's Country Holidays Fund
Stafford House, 91 Keymer Road, Hassock, Sussex BN6 8QJ

CCHF (registered charity number 206958) Volunteers required to help out on week long or weekend activity breaks for severely disadvantaged children. Meals and accommodation provided, subject to interview, CRB check and references.

Christian Aid Gap Year
2a Deans Court Lane, Wimborne, Dorset BH21 1EE

Have placements between September and June each year for volunteers in their offices around the UK.

Churchtown - A Vitalise Centre
Volunteering Team, Shap Road Industrial Estate, Shap Road
Kendal, Cumbria LA9 6NZ

Vitalise provide essential services for the disabled and visually impaired people. They always need volunteers. Registered Charity No.295072.

Conservation Volunteers Northern Ireland
Beech House, 159 Ravenhill Road, Belfast, County Antrim BT6 0BP

Conservation Volunteers, part of BTCV, provides all-year-round volunteering opportunities on a broad range of practical environmental projects across Northern Ireland.

CSV (Community Service Volunteers)
Head Office, 237 Pentonville Road, Islington, London N1 9NJ

CSV is the largest volunteering organisation in the UK. Has full-time volunteering programme provides hundreds of free gap-year placements at social care projects throughout the UK.

Dartington International Summer School
The Barn, Dartington Hall,
Totnes, Devon TQ9 6DE

Volunteer as a Steward or a Trog. The work is physically demanding and involves long hours but you do get free accommodation, food and the opportunity to gain experience in arts administration. Reg Charity No. 279756.

Dogs Trust
Personnel Officer, 17 Wakley Street, Pentonville, London EC1V 7RQ

Volunteers needed to help out in the following areas: fundraising, dog walking, dog socialising and pre-adoption home visiting. Registered Charity No. 227523.

Elizabeth Finn Care
1 Derry Street, South Kensington, London W8 5HY

Charity (No. 207812) that aims to help by giving financial support where needed to those with limited resources who live in their own homes, or by providing accommodation for older people in their own care homes. Volunteers always needed.

Emmaus UK
48 Kingston Street, Cambridge, Cambridgeshire CB1 2NU

Emmaus Communities (Registered Charity No. 1064470) offer homeless people a home and full time work refurbishing and selling furniture and other donated goods. They list various volunteer opportunities on their website.

English Heritage
Education Volunteers Manager, PO Box 569,
Swindon, Wiltshire SN2 2YP

English Heritage are looking for people who are aged 18 and over to assist with workshops, tours and other activities associated with learning and school visits.

Friends of The Earth
26-28 Underwood Street, Hoxton, London N1 7JQ

Friends of The Earth welcomes volunteers at their head office in London, or at any of their regional offices. Registered Charity No. 281681

Global Adventure Challenges Ltd
Red Hill House, Hope Street, Saltney, Chester, Cheshire CH4 8BU

Raise money for your chosen charity whilst having the adventure of a lifetime. Many adventures to choose from are listed on their website.

Greenpeace
Human Resources Department, Canonbury Villas, Islington, London N1 2PN

Greenpeace need volunteers either as an active supporter or in their London office to help out with their administration. Registered Charity No. 284934.

Groundwork Oldham & Rochdale
Environment Centre, Shaw Road, Higginshaw
Oldham, Lancashire OL1 4AW

Volunteering opportunities for people aged 16-25. Registered Charity No. 514726

Hearing Dogs for Deaf People
The Grange, Wycombe Road, Saunderton
Princes Risborough, Buckinghamshire HP27 9NS

Become a volunteer with Hearing Dogs for Deaf People (Registered charity No.293358). Contribute to the life changing work of this Charity by visiting their website and clicking on 'Work with us'.

ILA (Independent Living Alternatives)
Trafalgar House, Grenville Place,
Mill Hill, London NW7 3SA

Aims to enable people who need personal assistance, to be able to live independently in the community and take full control of their lives.

London 2012
One Churchill Place,
Canary Wharf, London E14 5LN

Recruitment of volunteers begins in 2010 and they advise early registration of your interest. Selection of successful candidates will not be on a first come, first served, basis but on volunteering experience and appropriate skills.

Macmillan Cancer Support (UK Office - Volunteering)
89 Albert Embankment, Vauxhall, London SE1 7UQ

Share your skills to improve the lives of people affected by cancer. Assist our fundraising activities or support us in our offices and gain new experience whilst having fun. Registered Charity No. 261017.

Mind
15-19 Broadway, Stratford, London E15 4BQ

Mind (Registered Charity No. 424348) would like to hear from you if you would like to take part in a fundraising event, or have an idea for fundraising for the charity.

Museum of London
150 London Wall, Barbican, London EC2Y 5HN

Volunteer at the Museum of London.

NSPCC
Weston House, 42 Curtain Road, Shoreditch, London EC2A 3NH

Volunteers needed to help with fundraising, office work, manning the switchboard at Childline or even helping on a specific project. (Reg. Charity No. 216401)

PDSA
Whitechapel Way, Priorslee, Telford, Shropshire TF2 9PQ

A wide range of volunteering opportunities offered. Use the contact form on their website to find out about opportunities in the UK and Ireland. Registered Charity No. 208217.

Plan UK
5-6 Underhill Street, Camden Town, London NW1 7HS

Plan UK works with children and their communities in the world's poorest countries aiming to vastly improve their quality of life. Volunteer opportunities and internships available.

Rainforest Concern
8 Clanricarde Gardens, Notting Hill, London W2 4NA

Sends volunteers to Ecuador, Costa Rica and Panama to work with important conservation programmes in the Amazon and the Andes, as well as the Leatherback Turtle project.

RNLI
HR Core Services, West Quay Road,
Poole, Dorset BH15 1HZ

Volunteer lifeguards required. Registered Charity No. 209603.

Royal Botanic Gardens
Volunteer Co-ordinator, Museum Number 1, Kew
Richmond, Surrey TW9 3AB

Volunteers can help out at the Royal Botanic Gardens in five different areas: School explainers, horticultural, friends of Kew, volunteer guides and in the climbers and crepers play zone.

RSPB (Royal Society for the Protection of Birds)
The Lodge, Potton Road,
Sandy, Bedfordshire SG19 2DL

Volunteers are always needed to help the RSPB (Registered Charity No. 207076) carry out their work.

RSPCA
Wilberforce Way, Southwater, Horsham, Surrey RH13 9RS

The RSPCA (registered charity no. 219099) are always looking for volunteers.

Samaritans
The Upper Mill, Kingston Road,
Ewell, Surrey KT17 2AF

The Samaritans (Registered Charity No. 219432) depend entirely on volunteers. They are there 24/7 for anyone who needs help. Can you spare the time to help them?

Sense
Head Office, 101 Pentonville Road,
Pentonville, London N1 9LG

Volunteers always required by Sense (Registered Charity No. 289868) in a variety of areas.

SHAD
5 Bedford Hill, Balham, London SW12 9ET

Are you aged over 18 years, with four months (or more) to spare? Personal Assistants are needed to enable physically disabled adults to live independently in their own homes.

Shelter
88 Old Street, St Luke's, London EC1V 9HU

Volunteering opportunities available throughout the UK. Registered Charity No. 263710.

The Blue Cross
Shilton Road, Burford, Oxfordshire OX18 4PF

The Blue Cross is Britain's pet charity (No. 224392), providing practical support, information and advice for pet and horse owners.

The Children's Trust
Tadworth Court, Tadworth, Surrey KT20 5RU

The Children's Trust (Registered Charity No. 288018) run a residential centre for about 80 severely disabled children, and is always looking for people to get involved.

The Monkey Sanctuary Trust
St Martins, Looe, Cornwall PL13 1NZ

Monkey Sanctuary Trust (Registered Charity No. 1102532) needs volunteer help all year round, making monkey food, cleaning enclosures, helping serve the public in the summer and maintenance and other projects in the winter. Volunteers do not work directly with the monkeys.

The National Trust
National Trust Central Volunteering Team, Heelis, Kemble Drive
Swindon, Wiltshire SN2 2NA

Learn new skills whilst helping to conserve the UK's heritage. Volunteering opportunities can be found on their website. Registered Charity No. 205846.

The National Trust for Scotland
Volunteering Office, Wemyss House, 28 Charlotte Square
Edinburgh, Midlothian EH2 4ET

The National Trust for Scotland is a conservation charity (No. SC 007410) that protects and promotes Scotland's natural and cultural heritage for present and future generations to enjoy. Contact them to find out about volunteering opportunities.

The Prince's Trust
Head Office, 18 Park Square East, Regent's Park, London NW1 4LH

Volunteer with the Prince's Trust (Registered Charity No. 1079675) and help young people achieve something with their lives. Opportunities in fundraising, personal mentoring, volunteer co-ordinator and training. See website for vacancies in your area.

The Simon Community
129 Malden Road, Camden, London NW5 4HS

The Simon Community is a partnership of homeless people and volunteers living and working with London's homeless. They need full-time residential volunteers all year round. Registered Charity No. 283938.

The Wildlife Trusts
The Kiln, Waterside, Mather Road
Newark, Nottinghamshire NG24 1WT

The Wildlife Trusts (Registered Charity No. 207238) always need volunteers. Check out their website or contact your local office for information about vacancies in your area.

Time for God
North Bank, 28 Pages Lane,
Muswell Hill, London N10 1PP

Time for God co-ordinates national and international projects, including youth and community work, homeless and rehabilitation projects. Registered Charity No. 1101997.

UNICEF (United Nations Childrens Fund)
Africa House, 64-78 Kingsway, Holborn, London WC2B 6NB

UNICEF normally has two or three volunteers working in its main office at any one time, and local offices will always need help: apply to them direct. Registered Charity No. 1072612.

Vinspired
5th Floor, Dean Bradley House,
52 Horseferry Road
Westminster, London SW1P 2AF

Formerly the Millennium Volunteer Programme, Vinspired is a volunteering site for those aged between 16 and 25. Registered Charity No. 1113255.

Vitalise
Volunteer Team, Shap Road Industrial Estate, Shap Road
Kendal, Cumbria LA9 6NZ

Vitalise runs centres providing holiday and respite opportunities for people with disabilities and their carers. Volunteers are welcomed and needed, and will receive accommodation and board.

Volunteer Reading Help
Charity House, 14-15 Perseverance Works,
38 Kingsland Road, Hackney, London E2 8DD

National charity (No. 296454) that helps primary school children who find reading a struggle. Training takes six hours and volunteers work with the same children every week, giving at least an hour of their time.

Whizz-Kidz
Elliott House, 10-12 Allington Street,
Westminster, London SWIE 5EH

Whizz-Kidz aims to improve the lives of disabled under-18s by providing wheelchairs, trikes, walking aids and so on. Contact them direct to find out about overseas challenge events such as climbing Kilimanjaro or walking the Great Wall of China.

Youth Hostel Association
Trevelyan House, Dimple Road,
Matlock, Derbyshire DE4 3YH

The YHA has Youth Hostels around the country and needs volunteers to help with running them and maintaining the local environment and paths, as well as fundraising.

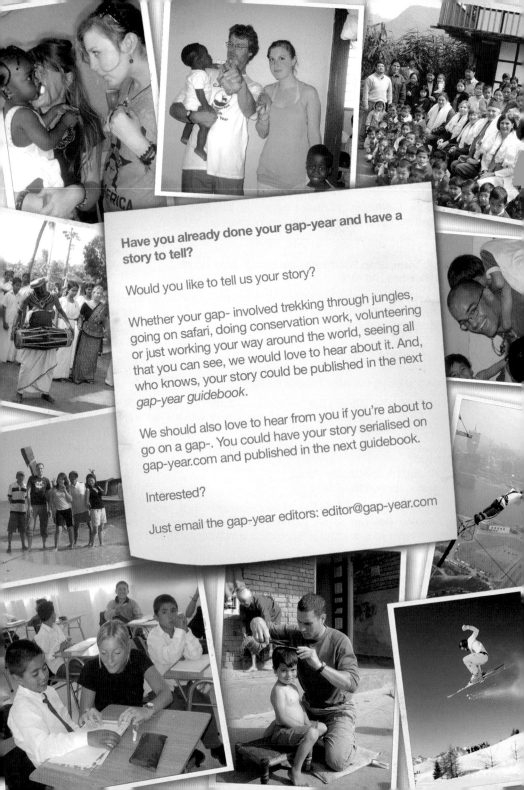

Have you already done your gap-year and have a story to tell?

Would you like to tell us your story?

Whether your gap- involved trekking through jungles, going on safari, doing conservation work, volunteering or just working your way around the world, seeing all that you can see, we would love to hear about it. And, who knows, your story could be published in the next *gap-year guidebook*.

We should also love to hear from you if you're about to go on a gap-. You could have your story serialised on gap-year.com and published in the next guidebook.

Interested?

Just email the gap-year editors: editor@gap-year.com

Chapter 12

Learning
in the UK

You don't have to spend your **gap**-year travelling the globe if that doesn't appeal to you. The point about taking a **gap-** is to try out new experiences that leave you feeling refreshed and stimulated, to learn something new and possibly come up with some new ideas about where you want your life to head next.

So if you're frustrated that hardly anything you were taught at school seems relevant to your life, why not use your **gap**-year to learn new skills that you choose yourself? You can make them as useful as you want.

There are plenty of evening classes available at local colleges, though usually only in term time, and, if you're thinking of training that doesn't involve university or are looking for ways to expand your skill set as part of a change of career direction, check out the Learning and Skills Council, which exists to promote lifelong learning, with the aim of young people and adults having skills to match the best in the world by the year 2010. There's lots of information on what's available, including financial help, on:
www.lsc.gov.uk/

A **gap-** is also a good opportunity to explore interests that may, up to now, have been hobbies; here are some suggestions:

Archaeology

Do relics from the past fascinate you? Would you love to find one? You could get yourself on an actual archaeological dig. One good place to start is with

345

your local county council's Archaeology Department, which may know of local digs you could join. Nowadays, whenever a major building development is going through the planning application process, permission to build often includes a condition allowing for archaeological surveys to be done before any work can begin; so another source of information could be the planning departments of local district councils.

Art

If you're seriously interested in painting, sculpting or other artistic subjects, but don't know if you want to carry it through to a full degree, there is the useful option of a one-year art foundation course. These are available from a wide variety of art colleges.

A foundation course at Art College doesn't count towards an art degree, in the sense that you can then skip the first year of your three-year degree course, but it can help you find out whether you are interested in becoming a practising artist, maybe an illustrator, an animator, a graphic designer, or are more interested in things like art history, or perhaps working in a gallery or a museum or in a field like interior design.

If you do want to go onto the three-year art school degree, competition for undergraduate places is based on the volume and standard of work in a candidate's entry portfolio. Having a portfolio from your foundation course puts you at a natural advantage. Course providers also advise against specialising in one discipline, say sculpture, before covering the more wide-ranging syllabus of a foundation course.

Cookery

Can you cook? There are really two types of cookery courses for gappers: basic skills and how to earn money.

The basic skills courses are for those who want to be able to feed themselves more than baked beans or packet soup. These courses can take you from boiling water through to quite a reasonable level - you may not be able to cook for a dinner party of 12, but you should finish the course with enough skills to be able to cook a variety of tasty meals without poisoning anyone. Cheap and cheerful cookery courses (standard, ethnic, exotic) can be found at day or evening classes at local colleges of further education. Usually the fees are low but you have to pay for, or provide your own, ingredients.

The second type of course is aimed at teaching you the skills needed to work as a cook during your **gap**-year. Working as a cook in ski resorts, on yachts in the Caribbean or in villas in Tuscany or the south of France not only allows you to see the world, but also pays you while you see it.

Cookery schools tell us that the majority of those who want to work after doing a cookery course do find cooking work.

What's involved in being a chalet cook depends on what a ski company or employer wants. Usually the day starts with a cooked breakfast for the ski party, then possibly a packed lunch, tea and cake when hungry skiers get

back, possibly canapés later, and a three- or four-course supper. The food does need more than the usual amount of carbohydrate.

Ski companies expect high standards and may ask for sample menus when you apply for chalet cooking jobs. Sometimes the menus are decided in advance and the shopping done locally by someone else; sometimes the cook has to do the shopping.

Perhaps surprisingly, ski companies and agencies rarely ask about language skills - the cooks seem to manage without (see Chapter 7 - Working Abroad, for ideas on making use of your new skills).

Drama

There are plenty of amateur dramatic and operatic societies in small towns across the UK. If you've always had a hankering to tread the boards, they're a great way to find out more about all the elements of putting on a production. You may be able to volunteer at your local theatre and gain valuable experience that way. Ring them up or check out their website to see if they have a volunteers bank.

Then there are short courses and summer schools. This site lists a wide range of programmes available over the summer holidays:
www.summer-schools.info

Driving

There may be a lot of pressure to minimise car use in an effort to reduce carbon emissions and tackle global warming, but there are still plenty of good reasons for learning to drive.

First, unless you're intending to live in an inner city indefinitely, you may need a driver's licence to get a job; secondly, it will give you independence and you won't have to rely on everyone else to give you lifts everywhere. Even though

you might not be able to afford the insurance right now, let alone an actual car, your **gap-**year is an ideal time to take driving lessons.

The test comes in two parts, theory and practical: and you need to pass the theory test before you apply for the practical one. However, you can start learning practical driving before you take the theory part, but to do that you need a provisional driving licence. You need to complete a driving licence application form and a photocard application form D1 (formerly D750) - available from most post offices. Send the forms, the fee and original documentation confirming your identity such as your passport or birth certificate (make sure you keep a photocopy) and a passport-sized colour photograph to the DVLA.

You also need to check that you are insured for damage to yourself, other cars or other people, and if you are practising in the family car, your parents will have to add cover for you on their insurance.

The DSA (Driving Standards Authority) is responsible for driving tests. However, to avoid duplication all information on learning to drive, including fees, advice on preparing for the test and booking one has been moved to the Direct Gov website:
www.direct.gov.uk/en/Motoring/LearnerAndNewDrivers/LearningToDriv eOrRide/index.htm

visit: www.gap-year.com

Theory

The theory test is in two parts: a multiple-choice part and a hazard perception section. You have to pass both. If you pass one and fail the other, you have to do both again.

The multiple-choice is a touch-screen test where you have to get at least 43 out of 50 questions right. You don't have to answer the questions in turn and the computer shows how much time you have left. You can have 15 minutes practice before you start the test properly. If you have special needs you can get extra time for the test - ask for this when you book it.

In the hazard test, you are shown 14 video clips filmed from a car, each containing one or more developing hazards. You have to indicate as soon as you see a hazard developing, which may necessitate the driver taking some action, such as changing speed or direction. The sooner a response is made the higher the score. Test results and feedback information are given within half an hour of finishing. The fee for the standard theory test is currently £31.00

Your driving school, instructor or local test centre should have an application form, although you can book your test over the phone (0300 200 1122) or online at:
www.direct.gov.uk/en/Motoring/LearnerAndNewDrivers/TheoryTest/DG_4022537

Practical test

You have two years to pass the practical test once you have passed the theory part. The practical test for a car will cost £62.00, unless you choose to take it in the evening or on Saturday, in which case the cost will increase to £75. It's more expensive for a motorbike and the test is now in two modules - module 1 is £10 for both evenings and weekends, module 2 is £70.00 for weekday and £82 for weekend and evening tests. You can book the practical test in the same way as the theory test. The bad news is that the tests are tough and it's quite common to fail twice or more before a pass. The practical test requires candidates to drive on faster roads than before - you'll need to negotiate a dual carriageway as well as a suburban road. You'll fail if you commit more than 15 driving faults. Once you pass your practical test, you can exchange your provisional licence for a full licence.

Instructors

Of course some unqualified instructors (including parents) are experienced and competent, as are many small driving schools - but some checking out is a good idea if a driving school is not a well-known name. You can make sure that it is registered with the Driving Standards Agency and that the instructor is qualified. AA and BSM charges can be used as a benchmark if you're trying other schools. There's information about choosing an instructor and what qualifications they must have if they're charging you here:
www.direct.gov.uk/en/Motoring/LearnerAndNewDrivers/LearningToDriveOrRide/DG_4022528

Language courses

Even if the job you are applying for doesn't require them, employers are often impressed by language skills. With the growth of global business, most companies like to think of themselves as having international potential at the very least.

If you didn't enjoy language classes at school, that shouldn't necessarily put you off. College courses and evening classes are totally different - or at least they should be. If in doubt, ask to speak to the tutor, or to someone who has already been on the course, before you sign up.

And even if you don't aspire to learn enough to be able to use your linguistic skills in a job, you could still take conversation classes so you can speak a bit of the language when you go abroad on your holidays. It is amazing what a sense of achievement and self confidence you can get when you manage to communicate the simplest things to a local in their own language: such as ordering a meal or buying stamps for your postcards home.

The best way to improve your language skills is to practice speaking; preferably to a native speaker in their own country. But if you don't have the time or the money to go abroad yet, don't worry. There are plenty of places in the UK to learn a wide variety of languages, from Spanish to Somali. We've listed some language institutions in the directory, but also find out what language courses your local college offers, and what evening classes there are locally.

Online learning

There are plenty of online language learning courses for those who are welded semi-permanently to their computers.

You can now get very comprehensive language courses on CD-ROM, which include booklets or pages that can be printed off. The better ones use voice recognition as well, so you can practise your pronunciation. These can also be found in bookstores.

The internet itself is also a good source of language material. There are many courses, some with free access, some that need a very healthy credit card. If all you want is a basic start, then take a look at:
www.bbc.co.uk/languages/

This site offers you the choice of beginner's French, German, Italian, Mandarin, Portuguese, Greek, Spanish, Japanese, Urdu and some other languages, complete with vocabulary lists to download, all for free.

As well as courses, there are translation services, vocabulary lists and topical forums - just do a web search and see how many sites come up. Many are free but some are extremely expensive so check before you sign up.

Practice makes perfect

When you need to practise, find out if there are any native speakers living in your town - you could arrange your own language and cultural evenings.

Terrestrial TV stations run some language learning programmes, usually late at night. If you have satellite or cable TV you can also watch foreign shows though this can be a bit frustrating if you're a beginner. It's best to record the programmes so you can replay any bits that you didn't understand the first time round.

Once you get a bit more advanced then you can try tuning your radio into foreign speech-based shows from the relevant countries. This is also a good way to keep up-to-date with current affairs in your chosen country, as well as keeping up your listening and understanding skills. Subjects are wide-ranging, and there's something to interest everyone.

Most self-teach language tapes have been well received by teachers and reviewers, but can be a bit expensive for the average **gap-**year student. So, you might be glad to hear that, if you have iTunes, you can download language podcasts from the store. Most of these are free and you have the option of subscribing so that new podcasts are automatically downloaded next time you log on.

Music

Perhaps you always wanted to learn the saxophone, but never quite got round to it? Now would be an ideal time to start. If you're interested, your best bet is to find a good private tutor. Word of mouth is the best recommendation, but some teachers advertise in local papers, and you could also try an online search engine like Musicians' Friend: **www.musiciansfriend.co.uk**

If you already play an instrument, you could broaden your experience by going on a residential course or summer school. These are available for many different ability levels, although they tend to be quite pricey. There's no central info source on the net, as there is for drama courses, but we searched the internet for residential summer music schools and found loads of individual schools offering courses, so there are bound to be some near you. See the directory for more information.

Photography

There are lots of photography courses available, from landscape photography to studio work. Don't kid yourself that a photography course is going to get you a job and earn you pots of money, but there's nothing to stop you enjoying photography as a hobby or sideline.

If you do want to find out more about professional photography you could try contacting local studios and asking about the possibility of spending some time with them as a studio assistant. Another option is to contact your local paper and ask if you can shadow a photographer, so you can get a feel for how they work and perhaps start building a portfolio of your own.

Sport

After all that studying maybe all you want to do is get out there and do something. The same applies if you've been stuck in an office at a computer for most of your working life. If you're the energetic type and hate the thought of spending your **gap**-year stuck behind a desk, why not get active and do some sport? There are sports courses for all types at all levels, from scuba diving for beginners to advanced ski instructor qualification courses. Of course if you manage to get an instructor's qualification you may be able to use it to get a job (see Chapter 7 - Working Abroad).

TEFL

Teaching English as a Foreign Language qualifications are always useful for earning money wherever you travel abroad. The important thing to check is that the qualification you will be gaining is recognised by employers. Most courses should also lead on to help with finding employment. There's more on TEFL courses in Chapter 7 - Working Abroad.

X-rated

If you hated sport at school, try giving it another chance during your **gap**-year - you may be surprised how much you like it. There are plenty of unusual sports to try.

For a real adrenalin rush, go for one of the extreme sports like sky boarding, basically a combination of skydiving and snowboarding - you throw yourself out of a plane wearing a parachute and perform acrobatic stunts on a board. Or, if you like company when you're battling against the elements, then you could get involved in adventure racing: teams race each other across rugged terrain without using anything with a motor, *eg* skiing, hiking, sea kayaking. Team members have to stay together throughout the race. Raid Gauloises (five person teams, two weeks, five stages, half the teams don't finish!) and Eco-Challenge (ten days, 600km, several stages and an environmental project) are the two most well known adventure race events.

The annual X Games feature a wide range of extreme sports and take place during one week in summer (including aggressive in-line skating) and another week in winter (including mountain bike racing on snow). Check out their website (**www.expn.go.com**) for the full details.

If you want to get wet, then try diving, kayaking, sailing, surfing, water polo, windsurfing, or white-water rafting.

And if those don't appeal then there's always abseiling, badminton, baseball, basketball, bungee jumping, cave diving, cricket, fencing, football, golf, gymnastics, hang gliding, hockey, horse riding, ice hockey, ice skating, jet skiing, motor racing, mountain biking, mountain boarding, netball, parachuting, polo, rock climbing, rowing, rugby, running, skateboarding, skating, ski jumping, skiing, skydiving, sky surfing, snooker, snow mobiling, snowboarding, squash, stock car racing, tennis or trampolining! If the sport you are interested in isn't listed in our directory then try contacting the relevant national association (*eg* the LTA for tennis) and asking them for a list of course providers.

Have a look at what's on offer here:
www.extremesportscafe.com/
http://library.thinkquest.org/13857/–

Volunteering in South America

Anna, 22, took time out after graduation to travel in South America for just short of six months.

Here's her itinerary:

Brazil: Rio de Janeiro, Itacare, Chapada Diamantina, Salvador, Jerricoacoara, Manaus, Campo Grande, The Pantenal, Iguazu Falls.

Argentina: Buenos Aires, Bariloche, El Calefate, Cordoba, Salta.

Chile: San Pedro de Atecama.

Bolivia: Salt Flats, Uyuni, Potosi, Sucre, La Paz, Rurrenbaque, Copacabana.

Peru: Arequipa, Cusco, Lima.

She volunteered with a project in Rio de Janeiro, then travelled to Brazil with the same organisation before doing a stretch of independent travel in the rest of South America.

Anna said it was: "Amazing, saw the most spectacular sights I've ever seen, met the friendliest people and ate the most incredible food… Somewhere like South America is so diverse I could be in tropical rainforest one week, a metropolitan city for the weekend and then on a boat surrounded by glaciers the next. Travelling, particularly on your own, can be tiring and stressful at times, but the things you find yourself doing and experiencing, things you would never imagine you'd get chance to do, more than make up for it."

She has this advice for other travellers: "Don't expect everything to go to plan; buses/trains/planes get cancelled and delayed, roads get closed, whole countries go on strike and you end up staying in places longer than planned, or not making it to some places at all… You have to learn to relax about it and just see where you end up!

"Secondly, talk to other travellers; you'll meet loads of people in hostels who have just been to the places you're going to next. They'll be the best people to tell you where to (and where not to) stay and eat, sights worth seeing, places to avoid and other travel tips…"

We asked if she'd have done anything differently: "I would have packed less of everything! There are very few things you can't pick up

while you're away, so it's not necessary to pack for every possible scenario, plus there were souvenirs and nice clothes that I wanted to buy but I just didn't have the space to carry them.

"I might have also had a few Spanish lessons before I went, as it would have been nice to be able to talk to the local people beyond the complete basics I picked up as I went along."

It took her surprisingly little time to readjust as she went straight back to work and caught up with friends, but she's hoping to be off again next year!

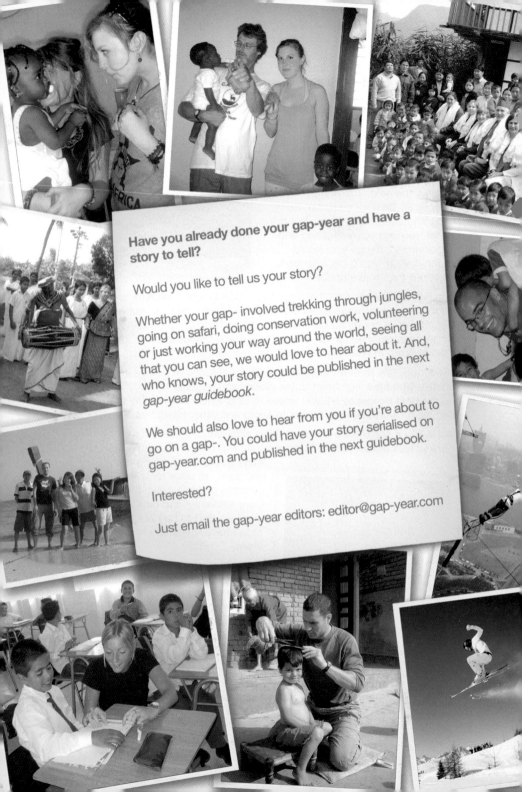

Have you already done your gap-year and have a story to tell?

Would you like to tell us your story?

Whether your gap- involved trekking through jungles, going on safari, doing conservation work, volunteering or just working your way around the world, seeing all that you can see, we would love to hear about it. And, who knows, your story could be published in the next gap-year guidebook.

We should also love to hear from you if you're about to go on a gap-. You could have your story serialised on gap-year.com and published in the next guidebook.

Interested?

Just email the gap-year editors: editor@gap-year.com

Archaeology

Archaeology Abroad
Institute of Archaeology, University College,
31-34 Gordon Square
Bloomsbury, London WC1H OPY

For info on digs abroad try the Archaeology Abroad bulletin and web pages.

Council for British Archaeology
St Mary's House, 66 Bootham,
York YO30 7BZ

CBA's magazine, British Archaeology, contains information about events and courses as well as digs. Reg Charity 287815.

School of Archaeology & Ancient History
University of Leicester, University Road,
Leicester LE1 7RH

Offers a series of modules in archaeology which can be studied purely for interest, or as part of a programme towards a Certificate in Archaeology.

University College London - Institute of Archaeology
31-34 Gordon Square,
St Pancras, London WC1H 0PY

UCL offers a range of short courses in archaeology many of which are open to members of the public.

University of Bristol - Department of Archaeology & Anthropology
Short Courses, 43 Woodland Road, Clifton
Bristol, Gloucestershire BS8 1UU

A variety of short courses offered, including: anthropology, archaeology, egyptology, history, Latin, Minoan, Roman and techniques. They also have a new one week intensive 'get started in archaeology' course.

Art

Burton Manor
The Village, Burton,
Neston, Cheshire CH64 5SJ

Various residential courses available in art and other subjects.

Camberwell College of Arts
Peckham Road,
Camberwell, London SE5 8UF

Offers various short courses in art and art related subjects.

Heatherley School of Art
75 Lots Road,
Chelsea, London SW10 0RN

Offers various summer courses in art as well as part-time and full-time courses.

The Prince's Drawing School
19-22 Charlotte Road, Broadgate, London EC2A 3SG

The Prince's Drawing School is an educational charity (No. 1101538) dedicated to teaching drawing from observation. Daytime, evening and summer school courses are run for artists and the general public.

University College London - Slade School of Fine Art
Slade Studios, Woburn Square, Bloomsbury, London WC1H 0AB

The Slade Summer School for Fine Art runs each summer.

University of the Arts - Central Saint Martins College of Art and Design
Southampton Row, Holborn, London WC1B 4AP

Short courses available in fashion, photography, graphic design, textiles and more.

University of the Arts - Wimbledon College of Art
Main Building, Merton Hall Road, Wimbledon, London SW19 3QA

They have a series of short courses in fashion, etching, filmmaking, sewing and more.

University of the Arts London - Chelsea College of Art and Design
16 John Islip Street, Westminster, London SW1P 4JU

Short courses available in interior design, drawing, painting and life drawing.

University of Wales Institute - Cardiff School of Art and Design
Howard Gardens, Cardiff, Glamorgan CF24 0SP

They run a ten week summer school programme designed to introduce you to the variety of art and design.

Cookery

Ashburton Cookery School
Hare's Lane Cottage, 76 East Street,
Ashburton, Devon TQ13 7AX

Cookery courses available from one to five days.

Belle Isle School of Cookery
Lisbellaw, Enniskillen,
County Fermanagh BT94 5HG

Essential Cooking is an intensive four week course designed for people who are interested in learning the key skills for a gap-year job in cooking

CookAbility
Sherlands, 54 Stonegallows,
Taunton, Somerset TA1 5JS

CookAbilty caters for all types of gap-year students. Whether you have set your sights on a chalet cooking season, self-catering at university or a new life skill, then this is the place to become inspired in the culinary arts.

Cookery at The Grange
The Grange, Whatley,
Frome, Somerset BA11 3JU

Cookery at the Grange in Somerset offers immensely popular four week residential cookery courses. The course leads on to cooking for family and friends or to working professionally – in chalets, on boats or outside catering – ideal for generating a little cash.

Cookery School at Little Portland Street
15b Little Portland Street, Soho, London W1W 8BW

Cookery School aims to turn out confident, inspired cooks not chefs. Courses for university and pre-university students are run during the summer holidays.

Cutting Edge Food & Wine School
Hackwood Farm, Robertsbridge, East Sussex TN32 5ER

Based in a 16th century farmhouse you will be taught in small groups by the Cutting Edge London Chef, who has an excellent reputation.

Edinburgh School of Food and Wine
The Coach House, Newliston,
Edinburgh, Midlothian EH29 9EB

Courses of interest to gappers are the four week Intensive Certificate Course which is geared towards chalet work, and the one week Survival Course which is ideally suited to those leaving home for the first time.

Food of Course
Middle Farm House, Sutton,
Shepton Mallet, Somerset BA4 6QF

They have an essential chalet course which will provide you with a thorough grounding in the cooking skills needed for running a ski chalet.

Gordon Ramsay's Tante Marie School of Cookery E: info@tantemarie.co.uk
Woodham House, Carlton Road, T: +44 (0) 1483 726957
Woking, Surrey GU21 4HF F: +44 (0) 1483 724173
www.tantemarie.co.uk

Tante Marie, accredited by the BAC and under the ownership of Gordon Ramsay, offers gap-year courses ranging from one to 11 weeks, including our acclaimed four week course and 11 week Cordon Bleu Certificate, both suitable for short-term employment, and ski or yacht season work.

Japan Centre Sushi Academy
Restaurant Toku, Japan Centre, 212 Picadilly, London W1J 9HX

Learn how to make sushi at the Sushi Academy in London.

Le Cordon Bleu
114 Marylebone Lane, Mayfair, London W1U 2HH

Le Cordon Bleu has courses ranging from their famous diplomas in 'Cuisine and Pâtisserie' to shorter courses in techniques, seasonal cooking, essentials and healthy eating.

Leiths School of Food & Wine
16-20 Wendell Road, Shepherd's Bush, London W12 9RT

Leiths' most popular gap-year courses, useful for chalet-people-to-be, are the Beginner's Certificate in Food and Wine and the Basic Certificate in Practical Cookery.

Murray School of Cookery
Glenbervie House, Holt Pound,
Farnham, Surrey GU10 4LE

The Murray School of Cookery offers two non-residential courses for gappers, including a one week Chalet Chef Course which teaches students how to be a successful chalet host.

The Avenue Cookery School
74 Chartfield Avenue, Putney, London SW15 6HQ

Offer courses aimed specifically at gap-year students, chalet assistants and undergraduates.

The Bertinet Kitchen
12 St Andrew's Terrace, Bath BA1 2QR

They run a beginners' course for those who have no clue what a kitchen is actually for.

The Cordon Vert
Parkdale, Dunham Road,
Altrincham, Cheshire WA14 4QG

Cookery school run by the Vegetarian Society (Charity No. 259358). One and two day courses available.

The Gables School of Cookery
Pipers Lodge, Bristol Road,
Falfield, Gloucestershire GL12 8DF

Achieve your dreams through a professional four week cookery course where you can learn the skills required to work your gap-year in a ski resort or on a yacht.

Fashion & Design

Leicester College - St Margaret's
St Margaret's Campus, St John Street, Leicester LE1 3WL

Has part-time courses in footwear, fabrics and pattern cutting.

Newcastle College
Rye Hill Campus, Scotswood Road,
Newcastle upon Tyne NE4 7SA

Short courses available in fashion illustration, bridalwear design, textile dyeing and printing, pattern cutting and embroidery.

The Fashion Retail Academy
15 Gresse Street, Soho, London W1T 1QL

Short courses available in visual merchandising, styling, PR, buying and range planning there are also tailor-made courses for those wishing to run their own retail business.

University of the Arts - London College of Fashion
20 John Princes Street, Mayfair, London W1G 0BJ

Short courses available in pattern cutting, principles of styling techniques, film and TV make up, childrenswear and maternitywear, retro fashion design and how to recycle your second-hand clothes.

University of the Arts - London Milan Courses
Short Course Office, Central Saint Martins, 10 Back Hill
Clerkenwell, London EC1R 5EN

Short courses in London and Milan in fashion design, fashion styling, graphic design, interior and product design.

University of Westminster - School of Media, Arts & Design
Watford Road, Northwick Park, Harrow, Middlesex HA1 3TP

Westminster offers a range of short courses in fashion, including fashion design, textile printing, and pattern cutting.

DramaScene
Kemp House, 152-160 City Road, St Luke's, London EC1V 2DW

Weekend and evening courses in drama

Metropolitan Film School
Ealing Studios, Ealing Green, London W5 5EP

Practical courses for aspiring filmmakers. Short courses and one year intensive course available.

RADA (Royal Academy of Dramatic Art)
62-64 Gower Street, Bloomsbury, London WC1E 6ED

This legendary drama college runs a variety of summer school courses.

The Central School of Speech and Drama
Embassy Theatre, Eton Avenue, Belsize Park, London NW3 3HY

Central offers short courses in acting, singing, stand-up comedy, puppetry, cabaret and burlesque, and directing.

The Oxford School of Drama
Sansomes Farm Studios, Woodstock,
Oxford OX20 1ER

The Oxford School of Drama runs a six-month Foundation Course, including acting, voice, movement, music and stage fighting. Registered Charity No. 1072770.

The Year Out Group
Queensfield, 28 King's Road,
Easterton, Wiltshire SN10 4PX

E: info@yearoutgroup.org
T: +44 (0) 1380 816696
www.yearoutgroup.org

See main entry under volunteering.

Year Out Drama
Stratford upon Avon Further Education College,
The Willows North, Alcester Road
Stratford upon Avon, Warwickshire CV37 9QR

E: yearoutdrama@stratford.ac.uk
T: +44 (0) 1789 266 245
www.yearoutdrama.co.uk

Full-time practical drama course with a unique company feel; work with theatre professionals to develop a wide range of skills; perform in a variety of productions; write and direct your own work; benefit from close contact with the RSC. Enjoy numerous theatre trips. Expert guidance with university and drama school applications.

Berkshire College of Agriculture
Hall Place, Burchetts Green,
Maidenhead, Berkshire SL6 6QR

Short courses in wildlife care, animal behaviour, lambing management, poultry breeding, BHS stages 1 & 2, BHS teaching test, pasture management, horticulture, garden design, hedge laying, wildlife gardening, hurdle making, machinery management, tractor management and more ...

Bishop Burton College
York Road, Bishop Burton, Beverley HU17 8QG

Short courses available in tractor driving, pest control, tree felling, sheep shearing, animal husbandry and more...

Capel Manor College
Bullsmoor Lane, Enfield, Middlesex EN1 4RQ

They have short courses in lorinery, flower arranging, CAD in garden design, practical gardening, aboriculture, botanical illustration, leathercraft and more ...

Chichester College
Westgate Fields, Chichester, Sussex PO19 1SB

Short courses available in animal care, farming, bushcraft, coppicing, hedgerow planting and managment, watercourse management, moorland management and more ...

Plumpton College
Ditchling Road, Lewes, Sussex BN7 3AE

Courses available in animal care, welding, tractor driving, machinery, wine trade, aboriculture, chainsaw, bushcraft, pond management, wildlife, woodcraft and more...

Rodbaston College
Penkridge, Staffordshire ST19 5PH

Short courses available in keeping chickens, tractor driving, animal care, hurdle fencing, machinery, pest control and chainsaws.

Royal Agricultural College
Cirencester, Gloucestershire GL7 6JS

Have a two day residential taster course in April which gives an insight into the career options in land-based industries.

Sparsholt College
Westley Lane, Sparsholt,
Winchester, Hampshire SO21 2NF

Have part-time courses in forklift operation, tractor driving, health and safety, horticulture, floristy, landscaping and more.

The Open College of Equine Studies
Boxted, Bury St Edmunds, Suffolk IP29 4JT

Have a series of short courses available in horse training, estate management, business *etc*.

Warwickshire College - Moreton Morrell
Moreton Morrell Campus,
Warwick, Warwickshire CV35 9BL

Have taster days in land-based studies. Also have an Equine Centre and the first purpose built School of Farriery in the UK.

Languages

Berlitz - London
Lincoln House, 296-302 High Holborn, Holborn, London WC1V 7JH

International language school. Intense courses in Chinese French, German, Italian, Japanese, Portuguese, Russian and Spanish available. Other schools in the can be found in Birmingham, Brighton, Bristol, Edinburgh, Manchester and Oxford.

Canning House
2 Belgrave Square, Belgravia, London SW1X 8PJ

Canning House runs evening courses in Brazilian Portuguese, as well as a wide range of events on Latin America, Spain and Portugal

International House London
Unity Wharf, 13 Mill Street, Bermondsey, London SE1 2BH

Worldwide network of language schools offering courses in Arabic, Chinese, French, German, Italian, Japanese and Spanish.

Italian Cultural Institute in London
39 Belgrave Square, Belgravia, London SW1X 8NX

Has a wide programme of Italian language courses as well as a mass of information about Italy and its culture.

Languages @ Lunchtime
Modern Foreign Languages Section,
Hetherington Building, Bute Gardens
Glasgow, Lanarkshire G12 8RS

Small informal classes run at Glasgow University for two hours per week over 18 weeks.

The Japan Foundation - London Language Centre
6th Floor, Russell Square House,
10-12 Russell Square, Bloomsbury, London WC1B 5EH

Provides courses in Japanese. Also has regular newsletter and resource library.

University of London - School of Oriental and African Studies
Thornhaugh Street, Russell Square, Bloomsbury, London WC1H 0XG

The SOAS (part of the University of London) runs courses for numerous African and Asian languages. Small classes of not more than 12.

Music

BIMM - Brighton Institute of Modern Music
7 Rock Place, Brighton, Sussex BN2 1PF

Various part-time courses available, also summer schools, for bass, drums, guitar, vocals, songwriting and live sound/tour management.

Dartington International Summer School
The Barn, Dartington Hall, Totnes, Devon TQ9 6DE

Dartington International Summer School (Registered Charity No. 279756) is both a festival and a music school. Teaching and performing takes place all day, every day.

Lake District Summer Music
Stricklandgate House, 92 Stricklandgate,
Kendal, Cumbria LA9 4PU

Offers an ensemble-based course for string players and pianists intending to pursue careers as professional musicians. Registered Charity no 516350.

London Music School
9-13 Osborn Street, Whitechapel, London E1 6TD

Offers a Diploma in Music Technology, open to anyone with musical ability aged 17 or over. The course explores professional recording and you get to use a 24-track studio.

London School of Sound
35 Britannia Row, Islington, London N1 8QH

Based in the recording studio previously owned by Pink Floyd, they offer part and full-time courses of between five weeks and two years in music production, sound engineering and DJ skills.

Music Worldwide Drum Camp
Music Worldwide Ltd, 4 Dencora Apartments,
Chapel Field East, Norwich NR2 1SF

Drum Camp is an annual worldwide percussion event in Norfolk specialising in world rhythms and drum and dance programs. Offers an amazing variety of classes over four days, in music, singing and dance.

NLMS Music Summer School
5 Thame Road, Sydenham,
Chinnor, Oxfordshire OX39 4LA

Each year over 100 enthusiastic adult amateur musicians get together for a week of enjoyment.

North London Piano School
78 Warwick Avenue,
Edgware, Middlesex HA8 8UJ

The North London Piano School offers a residential summer course.

Oxford Flute Summer School
12 Jesse Terrace, Reading, Berkshire RG1 7RT

The Oxford Flute Summer School runs from mid-August. Tuition is available at different levels to suit your standard.

The British Kodály Academy
c/o 13 Midmoor Road, Wimbledon, London SW19 4JD

A registered charity (No. 326552) working towards the improvement of music education in the UK. They run various music courses for teachers and young children but also have courses for those wishing to improve their skills.

The DJ Academy Organisation
1 Damaskfield, Worcester WR4 0HY

Offer an eight week part time DJ course (in various cities in the UK), private tuition, one day superskills course, the ultimate mobile DJ course and the superclub experience.

The Recording Workshop
Unit 10, Buspace Studios, Conlan Street, Kensal Town, London W10 5AP

Offer part time and full time courses on all aspects of music production, sound engineering and music technology.

UK Songwriting Festival
Bath Spa University, Newton Park, Bath BA2 9BN

This festival is a five-day event held at Bath Spa University every August. Workshop includes daily lectures on the craft of songwriting, small group sessions, live band sessions and an acoustic live recording on CD. Includes studio sessions with a producer.

Photography

Brook School of Photography
113 Penn Hill Avenue, Poole, Dorset BH14 9L9

Offer portrait and wedding photography courses and workshop diploma.

Digitalmasterclass
105 Barton Road, Dover, Kent CT16 2LX

Small group classes in digital photography for beginners and those wishing to improve their basic skills.

Experience Seminars
Unit 1-4, Hill Farm, Wennington,
Huntingdon, Cambridgeshire PE28 2LU

Hosts a range of workshops throughout the UK, which are designed to provide a fast track way of learning photography and digital imaging techniques.

London School of Photography
Coaching & Training, 77 Oxford Street, Soho, London W1D 2ES

Short courses available in digital photography, photojournalism, as well as travel, adventure and street photography. Small classes of up to eight people. One-to-one training also available.

Photo Opportunity Ltd
Unit 8, Cedar Way, Camley Street, Camden Town, London NW1 0PD

Courses offered lasting from one to five days in length. Courses tailored to suit your own particular needs and classes are small.

Photofusion
17a Electric Lane, Brixton, London SW9 8LA

This independent photography resource centre, situated in Brixton, offers digital photography courses.

Picture Weddings - Digital wedding photography workshops
2 Farriers Mews, Bourton Grange, Bourton, Swindon SN6 8HZ

Fast-track workshops in digital wedding photography.

Shoot Experience Ltd
32b Kingsland Rd, Hackney, London E2 8DA

Offer fun photography workshops and courses in London

Simon Watkinson Photo Training
The Spout Farmhouse Studio, Reapsmoor,
Longnor near Buxton, Derbyshire SK17 0LL

Offer a range of courses for beginners upwards, including landscape, portraits, weddings, and courses in the Dales and the Lake district

The Photography School
Oakview House, 1 Newlands Avenue, Caversham
Reading, Berkshire RG4 8NS

Offers intensive photography courses for beginners and professionals.

The Royal Photographic Society
Fenton House, 122 Wells Road, Bath BA2 3AH

Holds photography courses, from landscape photography to studio work, throughout the year.

The Trained Eye
The Studios, Luckings Estate, Magpie Lane, Coleshill, Buckinghamshire HP7 0LS

Offer creative courses in wedding and portrait photography, for amateurs or advanced photographers to improve their skills.

Sport

BASP UK Ltd
20 Lorn Drive, Glencoe, Argyll-shire PH49 4HR

BASP offers First Aid and Safety Training courses designed specifically for the outdoor user, suitable for all NGB Awards.

Big Squid Scuba Diving Training and Travel
Unit 2F, Clapham North Arts Centre, 26-32 Voltaire Road
Clapham, London SW4 6DH

Big Squid offers a variety of dive courses using the PADI and TDI systems of diver education.

British Hang Gliding & Paragliding Association Ltd
The Old Schoolroom, Loughborough Road, Leicester LE4 5PJ

The BHPA oversees the standards of instructor training and runs coaching course for pilots. They also list all approved schools in the field of paragliding, hang gliding and parascending.

British Mountaineering Council
The Old Church, 177-179 Burton Road, West Didsbury
Manchester, Lancashire M20 2BB

BMC travel insurance covers a range of activities and is designed by experts to be free from unreasonable exclusions or restrictions, for peace of mind wherever you travel.

British Offshore Sailing School - BOSS
Hamble Point Marina, School Lane, Hamble
Southampton, Hampshire SO31 4NB

BOSS offers complete RYA shore-based and practical training courses, also women only courses, from Hamble Point Marina.

British Sub Aqua Club
Telford's Quay, South Pier Road, Ellesmere Port, Cheshire CH65 4FL

Why not discover scuba diving or snorkelling during your gap-year?

visit: www.gap-year.com

CricketCoachMaster Academy
2 Bolsover Close, Long Hanborough, Witney, Oxfordshire OX29 8RA

The CCM Academy has a coaching programme to further develop players with the recognised potential to play at county and international level.

Curling in Kent
Fenton's Rink, Dundale Farm, Dundale Road
Tunbridge Wells, Kent TN3 9AQ

Come to Fenton's Rink and try your hand at this exciting Olympic sport. New season begins 1st October.

Earth Events
Franks Yard, Baileys Hard, Beaulieu
Brockenhurst, Hampshire SO42 7YF

Organises group activities such as canoeing, rope work, cycling and climbing. Also offer environmental courses in the New Forest.

East Kilbride Curling Club
c/o East Kilbride Ice Rink, Olympia Shopping Centre,
East Kilbride, Lanarkshire G74 1PG

New members and beginners always welcome. They offer a 'come and try' session - see if this sport is for you!

Flybubble Paragliding
1 Manor Close, Ringmer, Lewes, Sussex BN8 5PA

Paragliding school registered with the British Hang Gliding and Paragliding Association (BHPA).

Glasgow Ski & Snowboard Centre
Bellahouston Park, 16 Drumbreck Road,
Glasgow, Lanarkshire G41 5BW

Learn to ski, improve your existing skills or learn to snowboard.

Green Dragons
Warren Barn Farm, Slines Oak Road,
Woldingham, Surrey CR3 7HN

Paragliding and hang gliding centre. You do not need any experience or knowledge, just the desire to fly and follow your instructor's guidance on positions for take off, time spent in the air and landing.

Jubilee Sailing Trust
Hazel Road, Woolston,
Southampton, Hampshire SO19 7GB

Tall Ships Sailing Trust. Join their JST Youth Leadership@Sea Scheme, no sailing experience needed. Registerd Charity No. 277810.

London Fencing Club
Finsbury Leisure Centre, Norman Street, St Luke's, London EC1V 3QN

Fencing tuition available in various centres in London - beginners to advanced training available.

London Scuba Diving School
Raby's Barn, Newchapel Road, Lingfield, Surrey RH7 6LE

The London Scuba Diving School teaches beginners in swimming pools in Battersea and Bayswater. They also offer advanced courses for the experienced diver.

Mendip Outdoor Pursuits
**The Warehouse, Silver Street,
Congresbury BS49 5EY**

Lessons in abseiling, archery, bridge building, caving, climbing, bush craft, kayaking, navigation, orienteering and more available.

National Mountaineering Centre
Plas y Brenin, Capel Curig, Conwy, Caernarfonshire LL24 OET

For those hoping to reach dizzy heights, the National Mountaineering Centre offers a vast range of activities and courses.

North London Parachute Centre Ltd
Block Fen Drove, Wimblington, March PE15 0FB

They have different sky diving and parachuting experiences and various courses for the complete beginner.

Pod Zorbing
393 Selsdon Road, Croydon, Surrey CR2 7AW

Harness zorbing in London - two person ball. Also do aqua zorbing.

Poole Harbour Watersports
284 Sandbanks Road, Lilliput, Poole, Dorset BH14 8HU

Learn to windsurf and kitesurf at Poole in Dorset. For both beginners and improvers.

ProAdventure Limited
23 Castle Street, Llangollen, Denbighshire LL20 8NY

Based in Wales, ProAdventure offers different activity courses around the UK, including canoeing, kayaking, rock climbing and mountain biking.

Province of London Curling Club
**c/o James Hustler, Secretary, 524 Galleywood Road,
Chelmsford, Essex CM2 8BU**

New curlers always welcome. Free coaching and equipment available. New season starts 1st October.

Skydive Brid
East Leys Farm, Grindale, Bridlington, Yorkshire YO16 4YB

Skydiving courses for complete beginners. Free skydiving in aid of charity and jumps organised for more experienced people.

South Cambridgeshire Equestrian Centre
Barrington Park Farm, Foxton Road,
Barrington, Cambridgeshire CB22 7RN

This riding school is set in 260 acres of Cambridgeshire countryside. They offer riding tuition to the beginner and also more advanced teaching for experienced riders.

Sportscotland National Centre Cumbrae
Isle of Cumbrae, Ayrshire KA28 0HQ

Sportscotland national watersport centre offer a range of courses from a fully residential three weeks powerboat instructor or 18 weeks professional yachtmaster training, to a one day introduction to windsurfing.

Suffolk Ski Centre
Bourne Hill, Wherstead,
Ipswich, Suffolk IP2 8NQ

Learn to ski or snowboard in Suffolk. Courses also available for those wishing to improve their existing skills.

Sussex Hang Gliding & Paragliding
Tollgate, Lewes, Sussex BN8 6JZ

Learn to paraglide or hang glide over the beautiful Sussex countryside.

Sussex Polo Club
Landfall House, Sandhill Lane,
Crawley Down, Sussex RH10 4LE

Learn something new - learn to play polo.

The Lawn Tennis Association
The National Tennis Centre,
100 Priory Lane, Roehampton,
London SW15 5JQ

You're never too young or too old to learn to play tennis and the LTA will help you.

The Talland School of Equitation
Dairy Farm, Ampney Knowle,
Cirencester, Gloucestershire GL7 5ED

BHS and ABRS approved equestrian centre offering top class training for professional qualifications. Variety of courses including competition training.

371

Tollymore Mountain Centre
Bryansford, Newcastle, County Down BT33 0PT

Tollymore have a range of courses designed to suit your own skills and experience. Their courses include rambling, mountaineering, climbing, canoeing and first aid.

UK Parachuting
Old Buckenham Airfield,
Attleborough, Norfolk NR17 1PU

AFF courses available. Also tandem skydiving and Accelerated Free Fall tuition slots available every day.

UK Skydiving Ltd
Globe House,
Love Lane, Cirencester,
Gloucestershire GL7 1YG

UK Skydiving is a company run by British Parachute Association (BPA) Instructors. They have courses for the absolute beginner, which are tailored to suit the individual.

UKSA (United Kingdom Sailing Academy)
The Martime Academy, Artic Road,
West Cowes, Isle of Wight PO31 7PQ

E: info@uksa.org
T: +44 (0) 1983 203038
www.uksa.org

UKSA have a wealth of options for a thrilling gap-year to suit all budgets, from extreme watersports instructor programmes to the six-week crew training course, designed to provide the yachting skills and experience for a career on luxury yachts and superyachts!

Wellington Riding
Heckfield, Hook, Hampshire RG27 OLJ

Riding lessons available for any level - children and adults.

X-isle Sports
Unit 6a, Embankment Road,
Bembridge, Isle of Wight PO25 5NR

Centre on the Isle of Wight offering courses in waterskiing, kitesurfing, windsurfing, surfing, sailing and wakeboarding.

TEFL

CILC - Cheltenham International Language Centre
University of Gloucestershire, Cornerways, The Park
Cheltenham, Gloucestershire GL50 2RH

Gloucestershire University offer intensive courses in TEFL leading to the Cambridge ESOL CELTA award.

ETC - The English Training Centre
53 Greenhill Road, Moseley,
Birmingham, Warwickshire B13 9SU

Professionally-designed TESOL courses offered accredited by ACTDEC. Experienced tutors provide comprehensive feedback and helpful support. Free grammar guide and teaching resource book.

Golders Green Teacher Training Centre
11 Golders Green Road, Golders Green, London NW11 8DY

Full-time and part-time TEFL/TESOL courses available.

ITC - Intensive TEFL Courses
26 Cockerton Green,
Darlington, County Durham DL3 9EU

E: info@tefl.co.uk
T: +44 (0) 8456 445464
F: +44 (0) 1325 366167
www.tefl.co.uk

Intensive TEFL Courses (ITC) have been running weekend TEFL (Teach English as a Foreign Language) courses throughout the UK since 1993. The certificate allows you to teach conversational English worldwide with an optional Distance Learning Course resulting in a 100hr TEFL certificate. Job contacts given free to all students.

LTTC - London Teacher Training College
Dalton House, 60 Windsor Avenue,
Wimbledon, London SW19 2RR

Over the years the college has trained a vast number of teachers from around the world, and prides itself on the quality of its courses and the individual attention it provides every student who enrols.

TEFL Training LLP
Friends Close, Stonesfield,
Witney, Oxfordshire OX29 8PH

Teaching English UK or Abroad? - Prepare yourself while still working or studying. Our weekend course will give you a very practical introduction to Teaching English as a Foreign Language.

Windsor TEFL
21 Osborne Road,
Windsor, Berkshire SL4 3EG

Offer their TEFL course in their centres in London and Windsor as well as in Europe. Also offer the CELTA TEFL course in various places worldwide.

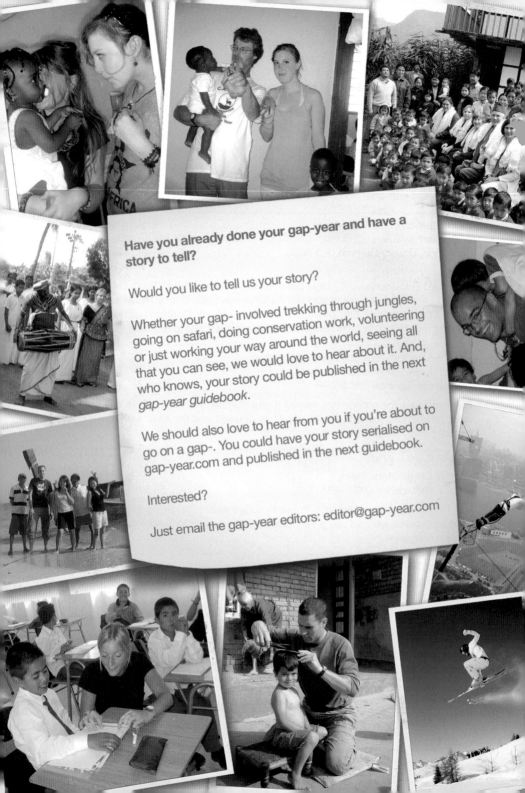

Have you already done your gap-year and have a story to tell?

Would you like to tell us your story?

Whether your gap- involved trekking through jungles, going on safari, doing conservation work, volunteering or just working your way around the world, seeing all that you can see, we would love to hear about it. And, who knows, your story could be published in the next *gap-year guidebook*.

We should also love to hear from you if you're about to go on a gap-. You could have your story serialised on gap-year.com and published in the next guidebook.

Interested?

Just email the gap-year editors: editor@gap-year.com

Appendices

Choosing a tutorial college

Standards vary and it's best to check out two or three colleges before you make your final choice. Here are some things to check before you decide:

- Does the college get results? For the last few years the *Daily Telegraph* has regularly published a table in early September giving the average A level retake grade improvements at tutorial colleges.

- Does the college have a good reputation? Get references from former students - the college should be happy to supply you with contact names.

- Has the college been inspected by the Department for Children, Schools and Families (DCSF) or an independent body such as BAC (the British Accreditation Council for Independent Further and Higher Education) or CIFE (the Council for Independent Further Education)?

- Does the college teach the right subjects?

- Does the college teach the same syllabus (*eg* OCR/French) that you studied at school?

- What time of year are the courses run? This affects what you can do during the rest of your year out.

- Who will be teaching you? Check their qualifications and how familiar they are with the syllabus.

- Is the place up-to-date? Near transport? Does it have quiet study rooms and good facilities?

- What does it cost? What are the hourly rates?

- What do get for your money? How many hours of group teaching each week and how many one-to-one tutorials?

Retakes

Please note: The information contained in these appendices is for guidance only. We would strongly advise you to talk to your school or college examination officer, chosen university or exam board for up-to-the-minute advice and information.

Retakes

There are several reasons why you might find yourself considering retakes: maybe because your grades are too low to meet a conditional offer (and the university won't negotiate with you to admit you on lower grades), or because illness interfered with exams.

But beware, getting better grades second time round doesn't guarantee you a university place - often universities will demand even higher grades if it's taken you two bites at the cherry (unless of course you've got a really good excuse, like illness).

Grade appeals

The now almost habitual media comment about the devaluation of A level marks has left many people wondering just how much we can trust exam results. If you really think you've been done down by a tired exam marker, a misleading or misprinted question or some other factor, you can appeal against your result.

You appeal first to the examination board that set the exam, and if you don't think the adjudication is just, you can go on to appeal to the Examination Appeals Board (EAB) (see page 379). But be warned: this process takes a long time and there's no guarantee the appeal will go your way.

Retake timing

Now that modular A levels are firmly entrenched, you may be able to retake the modules you did badly while you are still at school, instead of having to retake them in your year out.

However, you need to check with both your exam board and chosen university before you make any plans.

Every exam board has its own timetable for retakes (see below for contact details) and universities also vary considerably in their regulations on retakes.

You need to make sure your chosen university course doesn't set higher entry grades for exams taken at a second sitting.

In some cases you may find that when you retake a certain exam you have to change exam board - this can be a problem in some subjects (*eg* languages with set texts) and you may therefore have to resit your A levels a whole year after the original exams, which can seriously disrupt your **gap**-year. Check with your exam board as early as you can.

Tutorial colleges like to keep students working on A levels for a full year. That keeps the college full and tutors paid. But many agree that the best thing is to get resits over before you forget the work you've already done. So the best timing, if you are academically confident and want to enjoy your **gap**-year, is to go to a tutorial college in September and resit the whole exam or the relevant modules in January - if sittings are available then.

Languages

If you have only language AS levels, A2 levels or A levels to retake, there are several options:

- Take an extra course or stay in the country of the relevant language and return to revise for a summer resit, choosing the same exam board (courses abroad, however, are not usually geared to A level texts).

- Check with tutorial colleges how much of your syllabus module or modules (the chosen literature texts are crucial) overlap with those of other exam boards. This may give you the chance to switch exam boards and do a quick retake in January.

- Cram for as long as necessary at a specialist language college. Some British tutorial colleges and language course organisers have links with teaching centres in other countries so it's worth checking this out before signing on.

Retake results

Those who sit A level retakes in January, and get the grades needed for a chosen place, will not have to wait until August for that place to be confirmed.

Examining boards will feed the result directly into UCAS so you will know your place has been clinched. A technicality, but comforting for **gap**-year students who want to travel.

And don't forget that if you have a firm choice conditional offer and you make the grades asked for, the university can't back out. It has an obligation to admit you.

A level examining boards

There are five A level examining boards: AQA (Assessment and Qualifications Alliance), Edexcel, OCR (Oxford, Cambridge & RSA), Northern Ireland (CCEA) and Wales (WJEC). There's also the IB, which has its own curriculum and syllabus, geared towards the IB Diploma. All these boards now provide their exam timetables on the internet about nine months in advance: we've provided their contact details below, along with those of other exam-related organisations.

visit: *www.gap-year.com*

AQA (Assessment and Qualifications Alliance)
Stag Hill House,
Guildford, Surrey GU2 7XJ

www.aqa.org.uk
Tel: +44 (0) 1483 506506
Email: mailbox@aqa.org.uk

CCEA (Northern Ireland Council for the Curriculum, Examinations and Assessment)
29 Clarendon Road, Clarendon Dock
Belfast, County Antrim BT1 3BG

www.ccea.org.uk
Tel: +44 (0) 28 9026 1200
Fax: +44 (0) 28 9026 1234
Email: info@ccea.org.uk

EAB (Examination Appeals Board)
83 Piccadilly,
London W1J 8QA

www.theeab.org.uk
Tel: +44 (0) 20 7509 5995

This is the final court of appeal for exam grades. Centres and private candidates only go to the EAB if an appeal to the relevant examination board has failed. The EAB website has a notice board showing when appeals are going to be heard.

EDEXCEL
190 High Holborn,
London WC1V 7BH

www.edexcel.org.uk
Tel: see website for contact numbres

IB (International Baccalaureate)
Peterson House, Malthouse Avenue
Cardiff Gate
Cardiff CF23 8GL

www.ibo.org
Tel: +44 (0) 29 2054 7777
Fax: +44 (0) 29 2054 7778
Email: ibca@ibo.org

Currrently the UK office and central body for the development, administration and assessment of the International Baccalaureate Diploma Programme.

OCR (Oxford Cambridge & RSA Examinations)
1 Hills Road,
Cambridge,
Cambridgeshire CB1 2EU

www.ocr.org.uk
Tel: +44 (0) 1223 553 998
Fax: +44 (0) 1223 552 627
Email: general.qualifications@ocr.org.uk

QCA (Qualifications and Curriculum Authority)
83 Piccadilly,
London W1J 8QA

www.qca.org.uk
Tel: +44 (0) 20 7509 5555
Fax: +44 (0) 20 7509 6666
Email: info@qca.org.uk

The QCA is the body that (along with the Qualifications, Curriculum and Assessment Authority for Wales: ACCAC) approves all syllabuses and monitors exams (grading standards, for example).

SQA (Scottish Qualifications Authority)
The Optima Building, 58 Robertson Street,
Glasgow, Lanarkshire G2 8DQ

www.sqa.org.uk
Tel: +44 (0) 845 279 1000
Fax: +44 (0) 845 213 5000
Email: customer@sqa.org.uk

Central body for the development, administration and assessment of Scottish qualifications, including Standard Grade, Highers, Advanced Highers, HNCs, HNDs and SVQs.

the gap-year guidebook 2010

WJEC
245 Western Avenue,
Cardiff, Glamorgan CF5 2YX

www.wjec.co.uk
Tel: +44 (0) 29 2026 5000
Email: info@wjec.co.uk

WJEC's qualifications include Entry Level, GCSE and AS/A level, as well as Key Skills. They also handle the Welsh Baccalaureate and provide examinations, assessment, educational resources and support for adults who wish to learn Welsh.

Colleges accredited by BAC and CIFE

The following independent sixth form and tutorial colleges offering A level tuition (one-year, two-year, complete retakes, modular retakes or intensive coaching) are recognised by the British Accreditation Council (BAC, Tel: 020 7447 2584, www.the-bac.org) and/or the Council for Independent Further Education (CIFE, Tel: 020 8767 8666, www.cife.org.uk). Of course a college can have a good reputation and achieve excellent results without accreditation.

Abacus College (Oxford)	BAC	Tel:+44 (0) 1865 240 111
Abbey College Birmingham	BAC	Tel:+44 (0) 121 236 7474
Abbey College Cambridge	BAC	Tel:+44 (0) 1223 578 280
Abbey College London (SW1)	BAC	Tel:+44 (0) 20 7824 7300
Abbey College Manchester	BAC	Tel:+44 (0) 161 817 2700
Acorn Independent College (Southall)	BAC	Tel:+44 (0) 20 8571 9900
Ashbourne Independent Sixth Form College, (London W8)	BAC/CIFE	Tel:+44 (0) 20 7937 3858
Bales College (London W10)	BAC/CIFE	Tel:+44 (0) 20 8960 5899
Basil Paterson Tutorial College (Edinburgh)	BAC	Tel:+44 (0) 131 225 3802
Bath Academy (Bath)	BAC/CIFE	Tel:+44 (0) 1225 334 577
Bellerbys College – Brighton	BAC	Tel:+44 (0) 1273 339 200
Bellerbys College – Cambridge	BAC	Tel:+44 (0) 1223 517 037
Bellerbys College – London	BAC	Tel:+44 (0) 20 8694 7000
Bosworth Independent College (Northampton)	CIFE	Tel:+44 (0) 1604 239 995
Brampton College (London NW4)	BAC	Tel:+44 (0) 20 8203 5025

Brooke House College (Market Harborough)	BAC/CIFE	Tel:+44 (0) 1858 462 452
CATS (Cambridge)	BAC	Tel:+44 (0) 1223 314 431
CATS (Canterbury)	BAC	Tel:+44 (0) 1227 866 540
Cambridge Centre for Sixth Form Studies	CIFE	Tel:+44 (0) 1223 716 890
Cambridge Seminars	BAC	Tel:+44 (0) 1223 313 464
Cambridge Tutors College	CIFE	Tel:+44 (0) 20 8688 5284
Chelsea Independent College	BAC/CIFE	Tel:+44 (0) 20 7610 1114
Cherwell College (Oxford)	BAC	Tel:+44 (0) 1865 242 670
College of International Education (Oxford)	BAC	Tel:+44 (0) 1865 202238
Collingham (London SW5)	BAC/CIFE	Tel:+44 (0) 20 7244 7414
Commonwealth Law College	BAC	Tel:+44 (0) 20 7247 8082
David Game College (London W11)	BAC	Tel:+44 (0) 20 7221 6665
Davies, Laing & Dick (London, W1)	BAC/CIFE	Tel:+44 (0) 20 7935 8411
Duff Miller College (London SW7)	BAC/CIFE	Tel:+44 (0) 20 7225 0577
Ealing Independent College (London, W5)	BAC	Tel:+44 (0) 20 8579 6668
EF Brittin College – Torquay	BAC	Tel:+44 (0) 1803 202 932
Exeter Tutorial College (Exeter)	BAC/CIFE	Tel:+44 (0) 1392 278 101
Harrogate Tutorial College	BAC/CIFE	Tel:+44 (0) 1423 501 041
Holborn College	BAC	Tel:+44 (0) 20 8317 6000
International College Britain	BAC	Tel:+44 (0) 131 313 1988
King's School, Oxford	BAC	Tel:+44 (0) 1865 711 829
Lansdowne College (London W2)	CIFE	Tel:+44 (0) 20 7616 4400
London College Wimbledon	BAC	Tel:+44 (0) 20 8944 1134

London School of Science & Technology	BAC	Tel:+44 (0) 208 795 3863
Mander Portman Woodward (Birmingham)	BAC	Tel:+44 (0) 121 454 9637
Mander Portman Woodward (London SW7)	BAC/CIFE	Tel:+44 (0) 20 7835 1355
Mander Portman Woodward (Cambridge)	BAC	Tel:+44 (0) 1223 350 158
Middlesex College of Law	BAC	Tel:+44 (0) 20 8424 2442
Midlands Academy of Business & Technology (MABT)	BAC	Tel:+44 (0) 116 261 9426
Oxford Business College (Oxford)	BAC	Tel:+44 (0) 1865 791 908
Oxford Tutorial College (Oxford)	BAC/CIFE	Tel:+44 (0) 1865 793 333
Pinnacle International College (Formerly CRTS International College)	BAC	Tel:+44 (0) 20 8885 5577
Rayat London College	BAC	Tel:+44 (0) 20 8754 3330
Reach Cambridge	BAC	Tel:+44 (0) 870 8031 732
Regent College (Harrow)	BAC	Tel:+44 (0) 20 8966 9900
San Michael College	BAC	Tel:+44 (0) 121 454 7949
St Andrew's (Cambridge)	BAC	Tel:+44 (0) 1223 358 073
The Abbey College (Malvern)	BAC	Tel:+44 (0) 1684 892300
Tudor College London	BAC	Tel:+44 (0) 20 7837 8382

visit: www.gap-year.com

Applying to university

At the time of writing, UCAS was reporting that the number of students taking up university and college places has risen again this year (up 8.8% on 2008 figures as of 24 March 2009). The previous record was set in autumn 2008 when, according to annual figures released by UCAS, the highest ever uptake was recorded. The total number of applicants rose in 2008 to 588,689 from 534,495 in 2007. The number of full-time students accepted on to undergraduate courses starting in 2008 rose by 10.4%, and 43,197 more students were accepted in 2008, taking the total from 413,430 in 2007 to 456,627.

For some, the decision to take a year off is made well in advance. Often students make the decision to defer their entry into higher education, with specific projects in mind. Some choose not to apply at all until after their A level results. Others find themselves taking a **gap**-year at much shorter notice, once they receive their grades. If UCAS applicants have not met the conditions of the offers they are holding, then a **gap**-year can allow them to reassess their plans. Equally one option for those who have done better than expected can use the time to aim for something they had originally considered beyond them.

Application process

UCAS (the Universities and Colleges Admissions Service) handles applications to all UK universities (except the Open University) as well as to most other institutions that offer full-time undergraduate higher education courses. This includes applications for Oxford, Cambridge and for degrees in medicine, dentistry and veterinary science/medicine, although they have to be in earlier than for other universities and colleges and for other subjects.

UCAS
PO Box 28,
Cheltenham GL52 3LZ

www.ucas.com
Tel: +44 (0) 871 468 0468
Email: enquiries@ucas.co.uk

Sending an email to this address will get you an automated response with general information and guidance on UCAS procedures. If you have hearing difficulties, you can call the RNID Typetalk service on 18001 0871 468 0 468 from within the UK, or on +44 151 494 1260 (text phone) or +44 151 494 2022 (for those with impaired hearing) from outside the UK. There is no extra charge for this service, and calls are charged at normal rates.

UCAS offers a distribution service to companies who wish to send promotional material to students. UCAS handles the distribution itself and does not pass on your personal details, which remain confidential. If you prefer not to receive this kind of material however, you can opt out when completing your UCAS application.

You can apply for five different courses at any UCAS institution, except for medicine courses A100, A101, A102, A103, A104, A105, A106, dentistry courses: A200, A201, A202, A203, A204, A205, A206, A300, A400 and veterinary science/medicine courses D100, D101, and D102, for each of which you can make just four choices. Note that some art and design courses use the deadline of 24 March for entries while others use 15 January - be sure to check on Course Search for the deadline that applies to your chosen courses. You can hold on to no more than two of the offers you get: one 'firm (first) choice' and one 'insurance (second choice) place'. So you may have to be cautious about the courses you pitch for.

Online application

UCAS has a secure, web-based application system called Apply. Each school, college, careers agency or British Council Office that has registered with UCAS to use Apply, appoints a coordinator who manages the way it is used. For students, registering to the new system takes a few minutes and costs nothing. Once a student has registered, they are given a username and are asked to choose a password that they will need to use each time they want to access their application. Applicants can use this system anywhere that has access to the web. The service works in tandem with the online Course Search service. Check out the UCAS website for more information at: **www.ucas.com**

Students who are not at a school or college also make their applications using the online Apply system. Individual applicants can either cut and paste a reference previously sent to them, or contact their old school or college and ask whether they will supply a reference online. In either case they send the completed application, together with their payment, to UCAS.

Please remember you do *not* have to apply for all your choices at the same time. You can add further choices as long as you have not used up all your choices and have not accepted a place.

A level results

A level results come out in mid-August. Depending on your grades, one of the following will happen:

- Firm (first) choice university confirms offer of a place. (If your grades meet and exceed your offer, you may research alternatives for up to five days while retaining your firm offer, a process known as Adjustment.)

- Insurance (second choice) university confirms offer of a place.

- Clearing.

- Retakes.

Before you make any decisions, make sure you know all the angles. Retakes may be the only way for you to get to university, but most universities will demand even higher results the second time around. A point confirmed by Glasgow University: "We expect slightly higher requirements if you don't get good enough grades in one A level attempt."

visit: www.gap-year.com

The UCAS Tariff

The UCAS Tariff was first used for those applying to enter higher education (HE) in 2002. Since its introduction it has expanded to cover additional qualifications. It is a points-based system that establishes agreed equivalences between different types of qualifications, and provides admissions tutors with a way of comparing applicants with different types and volumes of achievement.

UCAS is keen to encourage all universities and colleges to use the Tariff in order to make the application system more uniform across the country. Over three quarters of universities and colleges now use the Tariff, but some admissions tutors still choose to make offers in terms of grades.

More information and a copy of the latest Tariff is available at:
www.ucas.com/students/ucas_tariff/

Newly tariffed qualifications include the Advanced Diploma, Asset Languages, Cambridge Pre-U, International Baccalaureate Certificate, OCR Level 3 Certificate/Diploma for iMedia Professionals (iMedia), and Progression Diploma.

Key dates

This is what will happen if you apply for a university course starting in autumn 2010 or for deferred entry in 2011, so if you are thinking of taking a **gap**-year you'll need to know that:

- The main deadline for applications for all universities (except Oxford, Cambridge, medicine, dentistry, veterinary medicine or veterinary science courses and certain art and design programmes) is 15 January. See list of dates below.

- There is a 'commitment to clear, transparent admissions policies'. More than 85% of courses on Course Search universities include 'Entry Profiles' to tell students about entry requirements, including skills, personal qualities, or experience not necessarily connected with academic qualifications. These are often included on universities' own websites as well.

- Extra has been designed for applicants who have used all five of their choices, but who do not have a place. Extra allows them to make additional choices through UCAS, one at a time. The service runs from mid-March to the end of June, so you won't have to wait until Clearing to find a place. If you are eligible for Extra, UCAS will tell you how to refer your application to a university or college with vacancies, using the Track service on its website.

- 'Invisibility of choices' means that universities and colleges cannot see which other universities or colleges a student has applied to, until that applicant has replied to an offer or has no live choices.

The autumn term is when Year 13 students usually begin to apply for university and college places through the UCAS system (though some super-organised schools and students start preparations in the summer of Year 12).

The information you need for applying to university or college is online at **www.ucas.com** where an up-to-date list of courses is always available.

Here are some key dates:

- University open days are organised from spring each year.

- UCAS has three main application deadlines. The first is 15 October for all applications to Oxford and Cambridge universities and applications for medicine, dentistry and veterinary medicine/science as listed above. The deadline for all other courses, except some art and design courses, is 15 January. The third deadline is 24 March, which applies to all art and design courses not using the 15 January deadline.

- Universities and colleges do not guarantee to consider applications they receive after 15 January, and some popular courses may not have vacancies after that date. Please check with individual universities and colleges if you are not sure. You are advised to apply as early as possible.

- Not all courses start in September or October - some start between January and May. Check the start dates for the courses you are interested in on the 'Course information' screen in Course Search. For courses that start between January and May, you may need to apply before the three application deadlines above, as the universities and colleges will need time to consider your application. Contact the university or college direct for advice about when they need your application. Although some will be happy to receive applications right up to the start of the course, be prepared to send your application early.

- Applications for 2010 entry, which include any Oxford or Cambridge choices or any medicine courses A100, A101, A102, A103, A104, A105, A106, dentistry courses A200, A201, A202, A203, A204, A205, A206, A300, A400 or veterinary science/medicine courses D100, D101 and D102, must be at UCAS by 15 October 2009.

- When your application is processed, UCAS sends you a welcome letter stating your choices and your Personal ID. If there seems to be a mistake, call UCAS immediately, quoting your Personal ID.

Universities and colleges start to notify UCAS of their decisions for 2010 entry from October 2009. Applicants receive decisions via UCAS (unconditional offer, conditional offer or unsuccessful application). If the university or college want you to attend an interview, or submit a portfolio or other additional material, they will contact you directly or send you an invitation letter via UCAS.

You should reply to offers by the deadline given when you receive all your university decisions from UCAS. Remember:

- A level results will be published on 19 August 2010.

- UCAS Track automatically notifies all eligible applicants about Clearing - in other words, all those who have: missed their grades and have been turned down; not received offers earlier in the year; declined all offers made to them; applied after the final closing date (see above); or not found a place using Extra.

- A list of vacancies for degrees, HNDs and other undergraduate courses is published on the UCAS website as soon as results have been processed. This online vacancy service is updated several times a day, see **www.ucas.com**

visit: www.gap-year.com

Vacancy listings are also published by *The Independent* and *The Belfast Telegraph*.

- Clearing closes on 20 September.

Track

The Track facility on the UCAS website enables those who have applied, not only to check the progress of their application, but also to reply to offers online, to cancel choices from which they no longer wish to hear and even to change their address for correspondence. It is an invaluable tool for managing an application, but particularly useful to those who apply during a **gap**-year and who are overseas when important decisions are being made.

Deferred entry, rescheduled entry, or post A level application?

There are three ways to handle university entrance if you want to take a **gap**-year. The safest is usually to apply for deferred entry, but not all courses accept deferred entry candidates.

Our advice is to talk to the admissions office before making a decision about taking a **gap**-year.

1. Deferred entry

- Check first with the appropriate department of the university you want to go to, that they are happy to take students after a **gap**-year. If it's a popular course, preference may go to the current year applications.

- On your UCAS application there is a 'Start date' field in the 'Choices' section. For each choice click on the 'see list' button to the right of the 'Start date' field and choose a deferred entry start date or current entry start date. Talk to your teachers first and follow instructions in the Apply online help text.

- If you are planning to take a **gap**-year, you will need to explain why in your Personal Statement on the UCAS application. You need to convince the university that a year off will make you a better applicant, so give an outline of what you plan to do and why.

- Send your completed application to UCAS, just like any other student applying for entry without taking a **gap**-year. Those who do so well before the appropriate deadline, however, may be among the first to start receiving replies (via UCAS). You will get a call for selection interview(s) (directly from the university or college or through UCAS), an unsuccessful decision, an offer which is conditional on getting specific exam grades or Tariff points score, or an unconditional offer.

- Up until 30 June, UCAS will continue to forward applications to universities 'for consideration at their discretion'. Applications received after 30 June go straight into Clearing.

387

NOTE: Some academics are not happy with deferred entry because it means it might be nearly two years before you start your higher education. During that time a course may have changed, or *you* may have changed. So your application may be looked on unfavourably without your knowing why. Most departments at many universities are in favour of a **gap**-year but they are not all in favour of deferred entry. If they interview you in November 2009 for a place in October 2011 it will be 23 months before they see you again. Check it out with the university department first.

2. Deferring entry after you have applied

If you apply for a place in the coming university year and, after A level results decide to defer, you can negotiate direct with the university or college at which you are holding a place. If they agree to defer your place they will inform UCAS, who will confirm this to you in writing.

NOTE: Some admissions tutors say that to give up a place on a popular course is risky, because the university will not be happy after you have messed them about. Others say that if a course has over-recruited, your deferral will be welcome. Tread carefully.

3. Post A level applications

If you take A levels in June 2010, you can still apply through UCAS after the results come out in August. You will go straight into Clearing. If you do not send in a UCAS application before the end of the 2010 entry cycle, (20 September 2010) you should apply - between early September 2010 and the appropriate deadlines for your universities or courses - for entry in the following year. Universities and colleges will not accept those who do not apply through UCAS.

Faculty check: all subjects

If you want to take a **gap**-year, remember (before you apply) to contact the appropriate department or faculty at the university you would like to go to, and find out if they approve of a **gap**-year or not. Prepare a good case for it before you phone. It is advisable to do this even if you are an absolutely outstanding candidate, because on some courses a year off is considered a definite disadvantage. This is usually the case where a degree course is very long or requires a large amount of remembered technical knowledge at the start.

Art and design

Applying through UCAS to your chosen college of art and design might involve applying to courses using either of two deadline dates, 15 January or 24 March. Check the dates for the courses you are interested in on Course Search.

Medicine, dentistry and veterinary science/medicine

If you hope to pursue a career in medicine, dentistry or veterinary science/medicine, you can use no more than four (of your possible five) choices in any one of those three subject areas. The courses involved are:

visit: www.gap-year.com

- Medical courses: A100, A101, A102, A103, A104, A105, A106.
- Dentistry courses: A200, A201, A202, A203, A204, A205, A206, A300, A400.
- Veterinary science/medicine courses: D100, D101 and D102.

Don't forget that UCAS must receive *all* applications for these courses by 15 October.

Foundation degrees

Foundation degrees are the equivalent of the first two years of an Honours degree, may be studied full- or part-time, and consist of academic study integrated with relevant work-based learning undertaken with an employer. It may be studied as a stand-alone qualification or, upon completion, you may progress to the final year of an Honours degree.

Financing your studies

How you obtain finance for your study depends on where you live (your family home), because there are significant differences between the systems in England, Scotland, Wales and Northern Ireland. The government-funded student finance systems are studentfinanceengland, the Student Awards Agency for Scotland, studentfinancewales and studentfinancenorthernireland.

Over 90% of all UK students are domiciled in England, so the following advice is aimed at them, with a recommendation that those applying from elsewhere visit the website that serves their part of the UK.

In England, the whole process is being changed gradually over the next few years. Where applicants will be most affected by these changes is in the gradual switchover from being assessed by local authorities to being assessed by studentfinanceengland.

Those applying for their first student loan for the academic year beginning in September 2009 will apply direct to studentfinanceengland. Over the following three years, *all* English applicants will apply to studentfinanceengland, rather than to a local authority. Use this link to find out more:

www.direct.gov.uk/en/EducationAndLearning/UniversityAndHigherEduc ation/StudentFinance/index.htm

For English students, there is a varied package of available finance (and there are equivalents elsewhere in the UK). Everyone on an eligible course is automatically entitled to 72% of the maximum maintenance loan (determined by whether you are living at home, or away from home, during the academic year, and whether you are studying in London, where the amount is higher). The remaining 28% is means-tested against an applicant's family income. There are now very generous grants available, on a sliding scale, for applicants whose family income is less than £50,788, the maximum amount (£2,906) being available to all those with a family income of less than £25,000. Universities now have to sign an access agreement with the Office for Fair Access to be allowed to charge the full permitted tuition fee, in return for which they *must* provide bursaries of a minimum of £319 for all students who qualify

389

for grant funding. In addition, *all* students based in England are entitled to tuition fee loans. These are not means-tested and everyone may borrow up to the full tuition fee amount (capped at £3,225). Only the maintenance loan and the tuition fee loan need to be repaid - all other financing is given free.

Loans don't have to be paid back until your income reaches £15,000 a year before tax and what you repay will always be 9% of your earnings above £15k, collected automatically by Her Majesty's Revenue & Customs from your employer. If you earn less, you don't pay.

To keep up-to-date with progress on this:

www.direct.gov.uk/en/EducationAndLearning/UniversityAndHigherEduc ation/StudentFinance/FinanceForNewStudents/DG_070693

Scholarships and sponsorship

Every university is an independent institution with its own rules and most have their own special bursaries and scholarships for academic excellence, which they award on their own criteria.

In addition, there are still many organisations that offer sponsorship to students to study for a degree. This is sometimes on the condition that they join the sponsoring company or institution for a period when they graduate. The Army is one example from the public sector, information is available on:

www.armyjobs.mod.uk/education/grants/Pages/default.aspx

If you're looking for sponsorship, The Year in Industry improves your chances and removes the need to write endless letters. Go to: **www.yini.org.uk**

Universities in the UK

| University of Aberdeen | www.abdn.ac.uk |
| | Tel: +44 (0) 1224 272 000 |

| University of Abertay Dundee | www.abertay.ac.uk |
| | Tel: +44 (0) 1382 308 000 |

| Aberystwyth University | www.aber.ac.uk |
| | Tel: +44 (0) 1970 623 111 |

| Anglia Ruskin University | www.anglia.ac.uk |
| | Tel: +44 (0) 845 271 3333 |

| Arts University College at Bournemouth | www.aib.ac.uk |
| | Tel: +44 (0) 1202 533 011 |

| Aston University | www.aston.ac.uk |
| | Tel: +44 (0) 121 204 3000 |

| Bangor University | www.bangor.ac.uk |
| | Tel: +44 (0) 1248 351 151 |

| University of Bath | www.bath.ac.uk |
| | Tel: +44 (0) 1225 388 388 |

| Bath Spa University | www.bathspa.ac.uk |
| | Tel: +44 (0) 1225 875 875 |

| University of Bedfordshire | www.beds.ac.uk |
| | Tel: +44 (0) 1234 400 400 |

| University of Birmingham | www.bham.ac.uk |
| | Tel: +44 (0) 121 414 3344 |

| Bishop Grosseteste University College, Lincoln | www.bishopg.ac.uk |
| | Tel: +44 (0) 1522 527347 |

| University of Bolton | www.bolton.ac.uk |
| | Tel: +44 (0) 1204 900 600 |

| Bournemouth University | www.bournemouth.ac.uk |
| | Tel: +44 (0) 1202 524 111 |

The Gap-Year Guidebook 2010

University of Bradford	www.bradford.ac.uk Tel: +44 (0) 1274 232 323
University of Brighton	www.brighton.ac.uk Tel: +44 (0) 1273 600 900
University of Bristol	www.bristol.ac.uk Tel: +44 (0) 117 928 9000
Brunel University, West London	www.brunel.ac.uk Tel: +44 (0) 1895 274 000
University of Buckingham	www.buckingham.ac.uk Tel: +44 (0) 1280 814 080
Bucks New University	http://bucks.ac.uk Tel: +44 (0) 1494 522 141
University of Cambridge	www.cam.ac.uk Tel: +44 (0) 1223 337 733
Cardiff University	www.cardiff.ac.uk Tel: +44 (0) 29 2087 4000
Canterbury Christ Church University	www.canterbury.ac.uk Tel: +44 (0) 1227 767 700
Birmingham City University	www.bcu.ac.uk Tel: +44 (0) 121 331 5000
University of Central Lancashire	www.uclan.ac.uk Tel: +44 (0) 1772 201 201
University of Chester	www.chester.ac.uk Tel: +44 (0) 1244 511000
University of Chichester	www.chi.ac.uk Tel: +44 (0) 1243 816000
City University, London	www.city.ac.uk Tel: +44 (0) 20 7040 5060
Coventry University	www.coventry.ac.uk Tel: +44 (0) 2476 88 76 88
Cranfield University	www.cranfield.ac.uk Tel: +44 (0) 1234 750 111

visit: www.gap-year.com

University of Cumbria	www.cumbria.ac.uk Tel: +44 (0) 1524 384 384
De Montfort University	www.dmu.ac.uk Tel: +44 (0) 116 255 1551
University of Derby	www.derby.ac.uk Tel: +44 (0) 1332 590 500
University of Dundee	www.dundee.ac.uk Tel: +44 (0) 1382 383 000
Durham University	www.dur.ac.uk Tel: +44 (0) 191 334 2000
University of East Anglia	www.uea.ac.uk Tel: +44 (0) 1603 456 161
University of East London	www.uel.ac.uk Tel: +44 (0) 20 8223 3000
Edge Hill University	www.edgehill.ac.uk Tel: +44 (0) 1695 575 171
The University of Edinburgh	www.ed.ac.uk Tel: +44 (0) 131 650 1000
University of Essex • Writtle College	www.essex.ac.uk Tel: +44 (0) 1206 873 333 www.writtle.ac.uk +44 (0) 1245 424 200
University of Exeter	www.exeter.ac.uk Tel: +44 (0) 1392 661 000
University College Falmouth	www.falmouth.ac.uk Tel: +44 (0) 1326 211077
University of Glamorgan	www.glam.ac.uk Tel: +44 (0) 1443 480 480
University of Glasgow	www.gla.ac.uk Tel: +44 (0) 141 330 2000
Glasgow Caledonian University	www.caledonian.ac.uk Tel: +44 (0) 141 331 3000

University of Gloucestershire	www.glos.ac.uk Tel: +44 (0) 844 801 0001
University of Greenwich	www.gre.ac.uk Tel: +44 (0) 20 8331 8000
Harper Adams University College	www.harper-adams.ac.uk Tel: +44 (0) 1952 820280
Heriot-Watt University	www.hw.ac.uk Tel: +44 (0) 131 449 5111
University of Hertfordshire	www.herts.ac.uk Tel: +44 (0) 1707 284 000
University of Huddersfield	www.hud.ac.uk Tel: +44 (0) 1484 422 288
The University of Hull	www.hull.ac.uk Tel: +44 (0) 1482 346 311
Institute for System Level Integration	www.sli-institute.ac.uk Tel: +44 (0) 1506 469 300
Keele University	www.keele.ac.uk Tel: +44 (0) 1782 732 000
University of Kent	www.kent.ac.uk Tel: +44 (0) 1227 764 000
Kingston University	www.kingston.ac.uk Tel: +44 (0) 20 8417 9000
Lancaster University	www.lancs.ac.uk Tel: +44 (0) 1524 65201
Leeds College of Music	www.lcm.ac.uk Tel: +44 (0) 113 222 3400
Leeds Metropolitan University	www.leedsmet.ac.uk Tel: +44 (0) 113 812 0000
Leeds Trinity & All Saints	www.leedstrinity.ac.uk Tel: +44 (0) 113 283 7100
University of Leeds	www.leeds.ac.uk Tel: +44 (0) 113 243 1751

| University of Leicester | www.le.ac.uk |
| | Tel: +44 (0) 116 252 2522 |

| University of Lincoln | www.lincoln.ac.uk |
| | Tel: +44 (0) 1522 882 000 |

| University of Liverpool | www.liv.ac.uk |
| | Tel: +44 (0) 151 794 2000 |

| Liverpool Hope University | www.hope.ac.uk |
| | Tel: +44 (0) 151 291 3000 |

| Liverpool John Moores University | www.ljmu.ac.uk |
| | Tel: +44 (0) 151 231 2121 |

University of London
(contact colleges directly)
www.london.ac.uk
Tel: +44 (0) 20 7862 8360

- Barts and The London School of
  Medicine and Dentistry
  www.smd.qmul.ac.uk
  Tel: +44 (0) 20 7882 2239

- Birkbeck College
  www.bbk.ac.uk
  Tel: +44 (0) 20 7631 6000

- Courtauld Institute of Art
  www.courtauld.ac.uk
  Tel: +44 (0) 20 7872 0220

- Goldsmith's College
  www.gold.ac.uk
  Tel: +44 (0) 20 7919 7171

- Heythrop College
  www.heythrop.ac.uk
  Tel: +44 (0) 20 7795 6600

- Imperial College
  www.imperial.ac.uk
  Tel: +44 (0) 20 7589 5111

- Institute of Advanced Legal Studies
  www.ials.sas.ac.uk
  Tel: +44 (0) 20 7862 5800

- Institute of Education
  www.ioe.ac.uk
  Tel: +44 (0) 20 7612 6000

- Institute in Paris
  www.bip.lon.ac.uk
  Tel: +33 (0) 1 44 11 73 76

- King's College London
  www.kcl.ac.uk
  Tel: +44 (0) 20 7836 5454

- London School of Economics and Political Science

  www.lse.ac.uk
  Tel: +44 (0) 20 7405 7686

- London School of Hygiene and Tropical Medicine

  www.lshtm.ac.uk
  Tel: +44 (0) 20 7636 8636

- Queen Mary

  www.qmul.ac.uk
  Tel: +44 (0) 20 7882 5555

- Royal Academy of Music

  www.ram.ac.uk
  Tel: +44 (0) 20 7873 7373

- Royal Free and University College Medical School

  www.ucl.ac.uk/medicalschool
  Tel: +44 (0) 20 7679 2000

- Royal Holloway

  www.rhul.ac.uk
  Tel: +44 (0) 1784 434 455

- School of Advanced Study

  www.sas.ac.uk
  Tel: +44 (0) 20 7862 8659

- School of Oriental and African Studies

  www.soas.ac.uk
  Tel: +44 (0) 20 7637 2388

- School of Slavonic and East European Studies

  www.ssees.ac.uk
  Tel: +44 (0) 20 7679 8700

- St George's

  www.sgul.ac.uk
  Tel: +44 (0) 20 8672 9944

- The Royal Veterinary College

  www.rvc.ac.uk
  Tel: +44 (0) 20 7468 5000

- The School of Pharmacy

  www.pharmacy.ac.uk
  Tel: +44 (0) 20 7753 5800

- University College London

  www.ucl.ac.uk
  Tel: +44 (0) 20 7679 2000

London Metropolitan University

www.londonmet.ac.uk
Tel: +44 (0) 20 7423 0000

London South Bank University

www.lsbu.ac.uk
Tel: +44 (0) 20 7815 7815

Loughborough University

www.lboro.ac.uk
Tel: +44 (0) 1509 263 171

The University of Manchester	www.manchester.ac.uk Tel: +44 (0) 161 306 6000
• Manchester Business School	www.mbs.ac.uk Tel: +44 (0) 161 3061 320
Manchester Metropolitan University	www.mmu.ac.uk Tel: +44 (0) 161 247 2000
Middlesex University	www.mdx.ac.uk Tel: +44 (0) 20 8411 5000
Napier University	www.napier.ac.uk Tel: +44 (0) 8452 606 040
Newcastle University	www.ncl.ac.uk Tel: +44 (0) 191 222 6000
Newman College of Higher Education	www.newman.ac.uk Tel: +44 (0) 121 476 1181
The University of Northampton	www.northampton.ac.uk Tel: +44 (0) 1604 735500
Northumbria University	www.northumbria.ac.uk Tel: +44 (0) 191 232 6002
The University of Nottingham	www.nottingham.ac.uk Tel: +44 (0) 115 951 5151
Nottingham Trent University	www.ntu.ac.uk Tel: +44 (0) 115 941 8418
The Open University	www.open.ac.uk Tel: +44 (0) 845 300 6090
University of Oxford	www.ox.ac.uk Tel: +44 (0) 1865 270 000
Oxford Brookes University	www.brookes.ac.uk Tel: +44 (0) 1865 741 111
University of Plymouth	www.plymouth.ac.uk Tel: +44 (0) 1752 600 600
University of Portsmouth	www.port.ac.uk Tel: +44 (0) 2392 84 84 84

Queen Margaret University	www.qmu.ac.uk Tel: +44 (0) 131 474 0000
Queen's University Belfast	www.qub.ac.uk Tel: +44 (0) 28 9024 5133
• Stranmillis University College	www.stran.ac.uk Tel: +44 (0) 28 9038 1271
University of Reading	www.reading.ac.uk Tel: +44 (0) 1189 875 123
Roehampton University	www.roehampton.ac.uk Tel: +44 (0) 20 8392 3000
Royal College of Art	www.rca.ac.uk Tel: +44 (0) 20 7590 4444
Royal College of Music	www.rcm.ac.uk Tel: +44 (0) 20 7589 3643
University of Salford	www.salford.ac.uk Tel: +44 (0) 161 295 5000
The University of Sheffield	www.sheffield.ac.uk Tel: +44 (0) 114 222 2000
Sheffield Hallam University	www.shu.ac.uk Tel: +44 (0) 114 225 5555
University of Southampton	www.soton.ac.uk Tel: +44 (0) 23 8059 5000
Southampton Solent University	www.solent.ac.uk Tel: +44 (0) 23 8031 9000
Staffordshire University	www.staffs.ac.uk Tel: +44 (0) 1782 294 000
St Mary's University, Belfast	www.smucb.ac.uk Tel: +44 (0) 28 9032 7678
University of Strathclyde	www.strath.ac.uk Tel: +44 (0) 141 552 4400
University of St Andrews	www.st-andrews.ac.uk Tel: +44 (0) 1334 476 161

visit: www.gap-year.com

University of Stirling	www.stir.ac.uk Tel: +44 (0) 1786 473 171
University of Sunderland	www.sunderland.ac.uk Tel: +44 (0) 191 515 2000
University of Surrey	www.surrey.ac.uk Tel: +44 (0) 1483 300 800
University of Sussex	www.sussex.ac.uk Tel: +44 (0) 1273 606 755
Swansea University	www.swansea.ac.uk Tel: +44 (0) 1792 205 678
University of Teesside	www.tees.ac.uk Tel: +44 (0) 1642 218 121
Thames Valley University	www.tvu.ac.uk Tel: +44 (0) 208 579 5000
The Liverpool Institute for Performing Arts	www.lipa.ac.uk Tel: +44 (0) 151 330 3000
The Robert Gordon University	www.rgu.ac.uk Tel: +44 (0) 1224 262 000
Trinity College of Music	www.tcm.ac.uk Tel: +44 (0) 20 8305 4444
University of Ulster	www.ulster.ac.uk Tel: +44 (0) 8 700 400 700
University College for the Creative Arts	www.ucreative.ac.uk
• Canterbury	Tel: +44 (0) 1227 817302
• Epsom	Tel: +44 (0) 1372 728811
• Farnham	Tel: +44 (0) 1252 722441
• Maidstone	Tel: +44 (0) 1622 620000
• Rochester	Tel: +44 (0) 1634 888702
University Marine Biological Station Millport	www.gla.ac.uk/marinestation Tel: +44 (0) 1475 530 581

University of Wales
(contact institutions directly)

www.wales.ac.uk
Tel: +44 (0) 29 2037 6999

• University of Wales – Glyndwr University

www.glyndwr.ac.uk
Tel: +44 (0) 1978 290 666

• University of Wales – Royal Welsh College
of Music and Drama

www.rwcmd.ac.uk
Tel: +44 (0) 29 2034 2854

• University of Wales – Swansea Metropolitan
University

www.sihe.ac.uk
Tel: +44 (0) 1792 481 000

• University of Wales –
Trinity University College, Carmarthen

www.trinity-cm.ac.uk
Tel: +44 (0) 1267 676 767

• University of Wales, Newport

www.newport.ac.uk
Tel: +44 (0) 1633 430 088

• University of Wales Institute, Cardiff

www.uwic.ac.uk
Tel: +44 (0) 29 2041 6070

• University of Wales, Lampeter

www.lamp.ac.uk
Tel: +44 (0) 1570 422 351

• University of Wales, Coleg Harlech WEA

www.harlech.ac.uk
Tel: +44 (0) 1766 781 900

• University of Wales, Llandrillo College

www.llandrillo.ac.uk
Tel: +44 (0) 1492 546 666

University of Warwick

www.warwick.ac.uk
Tel: +44 (0) 2476 523 523

University of Westminster

www.wmin.ac.uk
Tel: +44 (0) 20 7911 5000

University of The Arts

www.arts.ac.uk
Tel: +44 (0) 20 7514 6000

University of the West of England, Bristol

www.uwe.ac.uk
Tel: +44 (0) 117 965 6261

University of the West of Scotland

www.paisley.ac.uk
Tel: +44 (0) 141 848 3000

The University of Winchester

www.winchester.ac.uk
Tel: +44 (0) 1962 841515

University of Wolverhampton	**www.wlv.ac.uk** Tel: +44 (0) 1902 321 000
University of Worcester	**www.worcester.ac.uk** Tel: +44 (0) 1905 855 000
University of York	**www.york.ac.uk** Tel: +44 (0) 1904 430 000
York St John University	**www.yorksj.ac.uk** Tel: +44 (0) 1904 624 624

Appendix | 1C - Universities in the UK

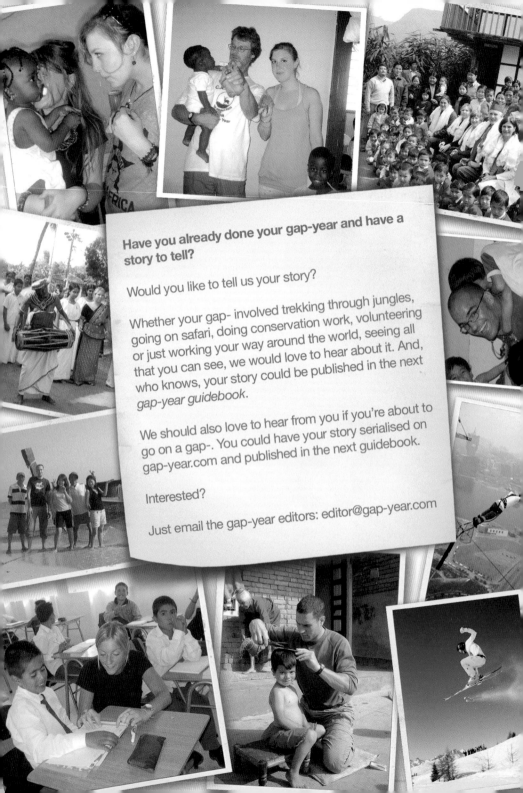

Have you already done your gap-year and have a story to tell?

Would you like to tell us your story?

Whether your gap- involved trekking through jungles, going on safari, doing conservation work, volunteering or just working your way around the world, seeing all that you can see, we would love to hear about it. And, who knows, your story could be published in the next *gap-year guidebook*.

We should also love to hear from you if you're about to go on a gap-. You could have your story serialised on gap-year.com and published in the next guidebook.

Interested?

Just email the gap-year editors: editor@gap-year.com

Country info

Once you have chosen where you want to go, whether one country or a dozen, do some research. It would be a shame to travel to the other side of the world and then miss what it has to offer. There are loads of websites giving interesting and useful factual advice (weather, geographical, political, economic) as well as those that are more touristy.

Foreign Office warnings

It's worth bearing in mind that economic and political situations can change rapidly in countries, so check with the Foreign and Commonwealth Office that the country is still safe to travel to before you go. There's a link to their website on: **www.gap-year.com**

It's important to look at the lists of specific areas which travellers should avoid. It's also worth noting the phone numbers of all British embassies and consulates in areas where you may be travelling, in case you need to contact them for help.

Telephone or email home regularly to save your family a lot of worry and British embassies a lot of wasted time. The following pages contain data for individual countries: make sure you check with the FCO for up-to-date information.

Afghanistan, The Islamic Republic of
- Population: estimated to be 28.7 million (UN)
- Location: South Asia
- Capital: Kabul
- Currency: Afghani (AFN)
- Religion: mainly Sunni Muslim
- Languages: Farsi (Dari), Pashtu (Pashto or Pukhto)
- British Embassy, Kabul: +93 (0) 700 102 000

Albania, The Republic of
- Population: estimated to be 3.6 million
- Location: South-east Europe
- Capital: Tirana
- Currency: Lek (ALL)
- Religion: Sunni Muslim, Albanian Orthodox, Roman Catholic
- Languages: Albanian (Tosk is the official dialect), Greek, Vlach, Romani, Slavic dialects
- British Embassy, Tirana: +355 4 223 4973/4/5

403

Algeria, The People's Democratic Republic of

- Population: 32 million
- Location: North Africa
- Capital: Algiers
- Currency: Algerian Dinar (DZD)
- Religion: Sunni Muslim, Christian, Jewish
- Language: Arabic (official language), French and Amazigh
- British Embassy, Algiers: +213 21 23 00 68

Andorra, The Principality of

- Population: 76,875
- Location: Southern Europe
- Capital: Andorra la Vella
- Currency: Euro (EUR)
- Religion: Roman Catholic
- Language: Catalan (official), French, Spanish
- British Consulate-General, Barcelona: +34 933 666 200

Angola, The Republic of

- Population: 16.4 million (2006 estimate)
- Location: Southern Africa
- Capital: Luanda
- Currency: Kwanza (AOA)
- Religion: Indigenous beliefs, Roman Catholic, Christian, Muslim
- Language: Portuguese (official), local African languages
- British Embassy, Luanda: +244 (222) 334582

Anguilla (British Overseas Territory)

- Population: 13,600 (2005 estimate)
- Location: Caribbean
- Capital: The Valley
- Currency: Eastern Caribbean Dollar (XCD); US dollars accepted (USD)
- Religion: Christian
- Language: English
- Government House, Anguilla: +1 (264) 497 2621/2

visit: www.gap-year.com

Antigua and Barbuda

- Population: 85,700 (EIU 2007 estimate)
- Location: Caribbean
- Capital: Saint John's City
- Currency: East Caribbean dollar (XCD)
- Religion: Anglican, Moravian, Methodist and Roman Catholic
- Language: English
- British High Commission, Barbados: +1 246 430 7800

Argentina (The Argentine Republic)

- Population: 36.2 million
- Location: Southern South America
- Capital: Buenos Aires
- Currency: Peso (ARS)
- Religion: Roman Catholic, Protestant, Jewish and Muslim
- Language: Spanish
- British Embassy, Buenos Aires: +54 (11) 4808 2200

Armenia, The Republic of

- Population: 3.2 million
- Location: Europe
- Capital: Yerevan
- Currency: Dram (AMD)
- Religion: Armenian Orthodox, Christian, Yezidi
- Language: Armenian, Russian, Yezidi
- British Embassy, Yerevan: +374 (0) 10 264 301

Ascension Island (British Overseas Territory)

- Population: 1000
- Location: Atlantic Ocean
- Capital: Georgetown
- Currency: St Helena/Ascension Pound (SHP)
- Religion: Christian
- Language: English
- Government House, Georgetown: +00 247 7000

Australia, The Commonwealth of
- Population: 20.7 million
- Location: Australasia
- Capital: Canberra
- Currency: Australian dollar (AUD)
- Religion: Christian, Buddhist, Jewish, Muslim
- Language: English, Aboriginal
- British High Commission, Canberra: +61 (0) 2 6270 6666

Austria, The Republic of
- Population: 8.3 million
- Location: Central Europe
- Capital: Vienna
- Currency: Euro (EUR)
- Religion: Roman Catholic, Muslim and Protestant
- Language: German
- British Embassy, Vienna Tel: +43 (1) 716 130

Azerbaijan, The Republic of
- Population: 8.5 million
- Location: South-west Asia
- Capital: Baku
- Currency: Manat (AZN)
- Religion: Muslim, Russian Orthodox, Armenian Orthodox,
- Language: Azeri, Russian, Armenian
- British Embassy, Baku: +994 (12) 497 5188/89/90

Bahamas, The Commonwealth of The
- Population: 333,800
- Location: Caribbean
- Capital: Nassau
- Currency: Bahamian Dollar (BSD)
- Religion: Baptist, Anglican, Roman Catholic, Methodist, Church of God, Evangelical Protestants
- Language: English, Creole (among Haitian immigrants)
- refer to British High Commission, Kingston, Jamaica: +1 (876) 510 0700

visit: www.gap-year.com

Bahrain, The Kingdom of

- Population: 698,585 (including expatriate residents)
- Location: Middle East
- Capital: Manama (Al Manamah)
- Currency: Bahraini Dinar (BHD)
- Religion: Muslim
- Language: Arabic, English
- British Embassy, Manama: +973 1757 4100; +973 1757 4167 (Information)

Bangladesh, The People's Republic of

- Population: 135 million (2003 estimate)
- Location: South Asia
- Capital: Dhaka
- Currency: Taka (BDT)
- Religion: Muslim, Hindu, Buddhist, Christian
- Language: Bangla, English, some tribal languages
- British High Commission, Dhaka: +880 (2) 882 2705/6/7/8/9

Barbados

- Population: 274,000 (June 2006)
- Location: Caribbean
- Capital: Bridgetown
- Currency: Barbadian Dollar (BBD)
- Religion: Protestant, Roman Catholic, Jewish, Muslim
- Language: English
- British High Commission, Bridgetown: +1 (246) 430 7800

Belarus, The Republic of

- Population: 9.7 million (2007 estimate)
- Location: Eastern Europe
- Capital: Minsk
- Currency: Belarusian Ruble (BYR)
- Religion: Eastern Orthodox Christian, Roman Catholic, Protestant, Jewish, Muslim
- Language: Belarusian, Russian
- British Embassy, Minsk: +375 (17) 210 5920/1

407

Belgium

- Population: 10.25 million
- Location: Central Europe
- Capital: Brussels
- Currency: Euro (EUR)
- Religion: Roman Catholic, Protestant
- Language: Dutch, French, German
- British Embassy, Brussels: +32 (2) 287 6211

Belize

- Population: 291,600 (June 2005)
- Location: Central America
- Capital: Belmopan
- Currency: Belizean Dollar (BZD)
- Religion: Roman Catholic, Protestant, Muslim, Buddhist, Hindu, Bahá'í
- Language: English, Creole, Spanish, indigenous languages
- British High Commission, Belmopan: +501 822 2981/2717

Benin, The Republic of

- Population: 8.4 million (UN Estimate 2005)
- Location: West Africa
- Capital: Porto-Novo
- Currency: CFA Franc BCEAO (XOF)
- Religion: Indigenous beliefs, Christian, Muslim
- Language: French, Fon, Yoruba, other African languages
- Community Liaison Officer, Contonou: +229 21 30 32 65

Bermuda (British Overseas Territory)

- Population: 64,000 (2007)
- Location: Atlantic Ocean
- Capital: Hamilton
- Currency: Bermuda Dollar (BMD)
- Religion: Christian, African Methodist Episcopalian
- Language: English, Portuguese
- Government House, Hamilton: +1 (441) 292 3600

visit: www.gap-year.com

Bhutan, The Kingdom of

- Population: 658,888 (2007)
- Location: South Asia
- Capital: Thimphu
- Currency: Ngultrum (BTN), Indian Rupee (INR)
- Religion: Buddhist, Hindu
- Language: Dzongkha, various Tibetan and Nepalese dialects, English widely spoken
- UK has no diplomatic representative in Bhutan. Contact British Deputy High Commission, Kolkata (Calcutta), India: +91 33 2288 5173-76

Bolivia, The Republic of

- Population: 9.7 million (2008)
- Location: Central South America
- Capital: La Paz
- Currency: Boliviano (BOB)
- Religion: Roman Catholic, Evangelical Methodist
- Language: Spanish, Quechua, Aymara and Indigenous dialects
- British Embassy, La Paz: +591 (2) 243 3424

Bosnia and Herzegovina

- Population: 4 million (estimated 2005)
- Location: South-east Europe
- Capital: Sarajevo
- Currency: Convertible Mark (BAM)
- Religion: Roman Catholic, Orthodox, Muslim
- Language: Bosnian, Serbian, Croatian
- British Embassy, Sarajevo: +387 33 282 200 (main); +387 33 20 4780 (Consular/Visa)

Botswana, The Republic of

- Population: 1.8 million (2007)
- Location: Southern Africa
- Capital: Gaborone
- Currency: Pula (BWP)
- Religion: Christian, indigenous beliefs
- Language: English, Setswana
- British High Commission, Gaborone: +267 395 2841

Brazil, The Federative Republic of

- Population: 189.6 million (2008 estimate)
- Location: Eastern South America
- Capital: Brasilia
- Currency: Real (BRL)
- Religion: Roman Catholic, Pentecostal, Animist
- Language: Portuguese
- British Embassy, Brasilia: +55 61 3329 2300

British Antartic Territory

- Population: no indigenous population; scientific stations only
- Location: South Pole
- Currency: Sterling
- Language: English
- refer to Foreign & Commonwealth Office, London: +44 (0) 20 7008 1500

British Virgin Islands

- Population: 27,000 (2005 estimate)
- Location: Caribbean
- Capital: Road Town, Tortola
- Currency: US Dollar (USD)
- Religion: Christian
- Language: English
- Government House, Tortola: +1 284 494 2345/2370

Brunei (Darussalam)

- Population: 390,000 (2007 estimate)
- Location: South-east Asia
- Capital: Bandar Seri Begawan
- Currency: Brunei Dollar (BND)
- Religion: Muslim
- Language: Malay, English, Cantonese, Mandarin, Hokkein, Hakka
- British High Commission, Bandar Seri Begawan: +673 (2) 222 231; +673 (2) 226 001 (Consular/Visa)

Bulgaria, The Republic of
- Population: 7.6 million (UN 2007)
- Location: South-east Europe
- Capital: Sofia
- Currency: Lev (BGN)
- Religion: Bulgarian Orthodox, Muslim, Roman Catholic, Jewish
- Language: Bulgarian
- British Embassy, Sofia: +359 (2) 933 9222

Burkina Faso
- Population: 15.02 million (2008 UN estimate)
- Location: West Africa
- Capital: Ouagadougou
- Currency: CFA Franc BCEAO (XOF)
- Religion: Animist, Muslim, Christian
- Language: French, indigenous languages
- British Honorary Consul, Ouagadougou: +226 (50) 30 88 60

Burma (The Union of Myanmar)
- Population: 52 million
- Location: South-east Asia
- Capital: Rangoon
- Currency: Kyat (MMK)
- Religion: Buddhist, Christian, Muslim, Animist
- Language: Burmese, ethnic minority languages
- British Embassy, Rangoon: +95 (1) 370 863

Burundi, The Republic of
- Population: 8.3 million
- Location: Central Africa
- Capital: Bujumbura
- Currency: Burundi Franc (BIF)
- Religion: Muslim, Roman Catholic, Animist
- Language: Kirundi, French, Swahili
- British Embassy, Liaison Office, Bujumbura: +257 22 246 478

Cambodia, The Kingdom of

- Population: 13.995 million (2007 estimate)

- Location: South-east Asia

- Capital: Phnom Penh

- Currency: Riel (KHR), and US Dollar (USD)

- Religion: Buddhist, Muslim, Christian

- Language: Khmer, Cambodian

- British Embassy, Phnom Penh: +855 23 427124/48153

Cameroon, The Republic of

- Population: 16.3 million (2005 UN estimate)

- Location: West Africa

- Capital: Yaounde

- Currency: CFA Franc BEAC (XAF)

- Religion: Christian, Muslim, indigenous beliefs

- Language: French, English, Pidgin, numerous African dialects

- British High Commission, Yaounde: +237 2222 05 45

Canada

- Population: 33.4 million (2008)

- Location: North America

- Capital: Ottawa

- Currency: Canadian Dollar (CAD)

- Religion: Roman Catholic, Protestant, Muslim

- Language: English, French

- British High Commission, Ottawa: +1 (613) 237 1530

Cape Verde, The Republic of

- Population: 426,800 (2008 estimate)

- Location: West Africa

- Capital: Praia

- Currency: Escudo (CVE)

- Religion: Roman Catholic

- Language: Portuguese, Crioulo

- British Honorary Consulate, Sao Vincente: +238 232 3512

visit: www.gap-year.com

Cayman Islands (British Overseas Territory)

- Population: 53,252 (2006 estimate)
- Location: Caribbean
- Capital: George Town (Grand Cayman)
- Currency: Caymanian Dollar (KYD)
- Religion: Christian
- Language: English
- Government House, George Town, Grand Cayman: +1 345 244 2401

Central African Republic, The

- Population: 4.3 million (2007 estimate)
- Location: Central Africa
- Capital: Bangui
- Currency: CFA Franc BEAC (XAF)
- Religion: Christian, Muslim, indigenous beliefs
- Language: French, Sangho
- refer to British High Commission, Yaoundé, Cameroon: +237 2222 05 45

Chad, The Republic of

- Population: 9.8 million (2006 estimate)
- Location: Central Africa
- Capital: N'Djamena
- Currency: CFA Franc BEAC (XAF)
- Religion: Muslim, Christian, indigenous beliefs
- Language: French, Arabic, local languages
- refer to British High Commission, Yaoundé, Cameroon: +237 2222 05 45

Chile, The Republic of

- Population: 15.1 million
- Location: Southern South America
- Capital: Santiago de Chile
- Currency: Peso (CLP)
- Religion: Roman Catholic, Evangelical, Jewish, Muslim
- Language: Spanish, Mapuche, Aymara, Quechua
- British Embassy, Santiago: +56 (2) 370 4100

413

China, The People's Republic of

- Population: 1.29 billion
- Location: East Asia
- Capital: Beijing
- Currency: Yuan Renminbi (CNY)
- Religion: Officially atheist. Daoist, Buddhist, Muslim, Roman Catholic, Protestant (the 5 state-registered religions)
- Language: Putonghua (Mandarin), many local Chinese dialects
- British Embassy, Beijing: +86 (10) 5192 4000

Colombia, The Republic of

- Population: 42 million
- Location: Northern South America
- Capital: Bogotá
- Currency: Peso (COP)
- Religion: Roman Catholic, Evangelical
- Language: Spanish, indigenous languages
- British Embassy, Bogotá: +57 (1) 326 8300

Comoros, The Union of The

- Population: 711,417 (2007 estimate)
- Location: Southern Africa, group of islands in the Mozambique Channel
- Capital: Moroni (Ngazidja)
- Currency: Comoros Franc (KMF)
- Religion: Muslim, Roman Catholic
- Language: Comoran, French, Arabic
- refer to British High Commission, Port Louis, Mauritius: +230 202 9400

Congo, The Republic of The

- Population: 4 million (2005)
- Location: West Africa
- Capital: Brazzaville
- Currency: CFA Franc BEAC (XAF)
- Religion: Roman Catholic, Christian, Muslim, traditional beliefs
- Language: French (official), Lingala, Kikongo, Munukutuba
- refer to British Embassy, Kinshasa, Democratic Republic of Congo: +243 81 715 0761

visit: www.gap-year.com

Congo, The Democratic Republic of the

- Population: 58.7 million
- Location: Central Africa
- Capital: Kinshasa
- Currency: Congolese Franc (CDF)
- Religion: Roman Catholic, Protestant, Kimbanguist, Muslim, indigenous beliefs
- Language: French (official), Lingala (trade language), Swahili, Kikongo, Tshiluba
- British Embassy, Kinshasa: +243 81 715 0761

Costa Rica, The Republic of

- Population: 4.2 million
- Location: Central America
- Capital: San José
- Currency: Colon (CRC)
- Religion: Roman Catholic, Evangelical Protestant
- Language: Spanish
- British Embassy, San José: +506 2258 2025

Côte d'Ivoire, The Republic of (Ivory Coast)

- Population: 20 million (2008 UN estimate)
- Location: West Africa
- Capital Yamoussoukro
- Currency: CFA Franc BCEAO (XOF)
- Religion: Muslim, Christian, indigenous beliefs
- Language: French (official), Dioula, Baoule and other local native dialects
- refer to British High Commission, Accra, Ghana: +233 (21) 221 665

Croatia, The Republic of

- Population: 4.5 million (2004 estimate)
- Location: South-east Europe
- Capital: Zagreb
- Currency: Kuna (HRK)
- Religion: Roman Catholic, Orthodox, Muslim
- Language: Croatian
- British Embassy, Zagreb: +385 (1) 6009 100

Cuba, The Republic of
- Population: 11.2 million
- Location: Caribbean
- Capital: Havana
- Currency: Convertible Peso (CUC) or Peso (CUP)
- Religion: Roman Catholic, Santeria, Protestant
- Language: Spanish
- British Embassy, Havana: +53 (7) 214 2200

Cyprus, The Republic of
- Population: 754,064
- Location: Mediterranean
- Capital: Nicosia
- Currency: Euro (EUR), Turkish Lira (in the north) (TRY)
- Religion: Greek Orthodox, Muslim, Maronite, Armenian Apostolic
- Language: Greek, Turkish, English
- British High Commission, Nicosia: +357 22 861100

Czech Republic, The
- Population: 10.47 million
- Location: Central Europe
- Capital: Prague
- Currency: Czech Koruna (Crown) (CZK)
- Religion: Roman Catholic, Protestant, Orthodox, Atheist
- Language: Czech
- British Embassy, Prague: +420 257 402 111

Denmark, The Kingdom of
- Population: 5.4 million
- Location: Northern Europe
- Capital: Copenhagen
- Currency: Danish Krone (DKK)
- Religion: Evangelical Lutheran, Christian, Muslim
- Language: Danish, Faroese, Greenlandic (an Inuit dialect), English is the predominant second language
- British Embassy, Copenhagen: +45 35 44 52 00

visit: www.gap-year.com

Djibouti, The Republic of
- Population: 852,844 (2008 estimate)
- Location: East Africa
- Capital: Djibouti
- Currency: Djiboutian Franc (DJF)
- Religion: Muslim, Christian
- Language: French (official), Arabic (official), Somali, Afar
- British Honorary Consul, Djibouti: +253 (3) 85007

Dominica, The Commonwealth of
- Population: 72,000
- Location: Caribbean
- Capital: Roseau
- Currency: East Caribbean Dollar (XCD)
- Religion: Roman Catholic, Protestant
- Language: English (official), French patois (Creole)
- British High Commission, Roseau: +767 255 3116 / 275 4000

Dominican Republic, the
- Population 8.9 million (2005 UN estimate)
- Location: Caribbean
- Capital: Santo Domingo
- Currency: Dominican Peso (DOP)
- Religion: Roman Catholic
- Language: Spanish
- British Embassy, Santo Domingo: +1 809 472 7111

East Timor - see Timor-Leste

Ecuador, The Republic of
- Population: 13.2 million (WHO 2005)
- Location: South America
- Capital: Quito
- Currency: US Dollar (USD)
- Religion: Roman Catholic
- Language: Spanish (official), Amerindian languages (especially Quechua)
- British Embassy, Quito: +593 (2) 2970 800/1

Egypt, The Arab Republic of
- Population: 76.5 million (2006)
- Location: North Africa
- Capital: Cairo
- Currency: Egyptian Pound (EGP)
- Religion: Muslim (mostly Sunni), Coptic Christian
- Language: Arabic (official), English and French
- British Embassy, Cairo: +20 (2) 2791 6000

El Salvador, The Republic of
- Population: 6.9 million
- Location: Central America
- Capital: San Salvador
- Currency: US Dollar (USD), Colon (SVC)
- Religion: Roman Catholic
- Language: Spanish
- British Honorary Consulate, El Salvador: +503 281 5555

Equatorial Guinea, The Republic of
- Population: 523,051 (2004)
- Location: West Africa
- Capital: Malabo
- Currency: CFA Franc BEAC (XAF)
- Religion: Christian (predominantly Roman Catholic), indigenous religions
- Language: Spanish (official), French (official), Fang, Bubi, Ibo
- Refer to British High Commission, Abuja, Nigeria: +234 (9) 413 2010

Eritrea
- Population: 4.9 million (2007 estimate)
- Location: East Africa
- Capital: Asmara
- Currency: Nafka (ERN)
- Religion: Christian, Muslim
- Language: Tigrinya, Tigre, Arabic, English
- British Embassy, Asmara: +291 1 12 01 45

visit: www.gap-year.com

Estonia, The Republic of

- Population: 1.34 million
- Location: East Europe
- Capital: Tallinn
- Currency: Kroon (EEK)
- Religion: Lutheran, Orthodox Christian
- Language: Estonian (official), Russian
- British Embassy, Tallinn: +372 667 4700

Ethiopia, The Federal Democratic Republic of

- Population: 76-78 million (2005 estimate)
- Location: East Africa
- Capital: Addis Ababa
- Currency: Ethiopian Birr (ETB)
- Religion: Orthodox Christian, Muslim, Animist, Protestant
- Language: Amharic, Tigrinya, Oromigna, Guaragigna, Sidaminga, Somali, Arabic, other local dialects, English (major foreign language taught in schools)
- British Embassy, Addis Ababa: +251 (11) 661 2354

Falkland Islands (British Overseas Territory)

- Population: 2955 (2006 census)
- Location: South Atlantic Ocean
- Capital: Stanley
- Currency: Falkland Island Pound (FKP)
- Religion: Christian, Roman Catholic, United Reformed Church, Anglican
- Language: English
- Government House, Stanley: +500 282 00

Fiji (The Republic of the Fiji Islands)

- Population: 837,271 (2007 Fiji national census)
- Location: Pacific Ocean
- Capital: Suva
- Currency: Fijian Dollar (FJD)
- Religion: Christian, Hindu, Muslim
- Language: English (official), Hindustani, Gujarati, numerous Fijian dialects
- British High Commission, Suva: +679 3229 100

Finland, The Republic of

- Population: 5.3 million
- Location: Northern Europe
- Capital: Helsinki
- Currency: Euro (EUR)
- Religion: Lutheran, Orthodox
- Language: Finnish (official), Swedish (official), growing Russian speaking minority and small Sami speaking community
- British Embassy, Helsinki: +358 (0) 9 2286 5100/5210/5216

France (The French Republic)

- Population: 63.4 million
- Location: West Europe
- Capital: Paris
- Currency: Euro (EUR)
- Religion: Roman Catholic, Protestant, Jewish, Muslim
- Language: French
- British Embassy, Paris: +33 1 44 51 31 00

Gabon (The Gabonese Republic)

- Population: 1.45 million (estimate 2007)
- Location: West Africa
- Capital: Libreville
- Currency: CFA Franc BEAC (XAF)
- Religion: Christian, Muslim, indigenous beliefs
- Language: French (official), Fang, Myene, Bateke, Bapounou/Eschira, Badjabi
- British Honorary Consulate, Libreville: +241 762 200

Gambia, The Republic of

- Population: 1.5 million
- Location: West Africa
- Capital: Banjul
- Currency: Dalasi (GMD)
- Religion: Muslim, Christian, indigenous beliefs
- Language: English (official), Mandinka, Wolof, Fula, indigenous languages
- British High Commission, Banjul: +220 449 5133

visit: www.gap-year.com

Georgia

- Population: 4.4 million
- Location: South-west Asia
- Capital: Tbilisi
- Currency: Lari (GEL)
- Religion: Georgian Orthodox, Muslim, Russian Orthodox, Armenian Apostolic
- Language: Georgian (official), Russian, Armenian, Azeri, Abkhaz
- British Embassy, Tbilisi: +995 32 274 747

Germany, The Federal Republic of

- Population: 82.5 million
- Location: Central Europe
- Capital: Berlin
- Currency: Euro (EUR)
- Religion: Protestant, Roman Catholic, Muslim
- Language: German
- British Embassy, Berlin: +49 (30) 20457-0

Ghana, The Republic of

- Population: 23.3 million (2008 estimate)
- Location: West Africa
- Capital: Accra
- Currency: Cedi (GHS)
- Religion: Muslim, Christian, indigenous beliefs
- Language: English (official), African languages (including Akan, Mossi, Ewe, and Hausa), Fante, Ga-Adangme, 75 spoken languages
- British High Commission, Accra: +233 (21) 221 665

Gibraltar (British Overseas Territory)

- Population: 29,257 (2007)
- Location: Atlantic Ocean
- Capital: Gibraltar
- Currency: Gibraltar Pound (GIP)
- Religion: Roman Catholic, Protestantism, Muslim, Hindu, Jewish
- Language: English
- Governor's Office, Main Street: +350 200 45 440

Greece (The Hellenic Republic)

- Population: 10.94 million (2001 census estimate)
- Location: South-east Europe
- Capital: Athens
- Currency: Euro (EUR)
- Religion: Greek Orthodox, Muslim
- Language: Greek
- British Embassy, Athens: +30 210 727 2600

Grenada

- Population: 89,703 (July 2006 estimate)
- Location: Caribbean
- Capital: St George's
- Currency: East Caribbean Dollar (XCD)
- Religion: Roman Catholic, Anglican, Protestant
- Language: English (official), French patois
- British High Commission, Bridge Town: +1 246 430 7800/7860 (resides in Barbados)

Guatemala

- Population: 12.7 million (2007 estimate)
- Location: Central America
- Capital: Guatemala City
- Currency: Quetzal (GTQ)
- Religion: Roman Catholic, Protestant, Judasim, Muslim, indigenous Mayan beliefs
- Language: Spanish, there are 23 officially recognized Amerindian languages
- British Embassy, Guatemala City: +502 2380 7300

Guinea, The Republic of

- Population: 9.2 million (2008 UN estimate)
- Location: West Africa
- Capital: Conakry
- Currency: Guinean Franc (GNF)
- Religion: Muslim, Christian, traditional beliefs
- Language: French (official), eight local languages taught in schools (Basari, Pular, Kissi, Koniagi, Kpelle, Loma, Malinke and Susu)
- British Embassy, Conakry: +224 63 35 53 29

visit: www.gap-year.com

Guinea-Bissau, The Republic of

- Population: 1.5 million (2008 UN estimate)
- Location: West Africa
- Capital: Bissau
- Currency: CFA Franc BCEAO (XOF)
- Religion: Muslim, Christian, indigenous beliefs
- Language: Portuguese (official), Crioulo, indigenous African languages
- Honorary British Consulate: +245 320 1224/1216

Guyana, The Co-operative Republic of

- Population: 751,000
- Location: South America
- Capital: Georgetown
- Currency: Guyanese Dollar (GYD)
- Religion: Christian, Hindu, Muslim
- Language: English, Amerindian dialects, Creole
- British High Commission, Georgetown: +592 226 58 81

Haiti, The Republic of

- Population: 8.5 million (2007 estimate)
- Location: Caribbean
- Capital: Port-au-Prince
- Currency: The Gourde (HTG)
- Religion: Roman Catholic, Protestant, Baptist, Pentecostal, Adventist, also Voodoo
- Language: French (official), Creole (official)
- British Consulate, Port-au-Prince: +509 257 3969

Holy See, Rome (Vatican City State)

- Population: 890
- Location: Italy
- Capital: Vatican City
- Currency: Euro (EUR)
- Religion: Roman Catholic
- Language: Latin, Italian, English and French
- British Embassy, Rome: +39 06 4220 4000

423

Honduras, The Republic of

- Population: 7.2 million (UN 2005)
- Location: Central America
- Capital: Tegucigalpa
- Currency: Lempira (HNL)
- Religion: Roman Catholic, Protestant
- Language: Spanish, English (business), Amerindian dialects
- British Embassy, Tegucigalpa: +504 237 6577/6459

Hong Kong (The Hong Kong Special Administration of China)

- Population: 6.8 million (2004)
- Location: East Asia
- Currency: Hong Kong Dollar (HKD)
- Religion: Buddhist, Taoist, Christian, Muslim, Hindu, Sikhist, Jewish
- Language: Chinese (Cantonese), English
- British Consulate General, Hong Kong: +852 2901 3281

Hungary, The Republic of

- Population: 10.1 million (2005)
- Location: Central Europe
- Capital: Budapest
- Currency: Forint (HUF)
- Religion: Roman Catholic, Calvinist, Lutheran, Jewish, Atheist
- Language: Hungarian
- British Embassy, Budapest: +36 (1) 266 2888

Iceland, The Republic of

- Population: 309,000 (April 2007)
- Location: North Europe
- Capital: Reykjavik
- Currency: Icelandic Krona (ISK)
- Religion: Evangelical Lutheran, Protestant, Roman Catholic
- Language: Icelandic
- British Embassy, Reykjavik: +354 550 5100

visit: www.gap-year.com

India, The Republic of

- Population: 1.13 billion (2007 estimate)
- Location: South Asia
- Capital: New Delhi
- Currency: Rupee (INR)
- Religion: Hindu, Muslim, Christian, Sikhist
- Language: Hindi (official), 18 main and regional official state languages, plus 24 further languages, 720 dialects and 23 tribal languages, English (officially an associate language, is used particularly for political, and commercial communication)
- British High Commission, New Delhi: +91 (11) 2687 2161

Indonesia, The Republic of

- Population: 234.7 million (2007)
- Location: South-east Asia
- Capital: Jakarta
- Currency: Rupiah (IDR)
- Religion: Muslim, Protestant, Roman Catholic, Hindu, Buddhist
- Language: Bahasa Indonesia (official), over 583 languages and dialects
- British Embassy, Jakarta: +62 (21) 2356 5200

Iran, The Islamic Republic of

- Population: 70 million (2000 UN estimate)
- Location: Middle East
- Capital: Tehran
- Currency: Rial (IRR)
- Religion: Shi'a Muslim, Sunni Muslim, Zoroastrian, Jewish, Christian, Bahá'i
- Language: Persian (Farsi), Azeri, Kurdish, Arabic, Luri, Baluchi
- British Embassy, Tehran: +98 (21) 6405 2000

Iraq, Republic of

- Population: 24.6 million (2003 estimate)
- Location: Middle East
- Capital: Baghdad
- Currency: New Iraqi Dinar (IQD)
- Religion: Muslim, Christian
- Language: Arabic, Kurdish, Assyrian, Armenian, Turkoman
- British Embassy, Bagdad: +964 7901 911 684

425

Ireland, Republic of
- Population: 4.2 million (preliminary 2006 census)
- Location: West Europe
- Capital: Dublin
- Currency: Euro (EUR)
- Religion: Roman Catholic, Church of Ireland
- Language: Irish, English
- British Embassy, Dublin: +353 (1) 205 3700

Israel, The State of
- Population: 7 million
- Location: Middle East
- Capital: Tel Aviv
- Currency: New Israeli Shekel (ILS)
- Religion: Jewish, Muslim, Christian
- Language: Hebrew, Arabic, English, Russian
- British Embassy, Tel Aviv: +972 (3) 5100 166

Italy
- Population: 59.1 million
- Location: South Europe
- Capital: Rome
- Currency: Euro (EUR)
- Religion: Roman Catholic, Jewish, Protestant, Muslim
- Language: Italian (official), German, French, Slovene
- British Embassy, Rome: +39 06 4220 0001

Ivory Coast - see Côte d'Ivoire

Jamaica
- Population: 2.7 million (2007 estimate)
- Location: Caribbean
- Capital: Kingston
- Currency: Jamaican Dollar (JMD)
- Religion: Anglican, Baptist and other Protestant, Roman Catholic, Rastafarian, Jewish, Seventh-Day Adventist
- Language: English, Patois
- British High Commission, Kingston: +1 (876) 510 0700

visit: www.gap-year.com

Japan

- Population: 127.7 million
- Location: East Asia
- Capital: Tokyo
- Currency: Yen (JPY)
- Religion: Shinto, Buddhist, Christian
- Language: Japanese
- British Embassy, Tokyo: +81 (3) 5211 1100

Jordan, The Hashemite Kingdom of

- Population: 5.3 million
- Location: Middle East
- Capital: Amman
- Currency: Jordanian Dinar (JOD)
- Religion: Sunni Muslim, Christian
- Language: Arabic (official), English
- British Embassy, Amman: +962 6 590 9200

Kazakhstan, The Republic of

- Population: 15.2 million
- Location: Central Asia
- Capital: Astana
- Currency: Kazakh Tenge (KZT)
- Religion: Muslim, Russian Orthodox, Protestant
- Language: Kazakh, Russian
- British Embassy, Almaty: +7 573 150 2200

Kenya, The Republic of

- Population: 38.6 million (2008 estimate)
- Location: East Africa
- Capital: Nairobi
- Currency: Kenyan Shilling (KES)
- Religion: Protestant (including Evangelical), Roman Catholic, indigenous beliefs, Muslim
- Language: English (official), Kiswahili, numerous indigenous languages
- British High Commission, Nairobi: +254 (20) 284 4000

Kiribati, The Republic of
- Population: 99,000 (2007 UN)
- Location: Pacific Ocean
- Capital: Tarawa
- Currency: Australian Dollar (AUD)
- Religion: Roman Catholic, Protestant (Congregational), Seventh-Day Adventist, Bahá'í, Latter-day Saints, Church of God
- Language: English (official), I-Kiribati
- refer to British High Commission, Suva, Fiji: +679 3229 100

Korea, The Democratic People's Republic of (North Korea)
- Population: 22.66 million (2003 UN estimate)
- Location: East Asia
- Capital: Pyongyang
- Currency: North Korean Won (KPW); foreigners are required to use Euros
- Religion: Buddhist, Christian, Chondo
- Language: Korean
- British Embassy, Pyongyang: +850 2 381 7980 (International); 02 382 7980 (Local dialling)

Korea, The Republic of (South Korea)
- Population: 48.49 million (2007 estimate)
- Location: East Asia
- Capital: Seoul
- Currency: South Korean Won (KRW)
- Religion: Shamanist, Buddhist, Confuciant, Chondogyo, Roman Catholic, Protestant
- Language: Korean
- British Embassy, Seoul: +82 (2) 3210 5500

Kosovo
- Population: 2 million (estimate)
- Location: Southern Europe
- Capital: Pristina
- Currency: Euro (EUR)
- Religion: Muslim, Serbian Orthodox, Roman Catholic
- Language: Albanian, Serbian, Bosniak, Turkish
- refer to British Embassy, Belgrade, Serbia: +381 (11) 2645 055

visit: www.gap-year.com

Kuwait, The State of

- Population: 2.6 million (estimate)
- Location: Middle East
- Capital: Kuwait City
- Currency: Kuwaiti Dinar (KWD)
- Religion: Muslim, Christian, other religions restricted
- Language: Arabic (official), English (second official language)
- British Embassy, Dasman: +965 2259 4320

Kyrgyzstan (The Kyrgyz Republic)

- Population: 5 million
- Location: Central Asia
- Capital: Bishkek
- Currency: Som (KGS)
- Religion: Muslim, Russian Orthodox, Christian minorities
- Language: Kyrgyz, Russian
- British Honorary Consul, Bishkek: +996 312 584 245

Laos (The Lao People's Democratic Republic)

- Population: 6.5 million (2007)
- Location: South-east Asia
- Capital: Vientiane
- Currency: Kip (LAK)
- Religion: Buddhist, Animist, Christian, Muslim
- Language: Lao
- British Embassy (resident at Bangkok): +66 (0) 2 305 8333

Latvia, The Republic of

- Population: 2.27 million
- Location: East Europe
- Capital: Riga
- Currency: Lat (LVL)
- Religion: Lutheran, Roman Catholic, Russian Orthodox
- Language: Latvian, Russian
- British Embassy, Riga: +371 6777 4700

Lebanon (The Lebanese Republic)

- Population: 4 million
- Location: Middle East
- Capital: Beirut
- Currency: Lebanese Pound (LBP)
- Religion: 18 registered sects including Druze, Maronite Christian, Shi'a and Sunni Muslim
- Language: Arabic (official), English, French, Armenian
- British Embassy, Beirut: +961 (1) 9608 00 (24 hours)

Lesotho, The Kingdom of

- Population: 2.1 million (2007 estimate)
- Location: Southern Africa
- Capital: Maseru
- Currency: Loti (LSL)
- Religion: Christian, indigenous beliefs
- Language: Sesotho, English
- British Honorary Consulate, Maseru: +266 2231 3929

Liberia, The Republic of

- Population: 3.35 million (2008 estimate)
- Location: West Africa
- Capital: Monrovia
- Currency: Liberian Dollar (LRD), US Dollar (USD)
- Religion: Christian, Muslim, indigenous beliefs
- Language: English (official), indigenous languages
- British Honorary Consulate, Monrovia: +231 226 056

Libya (The Great Socialist People's Libyan Arab Jamahiriya)

- Population: 5.41 million
- Location: North Africa
- Capital: Tripoli
- Currency: Dinar (LYD)
- Religion: Sunni Muslim
- Language: Arabic, Italian and English understood in major cities
- British Embassy, Tripoli: +218 (21) 340 3644/5

visit: www.gap-year.com

Liechtenstein, The Principality of

- Population: 35,000 (2006)
- Location: Central Europe
- Capital: Vaduz
- Currency: Swiss Franc (CHF)
- Religion: Roman Catholic, Protestant
- Language: German (official), Alemannic dialect
- refer to British Embassy, Berne, Switzerland: +41 (31) 359 7700

Lithuania, The Republic of

- Population: 3.4 million (2005)
- Location: East Europe
- Capital: Vilnius
- Currency: Litas (LTL)
- Religion: Roman Catholic
- Language: Lithuanian (official), Russian, English
- British Embassy, Vilnius: +370 5 246 29 00

Luxembourg, The Grand Duchy of

- Population: 451,000
- Location: Central Europe
- Capital: Luxembourg
- Currency: Euro (EUR)
- Religion: Roman Catholic, Protestant, Jewish, Muslim
- Language: Luxembourgish, German, French
- British Embassy, Luxembourg: + 352 22 98 64

Macao (The Macao Special Administrative Region of the People's Republic of China)

- Population: 488,100 (2005)
- Location: East Asia
- Currency: Pataca (MOP)
- Religion: Buddhist, Christian, Taoist
- Language: Cantonese, Portuguese, English
- British Honorary Consulate, Macao: +853 685 0886

431

Macedonia, republic of

- Population: 2 million (2004 estimate)
- Location: East Europe
- Capital: Skopje
- Currency: Macedonian Denar (MKD)
- Religion: Orthodox, Muslim
- Language: Macedonian, Albanian, Turkish, Serbian, Vlach, Roma
- British Embassy, Skopje: +389 (2) 3299 299

Madagascar, The Republic of

- Population: 20 million (2008 estimate)
- Location: Southern Africa
- Capital: Antananarivo
- Currency: Ariary (MGA)
- Religion: Christian, indigenous beliefs, Muslim
- Language: Malagasy, French
- British Consulate, Toamasina: +261 (20) 53 325 48/325 69

Malawi, The Republic of

- Population: 13.6 million (2006 estimate)
- Location: Southern Africa
- Capital: Lilongwe
- Currency: Kwacha (MWK)
- Religion: Protestant, Roman Catholic, Muslim, Hindu, indigenous beliefs
- Language: English (official), Chichewa (national)
- British High Commission, Liongwe: +265 (1) 772 400

Malaysia, The Federation of

- Population: 27.5 million (2008)
- Location: South-east Asia
- Capital: Kuala Lumpur
- Currency: Ringgit (MYR)
- Religion: Muslim, Buddhist, Taoist, Christian, Hindu, Animist
- Language: Bahasa Malay (national language), Iban, English widespread, Chinese, Tamil
- British High Commission, Kuala Lumpur: +60 (3) 2170 2200

visit: www.gap-year.com

Maldives, The Republic of
- Population: 400,000 (2004 estimate)
- Location: South Asia
- Capital: Malé
- Currency: Rufiyaa (MVR); resort islands accept US Dollar (USD)
- Religion: Sunni Muslim (other religions illegal)
- Language: Dhivehi, but English widely spoken in Malé and resort islands
- refer to British High Commission, Colombo, Sri Lanka: +94 (11) 539 0639

Mali, The Republic of
- Population: 12.5 million (2008)
- Location: West Africa
- Capital: Bamako
- Currency: CFA Franc BCEAO (XOF)
- Religion: Muslim, Christian, indigenous beliefs
- Language: French (official), Bambara, and numerous other African languages
- British Embassy Liaison Office, Bamako: +223 2021 3412

Malta, The Republic of
- Population: 402,700
- Location: South Europe
- Capital: Valletta
- Currency: Euro (EUR)
- Religion: Roman Catholic
- Language: Maltese, English
- British High Commission, Valletta: +356 2323 0000

Marshall Islands, Republic of the
- Population: 63,174 (2008)
- Location: Pacific Ocean
- Capital: Majuro
- Currency: US Dollar (USD)
- Religion: Christian (mostly Protestant)
- Language: English, two major Marshallese dialects, Japanese
- refer to British Embassy, Manilia: +63 (2) 858 2200

433

Mauritania, The Islamic Repubic of

- Population: 3.1 million (2005 estimate)
- Location: North Africa
- Capital: Nouakchott
- Currency: Ouguiya (MRO)
- Religion: Muslim
- Language: Hassaniya Arabic (official), Pulaar, Soninke, Wolof, French widely used in business
- British Honorary Consul, Nouakchott: +222 525 83 31

Mauritius, The Republic of

- Population: 1.27 million (2008 estimate)
- Location: Southern Africa
- Capital: Port Louis
- Currency: Mauritian Rupee (MUR)
- Religion: Hindu, Christian, Muslim
- Language: English, French, Creole
- British Honorary Consulate, Rodrigues: +230 832 0120

Mexico (The United Mexican State)

- Population: 110 million (2008 estimate)
- Location: Central America
- Capital: Mexico City
- Currency: Mexican Peso (MXN)
- Religion: Roman Catholic, Protestant
- Language: Spanish, at least 62 other regional languages
- British Embassy, Mexico City: +52 (55) 5242 8500

Micronesia, The Federated States of

- Population: 107,665 (2008 estimate)
- Location: Pacific Ocean
- Capital: Palikir
- Currency: US Dollar (USD)
- Religion: Roman Catholic, Protestant
- Language: English, Trukese, Pohnpeian, Yapese, Kosrean, Ulithian, Woleaian, Nukuoro, Kapingamarangi
- refer to British Embassy, Manila: +63 (2) 858 2200

434

Moldova, The Republic of

- Population: 4.32 million
- Location: East Europe
- Capital: Chisinau
- Currency: Moldovan Leu (MDL)
- Religion: Eastern Orthodox, Jewish, Baptist
- Language: Moldovan, Russian (official)
- British Embassy, Chisinau: +373 22 22 59 02;
  out of hours +373 69 10 44 42

Monaco, The Principality of

- Population: 32,543 (2006)
- Location: West Europe
- Capital: Monaco
- Currency: Euro (EUR)
- Religion: Roman Catholic
- Language: French (official), Italian, Monegasque, English
- British Honorary Consulate, Monaco: +377 93 50 99 54

Mongolia

- Population: 2.64 million (2007)
- Location: North Asia
- Capital: Ulaanbaatar
- Currency: Togrog (Tughrik) (MNT)
- Religion: Tibetan Buddhist, Shamanist, Muslim (south-west)
- Language: Khalkh Mongol, Kazakh
- British Embassy, Ulaanbaatar: +976 (11) 458 133

Montenegro, Republic of

- Population: 650,575
- Location: South-east Europe
- Capital: Podgorica
- Currency: Euro (EUR)
- Religion: Christian, Muslim
- Language: Montenegrin, Serbian, Bosnian, Albanian, Croatian
- British Embassy, Podgorica: +382 (20) 618 010

435

the gap-year guidebook 2010

Montserrat (British Overseas Territory)

- Population: 4655 (2006)
- Location: Caribbean
- Capital: Plymouth (destroyed by the last volcanic eruption)
- Currency: East Caribbean Dollar (XCD)
- Religion: Christian
- Language: English
- Governor's Office, Brades: +1 (664) 491 2688/9

Morocco, The Kingdom of

- Population: 30.5 million (2006 estimate)
- Location: North Africa
- Capital: Rabat
- Currency: Moroccan Dirham (MAD)
- Religion: Muslim, Christian, Jewish
- Language: Arabic (official), Berber dialects, French (commerce, diplomacy and government)
- British Embassy, Rabat: +212 (537) 63 33 33

Mozambique, The Republic of

- Population: 21.2 million (2008 estimate)
- Location: Southern Africa
- Capital: Maputo
- Currency: Metical (MZN)
- Religion: Roman Catholic, Christian, Muslim, indigenous beliefs
- Language: Portuguese (official), over 16 African languages and dialects
- British High Commission, Maputo: +258 21 356 000

Myanmar (see Burma)

Namibia, The Republic of

- Population: 2.08 million (2008 estimate)
- Location: Southern Africa
- Capital: Windhoek
- Currency: Namibian Dollar (NAD)
- Religion: Christian
- Language: English (official), Afrikaans, German, and several indigenous languages
- British High Commission, Windhoek: +264 (61) 274800

visit: www.gap-year.com

Nauru, The Republic of

- Population: 13,770 (2008 estimate)
- Location: Pacific Ocean
- Capital: Yaren District (unofficial)
- Currency: Australian Dollar (AUD)
- Religion: Protestant, Roman Catholic
- Language: Nauruan (official), English (commerce and government, widely understood)
- refer to British High Commission, Suva, Fiji: +679 322 9100

Nepal

- Population: 29.5 million (2008 estimate)
- Location: South Asia
- Capital: Kathmandu
- Currency: Nepalese Rupee (NPR)
- Religion: Hindu, Buddhist, Muslim
- Language: Nepali (official), Newari (mainly in Kathmandu), Tibetan languages (mainly hill areas), Indian languages (mainly Terai areas). Nepal has over 30 languages and many dialects.
- British Embassy, Kathmandu: +977 (1) 441 0583/1281/4588/1590

Netherlands, The Kingdom of The

- Population: 16.5 million (2009)
- Location: North Europe
- Capital: Amsterdam
- Currency: Euro (EUR)
- Religion: Roman Catholic, Protestant, Muslim
- Language: Dutch
- British Embassy, The Hague: +31 (0) 70 4270 427

New Zealand

- Population: 4.26 million (2008)
- Location: Pacific Ocean
- Capital: Wellington
- Currency: New Zealand Dollar (NZD)
- Religion: Anglican, Presbyterian, Roman Catholic, Methodist, Baptist
- Language: English, Maori
- British High Commission, Wellington: +64 (4) 924 2888

the gap-year guidebook 2010

Nicaragua, The Republic of
- Population: 5.1 million (2005)
- Location: Central America
- Capital: Managua
- Currency: Cordoba (NIO)
- Religion: Roman Catholic, Evangelical Protestant
- Language: Spanish (official), English, Miskito, Creole, Mayanga, Garifuna, Rama
- British Honorary Consul, Managua: +505 254 5454/3839

Niger, The Republic of
- Population: 12 million (2005 estimate)
- Location: West Africa
- Capital: Niamey
- Currency: CFA Franc BCEAO (XOF)
- Religion: Muslim
- Language: French (official), Arabic, local languages widely spoken
- British Honorary Consul, Niamey: +227 9687 8130

Nigeria, The Federal Republic of
- Population: 144.7 million (2006)
- Location: West Africa
- Capital: Abuja
- Currency: Naira (NGN)
- Religion: Muslim, Christian, traditional beliefs
- Language: English (official), Hausa, Yoruba, Igbo
- British High Commission, Abuja: +234 (9) 413 2010/2011/3885-7

Norway, The Kingdom of
- Population: 4.6 million (2006)
- Location: North Europe
- Capital: Oslo
- Currency: Norwegian Kroner (NOK)
- Religion: Church of Norway (Evangelical Lutheran)
- Language: Norwegian (bokmål and nynorsk), Sami
- British Embassy, Oslo: +47 23 13 27 00

Oman, The Sultanate of
- Population: 3.3 million (2007)
- Location: Middle East
- Capital: Muscat
- Currency: Oman Rial (OMR)
- Religion: Ibadhi Muslim, Sunni Muslim, Shi'a Muslim, Hindu, Christian
- Language: Arabic (official), English, Farsi, Baluchi, Urdu
- British Embassy, Muscat: +968 24 609 000; (out of hours emergencies) +968 9920 0865

Pakistan, The Islamic Republic of
- Population: 162.4 million
- Location: South Asia
- Capital: Islamabad
- Currency: Rupee (PKR)
- Religion: Muslim, Hindu, Christian
- Language: Punjabi, Sindhi, Pashtun, Urdu, Balochi, English and other local languages
- British High Commission, Islamabad: +92 51 201 2000

Palau, The Republic of
- Population: 827,900 (2007)
- Location: Pacific Ocean
- Capital: Suva
- Currency: United States Dollar (USD)
- Religion: Christian, Hindu, Muslim
- Language: English, numerous Fijian dialects, Gujarati, Fijian Hindi
- refer to British Ambassador, Manila, The Philippines: +63 (2) 858 2200

Palestine (The Occupied Palestinian Territories)
- Population: 4 million (2007 estimate)
- Location: Middle East
- Currency: New Israeli Shekel (ILS), Jordanian Dinar (JOD) (West Bank Only)
- Religion: Muslim, Christian
- Language: Arabic, English widely spoken
- British Consulate-General, Gaza: +972 (08) 283 7724

Panama, The Republic of
- Population: 3.23 million (2006)
- Location: Central America
- Capital: Panama City
- Currency: US Dollar (USD) (known locally as the Balboa (PAB))
- Religion: Roman Catholic, Protestant, Jewish, Muslim
- Language: Spanish (official), English
- British Embassy, Panama City: +507 269 0866

Papua New Guinea, The Independent State of
- Population: 6 million
- Location: South-east Asia,
- Capital: Port Moresby
- Currency: Kina (PGK)
- Religion: Christian according to its constitution, Roman Catholic, Evangelical Lutheran, Evangelical Alliance, Pentecostal, Baptist, Anglican, Seventh Day Adventist, United Church, Buddhist, Muslim, Hindu
- Language: English, Pidgin, Hiri Motu, over 820 different languages
- British High Commission, Port Moresby: +675 325 1677

Paraguay, The Republic of
- Population: 6.2 million
- Location: Central South America
- Capital: Asunción
- Currency: Guarani (PYG)
- Religion: Roman Catholic, Mennonite, Protestant, Latter-day Saints, Jewish, Russian Orthodox
- Language: Spanish (official), Guaraní (official)
- British Honorary Consulate, Asunción: +595 (21) 210 405

Peru, The Republic of
- Population: 28.22 million (2007 estimate)
- Location: Western South America
- Capital: Lima
- Currency: Nuevo Sol (PEN)
- Religion: Roman Catholic
- Language: Spanish (official), Quechua (official), Aymara and several minor Amazonian languages
- British Embassy, Lima: +51 (1) 617 3000 (main); 3053/3054 (consular)

visit: www.gap-year.com

Philippines, The Republic of the

- Population: 92.23 million (2009 estimate)
- Location: South-east Asia
- Capital: Metro Manila
- Currency: Peso (PHP)
- Religion: Roman Catholic, Protestant, Muslim
- Language: Filipino (official), English (official)
- British Embassy, Manila: +63 (2) 858 2200

Pitcairn, Henderson, Ducie & Oeno Islands (British Overseas Territory)

- Population: 51
- Location: South Pacific
- Capital: Adamstown
- Currency: New Zealand Dollar (NZD)
- Religion: Seventh Day Adventist
- Language: English, Pitkern (a mix of English and Tahitian)
- British High Commission, Auckland, New Zealand: +64 (9) 366 0186

Poland, The Republic of

- Population: 38.1 million
- Location: Central Europe
- Capital: Warsaw
- Currency: Zloty (PLN)
- Religion: Roman Catholic, Eastern Orthodox, Protestant
- Language: Polish
- British Embassy, Warsaw: +48 (22) 311 00 00

Portugal (The Portuguese Republic)

- Population: 10.6 million
- Location: South-west Europe
- Capital: Lisbon
- Currency: Euro (EUR)
- Religion: Roman Catholic, Protestant
- Language: Portuguese
- British Embassy, Lisbon: +351 (21) 392 4000

the gap-year guidebook 2010

Qatar, The State of
- Population: 1.4 million (2008)
- Location: Middle East
- Capital: Doha
- Currency: Qatari Riyal (QAR)
- Religion: Muslim
- Language: Arabic (official), English, Urdu
- British Embassy, Doha: +974 496 2000

Romania
- Population: 22.6 million
- Location: South-east Europe
- Capital: Bucharest
- Currency: New Leu (RON)
- Religion: Orthodox, Roman Catholic, Protestant, Reformed, Greek Catholic, Unitarian
- Language: Romanian (official), English, French, German
- British Embassy, Bucharest: +40 (21) 201 7200

Russia Federation, The
- Population: 142 million (2008)
- Location: North Asia
- Capital: Moscow
- Currency: Ruble (RUB)
- Religion: Orthodox Christian, Muslim, Jewish, Buddhist
- Language: Russian, Tatar
- British Embassy, Moscow: +7 (495) 956 7200

Rwanda, The Republic of
- Population: 8 million (estimated)
- Location: Central Africa
- Capital: Kigali
- Currency: Rwandan Franc (RWF)
- Religion: Roman Catholic, Protestant, Muslim, indigenous beliefs
- Language: Kinyarwanda (official), French (official), English (official), Kiswahili (used in commercial centres and by army)
- British Embassy, Kigali: +250 584 098/586 072

visit: www.gap-year.com

Saint Helena (British Overseas Territory)
- Population: 4000
- Location: Atlantic Ocean
- Capital: Jamestown
- Currency: St Helena Pound (SHP)
- Religion: Christiantiy, Bahá'í
- Language: English
- Governor's Office, Jamestown: +290 2555

Saint Kitts & Nevis (The Federation of St Christopher & Nevis)
- Population: 50,000
- Location: Caribbean
- Capital: Basseterre
- Currency: East Caribbean Dollar (XCD)
- Religion: Anglican, Roman Catholic, Evangelical Protestant
- Language: English
- British High Commission in Barbados: +1 (246) 430 7800

Saint Lucia
- Population: 171,100 (2007 estimate)
- Location: Caribbean
- Capital: Castries
- Currency: East Caribbean Dollar (XCD)
- Religion: Roman Catholic, Anglican, Methodist, Baptist, Jewish, Hindu, Muslim
- Language: English (official), French patois (Kweyol)
- British High Commission, Castries: +1 (758) 452 2484/5 (resides in Barbados)

Saint Vincent and the Grenadines
- Population: 109,022
- Location: Caribbean
- Capital: Kingstown
- Currency: East Caribbean Dollar (XCD)
- Religion: Anglican, Methodist, Roman Catholic, Seventh-Day Adventist, Hindu, other Protestant
- Language: English
- British High Commission, Kingstown: +784 456 5981 (resides in Barbados)

the gap-year guidebook 2010

Samoa, The Independent State of

- Population: 214,765 (2005 estimate)
- Location: South Pacific
- Capital: Apia
- Currency: Samoan Tala (WST)
- Religion: Roman Catholic, Methodist, Latter-day Saints
- Language: Samoan, English
- British Honorary Consulate, Apia: +685 27123

São Tomé & Príncipe, The Democratic State of

- Population: 158,000 (UN 2007 estimate)
- Location: West Africa
- Capital: São Tomé
- Currency: Dobra (STD)
- Religion: Christian
- Language: Portuguese, Lungwa Santomé, and other creole dialects
- Refer to the British Embassy in Luanda, Angola: +244 222 334582

Saudi Arabia, The Kingdom of

- Population: 27.6 million (2007 estimate)
- Location: Middle East
- Capital: Riyadh
- Currency: Saudi Riyal (SAR)
- Religion: Muslim (Sunni, Shia). The public practice of any other religion is forbidden
- Language: Arabic, English
- British Embassy, Riyadh: +966 (0) 1 488 0077

Senegal, The Republic of

- Population: 11.6 million (2005 UN estimate)
- Location: West Africa
- Capital: Dakar
- Currency: CFA Franc BCEAO (XOF)
- Religion: Muslim, Christian, indigenous beliefs
- Language: French (official), Wolof, Malinke, Serere, Soninke, Pular (all national)
- British Embassy, Dakar: +221 33 823 7392/9971

visit: www.gap-year.com

Serbia, The Republic of
- Population: 7.5 million (2002)
- Location: South-east Europe
- Capital: Belgrade
- Currency: Serbian Dinar (RSD)
- Religion: Serbian Orthodox, Muslim, Roman Catholic, Christian
- Language: Serbian (majority), Romanian, Hungarian, Slovak, Croatian, Albanian (Kosovan), Ukranian, Bosniak, Montenegrin, Bulgarian, Ruthenian, Roma. Vlach, Macedonian
- British Embassy, Belgrade: +381 (11) 2645 055

Seychelles, The Republic of
- Population: 82,247 (2007 estimate)
- Location: Indian Ocean
- Capital: Victoria
- Currency: Seychelles Rupee (SCR)
- Religion: Roman Catholic, Anglican, Muslim, Hindu
- Language: English, French, Creole (Seselwa)
- British High Commission, Mahe: +248 283 666

Sierra Leone, The Republic of
- Population: 6.2 million (2008 UN estimate)
- Location: West Africa
- Capital: Freetown
- Currency: Leone (SLL)
- Religion: Muslim, Christian, indigenous beliefs
- Language: English (official), Krio (English-based Creole), indigenous languages widely spoken
- British High Commission, Freetown: +232 (22) 232 961

Singapore, The Republic of
- Population: 4.84 million (2008)
- Location: South-east Asia
- Capital: Singapore
- Currency: Singapore Dollar (SGD)
- Religion: Taoist, Buddhist, Muslim, Christian, Hindu
- Language: Mandarin, English, Malay, Tamil
- British High Commission, Singapore: +65 6424 4200

445

Slovakia (The Slovak Republic)

- Population: 5.39 million (2002)
- Location: Central Europe
- Capital: Bratislava
- Currency: Euro (EUR)
- Religion: Roman Catholic, Atheist, Protestant, Orthodox
- Language: Slovak (official), Hungarian
- British Embassy, Bratislava: +421 (2) 5998 2000

Slovenia, The Republic of

- Population: 2 million
- Location: Central Europe
- Capital: Ljubljana
- Currency: Euro (EUR)
- Religion: Roman Catholic
- Language: Slovene, Italian, Hungarian, English
- British Embassy, Ljubljana: +386 (1) 200 3910

Solomon Islands

- Population: 530,000
- Location: Pacific Ocean
- Capital: Honiara
- Currency: Solomon Islands Dollar (SBD)
- Religion: Christian, traditional beliefs
- Language: English, Pidgin, 92 indigenous languages
- British High Commission, Honiara: +677 21705/6

Somalia (The Somali Democratic Republic)

- Population: 8.86 million (2006 estimate)
- Location: East Africa
- Capital: Mogadishu
- Currency: Somali Shilling (SOS)
- Religion: Sunni Muslim
- Language: Somali (official), Arabic, Italian, English
- British Embassy, Mogadishu: +252 (1) 20288/9

visit: www.gap-year.com

South Africa, Republic of

- Population: 43.8 million (2007 estimate)
- Location: Southern Africa
- Capital: Pretoria/Tshwane
- Currency: Rand (ZAR)
- Religion: Predominately Christian but all principal religions are represented
- Language: 11 official languages: Afrikaans, English, Ndebele, Sepedi, Sesotho, Swati, Tsonga, Tswana, Venda, Xhosa, Zulu
- British High Commission, Pretoria: +27 (12) 421 7500

South Georgia & South Sandwich Islands (British Overseas Territories)

- Population: no indigenous population
- Location: Atlantic Ocean
- Capital: King Edward Point
- Currency: United Kingdom Pound Sterling (GBP)
- Language: English
- Governor's Office, Stanley, Falkland Islands: +500 282 00

Spain, The Kingdom of

- Population: 44 million
- Location: South-western Europe
- Capital: Madrid
- Currency: Euro (EUR)
- Religion: Roman Catholic, Protestant
- Language: Castilian Spanish (official), Catalan, Galician, Basque
- British Embassy, Madrid: +34 (91) 700 8200

Sri Lanka, The Democratic Socialist Republic of

- Population: 19.4 million (2008, UN)
- Location: South Asia
- Capital: Colombo
- Currency: Rupee (LKR)
- Religion: Buddhist, Hindu, Muslim, Christian
- Language: Sinhalese, Tamil, English
- British High Commission, Colombo: +94 (11) 5390639

447

the gap-year guidebook 2010

Sudan, The Republic of
- Population: 33.61 million (2003)
- Location: North Africa
- Capital: Khartoum City
- Currency: Sudanese pound (SDG)
- Religion: Muslim, Christian, indigenous religions
- Language: Arabic (official), Nubian, Ta Bedawie, dialects of Nilotic, Nilo-Hamitic, Sudanic languages, English
- British Embassy, Khartoum: +249 (183) 777 105

Suriname, The Republic of
- Population: 437,024 (2004)
- Location: Northern South America
- Capital: Paramaribo
- Currency: Suriname Dollar (SRD)
- Religion: Hindu, Muslim, Roman Catholic, Dutch Reformed, Moravian, Jewish, Bahá'í
- Language: Dutch (official), English, Sranan Tongo (Creole), Hindustani, Javanese
- British Honorary Consulate, Paramaribo: +597 402 558

Swaziland, The Kingdom of
- Population: 1.1 million (2006 estimate)
- Location: Southern Africa
- Capital: Mbabane
- Currency: Lilangeni (SZL)
- Religion: Christian, indigenous beliefs
- Language: English, Siswati
- British Honorary Consulate, Mbabane: +268 551 6247

Sweden, The Kingdom of
- Population: 9.1 million (2008)
- Location: North Europe
- Capital: Stockholm
- Currency: Swedish Krona (SEK)
- Religion: Lutheran, Roman Catholic, Orthodox, Baptist, Muslim, Jewish, Buddhist
- Language: Swedish, English widely spoken
- British Embassy, Stockholm: +46 (8) 671 3000

visit: www.gap-year.com

Switzerland (The Swiss Confederation)

- Population: 7.5 million (2007)
- Location: Central Europe
- Capital: Berne
- Currency: Swiss Franc (CHF)
- Religion: Roman Catholic, Protestant, Muslim
- Language: Swiss German (official), French, Italian, Rhaeto-Rumantsch
- British Embassy, Berne: +41 (31) 359 7700

Syria (The Syrian Arab Republic)

- Population: 20 million
- Location: Middle East
- Capital: Damascus
- Currency: Syrian Pound (also called Lira) (SYP)
- Religion: Sunni Muslim, Shi'a Muslim, Alawite, Druze, other Muslim sects, Christian, Jewish
- Language: Arabic (official), Kurdish, Armenian, Aramaic, Circassian, some French, English
- British Embassy, Damascus: +963 (11) 339 1513/1541 (consular)

Taiwan (Province of the People's Republic of China)

- Population: 22.9 million (2007)
- Location: East Asia
- Capital: Taipei
- Currency: New Taiwan Dollar (TWD)
- Religion: Buddhist, Taoist, Christian
- Language: Mandarin Chinese (official), Taiwanese, Hakka
- British Trade & Cultural Office, Taipei: +886 (2) 8758 2088

Tajikistan, Republic of

- Population: 7 million (2004 UN)
- Location: Central Asia
- Capital: Dushanbe
- Currency: Somoni (TJS)
- Religion: Sunni Muslim, Ismaili Shiite, Russian Orthodox Christian, Jewish
- Language: Tajik, Russian
- British Embassy, Dushanbe: +992 372 24 22 21

Tanzania, United Republic of

- Population: 40.4 million (UN, 2007)
- Location: East Africa
- Capital: Dodoma (official)
- Currency: Tanzania Shilling (TZS)
- Religion: Christian, Muslim, indigenous beliefs
- Language: Kiswahili, English
- British High Commission, Dar es Salaam: +255 (022) 211 0101

Thailand, Kingdom of

- Population: 65 million (2007 estimate)
- Location: South-east Asia
- Capital: Bangkok
- Currency: Baht (THB)
- Religion: Buddhist, Muslim, Christian, Hindu
- Language: Thai, Yawi
- British Embassy, Bangkok: +66 (0) 2 305 8333

Tibet – see China

Timor-Leste, Democratic Republic of

- Population: 1.1 million (2008)
- Location: South-east Asia
- Capital: Dili
- Currency: US Dollar (USD)
- Religion: Roman Catholic (majority), Protestant, Muslim, Hindu, Buddhist
- Language: Tetum (official), Portuguese (official), Bahasa Indonesian, English
- refer to British Embassy, Jakarta: +62 (21) 2356 5200

Togo (Togolese Republic)

- Population: 4.7 million
- Location: West Africa
- Capital: Lomé
- Currency: CFA Franc BCEAO (XOF)
- Religion: Christian, Muslim, indigenous beliefs
- Language: French, Kabiye, Ewe
- The British Ambassador to Togo resides in Accra, Ghana: +223 21 221665; in a genuine emergency contact the Honorary Consul in Togo: +228 2222714

Tonga, Kingdom of

- Population: 101,991 (2006)
- Location: Pacific Ocean
- Capital: Nuku'alofa
- Currency: Pa'anga (TOP)
- Religion: Christian
- Language: Tongan, English
- refer to British High Commission, Suva, Fiji: +679 322 9100

Trinidad and Tobago, Republic of

- Population: 1.05 million (2007 estimate)
- Location: Caribbean
- Capital: Port of Spain
- Currency: Trinidad and Tobago Dollar (TTD)
- Religion: Roman Catholic, Hindu, Anglican, Muslim, Presbyterian
- Language: English (official), Spanish
- British High Commission, Port of Spain: +1 (868) 622 2748

Tristan da Cunha (British Overseas Territory)

- Population: 275
- Location: Atlantic Ocean
- Capital: Edinburgh of the Seven Seas
- Currency: Sterling (GBP)
- Religion: Christian
- Language: English
- Administrator's Office: +870 764 341 816

Tunisia (Tunisian Republic)

- Population: 9.92 million (2003)
- Location: North Africa
- Capital: Tunis
- Currency: Tunisian Dinar (TND)
- Religion: Muslim, Christian
- Language: Arabic, French
- British Embassy, Tunis: +216 71 108 700

Turkey, Republic of

- Population: 71.9 million (2008)
- Location: South-east Europe
- Capital: Ankara
- Currency: New Turkish Lira (TRY)
- Religion: Muslim
- Language: Turkish, Kurdish
- British Consulae, Izmir: +90 (232) 463 5151

Turkmenistan

- Population: 5.1-6.9 million
- Location: Central Asia
- Capital: Ashgabat
- Currency: Manat (TMM)
- Religion: Sunni Muslim
- Language: Russian, Turkmen
- British Embassy, Ashgabat: +993 (12) 363 462/63/64

Turks and Caicos Islands (British Overseas Territories)

- Population: 32,000 (2006)
- Location: Atlantic Ocean
- Capital: Grand Turk
- Currency: US Dollar (USD)
- Religion: Christian
- Language: English, some Creole
- Governor's Office, Grand Turk: +1 (649) 946 2309

Tuvalu

- Population: 12,177 (2008 estimate)
- Location: Pacific Ocean
- Capital: Funafuti
- Currency: Australian Dollar (AUD), Tuvaluan Dollar (TVD) (coinage only)
- Religion: Church of Tuvalu, Bahá'í
- Language: Tuvaluan, English, Samoan, Kiribati
- refer to British High Commission, Suva, Fiji: +679 322 9100

Uganda Republic

- Population: 28.9 million (2006 estimate)
- Location: Central Africa
- Capital: Kampala
- Currency: Uganda Shilling (UGX)
- Religion: Christian, Muslim
- Language: English (official national language), Luganda, Swahili
- British High Commission, Kampala: +256 (31) 231 2000

Ukraine

- Population: 46.2 million (estimate)
- Location: East Europe
- Capital: Kyiv (Kiev)
- Currency: Hryvna (UAH)
- Religion: Ukrainian Orthodox, Ukrainian Greek Catholic, Jewish, Muslim
- Language: Ukrainian (official), Russian, Romanian, Polish, Hungarian
- British Embassy, Kyiv: +380 44 490 3660

United Arab Emirates

- Population: 4.6 million (2005 estimate)
- Location: Middle East
- Capital: Abu Dhabi
- Currency: Dirham (AED)
- Religion: Muslim, Hindu
- Language: Arabic (official)
- British Embassy, Abu Dhabi: +971 (2) 610 1100

United Kingdom

- Population: 60.6 million (2006)
- Location: Western Europe
- Capital: London
- Currency: United Kingdom Pound Sterling (GBP)
- Religion: Church of England, although all other faiths are practised
- Language: English, Welsh (in Wales), Gaelic (in Scotland)
- Foreigh & Commonwealth Office: +44 (0) 20 7008 1500

United States of America
- Population: 306 million (2009 estimate)
- Location: North America
- Capital: Washington, DC
- Currency: US Dollar (USD)
- Religion: Protestant, Roman Catholic, Latter-day Saints, Jewish, Muslim
- Language: English, Spanish
- British Embassy, Washington DC: +1 (202) 588 6500

Uruguay
- Population: 3.5 million (2008)
- Location: Southern South America
- Capital: Montevideo
- Currency: Peso Uruguayan (UYU)
- Religion: Roman Catholic, Protestant, Jewish, Atheist
- Language: Spanish
- British Embassy, Montevideo: +598 (2) 622 36 30/50

Uzbekistan, Republic of
- Population: 26.5 million (2004 UN)
- Location: Central Asia
- Capital: Tashkent
- Currency: Som (UZS)
- Religion: Sunni Muslim
- Language: Uzbek, Russian, Tajik
- British Embassy, Tashkent: +998 71 120 1500/1516 (consular/visa)

Vanuatu, Republic of
- Population: 215,446 (2008 estimate)
- Location: South Pacific
- Capital: Port Vila
- Currency: Vatu (VUV)
- Religion: Presbyterian, Anglican, Roman Catholic, Seventh Day Adventist
- Language: Bislama (offical), English (official), French (official), plus over 130 vernacular languages
- refer to British High Commission, Suva, Fiji: +679 322 9100

Venezuela, The Bolivarian Republic of
- Population: 28.2 million (2008 estimate)
- Location: Northern South America
- Capital: Caracas
- Currency: Bolivar Fuerte (VEF)
- Religion: Roman Catholic
- Language: Spanish
- British Embassy, Caracas: +58 (212) 263 8411

Vietnam, The Socialist Republic of
- Population: 83 million
- Location: South-east Asia
- Capital: Hanoi
- Currency: Vietnamese Dong (VND) (US dollar widely accepted)
- Religion: Buddhist, Roman Catholic, Protestant, Cao Dai, Hoa Hao
- Language: Vietnamese, minority languages also spoken
- British Embassy, Hanoi: +84 (4) 3936 0500

Yemen, Republic of
- Population: 20 million (estimate)
- Location: Middle East
- Capital: Sana'a
- Currency: Yemeni Rial (YER)
- Religion: Muslim
- Language: Arabic
- British Embassy, Sana'a: +967 (1) 308 100

Zambia, Republic of
- Population: 11.8 million (2006)
- Location: Southern Africa
- Capital: Lusaka
- Currency: Kwacha (ZMK)
- Religion: Christian, Muslim, Hindu, indigenous beliefs
- Language: English (official language of government), plus six further official languages
- British High Commission, Lusaka: +260 (211) 423200

455

Zimbabwe, Republic of

- Population: 12.1 million (2007)
- Location: Southern Africa
- Capital: Harare
- Currency: Zimbabwean Dollar (ZWD)
- Religion: Christian, indigenous beliefs, small communities of Hindu, Muslim and Jewish
- Language: English (official), Shona, Ndebele
- British Embassy, Harare: +912 125 160/167

Business Colors

Office work is based on information technology, so being trained in this field is a great start to earning quick cash. Office temping is a very common job that pays reasonably well and there is usually plenty of it around.

Office skills are pretty basic to many careers and, in an increasingly global market, could lead to chances to work abroad - so you can even combine travel or living in another culture with work.

Work experience ASAP

The big question is: "How do I get work experience when everywhere I go rejects me because I haven't got work experience?" This could ruin your whole **gap**-year plan. For simple menial work, such as stacking shelves or fruit picking, it shouldn't be too much of a problem, but those types of jobs don't pay particularly well.

If you need money fast then you might have to look elsewhere.

Gap-year recruiters tend to expect their clients to have no work experience at all, so it could be a good idea to get ahead of the game and get some experience under your belt, before you leave school. Even if the work is basic (filing, making the tea), it shows that you can function within a working environment.

If you're reading this while you're in Year 12, then you have quite a lot of time left and we advise you to use it to get as much work experience as possible. This will seriously impress your future employers.

We're not saying that you have to spend every week of your holidays working, although many teenagers do now combine weekend and holiday working - such as retail jobs - with study.

You can always do with a bit more cash. It may seem tedious but think how much more impressive you'll be at job interviews later on, with a fatter CV and references in hand.

Skills for work

What are the skills that you need in order to get that vital job? Don't forget that you only have a limited time, so you don't want to be training for too long as that will cut down on your earning time and therefore enjoyment time. This is why many people choose to go into trades such as bartending or retail, where the company tends to provide the training, though this might not prove to be nearly as lucrative as office work.

If you've done a computer based course during sixth form, then that could well prove to be enough. If you can type at around 40-45 words per minute, or you're comfortable designing websites, then you stand a good chance of landing a fairly well-paid job.

457

Qualifications - who needs them?

Qualifications are needed when you can't otherwise prove that you're capable of whatever the job involves. For example, if you're not French and have never lived in France, then you'll have to have a qualification showing that you can *speak* French, if that's what the job involves. In office work the agency that you use will put you through some tests first, before putting your name forward to the employer.

More important than any paper qualification, is that your typing speed and accuracy are strong enough to take you through the tests agencies will ask you to undertake. Practice is vital in building up your speeds but you shouldn't despair if you don't reach that magic 45 words per minute, there are other options available to help you build up your speeds while you are working.

Many offices, especially the smaller ones, will offer a trial, for around three days, just to make sure that you have what it takes. This saves them from sorting through an array of paperwork and qualifications.

What if I'm just no good?

Well, you'll just have to get good then, won't you? Training for information technology has dramatically changed recently. Skills that used to take a full year can now take as little as one month. The prices have dropped too.

Evening courses at a local FE college can be under £100 and public libraries also run courses on the internet. IT is already very firmly in schools' curricula so most of you should already have the skills to cope within the office. If not, then get going and get trained.

Which college?

There are lots of different things to look at when choosing a college. Convenience (location, hours) is very important, along with price. However, you don't want to compromise the quality of the qualification you will receive because of practical concerns.

A good idea might be to check with an agency about the value of a qualification from particular colleges. Or check with the actual college on the employment record of their past students.

Finding the right course

Of course you want to start earning as soon as possible, so is it worth spending a longer time studying for a qualification that you don't really need?

How do you know which course is best for you? Can you compare different word processing courses against each other; surely word processing is just word processing? Also, you don't want to pay to learn something that you already know how to do. To help with this little dilemma the City & Guilds, which awards over a million certificates a year, defines the levels of its qualifications (which continue up to Level 7).

visit: www.gap-year.com

Level 1: Introductory awards for those new to the area covering routine tasks or basic knowledge and understanding.

Level 2: Qualifications for those with some knowledge of, and ability in, the areas that acknowledge individual responsibility.

Level 3: Qualifications that recognise complex work involving supervisory ability.

If you think that you already know level two, for example, then it's worth your while going straight onto level 3.

How much to pay?

The most important thing here is to get value for money. Of course the better the course the more expensive it's likely to be, but what things can you check for to make sure that you're not being conned? Be aware of the VAT and any other hidden costs that there might be. To test the value of the course compare the total hours of tuition to the price, check out each course and just be sure that what you are going to do will be of benefit, before parting with any money.

Over the next pages you'll find a list of colleges, from all over the country, which run intensive business skills courses. It is only an indicator of what's available, not a guarantee of quality.

We're happy to hear from (and report about) any training centres that offer short courses in office skills.

Aberdeen College of Further Education	enquiry@abcol.ac.uk www.abcol.ac.uk Tel: +44 (0) 1224 612 330
Abingdon and Witney College	enquiry@abingdon-witney.ac.uk www.abingdon-witney.ac.uk Tel: +44 (0) 1235 555 585
Accrington & Rossendale College	www.accross.ac.uk Tel: +44 (0) 1254 389 933
Alton College	enquiries@altoncollege.ac.uk www.altoncollege.ac.uk Tel: +44 (0) 1420 592 200
Amersham & Wycombe College	www.amersham.ac.uk Tel: +44 (0) 1494 735 555
Andover College	info@andovercollege.ac.uk www.andovercollege.ac.uk Tel: +44 (0) 1264 360 003
Aylesbury College	customerservice@aylesbury.ac.uk www.aylesbury.ac.uk Tel: +44 (0) 1296 588 588

Ayr College	enquiries@ayrcoll.ac.uk
	www.ayrcoll.ac.uk
	Tel: +44 (0) 1292 265 184

Banff & Buchan College	info@banff-buchan.ac.uk
	www.banff-buchan.ac.uk
	Tel: +44 (0) 1346 586 100

Barking College	admissions@barkingcollege.ac.uk
	www.barkingcollege.ac.uk
	Tel: +44 (0) 1708 770 000

Barnet College	admissions@barkingcollege.ac.uk
	www.barnet.ac.uk
	Tel: +44 (0) 20 8266 4000

Barnfield College	enquiries@barnfield.ac.uk
	www.barnfield.ac.uk
	Tel: +44 (0) 1582 569 500

Barnsley College	programme.enquiries@barnsley.ac.uk
	www.barnsley.ac.uk
	Tel: +44 (0) 1226 216 216

Barry College	enquiries@barry.ac.uk
	www.barry.ac.uk
	Tel: +44 (0) 1446 725 000

Barton Peveril College	enquiries@imail.barton.ac.uk
	www.barton-peveril.ac.uk
	Tel: +44 (0) 238 036 7200

Basingstoke College of Technology	information@bcot.ac.uk
	www.bcot.ac.uk
	Tel: +44 (0) 1256 354 141

Bedford College	info@bedford.ac.uk
	www.bedford.ac.uk
	Tel: +44 (0) 800 074 0234

Belfast Metroplitan College	central_admissions@belfastinstitute.ac.uk
	www.belfastmet.ac.uk
	Tel: +44 (0) 28 9026 5000

Bexhill College	enquiries@bexhillcollege.ac.uk
	www.bexhillcollege.ac.uk
	Tel: +44 (0) 1424 214 545

Bexley College	enquiries@bexley.ac.uk
	www.bexley.ac.uk
	Tel: +44 (0) 1322 442 331

Bishop Auckland College	enquiries@bacoll.ac.uk www.bacoll.ac.uk Tel: +44 (0) 1388 443 000
Blackburn College	www.blackburn.ac.uk Tel: +44 (0) 1254 551 44
Blackpool & The Fylde College	visitors@blackpool.ac.uk www.blackpool.ac.uk Tel: +44 (0) 1253 504 343
Bolton Community College	info@bolton-community-college.ac.uk www.bolton-community-college.ac.uk Tel: +44 (0) 1204 907 200
Borders College	enquiries@borderscollege.ac.uk www.borderscollege.ac.uk Tel: +44 (0) 8700 505 152
Boston College	info@boston.ac.uk www.boston.ac.uk Tel: +44 (0) 1205 365 701
Bournemouth & Poole College	enquiries@thecollege.co.uk www.thecollege.co.uk Tel: +44 (0) 1202 205 205
Bournville College	info@bournville.ac.uk www.bournville.ac.uk Tel: +44 (0) 1274 433 333
Bracknell & Wokingham College	study@bracknell.ac.uk www.bracknell.ac.uk Tel: +44 (0) 845 330 3343
Bradford College	admissions@bradfordcollege.ac.uk www.bradfordcollege.ac.uk Tel: +44 (0) 1274 433 333
Braintree College	enquiries@braintree.ac.uk www.braintree.ac.uk Tel: +44 (0) 1376 321 711
Bridgwater College	information@bridgwater.ac.uk www.bridgwater.ac.uk Tel: +44 (0) 1278 455464
Brockenhurst College	enquiries@brock.ac.uk www.brock.ac.uk Tel: +44 (0) 1590 625 555

Bromley College	info@bromley.ac.uk www.bromley.ac.uk Tel: +44 (0) 20 8295 7000
Brooklands College	info@brooklands.ac.uk www.brooklands.ac.uk Tel: +44 (0) 1932 797 797
Budmouth Technology College	peerc@budmouth.dorset.sch.uk www.budmouth.dorset.sch.uk Tel: +44 (0) 1305 830 500
Burnley College	student.services@burnley.ac.uk www.burnley.ac.uk Tel: +44 (0) 1282 711 200
Burton College	enquiries@burton-college.ac.uk www.burton-college.ac.uk Tel: +44 (0) 1283 494 400
Bury College	information@burycollege.ac.uk www.burycollege.ac.uk Tel: +44 (0) 161 280 8280
Cambridge Regional College	enquiry@camre.ac.uk www.camre.ac.uk Tel: +44 (0) 1223 418 20
Cannock Chase Technical College	enquiry@cannock.ac.uk www.cannock.ac.uk Tel: +44 (0) 1543 462 200
Canterbury College	courseenquiries@cant-col.ac.uk www.cant-col.ac.uk Tel: +44 (0) 1227 811 111
Cardonald College	enquiries@cardonald.ac.uk www.cardonald.ac.uk Tel: +44 (0) 141 272 3333
Carlisle College	info@carlisle.ac.uk www.carlisle.ac.uk Tel: + 44 (0) 1228 822 703
Castle College	learn@castlecollege.ac.uk www.castlecollege.ac.uk Tel: +44 (0) 845 845 0500
Causeway Institute	admissions@causeway.ac.uk www.causeway.ac.uk Tel: +44 (0) 28 7035 4717

visit: www.gap-year.com

Central Sussex College	www.centralsussex.ac.uk Tel: +44 (0) 845 155 0043
Chesterfield College	advice@chesterfield.ac.uk www.chesterfield.ac.uk Tel: +44 (0) 1246 500 500
Cirencester College	student.services@cirencestercollege.ac.uk www.cirencestercollege.ac.uk Tel: +44 (0) 1255 640 99
City & Islington College	courseinfo@candi.ac.uk www.candi.ac.uk Tel: +44 (0) 20 7700 9200
City College Brighton & Hove	info@ccb.ac.uk www.ccb.ac.uk Tel: +44 (0) 1273 667 788
City College Coventry	info@staff.covcollege.ac.uk www.covcollege.ac.uk Tel: +44 (0) 2476 791 000
City College Manchester	www.ccm.ac.uk Tel: +44 (0) 800 013 0123
City College Norwich	information@ccn.ac.uk www.ccn.ac.uk Tel: +44 (0) 1603 773 311
City College Plymouth	reception@cityplym.ac.uk www.cityplym.ac.uk Tel: +44 (0) 1752 305 300
City College Southampton	enquiries@southampton-city.ac.uk www.southampton-city.ac.uk Tel: +44 (0) 023 8048 4848
City Lit	www.citylit.ac.uk Tel: +44 (0) 207 492 2600
City of Bath College	www.citybathcoll.ac.uk Tel: +44 (0) 1225 312 191
City of Bristol College	enquiries@cityofbristol.ac.uk www.cityofbristol.ac.uk Tel: +44 (0) 117 312 5000
City of Sunderland College	www.citysun.ac.uk Tel: +44 (0) 191 511 6060
City of Westminster College	www.cwc.ac.uk Tel: +44 (0) 20 7723 8826

City of Wolverhampton College	www.wolverhamptoncollege.ac.uk Tel: +44 (0) 1902 836 000
Clydebank College	info@clydebank.ac.uk www.clydebank.ac.uk Tel: +44 (0) 141 951 2122
Coatbridge College	mail@coatbridge.ac.uk www.coatbridge.ac.uk Tel: +44 (0) 1236 422 316
Colchester Institute	www.colchester.ac.uk Tel: +44 (0) 1206 518 000
Coleg Abertawe	enquiries@swancoll.ac.uk www.swancoll.ac.uk Tel: +44 (0) 1792 284 000
Coleg Castell Nedd	enquiries@nptc.ac.uk www.nptc.ac.uk Tel: +44 (0) 1639 648 000
Coleg Glan Hafren	enquiries@glan-hafren.ac.uk www.glan-hafren.ac.uk Tel: +44 (0) 29 20 250 250
Coleg Glannau Dyfrdwy	www.deeside.ac.uk Tel: +44 (0) 1244 831 531
Coleg Gorseinon	admin@gorseinon.ac.uk www.gorseinon.ac.uk Tel: +44 (0) 1792 890 700
Coleg Gwent	info@coleggwent.ac.uk www.coleggwent.ac.uk Tel: +44 (0) 1495 333 333
Coleg Llysfasi	admin@llysfasi.ac.uk www.llysfasi.ac.uk Tel: +44 (0) 1978 790 263
Coleg Menai	student.services@menai.ac.uk www.menai.ac.uk Tel: +44 (0) 1248 370 125
Coleg Merthyr Tudful	www.merthyr.ac.uk Tel: +44 (0) 1685 726 006
Coleg Morgannwg	www.morgannwg.ac.uk Tel: +44 (0) 1685 887 500
Coleg Penybont	enquiries@bridgend.ac.uk www.bridgend.ac.uk Tel: +44 (0) 1656 302 302

visit: www.gap-year.com

Coleg Sir Gar	admissions@colegsirgar.ac.uk www.colegsirgar.ac.uk Tel: +44 (0) 1554 748 000
College of North East London	admissions@staff.conel.ac.uk www.conel.ac.uk Tel: +44 (0) 208 802 3111
College of North West London	courenq@cnwl.ac.uk www.cnwl.ac.uk Tel: +44 (0) 208 208 5000
College of West Anglia	enquiries@col-westanglia.ac.uk www.col-westanglia.ac.uk Tel: +44 (0) 1553 761 144
Collyer's, The College of Richard Collyer	admin@collyers.ac.uk www.collyers.ac.uk Tel: +44 (0) 1403 210 822
Cornwall College	enquiries@cornwall.ac.uk www.cornwall.ac.uk Tel: +44 (0) 1209 616 161
Craven College	www.craven-college.ac.uk Tel: +44 (0) 1756 791 41
Croydon College	info@croydon.ac.uk www.croydon.ac.uk Tel: +44 (0) 208 686 5700
CRTS International Study Centre	admission@crts.co.uk www.crts.co.uk Tel: +44 (0) 20 8801 0371
Cumbernauld College	info@cumbernauld.ac.uk www.cumbernauld.ac.uk Tel: +44 (0) 1236 731 811
Darlington College of Technology	enquire@darlington.ac.uk www.darlington.ac.uk Tel: +44 (0) 1325 503 050
Dearne Valley College	www.dearne-coll.ac.uk Tel: +44 (0) 1709 513 333
Derby College	enquiries@derby-college.ac.uk www.derby-college.ac.uk Tel: +44 (0) 1322 520 200
Derwentside College	www.derwentside.ac.uk Tel: +44 (0) 1207 585 900

Dewsbury College	info@dewsbury.ac.uk www.dewsbury.ac.uk Tel: +44 (0) 1924 436 221
Dudley College	www.dudleycol.ac.uk Tel: +44 (0) 1384 363 546
Dumfries & Galloway College	info@dumgal.ac.uk www.dumgal.ac.uk Tel: +44 (0) 1387 261 261
Dundee College	enquiry@dundeecollege.ac.uk www.dundeecoll.ac.uk Tel: +44 (0) 1382 834 800
Dunstable College	enquiries@dunstable.ac.uk www.dunstable.ac.uk Tel: +44 (0) 1582 477 776
Ealing, Hammersmith & West London College	cic@wlc.ac.uk www.wlc.ac.uk Tel: +44 (0) 20 8741 1688
East Berkshire College	info@eastberks.ac.uk www.eastberks.ac.uk Tel: +44 (0) 845 373 250
East Devon College	enquiries@admin.eastdevon.ac.uk www.edc.ac.uk Tel: +44 (0) 1884 235 200
East Riding College	info@eastridingcollege.ac.uk www.eastridingcollege.ac.uk Tel: +44 (0) 845 120 0037
East Surrey College	www.esc.ac.uk Tel: +44 (0) 1737 788 444
East Tyrone College of Further & Higher Education	info@etcfhe.ac.uk www.etcfhe.ac.uk Tel: +44 (0) 28 8772 2323
Eastleigh College	goplaces@eastleigh.ac.uk www.eastleigh.ac.uk Tel: +44 (0) 238 091 1299
Edinburgh's Telford College	mail@ed-coll.ac.uk www.ed-coll.ac.uk Tel: +44 (0) 131 559 4000
Enfield College	courseinformation@enfield.ac.uk www.enfield.ac.uk Tel: +44 (0) 20 8443 3434

visit: www.gap-year.com

Epping Forest College	informationcentre@epping-forest.ac.uk www.epping-forest.ac.uk Tel: +44 (0) 208 508 8311
Esher College	eshercollege@esher.ac.uk www.esher.ac.uk Tel: +44 (0) 20 8398 0291
Evesham & Malvern Hills College	www.evesham.ac.uk Tel: +44 (0) 1386 712 600
Exeter College	info@exe-coll.ac.uk www.exe-coll.ac.uk Tel: +44 (0) 1392 205 223
Fareham College	info@fareham.ac.uk www.fareham.ac.uk Tel: +44 (0) 1329 815 200
Farnborough College of Technology	info@farn-ct.ac.uk www.farn-ct.ac.uk Tel: +44 (0) 1252 407 040
Farnham College	enquiries@farnham.ac.uk www.farnham.ac.uk Tel: +44 (0) 1252 716 988
Fermanagh College	admissions@fermanaghcoll.ac.uk www.fermanaghcoll.ac.uk Tel: +44 (0) 28 6632 2431
Filton College	info@filton.ac.uk www.filton.ac.uk Tel: +44 (0) 117 931 2121
Franklin College	college@franklin.ac.uk www.franklin.ac.uk Tel: +44 (0) 1472 875 000
Furness College	www.furness.ac.uk Tel: +44 (0) 1229 825 017
Gateshead College	www.gateshead.ac.uk Tel: +44 (0) 191 4900 300
Gloscat	info@gloscat.ac.uk www.gloscat.ac.uk Tel: +44 (0) 1242 532 000
Godalming College	college@godalming.ac.uk www.godalming.ac.uk Tel: +44 (0) 1483 423 526

Great Yarmouth College	info@gyc.ac.uk
	www.gyc.ac.uk
	Tel: +44 (0) 1493 655 261
Guildford College	info@guildford.ac.uk
	www.guildford.ac.uk
	Tel: +44 (0) 1483 448 500
Halesowen College	info@halesowen.ac.uk
	www.halesowen.ac.uk
	Tel: +44 (0) 121 602 7777
Harrogate College	www.leedsmet.ac.uk/harrogate
	Tel: +44 (0) 1423 879 466
Hartlepool College of Further Education	enquiries@hartlepoolfe.ac.uk
	www.hartlepoolfe.ac.uk
	Tel: +44 (0) 1429 295 000
Hartpury College	enquire@hartpury.ac.uk
	www.hartpury.ac.uk
	Tel: +44 (0) 1452 700 283
Havant College	enquiries@havant.ac.uk
	www.havant.ac.uk
	Tel: +44 (0) 23 9248 3856
Havering College	information@havering-college.ac.uk
	www.havering-college.ac.uk
	Tel: +44 (0) 1708 455 011
Herefordshire College of Technology	enquiries@hct.ac.uk
	www.hereford-tech.ac.uk
	Tel: +44 (0) 800 032 1986
Highbury College	info@highbury.ac.uk
	www.highbury.ac.uk
	Tel: +44 (0) 23 9231 3373
Holy Cross Sixth Form College	information@holycross.ac.uk
	www.holycross.ac.uk
	Tel: +44 (0) 161 762 4500
Hopwood Hall College	enquiries@hopwood.ac.uk
	www.hopwood.ac.uk
	Tel: +44 (0) 161 643 7560
Hove College	courses@hovecollege.co.uk
	www.hovecollege.co.uk
	Tel: +44 (0) 1273 772577

visit: www.gap-year.com

Huddersfield Technical College	info@hudcoll.ac.uk www.huddcoll.ac.uk Tel: +44 (0) 1484 536 521
Hull College	info@hull-college.ac.uk www.hull-college.ac.uk Tel: +44 (0) 1482 329 943
Huntingdonshire Regional College	college@huntingdon.ac.uk www.huntingdon.ac.uk Tel: +44 (0) 1480 379 100
Interlink College London	ictbs@interlinktech.co.uk www.interlinktech.co.uk Tel: +44 (0) 208 531 1118
Inverness College	info@inverness.uhi.ac.uk www.inverness.uhi.ac.uk Tel: +44 (0) 1463 273 000
Isle of Man College	www.iomcollege.ac.im Tel: +44 (0) 1624 648 200
Itchen College	info@itchen.ac.uk www.itchen.ac.uk Tel: +44 (0) 23 8043 5636
Jewel & Esk Valley College	info@jevc.ac.uk www.jevc.ac.uk Tel: +44 (0) 131 660 1010
John Wheatley College	advice@jwheatley.ac.uk www.jwheatley.ac.uk Tel: +44 (0) 141 778 2426
Josiah Mason College	enquiries@jmc.ac.uk www.jmc.ac.uk Tel: +44 (0) 121 603 4757
Keighley College	www.keighley.ac.uk Tel: +44 (0) 1535 618 600
Kendal College	admissions@kendal.ac.uk www.kendal.ac.uk Tel: +44 (0) 1539 814 709
Kensington & Chelsea College	www.kcc.ac.uk Tel: +44 (0) 207 573 3600
Kidderminster College	www.kidderminster.ac.uk Tel: +44 (0) 1562 820 811
Kilmarnock College	www.kilmarnock.ac.uk Tel: +44 (0) 1563 523 501

Kingston College	info@kingston-college.ac.uk
	www.kingston-college.ac.uk
	Tel: +44 (0) 208 546 2151
Knowsley Community College	info@knowsleycollege.ac.uk
	www.knowsleycollege.ac.uk
	Tel: +44 (0) 845 155 1055
Lakes College	info@lcwc.ac.uk
	www.lcwc.ac.uk
	Tel: +44 (0) 1946 839 300
Lambeth College	courses@lambethcollege.ac.uk
	www.lambethcollege.ac.uk
	Tel: +44 (0) 207 501 5010
Lancaster & Morecambe College	www.lmc.ac.uk
	Tel: +44 (0) 800 306 306
Langside College	enquireuk@langside.ac.uk
	www.langside.ac.uk
	Tel: +44 (0) 141 272 3600
Lauder College	www.lauder.ac.uk
	Tel: +44 (0) 1383 845 010
Leeds College of Technology	info@lct.ac.uk
	www.lct.ac.uk
	Tel: +44 (0) 113 297 6300
Leeds Thomas Danby	info@leedsthomasdanby.ac.uk
	www.leedsthomasdanby.ac.uk
	Tel: +44 (0) 113 249 4912
Leicester College	info@leicestercollege.ac.uk
	www.leicestercollege.ac.uk
	Tel: +44 (0) 116 224 2240
Lewisham College	info@lewisham.ac.uk
	www.lewisham.ac.uk
	Tel: +44 (0) 208 692 0353
Lews Castle College	www.lews.uhi.ac.uk
	Tel: +44 (0) 1851 770 000
Lincoln College	enquiries@lincolncollege.ac.uk
	www.lincolncollege.ac.uk
	Tel: +44 (0) 1522 876 000
Liverpool Community College	www.liv-coll.ac.uk
	Tel: +44 (0) 151 252 1515

Loughborough College	info@loucoll.ac.uk www.loucoll.ac.uk Tel: +44 (0) 845 166 2952
Lowestoft College	www.lowestoft.ac.uk Tel: +44 (0) 1502 583 521
Ludlow College	info@ludlow-college.ac.uk www.ludlow-college.ac.uk Tel: +44 (0) 1584 872 846
Macclesfield College	info@macclesfield.ac.uk www.macclesfield.ac.uk Tel: +44 (0) 1625 410 000
Manchester College of Arts & Technology	enquiries@mancat.ac.uk www.mancat.ac.uk Tel: +44 (0) 161 953 5995
Matthew Boulton College of Further & Higher Education	ask@matthew-boulton.ac.uk www.matthew-boulton.ac.uk Tel: +44 (0) 121 446 4554
Merton College	info@merton.ac.uk www.merton.ac.uk Tel: +44 (0) 20 8408 6400
Middlesbrough College	courseinfo@mbro.ac.uk www.mbro.ac.uk Tel: +44 (0) 1642 333 333
Mid-Kent College	www.midkent.ac.uk Tel: +44 (0) 1634 402 020
Milton Keynes College	info@mkcollege.ac.uk www.mkcollege.ac.uk Tel: +44 (0) 1908 684 444
Moray College	www.moray.ac.uk Tel: +44 (0) 1343 576 000
Morley College	enquiries@morleycollege.ac.uk www.morleycollege.ac.uk Tel: +44 (0) 207 928 8501
Motherwell College	information@motherwell.ac.uk www.motherwell.ac.uk Tel: +44 (0) 1698 232 425
Nelson & Colne College	reception@nelson.ac.uk www.nelson.ac.uk Tel: +44 (0) 1282 440 200

Nescot	info@nescot.ac.uk www.nescot.ac.uk Tel: +44 (0) 20 8394 1731
New College Durham	help@newdur.ac.uk www.newdur.ac.uk Tel: +44 (0) 191 375 4000
New College Nottingham	enquiries@ncn.ac.uk www.ncn.ac.uk Tel: +44 (0) 115 9100 100
New College Pontefract	reception@newcollpont.ac.uk www.newcollpont.ac.uk Tel: +44 (0) 1977 702 139
New College Stamford	www.stamford.ac.uk Tel: +44 (0) 1780 484 300
New College Swindon	admissions@newcollege.ac.uk www.newcollege.ac.uk Tel: +44 (0) 808 172 1721
Newbury College	info@newbury-college.ac.uk www.newbury-college.ac.uk Tel: +44 (0) 1635 845 000
Newham College of Further Education	admissions@newham.ac.uk www.newham.ac.uk Tel: +44 (0) 208 257 4000
North Devon College	postbox@ndevon.ac.uk www.ndevon.ac.uk Tel: +44 (0) 1271 345 291
North East Worcestershire College	info@ne-worcs.ac.uk www.ne-worcs.ac.uk Tel: +44 (0) 1527 570 020
North Glasgow College	www.north-gla.ac.uk Tel: +44 (0) 141 558 9001
North Hertfordshire College	www.nhc.ac.uk Tel: +44 (0) 1462 424 239
North Nottinghamshire College	webcontact@nnc.ac.uk www.nnotts-col.ac.uk Tel: +44 (0) 1909 504 504
North Trafford College	www.ntc.ac.uk Tel: +44 (0) 161 886 7070

North Warwickshire & Hinckley College	the.college@nwhc.ac.uk www.nwhc.ac.uk Tel: +44 (0) 24 7624 3000
North West Kent College	course.enquiries@nwkcollege.ac.uk www.nwkcollege.ac.uk Tel: +44 (0) 1322 629 400
North West Regional College	info@nwrc.ac.uk www.nwrc.ac.uk Tel: +44 (0) 28 7127 6000
Northampton College	www.northamptoncollege.ac.uk Tel: +44 (0) 1604 734 567
Northern Regional College	info@nrc.ac.uk www.nrc.ac.uk Tel: +44 (0) 28 9085 5000
Northumberland College	advice.centre@northland.ac.uk www.northland.ac.uk Tel: +44 (0) 1670 841 200
Norton Radstock College	www.nortcoll.ac.uk Tel: +44 (0) 1761 433 161
Oaklands College	advice.centre@oaklands.ac.uk www.oaklands.ac.uk Tel: +44 (0) 1727 737 080
Orkney College	orkney.college@uhi.ac.uk www.orkney.uhi.ac.uk Tel: +44 (0) 1856 569 000
Orpington College	enquiries@orpington.ac.uk www.orpington.ac.uk Tel: +44 (0) 1689 899 700
Oxford & Cherwell Valley College	enquiries@ocvc.ac.uk www.ocvc.ac.uk Tel: +44 (0) 1865 550 550
Oxford Media & Business School	courses@oxfordbusiness.co.uk www.oxfordbusiness.co.uk Tel: +44 (0) 1865 240 963
Palmer's College	enquiries@palmers.ac.uk www.palmers.ac.uk Tel: +44 (0) 1375 370 121
Park Lane College	www.parklanecoll.ac.uk Tel: +44 (0) 845 045 7275

Paston College	enquiries@paston.ac.uk www.paston.ac.uk Tel: +44 (0) 1692 402 334
Penwith College	enquire@penwith.ac.uk www.penwith.ac.uk Tel: +44 (0) 1736 335 000
Perth College	pc.enquiries@perth.uhi.ac.uk www.perth.ac.uk Tel: +44 (0) 1738 877 000
Peterborough Regional College	info@peterborough.ac.uk www.peterborough.ac.uk Tel: +44 (0) 845 872 8722
Pitmans Training Group	www.pitman-training.com Tel: +44 (0) 1937 548500
Portsmouth College	registry@portsmouth-college.ac.uk www.portsmouth-college.ac.uk Tel: +44 (0) 23 9266 7521
Prior Pursglove College	www.pursglove.ac.uk Tel: +44 (0) 1287 280 800
Queen Mary's College	info@qmc.ac.uk www.qmc.ac.uk Tel: +44 (0) 1256 417 500
Quest Business Training	info@questcollege.co.uk www.questcollege.co.uk Tel: +44 (0) 20 7373 3852

Our ten week **gap-year** course covers the skills essential for temping and making your **gap-year** a truly challenging time. Lessons, seminars and workshops cover important interview techniques, skills and training. Alternatively, take a four or six week class to acquire practical office skills such as touch typing, MS Office and telephone techniques – they will be of lifelong benefit.

Redcar & Cleveland College	webenquiry@cleveland.ac.uk www.cleveland.ac.uk Tel: +44 (0) 1642 473 132
Reid Kerr College	sservices@reidkerr.ac.uk www.reidkerr.ac.uk Tel: +44 (0) 141 581 2222
Riverside College	www.riversidecollege.ac.uk Tel: +44 (0) 151 257 2800

Royal Forest of Dean	enquiries@rfdc.ac.uk www.rfdc.ac.uk Tel: +44 (0) 1594 833 416
Salisbury College	enquiries@salisbury.ac.uk www.salisbury.ac.uk Tel: +44 (0) 1722 344 344
Sandwell College	enquiries@sandwell.ac.uk www.sandwell.ac.uk Tel: +44 (0) 121 556 6000
Selby College	www.selby.ac.uk Tel: +44 (0) 1757 211 000
Shipley College	enquiries@shipley.ac.uk www.shipley.ac.uk Tel: +44 (0) 1274 327 222
Skelmersdale & Ormskirk Colleges	info@skelmersdale.ac.uk www.skelmersdale.ac.uk Tel: +44 (0) 1695 728 744
Solihull College	enquiries@solihull.ac.uk www.solihull.ac.uk Tel: +44 (0) 121 678 7000
South Cheshire College	info@s-cheshire.ac.uk www.s-cheshire.ac.uk Tel: +44 (0) 1270 654 654
South Devon College	enquiries@southdevon.ac.uk www.southdevon.ac.uk Tel: +44 (0) 1803 540 540
South Downs College	www.southdowns.ac.uk Tel: +44 (0) 23 9279 7979
South East Essex College	admissions@southend.ac.uk www.southend.ac.uk Tel: +44 (0) 1702 220 400
South East Regional College	www.serc.ac.uk Tel: +44 (0) 28 4461 5815
South Kent College	www.southkent.ac.uk Tel: +44 (0) 845 207 8220
South Lanarkshire College	admissions@slc.ac.uk www.south-lanarkshire-college.ac.uk Tel: +44 (0) 141 641 6600
South Leicestershire College	www.slcollege.ac.uk Tel: +44 (0) 116 288 5051

the gap-year guidebook 2010

South Nottingham College	enquiries@snc.ac.uk www.snc.ac.uk Tel: +44 (0) 115 914 6400
South Thames College	studentservices@south-thames.ac.uk www.south-thames.ac.uk Tel: +44 (0) 208 918 7777
South Trafford College	enquiries@stcoll.ac.uk www.stcoll.ac.uk Tel: +44 (0) 161 952 4600
South Tyneside College	www.stc.ac.uk Tel: +44 (0) 191 427 3500
South West College	www.swc.ac.uk Tel: +44 (0) 28 8224 5433
Southern Regional College	www.src.ac.uk Tel: +44 (0) 28 3752 2205
Southgate College	admiss@southgate.ac.uk www.southgate.ac.uk Tel: +44 (0) 208 982 5050
Southport College	www.southport-college.ac.uk Tel: +44 (0) 1704 500 606
Southwark College	info@southwark.ac.uk www.southwark.ac.uk Tel: +44 (0) 207 815 1500
St David's Catholic College	enquiries@st-davids-coll.ac.uk www.st-davids-coll.ac.uk Tel: +44 (0) 29 2049 8555
St Helens College	www.sthelens.ac.uk Tel: +44 (0) 1744 733 766
St Mary's College	reception@stmarysblackburn.ac.uk www.stmarysblackburn.ac.uk Tel: +44 (0) 1254 580 464
St Vincent College	info@stvincent.ac.uk www.stvincent.ac.uk Tel: +44 (0) 239 258 8311
Stafford College	www.staffordcoll.ac.uk Tel: +44 (0) 1785 223 800
Stanmore College	enquiry@stanmore.ac.uk www.stanmore.ac.uk Tel: +44 (0) 20 8420 7700

visit: www.gap-year.com

Stockport College	admissions@stockport.ac.uk www.stockport.ac.uk Tel: +44 (0) 161 958 3100
Stockton Riverside College	www.stockton.ac.uk Tel: +44 (0) 1642 865 400
Stoke on Trent College	info@stokecoll.ac.uk www.stokecoll.ac.uk Tel: +44 (0) 1782 208 208
Stourbridge College	info@stourbridge.ac.uk www.stourbridge.ac.uk Tel: +44 (0) 1384 344 344
Stow College	enquiries@stow.ac.uk www.stow.ac.uk Tel: +44 (0) 141 332 1786
Stratford-upon-Avon College	college@stratford.ac.uk www.strat-avon.ac.uk Tel: +44 (0) 1789 266 245
Strode College	courseinfo@strode-college.ac.uk www.strode-college.ac.uk Tel: +44 (0) 1458 844 400
Stroud College	enquire@stroudcol.ac.uk www.stroud.ac.uk Tel: +44 (0) 1453 763 424
Suffolk New College	info@suffolk.ac.uk www.suffolk.ac.uk Tel: +44 (0) 1473 255 885
Sussex Downs College	info@sussexdowns.ac.uk www.sussexdowns.ac.uk Tel: +44 (0) 1273 483 188
Swindon College	studentservices@swindon-college.ac.uk www.swindon-college.ac.uk Tel: +44 (0) 1793 491 591
Tameside College	www.tameside.ac.uk Tel: +44 (0) 161 908 6789
Tamworth & Lichfield College	enquiries@tamworth.ac.uk www.tamworth.ac.uk Tel: +44 (0) 1827 310 202
Taunton's College	email@tauntons.ac.uk www.tauntons.ac.uk Tel: +44 (0) 23 8051 1811

the gap-year guidebook 2010

Thames Valley University	www.tvu.ac.uk Tel: +44 (0) 118 967 5000
Thanet College	www.thanet.ac.uk Tel: +44 (0) 1843 605 040
The Adam Smith College	enquiries@adamsmith.ac.uk www.adamsmithcollege.ac.uk Tel: +44 (0) 800 413 280
The Blackpool Sixth Form College	enquiries@blackpoolsixth.ac.uk www.blackpoolsixth.ac.uk Tel: +44 (0) 1253 394 911
The City College	admissions@citycollege.ac.uk www.citycollege.ac.uk Tel: +44 (0) 20 7253 1133
The College Ystrad Mynach	enquiries@ystrad-mynach.ac.uk www.ystrad-mynach.ac.uk Tel: +44 (0) 1443 816 888
The Community College Hackney	enquiries@tcch.ac.uk www.tcch.ac.uk Tel: +44 (0) 207 613 9123
The Henley College	info@henleycol.ac.uk www.henleycol.ac.uk Tel: +44 (0) 1491 579 988
The Isle of Wight College	info@iwcollege.ac.uk www.iwightc.ac.uk Tel: +44 (0) 1983 526 631
The North Highland College	info@northhighland.ac.uk www.nhcscotland.com Tel: +44 (0) 1847 889 000
The Oldham College	info@oldham.ac.uk www.oldham.ac.uk Tel: +44 (0) 161 624 5214
The Sheffield College	www.sheffcol.ac.uk Tel: +44 (0) 114 260 2600
Thomas Rotherham College	enquiries@thomroth.ac.uk www.thomroth.ac.uk Tel: +44 (0) 1709 300 600
Thurrock & Basildon College	enquire@tab.ac.uk www.thurrock.ac.uk Tel: +44 (0) 845 601 5746

Totton College	info@totton.ac.uk www.totton.ac.uk Tel: +44 (0) 2380 874 874
Tower Hamlets College	advice@tower.ac.uk www.tower.ac.uk Tel: +44 (0) 207 510 7510
Tresham Institute of Further & Higher Education	info@tresham.ac.uk www.tresham.ac.uk Tel: +44 (0) 845 658 8990
Truro College	enquiry@trurocollege.ac.uk www.trurocollege.ac.uk Tel: +44 (0) 1872 267 000
Tyne Metropolitan College	www.ntyneside.ac.uk Tel: +44 (0) 191 229 5000
University of Derby – Buxton	www.derby.ac.uk Tel: +44 (0) 1298 71100
Uxbridge College	enquiries@uxbridgecollege.ac.uk www.uxbridgecollege.ac.uk Tel: +44 (0) 1895 853 333
Varndean College	www.varndean.ac.uk Tel: +44 (0) 1273 508 011
Wakefield College	info@wakefield.ac.uk www.wakcoll.ac.uk Tel: +44 (0) 1924 789 789
Walsall College	www.walsallcollege.ac.uk Tel: +44 (0) 1922 657 000
Waltham Forest College	info@waltham.ac.uk www.waltham.ac.uk Tel: +44 (0) 208 501 8000
Warrington Collegiate	learner.services@warrington.ac.uk www.warr.ac.uk Tel: +44 (0) 1925 494 494
Warwickshire College	enquiries@warkscol.ac.uk www.warkscol.ac.uk Tel: +44 (0) 1926 318 000
West Cheshire College	info@west-cheshire.ac.uk www.west-cheshire.ac.uk Tel: +44 (0) 1244 677 677

West Kent College	enquiries@wkc.ac.uk www.wkc.ac.uk Tel: +44 (0) 1732 358 101
West Lothian College	enquiries@west-lothian.ac.uk www.west-lothian.ac.uk Tel: +44 (0) 1506 418181
West Nottinghamshire College	www.wnc.ac.uk Tel: +44 (0) 1623 627 191
West Thames College	info@west-thames.ac.uk www.west-thames.ac.uk Tel: +44 (0) 20 8326 2000
Westminster Kingsway College	courseinfo@westking.ac.uk www.westking.ac.uk Tel: +44 (0) 870 060 9800
Weston College	enquiries@weston.ac.uk www.weston.ac.uk Tel: +44 (0) 1934 411 411
Weymouth College	lgs@weymouth.ac.uk www.weymouth.ac.uk Tel: +44 (0) 1305 761 100
Wigan & Leigh College	www.wigan-leigh.ac.uk Tel: +44 (0) 1942 761 600
Wiltshire College	info@wiltscoll.ac.uk www.wiltscoll.ac.uk Tel: +44 (0) 1249 464 644
Wirral Metropolitan College	www.wmc.ac.uk Tel: +44 (0) 151 551 7777
Woking College	www.woking.ac.uk Tel: +44 (0) 1483 761 036
Worcestershire College of Technology	college@wortech.ac.uk www.wortech.ac.uk Tel: +44 (0) 1905 725 555
Yale College	www.yale-wrexham.co.uk Tel: +44 (0) 1978 311 794
Yeovil College	info@yeovil.ac.uk www.yeovil.ac.uk Tel: +44 (0) 1935 423 921
Yorkshire Coast College	enquiries@ycoastco.ac.uk www.yorkshirecoastcollege.ac.uk Tel: +44 (0) 1723 372 105

visit: www.gap-year.com

index

482

Index | Index

483

the gap-year guidebook 2010

C

D

E

F

G

489

H

i

J

491

M

493

N

O

visit: www.gap-year.com

Q

R

499

U

V

W

Index | Index

505

the gap-year guidebook 2010

the gap-year guidebook 2010